I0132352

MAROTHODI

MAROTHODI

The Historical Archaeology of an African Capital

MARK S. ANDERSON

ATIKKAM

First pubished in the United Kingdom in 2009 by Atikkam Media Limited

This paperback edition first published 2013
by Atikkam Publishing
21 Milton Road, Willlen, Milton Keynes, Buckinghamshire, MK15 9JJ

Text copyright © 2013 Mark Steven Anderson
Design and layout copyright © 2013 Atikkam Media Limited

Atikkam Publishing is an imprint of Atikkam Media Limited

This book is in copyright. No distribution or reproduction of any part, in any form or by any means, digital or mechanical, may take place without the written permission of Atikkam Media Ltd, subject to statutory exception and to the provisions of relevant collective licensing agreements.

British Library Cataloguing in Publication Data
A catalogue record for this title is available from the British Library.

ATIKKAM
M E D I A

ISBN: 978-0-9561427-6-4 Paperback Edition

Additional copies of this title, including digital editions, are available from:
www.atikkam.com/marothodi

*This book is dedicated
to my Mother*

Namolelang! di makôrô di a lwa,
Pôô e ntšho e lwa le e khunou
Fa motlhabeng wa saka la Badimo
E tlhabile ya ga Boreyana philô!
Erile ke go bolêlêla, wa nyatsa—
Ke go reile ka re Pilwe ga pôtwe,
Go pôta Pilwe ke gona go latlhêga.
Kana Tsemane wa ga Moruiwane ga tšwarwe.

Help! the cattle with crooked horns fight,
The black bull (Bogatsu) fights the red one (Moseletsana) on the sand-ridge where the kraal of the
Badimo cattle is situated.
It has poked (Moseletsana) that (son) of Boreyana in the kidney!
You derided me when I told you—
When I told you that one does not go round Pilwe (Hill), that to go round Pilwe is to court trouble.
Tsemane (Bogatsu's wife) the daughter of Moruiwane is not held captive with impunity.

Praise peom for Bogatsu, chief of the Tlokwa, recounting his victory over the Fokeng at the battle
of Pilwe in the early 1800s. The battle was fought over Bogatsu's wife, Tsemane, who was allegedly
held captive by the Fokeng chief Moseletsana. Bogatsu was buried at Marothodi in around 1820.
(Translation by Vivien Ellenberger, 1939)

Contents

List of Illustrations

List of Tables

Preface

This book presents the results of archaeological research undertaken at the early 19th century Tswana town of Marothodi, in the Pilanesberg/Magaliesberg region of South Africa. The research was conducted by the author between 2002 and 2008 as part of a doctoral degree at the University of Cape Town (UCT).

In the following pages I introduce the archaeology of the settlement, with a particular emphasis on spatial arrangements and the organisation and cultural structure of metal production. The archaeological analysis is framed within a reasonably well-defined historical, biophysical and ethnographic context, with the overall aim of demonstrating the value of an interdisciplinary approach to the study of southern African Tswana towns.

As the first archaeological work to be undertaken at Marothodi, the research presented here should be seen as preliminary in nature. It is hoped that it might provide a useful reference for ongoing programmes at this and related sites, and perhaps capture the interest of readers who are as yet unfamiliar with this field of southern African Iron Age archaeology. With this in mind, the text is fully referenced throughout to aid further research, and the reader is encouraged to explore and engage with the rich collection of published archaeological, ethnographic and historical literature. Two excellent volumes with which to begin are Hammond-Tooke's *The Roots of Black South Africa* (1993) and Huffman's *Handbook to the Iron Age* (2007).

I precede the current work with a brief discussion of research methodology.

Mapping

The project began with the creation of maps of the site, and for this purpose aerial photographs of the area were consulted at the Chief Directorate Surveys and Mapping Office in Mowbray, Cape Town. Of the several available photographic 'runs' available, the images taken in 1994 were chosen, primarily because they offered the largest scale photography at 1:20,000 and consequently the clearest representation of the stone walling at Marothodi.

Enlargements at an approximate scale of 1:2000 were obtained, which was the highest level of magnification that could be printed at this facility. From these the visible stone walls of each homestead were traced on a digitizing tablet using ArchView GIS software, and a basic digital outline map of the site was created.

Some limitations in this method of map creation were encountered, particularly where certain areas of the site were not visible on the photograph due to missing walling or dense bush cover. Also, the limited scale of the image, even at the greatest enlargement, made the intricate stone walling difficult to trace accurately. To overcome some of these shortcomings, new maps were created by digitally tracing scanned images of the aerial photographs with Adobe Illustrator CS2 imaging software, which enabled the photographs to be enlarged on screen and manipulated for maximum visibility. The individual 'settlement units' were numbered sequentially according to the order in which they were mapped.

The traced digital maps were further adjusted and elaborated during ground survey at Marothodi, creating reasonably accurate maps of the main parts of the town. While most of the homesteads in which archaeological work was conducted were surveyed in sufficient detail to clarify walling arrangements and the position of dwelling structures, the 'Primary' *Kgosing* and 'Secondary' *Kgosing*, as the 'royal residences', received special attention, and the full range of visible structural features therein were plotted.

Settlement Unit 3 was almost completely invisible on aerial photographs, so the walls of this homestead and the adjacent hill slope were mapped on site via electronic distance measurement (EDM), using a Leica Total Station.

Fieldwork

The fieldwork team consisted of over 70 students, professionals and academics from around the world, who assisted the annual expeditions for varying lengths of time. Most participated as members of the Marothodi Archaeological Field School, convened and directed by the author (see Randall 2005/6). Excavations were conducted over a total period of approximately six months, and on a site of such scale they needed to follow a carefully structured sampling strategy.

As a combination of ethnographic data and archaeological survey had enabled the interpretation of political hierarchy in the macro spatial arrangement of the town, and helped to identify spatial components within individual homesteads, a general socio-political spatial framework could be established at Marothodi from the beginning.

Furthermore, preliminary ground survey revealed large quantities of metallurgical debris across the town, evidently associated with both iron and copper production. As the spatial distribution of this material appeared to traverse contextual socio-political boundaries, it provided a convenient and advantageous framework around which excavation sampling could be directed. Within this framework, individual settlement units were selected to ensure that both 'royal' and 'commoner' homesteads were sampled. Specific areas within homesteads that appeared to be associated with metal production were targeted, including *malapa* (households or domestic courtyards), middens from domestic and ceremonial contexts, and actual smelting sites.

Standard archaeological fieldwork procedures were utilised (Barker 1997; Hester *et al.* 1997; Roskams 2002). Structures and features were generally excavated according to their stratigraphy, with the exception of homogenous midden deposits which were excavated in arbitrary spits. As Marothodi is a single-component site, and was not under any immediate threat of destruction, the excavation of structural features proceeded only to the point of full exposure, and not complete removal. All deposit excavated from ash middens was screened through 5 mm mesh sieves to maximise the potential for recovery of small materials. A 100% artefact retrieval policy was applied to all excavations.

Archaeological features under investigation were recorded in detail on specially designed record forms, and in measured plans and photographs. Most features had been subjected to a certain degree of warping or degradation through various post-depositional processes, and the structural plans presented in this book are drawn at excavation resolution. That is, the lines of walls and other edges have not been artificially 'smoothed out' in the illustrations, but are drawn to accurately reflect the archaeological remains as they were plotted.

Radiocarbon dating methods are notoriously problematic when applied to sites of the last 300 years due to fluctuations in the atmospheric levels of radiocarbon over this period (Vogel & Fuls 1999), and consequently they have not been used in this research. While we do have the advantage of the high historical resolution provided by the oral traditions, an independent dating method would nevertheless be desirable. Preliminary research suggests that optically stimulated luminescence (OSL) might provide a more reliable alternative (Rosenstein 2008).

Post-excavation

Preliminary sorting of artefacts and the cleaning of some ceramics were carried out in the field. At the conclusion of fieldwork all excavated archaeological materials were transported back to the Department of Archaeology at the University of Cape Town, where they underwent further laboratory processing.

All excavated middens contained considerable quantities of bone, but a full analysis of this material did not form part of the current work. The only processing carried out on fauna was the identification and quantification of bones with abraded edges, which indicated that they had been used in secondary contexts as scraping tools (see Figure 1). Thus identified, they were treated thenceforth as artefacts, and are accounted for in chapters Six to Nine accordingly. The bone has been lodged with Dr. Elizabeth Voigt, an archaeozoologist associated with the McGregor Museum in Kimberley, and a full analysis of excavated fauna from Marothodi will be presented in a future publication.

All metallurgical slags retrieved from Marothodi were cleaned, then sorted and weighed according to morphology (see Miller & Killick 2004). Preliminary XRF and EDS analyses were conducted by Dr. Duncan Miller on some of the slags and metal objects retrieved from the first season of survey and excavation at SU25 (published in Hall *et al.* 2006). The results assisted in distinguishing between copper and iron production sites during subsequent fieldwork. All finished metal artefacts were photographed and are presented in this book.

Pottery associated with ancestral Sotho-Tswana is typically decoratively bland (Hall 1998), and this is certainly true of the Marothodi assemblages. The limited stylistic analysis that could be carried out on such a small, sparsely decorated sample was completed with the aim of describing diagnostic attributes for comparison with other sites, and to contribute to a discussion of identity. Generally however, the ceramic analysis did not form a pivotal element of the research, and should be seen as preliminary. All excavated ceramics were quantified and weighed, all diagnostic sherds were identified, and attributes of profile type, decorative technique and motif were recorded where possible. Sherds were considered to be diagnostic if they possessed at least a rim profile, and/or any surface decoration. A summary of diagnostic attributes is presented in the author's doctoral thesis (Anderson 2009).

Multi-dimensional analysis (Huffman 1980, 2007) was applied to the few decorated sherds that held sufficient profile information although this was curtailed by their often fragmentary nature. Most of the complete vessels were plain, and a lack of decoration was not considered a stylistic attribute.

All decorated sherds were illustrated and are presented in this book, along with representative examples of the profile types recovered from each excavated feature. The ceramic illustrations veer slightly from convention in that the few sherds of naturally black clay are depicted with shaded surfaces, and those made of red clay are shown white (all natural colours would normally be shown white). The accompanying descriptions should prevent any ambiguity over this concession to visual clarity. Sherds with abraded edges from secondary use as scraping tools were quantified with the rest of the ceramic assemblages, and then quantified separately and treated thenceforth as tools (see Figure 2). Quantities of ceramic scrapers are presented in the book alongside bone scraper statistics.

The primary project archive is held at the Department of Archaeology at the University of Cape Town.

Terminology

When referring to particular Tswana lineages I have not used the prefix 'Ba-' before the totem name, in keeping with currently accepted terminology. Thus, the Batlokwa are referred to simply as the Tlokwa, the Bakgatla as the Kgatla, the Bafokeng as the Fokeng, and so on.

Figure 1
A sample of bone scrapers
from Marothodi, arranged
with the most abraded
edges pointing downward.

Figure 2
A sample of ceramic
scrapers from Marothodi,
arranged with the
most abraded edges
pointing downward.

The term 'homestead' is used throughout the book to define the discrete physical units formed by the stone wall arrangements on the site. Ethnography supports the identification of these units (sometimes called 'hamlets' or 'villages') as an approximate physical expression of, but not directly synonymous with, a 'ward' (Schapera 1955). Wards (*dikgôrô*) are administrative social and political units of the community composed of one or more family groups under a headman, but are less clearly defined archaeologically than the walled homestead. Although the terms are sometimes used interchangeably, we refer to the archaeological settlement units at Marothodi as homesteads. The prefix 'SU' is often used when referring to a specific numbered homestead, for example 'SU25'.

When referring to the geographical area between the Vaal and Limpopo Rivers formerly known as the Transvaal (apart from when used in its historical context) the term 'trans-Vaal' is used here instead. This is a modern term of convenience first introduced in the historical literature in Hamilton's *The Mfecane Aftermath* (1995).

African achievement

Finally, while this book focuses on the results of a preliminary archaeological project at one particular settlement, it is hoped that it might also be received more generally as a celebration of the pre-colonial Tswana towns of South Africa, and of the remarkable achievements of the communities who built and occupied them. We are exploring a pivotal period in the subcontinent's history, during which African solutions to momentous challenges were negotiated within a climate of considerable turbulence and change. Their successes in this regard, prior to and during the colonial impact in southern Africa, should be recognised and respected. If this work could make a contribution to that end, I would consider one of its most important aims fulfilled.

Figure 3
The author discusses a
cluster of copper refining
furnaces at Marothodi with
archaeologists of the future.

Acknowledgements

Grateful acknowledgement is made to the South African National Research Foundation (NRF) for the doctoral bursary I enjoyed for three years, and for the research funding they awarded through the Tswana Town Research Group at the UCT Department of Archaeology, under which auspices my work was conducted.

Dr. Simon Hall, convenor of the Tswana Town Research Group, welcomed me into the world of African archaeology. As my doctoral thesis advisor, his academic encouragement, insight, and above all patience, were foundational and critical to the completion of this work. While all errors and omissions are entirely my own, these pages owe much to his teaching, and to his editorial input during the writing of the original thesis.

This book is built upon the achievements of many pioneering Africanist archaeologists and researchers, some of whom I have had the privilige of working with during the project, and others who have provided invaluable feedback on my work. I am particularly grateful to Jan Boeyens, Shadreck Chirikure, Francois Coetzee, Tom Huffman, Tim Maggs, Rod McIntosh, Duncan Miller, Mamakomoreng Nkhasi, Neil Parsons and Dana Rosenstein, all of whom continue to push back the boundaries of our disciplinary knowledge.

Thanks are due to the South African Heritage Resources Agency (SAHRA) for granting our excavation permit, and to the Department of Land Affairs for their support and advice. The Department of Archaeology at the University of South Africa (UNISA) kindly lent us some essential field equipment. I am also grateful to the people of Bapong for welcoming us into their community, and for allowing us to cross over their land twice a day to reach Marothodi. Grace Musuku and her colleagues at the Mphebatho Cultural Centre in Saulspoort offered our team a valuable insight into Tswana culture, and dished up many delicious meals. Tom Ferreira and family provided excellent accommodation at Bosele in the Pilanesberg National Park.

I would like to thank all staff and students of the Marothodi Archaeological Field School for their valuable assistance during the three seasons of excavation at Marothodi. I am also grateful to Judy Sealy and Simon Hall for permitting me to run the field school and for supporting the endeavour. I gratefully acknowledge the help of Charlie Arthur in 2003. Elizabeth Voigt assisted with excavations in 2005, and taught a field school module on archaeological fauna that was enjoyed and appreciated by all.

As assistant field director in 2004 and 2005, Sarah Court was critical to the success of the fieldwork and the preservation of my sanity. Her husband, Christian Biggi, also provided invaluable help in the field. I am very grateful for such dear and true friends.

Many others have offered vital moral and material support over the last few years, without which this book would not have been completed. Neil Henderson and Mario Ribas have been good friends as well as fellow researchers. Patrick Boucher, Paul Harris, Christian Gebranzig and Alan Zieg, your help and friendship will always be remembered and valued.

Finally, I am especially appreciative of my family. Your love and support throughout my time in South Africa has been constant and unconditional.

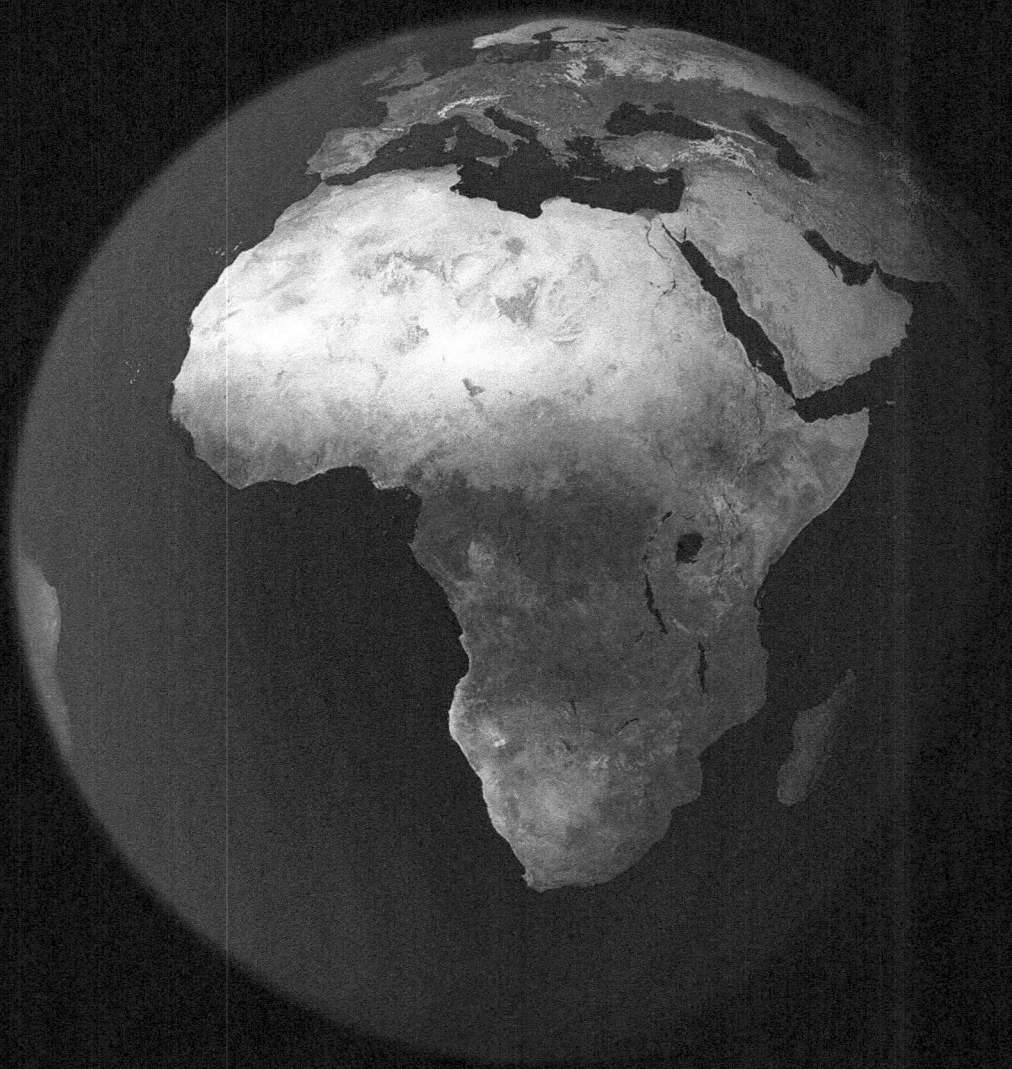

Introduction
Tswana Towns in Context

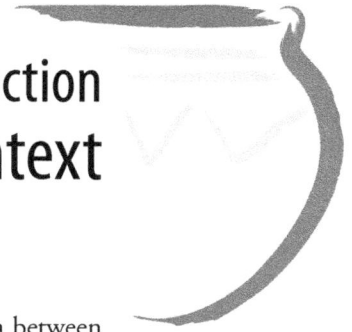

The innumerable stone ruins distributed across much of southern Africa between the Gariep and Zambezi rivers are some of the most vivid and remarkable elements of the subcontinent's abundant archaeological landscape. The vast majority of these started to appear from around AD 1600. They were occupied by various Bantu-speaking agropastoral communities who cultivated crops and venerated cattle as the source of both wealth and political power (Mason 1968, 1986; Maggs 1976a; Hammond-Tooke 1993; Huffman 2007).

But even against this rich archaeological backdrop, the immense Tswana towns of South Africa stand out as unique. Developing in the mid-1700s and reaching their ultimate expressions by the early 19th century, these extensive stone walled sites—typically associated with late Moloko ceramics—are concentrated in the Pilanesberg/Magaliesberg region to the north of the Highveld (Figs. 4 and 5).

Tswana towns were the capitals of aggregated Tswana-speaking communities—entire chiefdoms living together in a single town under the authority of their resident ruler (Boeyens 2000, 2003; Hall 1995a, 2007). With populations sometimes over 10,000 strong, their considerable size inspired the term 'mega-sites' in earlier archaeological literature (Mason 1986). Their density and scale bear testimony to significant changes that were underway in the Tswana world in the decades prior to their demise.

Most were eventually devastated during the catastrophic *Difaqane* wars that spread to the Pilanesberg/Magaliesberg region in the late 1820s, when the establishment of the Ndebele state in this area under Mzilikazi left many Tswana towns abandoned or destroyed.

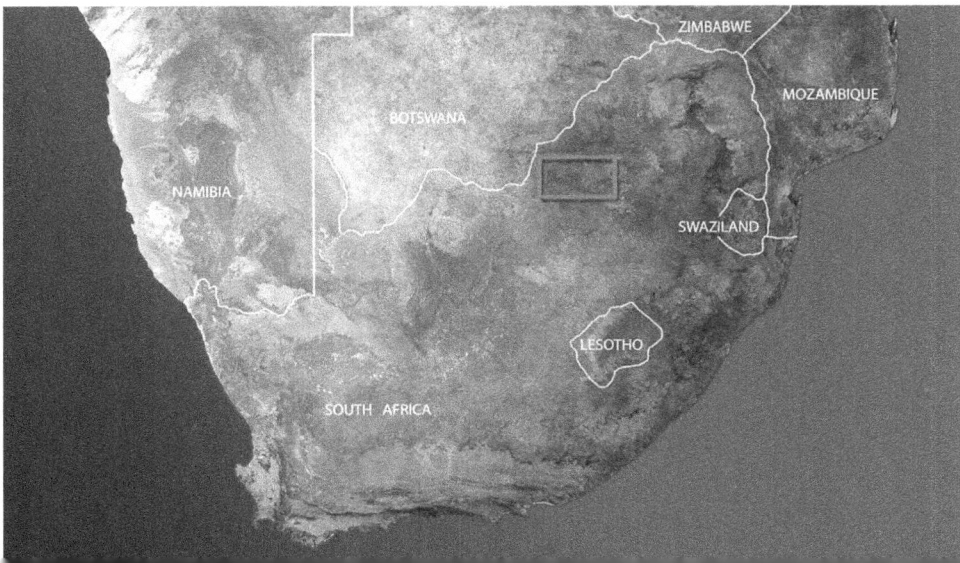

Figure 4
Map of southern Africa, showing the location of the Pilanesberg/Magaliesberg region (see Figure 5).

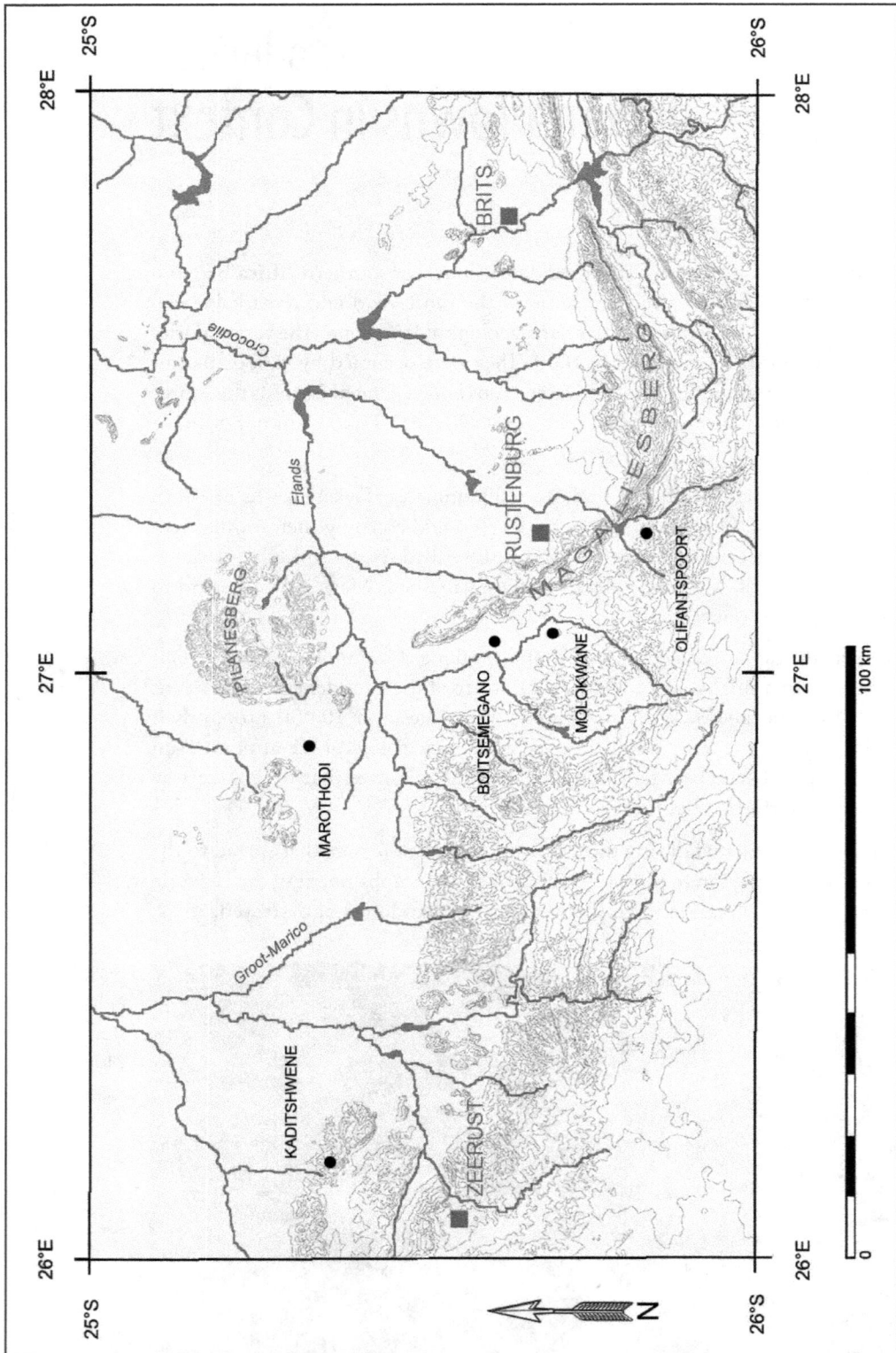

Figure 5

Map of the Pilanesberg/Magaliesberg region showing the main stone walled Tswana capitals of the early 19th century (circles) and present day towns (squares). Topography over 1200 metres and major rivers are also shown.

Archaeological research on Tswana towns has, since the 1980s, predominantly revolved around the application of an ethnographically derived normative model, known as the 'Central Cattle Pattern', for the interpretation of settlement space and organisation (Kuper 1982; Huffman 1986a, 2001; Pistorius 1992).

Although such models are useful and enlightening to archaeologists who study the organisation of 'prehistoric' or 'proto-historic' settlements, they operate on a very general scale, glossing over the detail, variability, and most importantly the historical processes that are important aspects of understanding a society.

Consequently, an exclusive focus on normative models exposes us to the risk of viewing the Tswana preference for town living as an inherent cultural norm, detached from the diachronic processes that led to the relatively sudden development of Tswana towns in the archaeological record from the middle of the 18th century. To continue with this approach would contribute nothing new, unless we change the scale of analysis and insert the insights yielded by normative models into historical contexts.

Our premise is that the study of this period falls within the realm of historical archaeology, and that Tswana capitals were home to historical identities (Reid & Lane 2004; Behrens & Swanepoel 2008). The organisation of a town was a culturally-driven response to a set of specific historical circumstances, and each should be examined as a unique expression of the people who built and occupied it. To understand Tswana towns more completely, therefore, we need to develop interdisciplinary research frameworks that combine ethnography, archaeology, and the historical resolution afforded by the careful use of associated oral traditions (Vansina 1961, 1971; Deetz 1988; Orser 1996).

The early 19th century site of Marothodi, which means 'raindrops' in Setswana, is situated near the Pilanesberg in today's North West Province in South Africa (Figs. 5 and 6). Marothodi was the capital of a Tlokwa chiefdom (Boeyens 2004) and is an historically-defined site through which we can explore the value of an interdisciplinary approach to Sotho-Tswana archaeology. Previous archaeological work at other Tlokwa centres has indicated that this lineage stems from early Nguni origins, which would distinguish them from the western Sotho-Tswana occupants of neighbouring aggregated capitals (Mason 1986, Coetzee 2005, Huffman 2007).

While the Tlokwa must, therefore, have become 'Tswana-ised' at a relatively recent point in their history, the settlement style and structure we see at Marothodi certainly seems to reflect a Tswana worldview by the early 19th century, and for this reason Sotho-Tswana ethnography will be predominantly relevant to our understanding of the capital. This is particularly pertinent to our discussion of the organisation and cultural structure of specialised metal production here. The evidence for a non-Tswana origin of the Tlokwa nevertheless offers an indication from the outset that Marothodi was not a 'typical' Tswana town, and that our archaeological analysis of the capital might reveal important elements of variablilty in the organisation of the settlement.

Our journey into the Tswana world begins with the journals of the first Europeans who made contact with Tswana communities in the early 19th century. These primary sources emphasise the historical nature of Tswana towns and contribute to our understanding of contemporary regional dynamics. They also demonstrate the time depth of the Tswana 'ethnographic present'. We follow this in Chapter Two with a review of the research background to the archaeology of Iron Age stone walled sites in South Africa. With increasing focus on the Tswana towns of the Pilanesberg/Magaliesberg region we examine the development of systematic archaeological research, and discuss the main theoretical frameworks that define the disciplinary milieu of the current work.

In Chapters Three, Four and Five we are introduced to the Marothodi region and to the site itself, as we explore the historical, biophysical and archaeological context of the town. As we will see, the oral traditions of the occupying Tlokwa community reveal that Marothodi was one of several sequential settlements established by this chiefdom in the Pilanesberg/Magaliesberg area, and that this sequence straddles a period of significant political shifts in the Tswana world. When considered against the deeper Nguni roots of the Tlokwa, we start to develop a unique historical backdrop against which the archaeology of Marothodi can be explored in more detail.

As no prior archaeological research had been undertaken at Marothodi, the gathering of new data was a key objective. In Chapters Six to Nine we take a closer look at some of the Marothodi homesteads, and present reports on the archaeological survey and excavations conducted there. While fieldwork was predominantly orientated around metal production sites within the settlement, spatial and material evidence was recorded across a range of domestic, ceremonial and industrial contexts.

From the gathered archaeological data, Chapter Ten presents a technological and ethnographic discussion of the practice and organisation of iron and copper production at Marothodi. Here, we discover that the organisation of production was guided by underlying Tswana cultural codes and values that were resiliently upheld, despite having to be adapted to the new challenges of living in a high-density town environment.

Figure 6
Oblique aerial photograph of the 'Secondary' Kgosing, one of the royal residences at Marothodi.

In Chapter Eleven we conclude with a review of our insights into the archaeological expression of identity at Marothodi, and reconsider some of the regional dynamics in which Marothodi participated. We also highlight the greater depth of interpretation obtained by viewing this Tswana capital against its historical, political and biophysical backdrop, within an interdisciplinary research framework. Finally, directions for future research are suggested, and we acknowledge the impressive achievement of this resourceful African community.

Chapter One
Early Contact

The earliest contacts between Europeans and Tswana-speaking communities in South Africa were recorded in the journals of explorers and missionaries in the early 19ᵗʰ century. Their manuscripts are delightfully entertaining and uniquely valuable in that they offer a contemporary record of Tswana communities who, in some cases, occupied settlements that are known archaeologically today (Boeyens 2000). These records demonstrate the time depth of the 'ethnographic present' from which much analogical data is drawn, and establish its relevance to the early 1800s.

The journals were written during a turbulent period in Tswana history, and can only be fully understood within the context of the highly-charged historical dynamics of the time. They capture an atmosphere of increasing tension between different Sotho-Tswana chiefdoms across the landscape, with the raiding of cattle described as an almost routine occurrence as different communities competed among themselves for precious resources.

Ominous rumours emerge in the texts of even larger scale unrest, attributed to roaming groups of so-called "Mantatees". We now understand these to have been a mixture of Sotho-speaking Fokeng and Tlokwa groups (not to be confused with the Tlokwa of Marothodi) who had been displaced from the Drakensberg region in the south-east by the Ndebele of the notorious chief Mzilikazi. Their arrival in Tswana areas was an early consequence of what became known as the *Mfecane* (Nguni) or *Difaqane* (Sotho) wars, and they were much feared among Tswana people. They caused a great deal of disruption, perhaps most vividly represented in the historical records by the battle at Dithakong in 1823 (Moffat 1842; Thompson 1967).

Shortly afterward, in 1827, Mzilikazi himself moved into the Pilanesberg/Magaliesberg region and occupied most of what had been Tswana territory. The Tswana who survived either fled from the area or were locally scattered, commonly being plunged into poverty. Whether as fugitives or as new subjects of the Ndebele state, the historical descriptions of their consequently miserable circumstances form a sharp contrast to the picture of prosperity captured by the earliest visitors to Tswana towns.

Some of the most common criticisms of these historical records focus not on what they contain, but on what they omit. Of course, none of the early European travellers who ventured into the southern African interior were trained ethnographers (there was no such thing at the time) and few, with the exception of Burchell, Lichtenstein and Smith, had any scientific training at all (Burchell 1822; Lichtenstein 1928; Lye 1973). All were burdened with Eurocentric prejudices that frequently gave rise to misinterpretation, patronising condescension, and sometimes outright disdain. Furthermore, the majority were enthusiastic Christian missionaries, and the religious zeal that emboldened them to risk

Figure 1.1
Map showing some of the Tswana towns mentioned in the historical journals, plus the archaeologically known capitals and the general territories of the major chiefdoms c.1800 to 1850.

their lives and endure the hardships of an 'untamed' Africa was the same fire that often blinded them to the cultural value of the "unclean attributes of 'heathenism'" they described among African people (Wallace 1945: xi).

With due consideration given to their limitations, however, these primary descriptions of living Tswana communities provide a valuable body of knowledge for the historical archaeologist. To get a feel for what it was like to walk into an inhabited Tswana town in the early 19th century we will engage with some of the most relevant texts, focussing upon the important details of Tswana settlement structure, style and organisation that they capture.

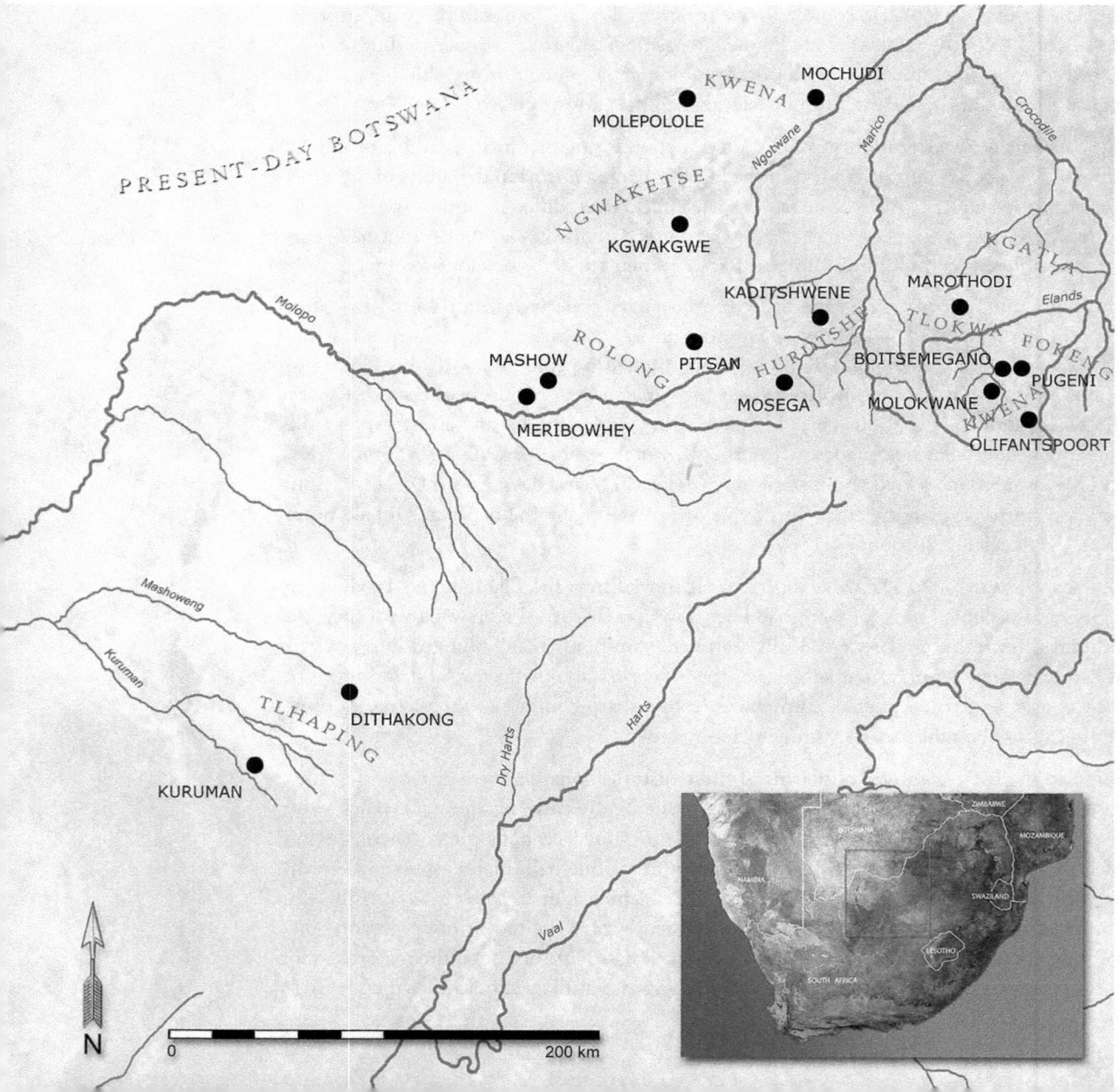

Journeys into the Interior

The first European visit to a Tswana town for which detailed records exist occurred in 1801, during an expedition organised by the British Government of the Cape Colony. The goals of the journey were largely economic in nature, being primarily to make contact with communities beyond the northern boundaries of the colony, with the aim of developing trade networks so that cattle could be bought. The expedition was led by Petrus Truter and William Somerville, and included Samuel Daniell as Secretary, who made numerous drawings of scenery and people they encountered on the trip (for example, Fig. 1.2). Truter's fourteen year-old nephew, Petrus Borcherds, accompanied the party as Assistant Secretary.

Somerville and Borcherds both kept first-hand accounts of the expedition, although Somerville's manuscript remained undiscovered and unpublished for nearly 180 years. Borcherds kept a journal "under the eye of Mr. Truter", as well as a second journal that he appears to have written for himself. Material from both of Borcherds' manuscripts was incorporated into his autobiographical account of the journey, published 60 years later, but a more contemporary account was recorded in an undated letter he wrote to his father soon after his return home (Borcherds 1861: 41; Bradlow & Bradlow 1979).

The journal that Borcherds kept for Truter formed the basis of Truter's official report of the expedition, which was handwritten in Dutch and presented to Sir John Barrow, a colonial official and explorer, when they returned to Cape Town in 1802. The Borcherds/Truter report, in combination with the personal accounts of the team members, forms the core of Barrow's account of the expedition, to which he added some of his own insights and

Figure 1.2
Booshwana Village. An engraving from Borcherds' autobiography, based on an original sketch drawn by Samuel Daniell at Dithakong in 1801.

observations, and published it as an annex to his *A Voyage to Cochinchina in the years 1792 and 1793* (1806). It includes engravings copied from Samuel Daniell's original sketches, many of which were also copied and published by the artist's brother, William Daniell, after Samuel's death (Daniell 1820).

The first community of Tswana-speakers encountered by the expedition were a mixed group of Tlhaping and Rolong, at the Tlhaping capital Dithakong (Figs. 1.1, 1.2 and 1.3). This settlement, located near the Mashoweng River, had hitherto been little more than a rumour in the colony (Saunders 1966). It was "calculated to contain about three thousand habitations, and from ten to fifteen thousand inhabitants" (Borcherds 1861: 84). The visitors were clearly impressed by the scale of what they did not hesitate to refer to as a "town", surrounded as it was by "extensive gardens, recently planted with water-melons, beans, and holcus or Kafir corn" (Borcherds 1861: 84).

> The area of the town of Letako (Dithakong) appeared to me to be as extensive as Cape Town, including the gardens. The houses were conveniently built in the usual circular form, with walls about six feet high and with a veranda. They are divided into two portions, which serve for sleeping and sitting apartments. They are stored with large earthen pots, to preserve provisions; each dwelling is separated from that adjoining by a thick hedge of reeds or twigs. (Borcherds 1861: 130)

Somerville also describes the "very large jars of Earth and cow dung" in which grain was stored, and the houses "with pillars of wood in front suporting the thatch roof", situated within the domestic courtyards (*malapa*), which were "paved with clay and cow dung" (Bradlow & Bradlow 1979: 121).

Barrow describes the houses in more detail:

> The ground plan of every house was a complete circle, from twelve to thirteen feet in diameter; the floor of hard beaten clay, raised about four inches above the general surface of the enclosure. About one fourth part of the circle, which was the front of the house and observed generally to face the east, was entirely open; the other three-fourths were walled up with clay and stones, to the height of about five feet. (Barrow 1806: 391)

However, Barrow's ground-plan of a house (Fig. 1.4, a), with its narrow ellipsoid 'inner apartment', seems at odds with the more commonly recorded design of Tswana houses with which we have since become familiar (see Walton 1956b; Frescura 1981; Larsson & Larsson 1984). It differs from those drawn by other early travellers and appears to represent a perception of what the ground plan might look like if it was based only on a cursory observation from outside the structure. It is possible that Barrow reproduced his plan from a drawing made by a member of the expedition which was thus flawed, or that he composed it from their descriptions alone. Alternatively, of course, he may have captured a genuine example of variability in Tswana house design.

The party inadvertently ventured into the realm of archaeological enquiry, in their observation of a nearby stone walled site:

> About half an hour from the camp was to be seen the ruins of a large town; the habitations were circular in shape, and the walls of stone, about four or five feet high, resembling the houses in the inhabited town; but none, not even the oldest of the natives, could give us the history of its origin or destruction. (Borcherds 1861: 84)

Although understandably lacking in historical detail, Borcherds' observation of these ruins attests to the presence of an aggregated stone walled Tswana settlement near Dithakong which, to precede contemporary Tlhaping/Rolong knowledge, must been built between the late 17th to early 19th centuries.

The 1801 expedition was ultimately considered a failure, as the Tlhaping were disinclined to part with their cattle and only a small number of animals could be purchased. While the visitors failed to understand their reluctance to sell "since they convert them to no useful purpose whatever, and seldom kill them for food" (Somerville, in Bradlow & Bradlow 1979: 140), this was a vivid demonstration of the deeper significance of cattle as wealth, and as a medium of exchange for wives in the Tswana world (Schapera 1953; Kuper 1982).

Truter and Somerville were followed in May 1805 by the German doctor and naturalist Heinrich Lichtenstein, who, guided by Petrus Truter's journal, accompanied an expedition to the north of the Gariep River (known at that time as the Orange River) at the invitation of Governor Janssens. While the principal aim of this trip was, again, to establish a trade in cattle, Lichtenstein himself was charged with gathering information about the land and its people. His success in this regard was facilitated to a considerable degree by the participation of John Mathias Kok, a missionary who had developed a strong relationship with Tswana-speaking people in the region, and who had joined the expedition as a guide and interpreter (Lichtenstein 1928).

When the party arrived at Dithakong they found a population considerably smaller than that which had received the earlier expedition. A few years previously, in an example of the mobility of Tswana chiefdoms in this period, the Rolong contingent of the community, under the chief Makraka, had separated from the Tlhaping and moved peaceably away from Dithakong. They left approximately one third of the occupants behind under the Tlhaping chief, Mulihawang, who then also moved to the Kuruman River some 50 kilometres to the south-west. It was Mulihawang's new capital, with its population of about 5000 inhabitants, that Lichtenstein visited in 1805.

With his European eyes, Lichtenstein struggled to recognise any order or pattern in the arrangement of the town. He describes it as "an absolute labyrinth of little alleys, large places, and broad streets", and concludes that "the streets are, properly speaking, little else than open spaces, having no regularity, either in their direction or their breadth" (1928: 373).

Figure 1.3
A painting by William Burchell, depicting his first view of the Tswana town Dithakong in 1812.

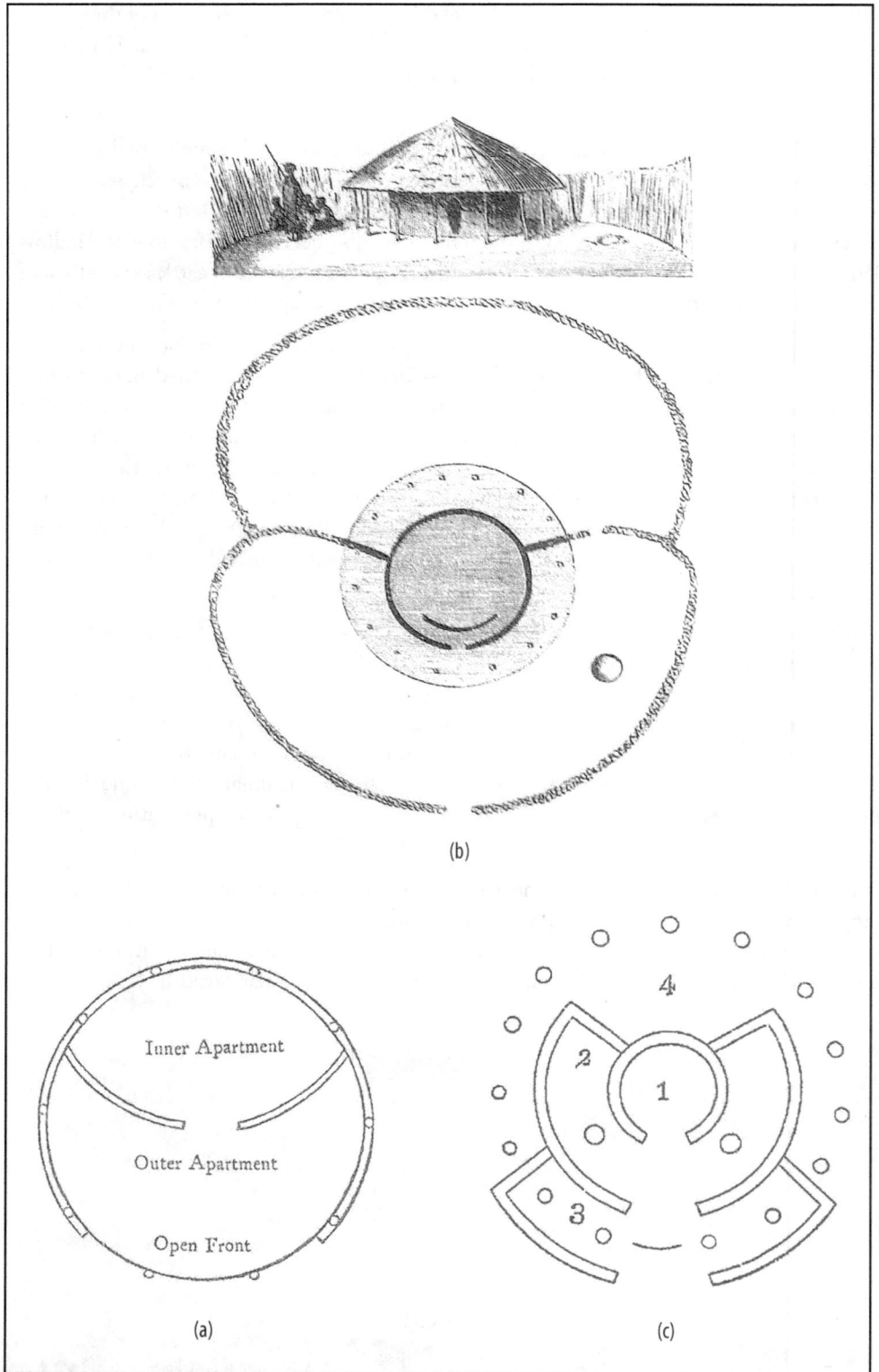

Figure 1.4
Historical plans of
Tswana houses:
(a) Barrow 1806: 392;
(b) Burchell 1824: 528;
(c) Kay 1833: 228
(numbered sections: "1, the
inner conoidal apartment;
2, the sleeping apartment;
3, the outer division half
under, and half beyond, the
roof; 4, the corn store").

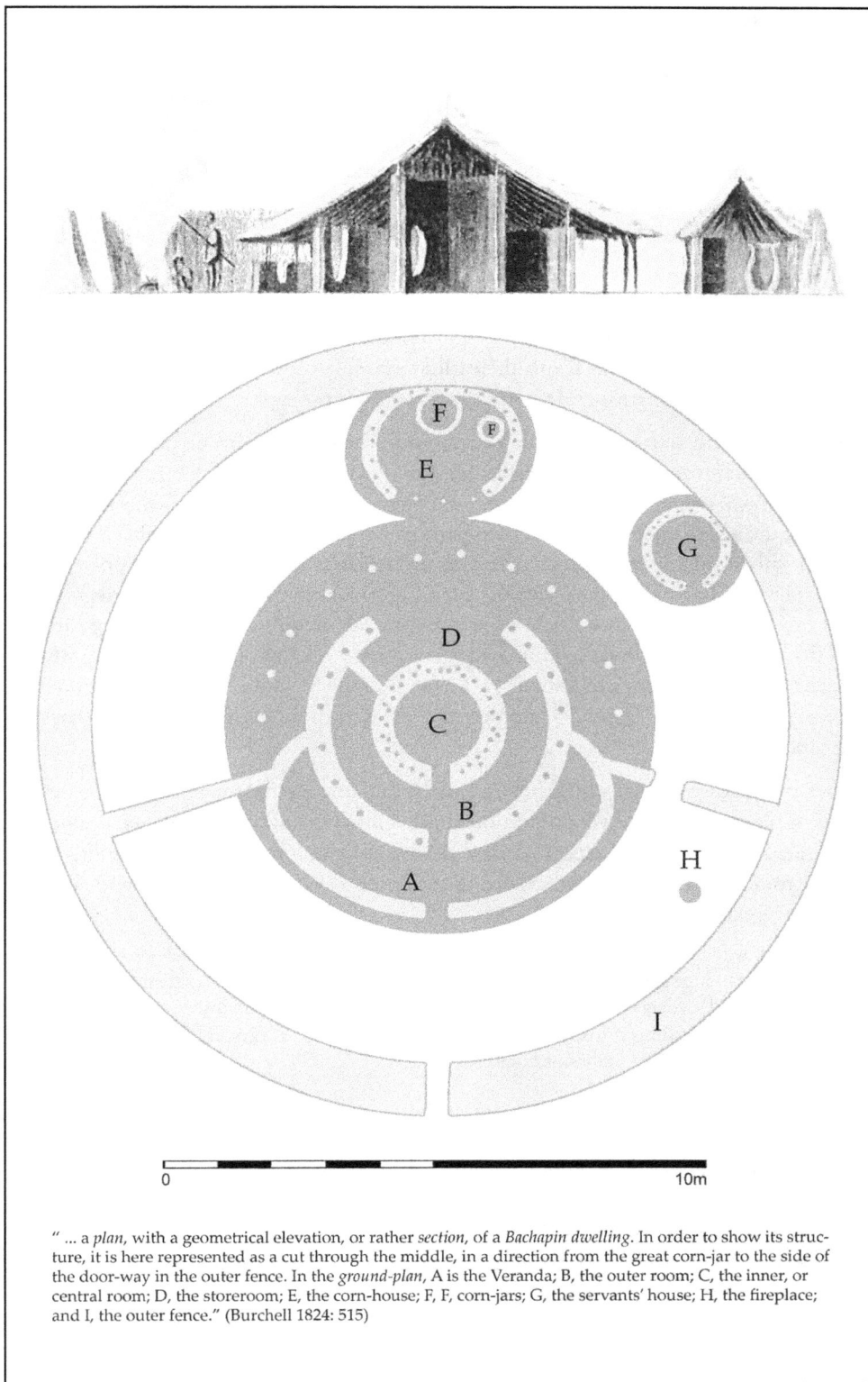

" ... a *plan*, with a geometrical elevation, or rather *section*, of a *Bachapin dwelling*. In order to show its structure, it is here represented as a cut through the middle, in a direction from the great corn-jar to the side of
the door-way in the outer fence. In the *ground-plan*, A is the Veranda; B, the outer room; C, the inner, or
central room; D, the storeroom; E, the corn-house; F, F, corn-jars; G, the servants' house; H, the fireplace;
and I, the outer fence." (Burchell 1824: 515)

Figure 1.5
"*Section and plan of a
Bachapin House*" from
Burchell 1824: Plate 9.
(Plan redrawn for clarity,
and metric scale substitutes
original imperial scale).

Lichtenstein does, however, describe the circular houses with their conical thatched roofs in considerable detail; from the number of mimosa posts used for the scaffolding, to the "argillaceous earth and ox-dung" composition of the wall plaster (377). He was clearly impressed by the "commodiousness and durability of the houses" (377), and alludes to the existence of a social hierarchy within the community with his description of separate servants' quarters, and the observation that "the huts of the poor are smaller, not being above eight or ten feet in diameter; sometimes even they consist only of a conical roof, resting upon the ground…" (378).

Although the Tlhaping had, by this time, experienced some limited contact with Europeans, (such as Kok, who had evidently offered them some instruction in animal husbandry), Lichtenstein's journal describes an 'Iron Age' Tswana community largely unchanged by European influence. His work forms the earliest example of what might perhaps, within the boundaries of its limitations, be termed a Tswana ethnography.

As an explorer with a strong scientific background, the observations of British naturalist William Burchell are particularly valuable. His four-year expedition left Cape Town in June of 1811, and was originally intended to reach Benguela on the west coast, with the aim of "exploring the less frequented or unknown parts of Africa, for the purpose of becoming acquainted with its inhabitants, and of increasing my own knowledge by the addition of whatever facts I might have the opportunity of observing" (Notcutt 1935: 8). Although growing unrest among Tswana communities of the interior prevented him from venturing further north than present-day Mafikeng, Burchell spent three weeks among the Tlhaping, whose capital had since moved back to Dithakong under the chief Mothibi. There, a new town had been established in 1806, some 10 kilometres to the west of the earlier Dithakong that the 1801 expedition visited.

Burchell was first struck, like others before him, by the "unexpected magnitude of the town" with its "multitude of houses which continued rising into view as far as I could see … not less than a mile and a half in diameter" (Notcutt 1935: 118), but it was not long before his keen scientific mind started to observe patterns in the town's organisation that had gone largely unnoticed by earlier visitors;

> In our way (sic) we passed through many *clusters of houses*; between which there were most frequently large spaces of unoccupied ground. Each of these clusters might generally be considered as the village of a different *kósi* or chieftain, and inhabited for the greater part, by his relations and connections; yet not necessarily, nor perhaps always, following this as a rule. (Burchell 1824: 313, italics original)

In his detailed descriptions of Tswana domestic households or *malapa*, which were built, he attests, entirely by the women, Burchell seems to have been impressed above all by "the neatness, good order and cleanness of their dwellings", and "the great carefulness which they show to remove all rubbish and every thing unsightly" (1824: 367). He describes a degree of variation in the size and interior design of the houses, as demonstrated in his plans and section drawings (Figs. 1.4, b and 1.5), but suggests that they are all "without a single exception, of the same general form and outward appearance" (1824: 364). He notes the distinction between the "front-court" and "back-yard" areas—significant features of Tswana household space. The latter, with their smooth plastered floors, were often used to house agricultural stores.

The arrangement of these household components formed, in some cases, what has been described more recently as a 'bilobial' dwelling style (Burchell 1824: 371; Maggs 1972).

Burchell also describes the location of men's "public enclosures" (courts or *kgotla*) and cattle kraals within each of the town's "divisions" (homesteads). He notes that the kraals are used as burial places for men, although "they have no wish to perpetuate a knowledge of the spot by setting up any mark over the grave". With limited pasturage available locally, most of the cattle are kept at "cattle-stations" some distance from the town (1824: 368).

As an independent explorer, Burchell's reporting was driven largely by personal curiosity which, combined with his training and experience in scientific data collection, led him to probe more deeply into the cultural significance of the things he witnessed at Dithakong than most other European visitors to the town. Although he did not evidently have access to the accounts of earlier expeditions, Burchell complemented and expanded upon the observations of his predecessors, and significantly deepened contemporary understanding of Tswana ethnography.

With a very different agenda to Burchell, the Rev. John Campbell of the London Missionary Society was initially sent to southern Africa to visit the mission stations that had recently been established in the region. On his first journey in 1813, he travelled up to Dithakong which, being clearly impressed by its scale, he described as an "African City" (Campbell 1815: 180).

Campbell's impression of the town, albeit relatively sweeping, resonated with the accounts of those who had visited Dithakong during the previous decade:

> The city is divided into a number of districts (homesteads or 'wards'), perhaps fifty, separated from each other, having each a Headman ... and a place enclosed for public resort (*kgotla*), where the men spend the greater part of the day together, dressing skins and making knives and various articles. We spent about three or four hours on this day in visiting some of those districts, but did not see above half of them (Campbell 1815: 187).

Figure 1.6
Painting of the Hurutshe capital Kaditshwene, based on a sketch drawn by John Campbell in 1820.

Figure 1.7
A domestic courtyard or
lapa at Kaditshwene in
1820, showing Hurutshe
women threshing grain.
The painting is based on
another of Campbell's
sketches.

While here, Campbell gathered reports about neighbouring Tswana communities; namely the Kwena to the north-east, who were reportedly wealthy and occupied a town three times the size of Dithakong; the Ngwaketse to the north-west, who frequently raided the Kwena; and the Hurutshe to the north who were also very prosperous, and whose "cattle kraal ... is so large that they frequently graze in it" (Campbell 1815: 216).

Although his first visit paved the way for the establishment of a mission station among the Tlhaping, it was during Campbell's second journey into Tswana territory in 1820, accompanied by the famous missionary Robert Moffat and his wife, that he recorded the most valuable information for historical archaeology (Campbell 1822). He visited the Tlhaping once again, who had since moved their capital back to Kuruman in 1817 in accordance with the wishes of the newly settled missionaries. On his way to their old settlement at Dithakong, which still accommodated a population similar in size to the new capital (Maggs 1976a: 278) he observed:

> On the road we passed several ancient inclosures (sic) built of stone, but by what nation the Matchappees (Tlhaping) have no tradition, only they are certain they could not be built by their ancestors, as Matchappee inclosures (sic) are all composed of bushes, and one generation adheres strictly to the customs of that which preceded it, but we afterwards discovered that it must have been built by the Marootzee (Hurutshe), or some other nation in that direction, who build their inclosures in stone exactly in the form of these ancient ruins. There is little doubt, therefore, but the ancient Marootzee nation had resided in that part of the country which is now possessed by the Matchapees, but the cause of their removing so far from it is now utterly unknown. (Campbell 1822: 126)

Campbell's observation is significant, not only because it supports the 1801 accounts of stone walled sites of greater antiquity on the local landscape (Barrow 1806; Borcherds 1861), but also because it includes the earliest recorded archaeological hypothesis in southern African Iron Age archaeology. Members of the Tlhaping community, utilising a combination of historical knowledge, ethnographic insight and archaeological observation, put forward the theory that the earlier stone walls were unlikely to have been built by their ancestors because they did not build in stone. This African genesis of our discipline, however rudimentary, should perhaps be acknowledged as a qualifier to the common assumption that southern African archaeology has entirely European disciplinary roots.

Having left the Moffats at Kuruman, Campbell ventured further north with the intention of visiting the Hurutshe, stopping briefly at the town of 'Meribowhey', more correctly spelt 'Maribôgô' (Schapera 1951: 102), and then at Mashow, where the Ratlou branch of Rolong lived (Campbell 1822; Maggs 1976a). Here he observed that the houses were very similar to those of the Tlhaping, with the exception of additional "stoops or terraces" (184). Campbell may be referring to the 'front veranda' feature that characterises many Tswana houses (Larsson & Larsson 1984), but which do not seem to have been ubiquitous at Dithakong. Again, he is struck by the scale of this Tswana town. He counted twenty-nine "districts" (homesteads), and estimated its population to be up to twelve thousand, surrounded by an area of cultivated land some twenty miles in circumference (Campbell 1822: 180-181).

Continuing on his journey, Campbell noted some more stone walled ruins, spanning about "two miles in length, and of considerable breadth". He observed that "a town had evidently once stood on that spot, and the kraals we saw had been attached to the different districts" (1822: 197).

Despite his growing familiarity with the size of Tswana towns, Campbell was nevertheless unprepared for the scale of Kaditshwene, the hilltop capital of the Hurutshe, when he arrived there in early May of 1820 (Campbell 1822; Boeyens 2000). In addition to the greater size of the town, which Campbell estimates to have been four times that of Kuruman, one of the most vivid differences would have been the use of stone walling to define the boundaries of cattle kraals and domestic households:

> Every house was surrounded, at a convenient distance, by a good circular stone wall. Some of them were plastered on the outside and painted yellow. One we observed painted red and yellow, with some taste. (Campbell 1822: 224)

Figure 1.8
One of John Campbell's original 1820 sketches of Kaditshwene, viewed from the west.

He echoes Burchell in his numerous references to the cleanliness of household floors, and reveals new details of artistic embellishment inside the houses: walls painted with figures of animals and adorned with cornices; carved or moulded pillars and figures, colourfully painted, which "would not have disgraced European workmen" (1822: 228). He witnessed how "for two miles in one direction the road was covered with droves of cattle" (256), and observed "extensive corn fields … two or three miles broad" (220). Earlier tales of such scenes must have sparked the rumours of Hurutshe wealth he picked up from the Tlhaping seven years earlier.

It is clear that Campbell was duly impressed by Kaditshwene, which he "found greatly to exceed, in point of importance, what I had previously conjectured. By the blessing of God it may prove a Jerusalem to the surrounding nations" (Campbell 1822: 253). His emotional statement serves as a reminder that some of his enthusiasm was related to the potential for the Hurutshe to receive a Christian mission.

Nevertheless, Campbell paints a picture of an extensive Tswana capital that is undeniably prosperous, well-organised and politically stable in the first quarter of the 19th century, and he reported that other such towns of comparable size and wealth existed elsewhere in the region at that time. Thanks to his contribution, it is at Kaditshwene that the historical archaeologist most vividly encounters the interface between archaeological, historical and ethnographic evidence (Boeyens 2000).

Stephen Kay, a Wesleyan-Methodist, travelled extensively around southern Africa in pursuit of missionary objectives, and his 1833 volume *Travels and Researches in Caffraria* was written with the aim of providing new missionaries with a guide, as the book's subtitle states, to the "character, customs and moral condition of the tribes" (Kay 1833). From the beginning, the accounts of his journeys through Tswana territories are coloured by the "melancholy effects" of escalating conflict between different chiefdoms. In this atmosphere of hostility he understandably interprets the aggregation of Tswana towns as a defensive response to the unrest:

> In order, as much as possible, to be prepared for attack, the population of the interior is in a great measure concentrated in towns, which are in many instances built on the very summits of mountains, commanding an extensive prospect every way. (Kay 1833: 215)

Kay describes his journey in 1821 from the mission at Kuruman, via the Tswana towns of "Meribawhey" (Maribôgô) and Mashow, to Kaditshwene, where Campbell had been the previous year. At Maribôgô, he describes little other than a disagreement over cattle plundering, and the value of visiting individual houses as an effective missionary tactic (1833: 217-218). Upon arriving at Mashow the following day, Kay describes a visit from Hurutshe headmen who had come to Mashow to seek military assistance against the Kwena, making it "evident that hostilities were kindling before us" (219). Indeed, the following day, Kay watched the Rolong army marching to war, but nevertheless found time to explore parts of the town, and found himself impressed by the "superior cleanliness, taste, and genius of the people" (220).

Arriving at Kaditshwene a week later, Kay found the Hurutshe in a state of "gloomy spiritlessness", with most of the men having gone off to fight (226). His observations of poverty and hunger among the "thirteen or fourteen thousand souls" (235) form a stark contrast to the impression of prosperity recorded by Campbell the previous year.

Kay describes several features of the town, including the stone walled cattle kraals and the position of threshing floors in back courtyard spaces. His description of the house structure is considerably detailed, and he remarks on the "germ of genius" represented in the painted animals and figures on the house walls (230). Kay provides a schematic house plan (Fig. 1.4, c) which appears similar in many respects to Burchell's plan of one of the larger houses at Dithakong (Fig. 1.5), although the latter also depicts the surrounding courtyard and associated structures.

Kay's sojourn at Kaditshwene ended on a sombre note. Having been repelled by the Kwena, the defeated Hurutshe warriors returned to Kaditshwene, begging for assistance from Kay and his firearms against their enemies. Kay refused, such an idea being contrary to his missionary objectives, and regretfully reports that "an invading host from the interior came down soon afterwards, and completely destroyed the town, routing and slaying all before them" (236). It seems likely that Kay is here referring to some of the so-called 'Mantatees', who drove the Hurutshe from Kaditshwene in early 1823. The survivors resettled at Mosega (Fig. 1.1) some 50 kilometres to the south (Boeyens 2000, 2003).

With a view to opening "new and more profitable channels of mercantile enterprise", the numerous journeys of British explorer George Thompson to regions beyond the colonial frontier were only partially driven by cultural curiosity (Thompson 1967: 1). He went to Kuruman in 1823 amidst rumours of the encroaching threat against the Tlhaping from the 'Mantatees', and records the eerie experience of visiting the recently abandoned Dithakong:

> We rode into the heart of it without seeing a human being; and a place which, a few hours ago, had contained a population of six or eight thousand souls, was now as solitary and silent as the most secluded wilderness. On looking into some of the huts, we perceived that the inhabitants must have fled in great haste, for the implements of cookery were standing with the food in them half dressed. It was, therefore, pretty evident that the approach of the enemy had taken them somewhat by surprise; and we naturally inferred that the invaders could not be far distant. (Thompson 1967: 108)

While the cooking fires may still have been smouldering, the living town of Dithakong had suddenly become an archaeological site in advance of the famous battle that was about to be fought there. Thompson's description of this "desolate city of the desert" (1967: 108) is a poignant premonition of the later historical records which, from this point onward, increasingly describe empty Tswana ruins.

Robert Moffat of the London Missionary Society was one of the early members of the mission station established at Kuruman in 1817. He first went there with Campbell in 1820, and returned again the following year, whereupon he took over the administration from the founder James Read. Moffat lived there among the Tlhaping for fifty years, and undertook several journeys through southern Africa during his ministry. Although he is best remembered as an evangelist, and for his extraordinary relationship with Mzilikazi, Moffat recorded comparatively little of the lives or customs of the Tswana he became so familiar with:

> My object here is not to give a description of the manners and customs of the Bechuanas, which would require a volume, while it would neither be very instructive nor very edifying". (Moffat 1842: 249)

Although somewhat muted by his own generally low opinion of Tswana lifestyle and moral character (Schapera 1951: xxvi), Moffat does record some details of Tswana house-building at Dithakong, describing the conical roofs and interior coolness and darkness of the structures. He emphasises the proactive role of the women in this and other domestic tasks, highlighting an evidently unequal division of labour between the sexes (Comaroff 1985). While her husband "spent the greater part of his life lounging in the shade", the woman is resigned to "labour under the rays of an almost vertical sun, in a hot and withering climate" (Moffat 1842: 251-252).

Moffat had, for some time, planned to visit the Ngwaketse, but his first attempt to do so in 1823 was thwarted by the imminent threat against Dithakong from the 'Mantatees'. The following year he tried again with more success. He stopped at Pitsan on the way, a Rolong capital that had previously been at Mashow where it was visited by Campbell in 1820, and by Kay in 1821 (Fig. 1.1). Moffat describes the town as covering a "large space" with, in his estimation, over twenty thousand inhabitants, including significant groups of Hurutshe and Ngwaketse who had been displaced by the 'Mantatees' (Moffat 1842: 388).

Later, they reached the "metropolis" of the Ngwaketse under chief Makaba at Kgwakgwe (Fig. 1.1), which "covered a large extent, so that the population must have been great compared with that of the towns of South Africa generally" (Moffat 1842: 398). Moffat describes aspects of the town in some detail, emphasising the cleanliness of the Ngwaketse utensils, domestic courtyards and house floors (their contrast with the Tlhaping in this regard being enthusiastically emphasised by Makaba), and elements of domestic organisation:

> Each of Makaba's wives, who were numerous, had a separate establishment, consisting of three or four houses, a corn-house, and a general storehouse. They had also a number of round jars for corn, from eight to twelve feet in diameter, and nearly the same in height, which are raised from the ground upon a circle of stones. (Moffat 1842: 398-399)

Figure 1.9
Hurutshe women preparing grain at Kaditshwene, painted by Charles Bell during the 1834 expedition led by Andrew Smith.

Moffat's description of the "front cattle-fold" (*kgotla*) indicates that it was formed from wooden posts rather than stone, and that the "proper cattle-fold" in Makaba's homestead could have accommodated "many thousand oxen" (Moffat 1842: 399). He was clearly impressed by the scale of the town, and upon ascending a nearby hill he "was able to count fourteen considerable villages; the farthest distant about one mile and a half; and I was informed that there were more towns, which I could not see" (Moffat 1842: 400).

Figure 1.10
A Tswana house, painted by Charles Bell during the 1834 expedition.

Andrew Smith was a Scottish doctor with military training who, among various medical and scientific posts, was the first Superintendent of the South African Museum in Cape Town. He was appointed by the South African Literary and Scientific Institution as leader of the 1834 Expedition into Central Africa, which was organised to gather natural and ethnographic data. The artist Charles Bell accompanied the team, charged with capturing images of the people and places they visited.

The expedition visited the Rolong at Thaba Nchu in November 1834. This town had been established for less than a year, and was estimated to be the largest contemporary Rolong settlement with five to six thousand inhabitants, including a well-established Methodist mission run by Broadbent and Hodgeson (Comaroff 1985).

Smith described the cultivated lands of grain and vegetable crops on the approach to the capital which, he noted, were situated some distance away from where their owners lived. His first impression of the place perhaps lacks the sense of awe that characterises earlier descriptions of Tswana towns, but he does allude to their complexity:

> It is impossible in the distance to judge of the character of a Bishuana (Tswana) town or to conjecture the number of its inhabitants. At first the lowness of the houses and their similarity to each other give it the appearance of a confused mass and, until the smoke from the huts or some other indication of the abode of man is discerned, it may be mistaken for a patch of dark soil. To this rule Thaba Unchu did not form an exception. (Lye 1975: 110)

Smith nevertheless observes that the houses, though recently built, were comfortable, and recognises that their organisation in clusters around the stone-built cattle kraals was related to social groups:

> In most parts they were closely huddled together and only separated from each other by the intervention of the cattlepans, each of which was the common property of several families who were connected either by the ties of relationship or by particular intimacy. (Lye 1975: 111)

In January of 1835 the party arrived at Kuruman, where Smith met Robert Moffat. During his stay, Smith made a number of sketches of Tlhaping implements and ornaments, including a drawing of a house plan and section (Lye 1975: 164) which is so similar in concept and detail to that of Burchell (Fig. 1.4, b) that it is difficult to believe it was not directly copied from the earlier drawing. He notes the separate clusters of houses, "such as is customary among the Bituana (Tswana) tribes, and which arises partly from the people who are attached to the different petty chiefs (headmen) being generally disposed to exist to a certain degree within a district of their own…" (Lye 1975: 166). Despite what he describes as "inferior workmanship", he was also impressed by the cleanliness of the house interiors and the domestic courtyards, and recognised gender-distinct spheres in the spatial organisation of the town.

Later that year, the missionary Peter Wright visited the Tlhaping at Dithakong, and spent a week with their chief, Mothibi (Wilson 1976). Although he did not leave much in the way of written descriptions of Tswana settlement style, a member of Wright's party illustrated the house of the chief during a meeting held under the eaves of its roof (Fig. 1.11).

In 1852, the Scottish journalist John Sanderson travelled through the Magaliesberg region on a "trading trip", and stopped at a Tswana settlement that he calls Pugeni, inhabited by a community of the same name under a chief called Mahata, some 16 kilometres north-west of Rustenburg (Sanderson 1981; Maggs 1976a).

Figure 1.11
A sketch from the missionary Peter Wright's visit to Dithakong in 1835, depicting a meeting with the Tlhaping chief Mothibi.

At Pugeni, Sanderson describes circular stone-built houses with clay surfacing over the walls, and with conical thatched roofs up to 30 feet high. He also provides the earliest description of wooden sliding doors, and notes that tree stems were sometimes planted in rear platforms inside the house, "the branches of which serve to hang articles upon". Each house was surrounded by a "broad eave or veranda", and situated within a plastered court-yard "kept scrupulously clean" (Sanderson 1981: 249).

> The towns appear to be a series of circles originally surrounding the cattle-kraals, and added to as occasion requires. There does not seem to be any regularity of plan, but streets lead from one part to another, sometimes 30 or 40 yards in width. In Pugeni, the chief town, there are several cattle-kraals: the principal one, a well-built oval, 93 yards in diameter between its axes. The wall is of dry stones, fully 4 feet in thickness, of equal height, and as well built as if the work of a European mason. Altogether, the cleanliness pervading these native kraals is such as ought to shame the Dutch Boers. (Sanderson 1981: 249)

With "some 300 huts" (248) Pugeni seems to have been relatively modest in scale when compared with the Tswana towns described in earlier decades. Indeed, oral traditions indicate that Sanderson is actually at Phokeng, where the Fokeng had a small capital under chief Moghatle from around 1837 (Breutz 1953a; Maggs 1993a). This synchronism between an early traveller's journal and Tswana oral tradition demonstrates the potential for a mutually supportive relationship between these two different scales of historical evidence. The Fokeng still reside at Phokeng today, under the Royal Bafokeng Administration.

Tswana ruins on the 19th century landscape

As we have seen in the works of Borcherds (1861), Barrow (1806) and Campbell (1815), Europeans have observed abandoned stone ruins on the landscape since they first ventured into Sotho-Tswana areas. There are many other such observations from travellers of the early- to mid-19th century that pass poignant comment on the upset of the *Difaqane*, and hold an important place in the body of early Tswana archaeological literature.

On his first journey to Mzilikazi in 1829, Robert Moffat describes "the ruins of innumerable towns, some of amazing extent" as he travels through the Magaliesberg. His observations form one of the earliest detailed descriptions of a southern African Iron Age archaeological site:

> The ruined towns exhibited signs of immense labour and perseverance, every fence being composed of stones, averaging five or six feet high, raised apparently without mortar, lime or hammer. Everything is circular, from the inner fence which surrounds each house to the walls which sometimes encompass the town. The remains of some of the houses which escaped the flames of marauders were large and showed a far superior style and taste to anything I had before witnessed. The walls were generally composed of clay with a small mixture of cow-dung, and so well plastered and polished with the former that they had the appearance of being varnished. The walls and doors were neatly ornamented with architraves and cornices, etc. The pillars supporting the roof in the form of pilasters, projecting from the wall and fluted, showed much taste. (Wallace 1945i: 8)

The contrast between the life and vibrancy of the Tlhaping at Kuruman with which he was so familiar, and the empty ruins now before him, seems to have put Moffat in a melancholy mood:

> Many an hour have I walked, pensively, among these scenes of desolation, - casting my
> thoughts back to the period when these now ruined habitations teemed with life and
> revelry, and when the hills and dales resounded to the burst of heathen joy. Nothing now
> remained but dilapidated walls, heaps of stones, and rubbish, mingled with human skulls,
> which, to a contemplative mind, told their ghastly tale. (Moffat 1842: 525)

On his 1835 journey to Mzilikazi, Andrew Smith frequently observed empty stone walled
sites, and attested to notable differences between Tswana and Ndebele settlement style
when seen as ruins:

> The mere difference (in walling arrangement) without regarding the difference in the
> forms of the houses, at once enable a traveller who is acquainted with the facts to conclude
> as to the description of people who occupy a country he may be visiting in South Africa
> … should he only come in contact with abandoned kraals. (Lye, 1975: 245)

Similar ruins were remarked upon by travellers such as Samuel Broadbent (1823: 46),
Andrew Geddes Bain (Lister 1949: 67), William Cornwallis Harris (1963: 142) and John
Sanderson (1981: 253), all of whom attributed their destruction to the Ndebele.

Andrew Anderson, a Cape colonial magistrate turned adventurer, travelled along the
northern banks of the Vaal River in the 1860s (Anderson 1974). Some of his descriptions
of stone ruins in the Marico area have courted controversy with regard to their accuracy
(Hoernlé & Hoernlé 1930; Maggs 1976a), and a somewhat romantic sentiment colours
his pondering of the displacement of Tswana groups who had lived in "large Kraals along
the river banks" (266), at the hands of Mzilikazi;

> … many of these stone kraals are still in existence, but in ruins … where they must have
> lived in peace for many generations, from the remains of extensive gardens now grown
> over with grass, proving, I think, they were not a wandering tribe, but a peaceful people
> … (Anderson 1974: 266)

While the existence of stone ruins along the Vaal is certainly not in doubt, Anderson here
presents a misconception that afterward became widely accepted—that the Tswana groups
of southern Africa lived in peace and stability prior to the disturbances surrounding the
Difaqane. But as these records have shown, and as we will explore further in Chapter
Three, deeper historical scrutiny reveals a more complex picture, characterised by almost
continuous skirmishing between Tswana lineages and the frequent movement of settlements from as early as the 17th century (Parsons 1996; Manson 1996).

Thus, a deserted Tswana settlement might, to the casual observer, have been abandoned
the previous month or the previous century—a fact that Mzilikazi was eager to convey to
Robert Moffat in an attempt to dilute his fearful reputation:

> In the course of our journeys, Moselekatse manifested great anxiety to convince me that
> the ruined towns we passed were the remains of former ages, and not the spoliations of his
> warriors; and in this instance he was correct". (Moffat 1842: 583)

In many cases today, only a combination of historical and archaeological evidence with
oral traditions can offer any clarity in re-establishing the identity of an individual site and
its place in Sotho-Tswana history where a direct link between the two has been lost. In the
next chapter we follow the development of systematic archaeological research on South
African stone walled sites.

Chapter Two
Research Background

I t would be half a century between Andrew Anderson's observation of Tswana ruins along the banks of the Vaal River (Anderson 1974), and the beginning of what might properly be termed systematic archaeological research on stone walled sites in South Africa. At that time the southern African discipline was largely focussed on the Stone Age, with the so-called "Bantu Period" being seen as something of an aside, or as falling within the realm of ethnography.

Since that time, we have progressed from an initial emphasis on simple descriptions of sites, through systems of classification and establishing cultural identities (including the development of ceramic sequences), and eventually to the incorporation of ethnographic data and the application of ethnographically derived normative models to interpret settlement organisation.

For the Late Iron Age, the analytical scale has recently shifted back towards the detail and variability of sites and the utilisation of an interdisciplinary approach to interpretation, drawing upon historical, ethnographic, ecological and archaeological data. In this chapter we discuss some of the key research initiatives and theoretical developments related to the archaeology of Sotho-Tswana stone walled sites.

Descriptive beginnings

The first peer-reviewed publication on a South African Iron Age stone walled site was that of Van Riet Lowe, who described ruins on the farm Vechtkop, some 24 kilometres south of Heilbron, in what is today the Free State (Van Riet Lowe 1927). His aim was simply to "elucidate the mystery" surrounding such ruins by attempting to "reconstruct and re-populate the settlement" (217).

A brief written description of the settlement layout is given, augmented by sketches of one of the houses in plan, section and front elevation (219), and a ground plan of a "typical stad" or homestead (220). Considerable space is devoted to describing and illustrating the artefacts recovered, reflecting the emphasis on collectable 'antiquities' prevalent at the time.

Drawing heavily from Stow's *Native Races of South Africa* (1905), Van Riet Lowe tries to present a broad historical context, within which he identifies the "Leghoya" (Taung) as the builders and occupants of the site from about 1787, and concludes that it was abandoned around 1820 as a result of the *Difaqane*. His conclusion was supported by a local informant, whose "account of the origin of the huts, and of the people who designed and built them, corroborated in detail my deductions from actual exploration and research" (Van Riet Lowe 1927: 228). Thus, despite the descriptive emphasis in his work, he did make an attempt to establish historical context and the identity of the occupants.

Hoernlé and Hoernlé followed Van Riet Lowe's work with a description of stone corbelled houses near Bethal, just north of the Vaal in present-day Mpumalanga (Hoernlé and Hoernlé 1930). The main aim of this research appears to have been to make a simple comparison with the site at Vechtkop.

Further west, Wells (1933) reported an extensive stone walled site on the Platberg, near Klerksdorp in present-day North West Province, which he described as "a labyrinth of passages and enclosures, bounded by massive walls of undressed stone" (582). The settlement is composed of several individual homesteads. Each is centred upon a distinct group of cattle kraals, and each dwelling structure is surrounded by a stone wall. Their foundations are suggestive of 'pole-and-daga' type walling with a thatched roof, and the "curved foundation before the entrance" (583) seems to indicate the presence of a front veranda.

Although his simple description resonates well with the character of more recently examined stone walled Tswana sites (Mason 1986; Pistorius 1992; Boeyens 2000), Wells only goes as far as to suggest a "Bantu" affiliation, and provides no plans or illustrations in his paper. However, he does make the earliest published call for interdisciplinary research that incorporates "historical, linguistic and other studies", an approach that Van Riet Lowe adopted intuitively but did not formally express (Wells 1933: 584).

A portion of the numerous sites in the Heilbron area, to the south-east of the Vredefort Dome in the Free State, were examined by Laidler (1935) with a comparatively well-organised expedition from the University of the Witwatersrand. Their aim was "to survey the main sites, obtain as much material as possible for investigating from certain middens, and to ascertain, if possible, the relative age and chronological sequence, if any, of the various types of stone-built settlement" (24).

Laidler identifies settlements that were evidently characterised by clay- or stone-walled thatched-roof houses, as well as the stone corbelled "bee-hive" variety, and suggests a chronological progression from the former to the latter. This shift, he attests, reflects the change from an early "pure Bantu" population of Rhodesian immigrants, via some catastrophe to a later mixed Bantu-Bush group (63). He also describes different forms of spatial layout and, while asserting that "the stone-building culture of the Transvaal and Free State is of the same origin as that of Zimbabwe" (51), makes a rudimentary attempt at a classification of local settlement style. The result of his only effort to engage with "local traditional history" (a claim by a Zulu informant that the ruins were built by Mzilikazi) is summarily dismissed, and instead he falls back on Ellenberger and MacGregor (1912) to identify the later phase of the site as Taung.

Although Laidler's historical interpretation was, like that of his colleagues, limited by the few published syntheses available at the time, his work was the first example of a systematic excavation of an Iron Age site, and it made a valuable contribution to the state of contemporary archaeological knowledge. As might be expected given the standards prevalent in this early period, however, he was criticised by later archaeologists for rushing the field work, failing to accurately record the location of the sites he worked on, and for losing two site plans which would have strengthened his paper considerably (Maggs 1976a: 7). These shortcomings are perhaps a reflection of the contemporary emphasis on artefacts, while provenance and context were accorded less importance.

In the Magaliesberg Valley, Trevor Jones described a group of settlement ruins on the farm Doornspruit, which were composed of circular homesteads with stone-built houses, granary platforms and "threshing floors" (Jones 1935). He rather tentatively affiliates the site with a pre-European Sotho-Tswana group who may, in light of the slag scatters in the vicinity, have been workers of metal. Otherwise, however, the paper is almost purely descriptive and lacks any serious attempt to suggest historical context or identity. Later historical and archaeological analysis has associated settlements of this type with Mzilikazi's Ndebele state (Pistorius 1996b, 1997).

Prompted by Van Riet Lowe, Daubenton continued the descriptive agenda with his report on three sites near Steynsrust in the Free State, nearly 200 kilometres south of Johannesburg (Daubenton 1938), and Pullen published a similar report on two groups of stone-built settlements atop ridges near Frankfort (Pullen 1942). The aims of both projects were to ascertain whether the sites warranted more detailed investigation, and to contribute to the records of the Historic Monuments Commission. Although Daubenton offers a short description of stone corbelled houses, the spatial settlement details in both papers are brief and vague, primarily asserting similarities with the previously published sites.

Early use of ethnography

With the exception of a brief report on some stone walling and dwelling structure floors on Brodie Hill, in today's Limpopo Province (Malan & Brink 1951), the period following the Second World War saw Iron Age archaeology in South Africa beginning to move beyond the simple descriptions and vague culture-historical assumptions that had characterised most research of the previous decades.

James Walton, an architectural historian, approached the archaeology of Sotho-Tswana-speakers from an ethnographic perspective, and was the first to synthesise the existing Sotho-Tswana ethnography and use it for archaeological interpretation.

Walton's work at Metlaeng in Lesotho, for example, directly incorporated ethnographic data from local informants in his interpretation of the adjacent archaeological site, which was occupied by the Fokeng-Hlakoana ancestors of the present-day community (Walton 1953). He also placed due emphasis on historical background, and although his historical sources were still largely limited to Ellenberger and MacGregor (1912), he was leading archaeology forward with his belief that "South African Bantu (Iron Age) archaeology is so closely bound up with ethnology that both approaches are needed for a satisfactory interpretation of the early Bantu sites" (Walton 1953: 11).

Ethnography also permeated Walton's discussion of Sotho settlements (Walton 1958), and his attempt to define a Fokeng settlement structure within the Sotho-Tswana archaeological record. He describes this as being characterised by linked cattle kraals, paved dwelling structure floors indicative of thatched 'bee-hive' structures, and ceramics with elaborate rim decoration (Walton 1956a). The historical background for his hypothesis was, however, somewhat inadequate, and his theory has been criticised as an over-simplification suffering from limited archaeological data (Mason 1962: 381; Maggs 1976a: 8).

Although he was not an archaeologist, Walton's *African Village* monograph (1956b) presents detailed Tswana architectural information that continues to contribute to archaeological interpretation. Its fusion of history, archaeology and ethnography demonstrates the potential held by an interdisciplinary approach to Tswana historical archaeology today, now that we enjoy the advantage of superior archaeological techniques, increasing historical resolution, and a well-developed body of ethnographic theory and data.

Regional distribution, site types and identities

While Walton focused his attention on Lesotho during the post-war decade, Revil Mason had started a series of archaeological investigations in areas north of the Vaal, and was the first to publish a definition of the term 'Iron Age' as applied to southern African archaeology (Mason 1952).

Mason also developed a "culture area concept", and applied it to the southern trans-Vaal and Free State (Mason 1952). He later extended the application to the western trans-Vaal area, and defined two distinct Late Iron Age Sotho-Tswana "culture historic areas" based on ceramic styles; *Buispoort* in the eastern region around the Magaliesberg and Witwatersrand, and *Uitkomst* in the westerly Zeerust and Rustenburg areas (Mason 1962). Although his analyses were grounded on a belief in a local Early Iron Age origin for the Sotho-Tswana (Mason 1983, 1986) and our definitions of culture historic units have evolved since Mason's early hypotheses, *Buispoort* and *Uitkomst* ceramic styles are still recognised and are now identified as terminal facies within the Moloko and Blackburn branches of the Urewe Tradition (Mason 1983, 1986; Evans 1983; Huffman 1980, 2002, 2007).

During his excavations at Late Iron Age sites during the 1960s, such as Melvile Koppies, Klipriviersberg, and the expansive site south of Zeerust that he incorrectly identified as the historical Kaditshwene (Mason 1986; Boeyens 2000), Mason began to focus on the importance of spatial organisation as an expression of social patterning and behaviour (Seddon 1968; Mason 1968). Recognising the advantages afforded by aerial photography for mapping large areas and defining settlement types, he conducted a preliminary regional survey of stone walled sites in small selected areas of the trans-Vaal and Free State using aerial photographs, simply counting the visible sites that met the criterion of a "contiguous walling system" (Mason 1965: 258). The survey area was subsequently extended by Seddon to include a larger block stretching westward from the Magaliesberg to the Botswana border, and again, involved a simple count of visible sites. Even at this preliminary stage variability in settlement style was noted, which Seddon tentatively attributed to chronological development (Seddon 1968).

Shortly afterwards, Mason observed that "settlement plan form is a direct function of so-cial organisation, and … one of the keys to the understanding of Iron Age social behaviour is the plan form of settlements" (Mason 1968: 168). In a subsequent aerial photograph survey of 47,733 square miles north of the Vaal he classified sites into five distinct 'classes', which he later redefined and expanded to ten (Mason 1968, 1986). From the accumulated spatial data, Mason started to explore a "possible relationship between structure and func-tion" in his attempts to interpret space within individual sites (Mason 1968: 175).

Although the aerial survey work achieved its primary goal to develop a general understand-ing of stone walled site distribution as a basis for further work, both Mason and Seddon based their early interpretations of settlement organisation in functional terms, in light of only archaeological evidence and some early historical descriptions. The variability of settlement styles and the clustering of site classes in different parts of the landscape are explained as "expressions of distinct Iron Age behaviour linked with the environmental variation from area to area, or merely as distinct behavioural developments due to relative geographical isolation" (Mason 1968: 175).

While rightly regarded as a pioneer archaeologist, Mason's work was largely characterised by what might be described as a "common sense" approach. He attributed his stone walled sites generally to Tswana-speakers, but made little use of oral traditions or ethnographic data in ascribing the identity of settlements or interpreting spatial organisation. Indeed, Mason's use of ethnography was notably muted in much of his research, the danger of which was demonstrated in his misinterpretation of the orientation of 'Hut S' at site 20/71 at Olifantspoort (Mason 1986: 241; Fredriksen 2007). As this book seeks to emphasise, local historical context and ethnography are critical to understanding the organisation of pre-colonial Sotho-Tswana settlements, and the variability between them.

The work of Tim Maggs further south in the Free State embraced these concepts more fully in his efforts to elucidate Sotho historical archaeology on the southern Highveld (Maggs 1972, 1976a, b). He approached Sotho archaeology from an historical perspec-tive, and was primarily concerned with linking different site types to historical identities. He conducted an aerial photograph survey of stone walled sites in an area extending from just north of the Vaal River, down to the Caledon River in the south, and extend-ing east to west from 26° to 30°E. From the survey he identified four main categories of site, named Types V, N, Z and R, and developed an excavation strategy based on this site typology.

In this work, Maggs established the time depth of stone walled sites and demonstrated the first expansion of farmers onto the Highveld south of the Vaal. Their earliest presence is represented by Type N sites around the Vaal and Klip rivers, dating from the fifteenth century, which Maggs associates with early Fokeng, Kwena, and possibly some Kgatla lin-eages. Type N sites developed into Type V before the seventeenth century, and the wider distribution of Type V sites, especially to the south-west, reflected the expansion of Taung lineages between the Vaal and Caledon rivers, where Type V became generally representa-tive of Sotho settlement style. Type Z sites were built by Kubung, and when compared with Type V, illustrate some of the general differences between Sotho and Tswana settle-ment characteristics (Maggs 1976a, b).

Maggs' recognition of cultural identities was strengthened by reference to regional history and ethnography, including some of the drawings and observations of early 19th century travellers that we discussed in the previous chapter, such as those of William Burchell (1824). Having noted the "network of typological similarities" between his Type Z sites and historically described Tlhaping and Rolong towns, Maggs could demonstrate the continuation of Type Z into the historic, ethnographic present, and was able to engage with the rich body of published Tswana ethnography in his interpretation of Type Z spatial organisation (Maggs 1976a: 319).

Furthermore, on the basis of the geographical, cultural and chronological resolution he had developed, Maggs was able to suggest an ecological impetus behind the extensive use of stone in Sotho-Tswana settlements. Due to the lack of timber in the southern Highveld region, Type V sites used stone extensively in their construction, as seen in the characteristic building of corbelled dwelling structures. Type Z sites, stemming from more westerly Tswana building styles, exchanged the wooden fences (described by early visitors to the Tlhaping and Rolong) for stone boundaries as they expanded into treeless areas, but retained their cone-on-cylinder house structure (Maggs 1976a).

Cognitive models

The work of Seddon, Mason and Maggs represented a phase in South African Iron Age research that was primarily concerned with recording regional site distributions, classifying settlement types, and relating them to historical identities and events. Their largely functionalist approach was to contrast markedly with the structuralist emphasis that characterised subsequent work, and which centred upon Tom Huffman's assertion that an understanding of prehistoric "Bantu cosmology" was not only an achievable objective, but was key to understanding Iron Age ways of life (Huffman 1986b: 330).

This stemmed from a study by Adam Kuper (1982), who synthesised a considerable body of ethnographic literature and identified large scale cultural structures for southern Bantu-speakers. He developed an ethnographic model that identified certain aspects of worldview shared by both Nguni- and Sotho-Tswana-speaking communities in the ethnographic present, which seemed to influence and characterise physical aspects of their settlement design.

With similarities recognised between the settlement organisation of communities in the ethnographic present and the spatial organisation of archaeological sites, Huffman then suggested that corresponding similarities should also have existed in their ideologies and worldview (Huffman 1982, 1986c). Therefore, Kuper's cognitive model, which Huffman re-labelled the 'Central Cattle Pattern', could also be applied to ancestral communities:

> The internal arrangement of a settlement reflects sociocultural organization because space is a cultural variable: its use is the result of a worldview, and people with the same worldview organize their settlements according to the same set of principles (Huffman 1986c: 89).

In its application to Iron Age archaeology, the Central Cattle Pattern has been invaluable in facilitating meaningful interpretation of settlement organisation and the spatial expression of concepts such as status, life forces and kinship (Huffman 2001). It has, however, received criticism from some archaeologists.

Paul Lane, for example, expresses some of the commonly held arguments against the validity of applying ethnographic models to archaeology of the more remote past (Lane 1994/1995). He suggests that to accept the application of an ethnographic model to a group of people throughout 2000 years of their existence is to accept that such communities were 'conservative' and unable to evolve without external stimuli, thereby encouraging a negative perception of prehistoric societies. For this reason he doubts the usefulness of the Central Cattle Pattern for Early Iron Age interpretation in particular (Lane 1994/1995).

Lane's critique for the recent past is less relevant, but nevertheless warrants a summary. He acknowledges that the African archaeological context offers a degree of cultural, historical and environmental continuity between source and subject that enables the application of a 'direct historical approach' to ethnographic analogy. But he is dissatisfied with what he perceives to be a lack of consideration of the historical context of the ethnographic data itself, both in terms of dynamics within the community and the methods of anthropological data collection. In short, normative models like the Central Cattle Pattern are by definition ahistoric, and do not account for change, variability, or the specific circumstances of the communities from which they are derived.

In his response to these criticisms, Huffman reiterates that one of the basic premises of the Central Cattle Pattern is the assumption that, although one worldview could lead to more than one type of settlement pattern, the reverse is unlikely to be true. That is, two different worldviews would be unlikely to create the same complex spatial organisation, and consequently, in the absence of another more convincing model, we can assume that a particular spatial settlement style can be used to recognise holders of a particular corresponding worldview (Huffman 2001).

Consequently, Huffman asserts that the Central Cattle Pattern applies to all Eastern Bantu speakers, including both Nguni and Sotho-Tswana. This inclusiveness illustrates that the model is not restricted to any particular identity group, or to environmental factors, but at a general level encompasses such smaller-scale variability. Huffman justifies his application of an ethnographically derived model to archaeological contexts by emphasising that the Central Cattle Pattern is based on a direct historical approach, and not formal analogy. The formation of the model begins by confirming a close relationship between ethnographic data and archaeological material of similar date. Then, when a model has been derived by exploring relationships between these two sets of data, it is applied back in time to the earlier archaeological record. He illustrates the applicability of the Central Cattle Pattern to specific archaeological examples, notably Kgaswe in Botswana, Broederstroom and KwaGandaganda, the latter two of which demonstrate the relevance of the model as far back as the 5th to 7th centuries. These examples also show that the model applies equally to identities associated with the Kalundu, Nkope and Kwale ceramic branches (western, central and eastern streams) (Huffman 2001, 2007).

Huffman emphasises the fact that the Central Cattle Pattern is an ahistoric normative model, operating on a scale general enough to incorporate regional, cultural and environmental variations without having to explain them. He asserts that "to challenge this model successfully, critics must propose an alternative that interprets the data better at the same scale of abstraction. At the normative scale, the evidence for the Central Cattle Pattern … is overwhelming" (Huffman 2001: 31).

Nevertheless, Huffman himself has described the relatively recent aggregation of Tswana communities from small dispersed settlements into large towns from the early 18th century (Huffman 1986a; Taylor 1979). This was a diachronic development prompted by a range of specific historical dynamics, and was paralleled by significant developments in scale and complexity within Tswana society. It is clear that, while ethnographically derived normative models are valid and valuable in their provision of a broad cognitive framework, it is also necessary to probe this historical detail, and to assess the influence it may have exerted over the development and organisation of individual towns. With much mainstream archaeological effort through the 1980s and 1990s focussed only on the application of normative models, the risk of 'glossing over' this kind of detail and variability became a cause for concern.

The work of Julius Pistorius at the large Kwena capital of Molokwane near present-day Rustenburg provides an example of the way in which ethnographic models like the Central Cattle Pattern can be used to explain spatial and social organisation of a Tswana town, but it also illustrates the consequent limitations of interpreting a settlement's physical expression as being 'inherently Tswana' (Pistorius 1992).

The research, conducted between 1981 and 1983, was "aimed at proving that the site's settlement style is representative of the settlement system of historical and contemporary Sotho-Tswana villages (*metse*) in its ground plan, composition and settlement layout", focussing on the settlement as a whole using aerial photography, and on a single settlement unit or homestead, SE1, through excavation (Pistorius 1992: 1). In common with earlier archaeological work this research is largely descriptive in nature, but it draws extensively upon ethnographic data to interpret the organisation of space and the function of archaeological features at Molokwane. Indeed, Pistorius' detailed synthesis of ethnographic data relating to Sotho-Tswana settlement organisation and function, from Kgatla, Ngwato, Kwena, Ntšhabeleng, Pedi and Tlokwa sources, is a valuable element of this work.

With the driving rationale of the research being simply to demonstrate that the town was organised according to the principles of the Central Cattle Pattern, it can be said to have achieved its goal. Indeed, Simon Hall (1995b) in his review of Pistorius (1992) agrees that "in the face of Pistorius' aims, I find little about this work which can be faulted" (88). But Molokwane is an historic site, clearly identified in the oral records as a Tswana town, and the Tswana ethnographic data with which Pistorius is working is also historical. Essentially then, he is comparing the 'ethnographic present' with the 'ethnographic present' and, as Hall points out, "given the unassailable tie between Molokwane and its Kwena occupants, Pistorius' general aim becomes somewhat spurious" (Hall 1995b: 88). The details of historical context forming the backdrop against which Molokwane developed as a town were glossed over in deference to an emphasis on ethnography and spatial organisation. Tapping into deeper levels of interpretation of Tswana towns would require the development of more progressive research frameworks that also engaged with history.

Embracing detail, variability and historical context

By the time Pistorius' work at Molokwane was published, new streams of archaeological enquiry were developing and structuralist interpretations were receiving criticism for their inability to address "smaller scale variability and specific historical circumstance", and the way in which these two factors related to one another (Hall 1995b: 88). Simon Hall suggested a need to place greater emphasis on the reasons behind the large size and population densities of Tswana towns, instead of treating this characteristic as "some inherent ethnographic principle whereby growth is axiomatic" (88). He identified a need to focus once again on the detail and variability within and between sites, as demonstrated by Mason and Maggs, but against a backdrop of established historical context.

In an attempt to address issues of change and cultural structure, Hall examined the dynamics of gender relations within Late Iron Age Sotho-Tswana domestic households, and how changes in these relations might be identifiable through archaeology. In particular, he explored the tight links between pottery, the social processes translated through pottery and the spatial settings of gender interaction (Hall 1998). He pointed to changes in the organisation of household space, from the multi-purpose dwelling structures of the Madikwe and Olifantspoort phases (early 16th to mid 17th centuries) within which a range of domestic activities were undertaken, to the comparatively empty houses of the late Moloko (18th century onward) when most activities occurred in the surrounding courtyard or *lapa*.

Hall suggested that this development might be reflected archaeologically in a parallel trend towards stylistically bland ceramics in the later period. His multi-dimensional analysis of Moloko ceramics supported his hypothesis that there may have been "a greater role for the mediation of boundaries through mobile symbols, particularly pottery" in the earlier phases than in the later period, when stone walling had been adopted and space/interaction had become more architecturally segmented (Hall 1998: 242).

Hall's study specifically attempted to address detail and change, and his attempt to move away from normative models and refocus on a smaller scale of analysis was a refreshing development. This sentiment was echoed in Lane's exploration of the Tswana house as a metaphor for the female body. He describes houses as "atoms" of the Tswana world, that were centres for procreation, and therefore the survival of the lineage. As such, great importance is attached to the house, and to a woman's body within it, as "the source of both practical and symbolic sustenance" (Lane 1998: 188).

Lane expands his association between a woman's body and the house by suggesting that some Tswana house plans resemble female reproductive anatomy, which might reflect the conceptual links between sex, childbirth, houses and women's bodies. He extends this idea further by pointing to physical similarities between the plans of whole settlements and female genitalia, and suggests that the nightly herding of cattle into the central byres of the settlement might symbolise reproductive conception.

While ethnography is explicit about the conceptual link between "the house and the female body that was its metaphoric referent" (Comaroff 1985: 56), it would seem somewhat speculative to extend this idea to the whole settlement plan. Lane bases his interpretation on aspects of the ethnography that indirectly point to a possible link between female physical bodies, procreation and settlement plan form, and concedes that there is certainly no direct indication of this in either ethnographic or historical sources.

Subsuming the weaknesses of his specific example, however, is the importance of Lane's assertion of the need to "develop interpretive frameworks that treat gender relations more as situational constructs than as fixed categories, and in ways that allow for as much consideration of the variations within social categories as between them" (Lane 1998: 201). In short, Lane echoes Hall's call for more attention to the detail and variability that exists in the Tswana world, both in the ethnographic present and in the archaeological record. This milieu has influenced recent research that continues to focus upon an intimate scale of Tswana life, emphasising aspects of social interaction and relationships between people, material culture and space within Tswana households (see Fredriksen 2007).

A pivotal element of this contextual detail is historical resolution. The work of Jan Boeyens at the Tswana town of Kaditshwene in the Marico district emphasised the importance of specific historical context (Boeyens & Cole 1999; Boeyens 2000). By fusing oral traditions, historical documents and archaeology, he was able to demonstrate that the extensive stone walled hill complex between the farms Kleinfontein and Bloemfontein, 25 kilometres north-east of Zeerust, was the early 19th century Hurutshe capital visited by John Campbell in 1820. The identification of this site as Kaditshwene put an end to the previous assumption, propagated by Seddon (1966) and Mason (1986), that the historical capital visited by Campbell was located on the farm Vergenoegd, some 30 kilometres to the south-west. With its historical context well established, our understanding of the scale and organisation of this important capital can be augmented by exploring it against a regional historical and political backdrop (Boeyens 2006).

Today, interdisciplinary approaches to southern African historical archaeology are being developed and invigorated by the Five Hundred Years Initiative (FYI), a collaborative research group centred at the University of the Witwatersrand with an agenda to encourage and facilitate synergistic research frameworks for the last half century of southern African history (Behrens 2007; Swanepoel *et al.* 2008). It is anticipated that this initiative will contribute significantly to the development of research into agropastoral communities of the Late Iron Age.

Thus, this book can be framed within the recent theoretical milieu nurtured by Hall, Lane and the FYI, that emphasises the importance of detail and variability within the Tswana world, and the vital role of contextual backdrop against which archaeological interpretation needs to be considered. It will be demonstrated that the interdisciplinary use of multiple data sets is vital if we are to approach a more complete interpretation of the complexities of Tswana town life. In the next few chapters we are introduced to Marothodi, the Tlokwa capital at the centre of our study, as we explore aspects of its historical, biophysical and archaeological context.

Chapter Three
Historical Context

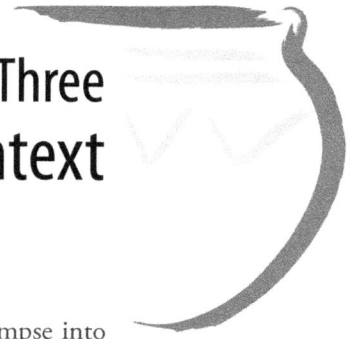

The early travellers' journals we examined in Chapter One offered a glimpse into a climate of increasing unrest among chiefdoms in the interior of South Africa in the early 19th century—tensions that culminated in the *Difaqane* wars of the 1820s and 30s. But prior to these turbulent events, Tswana oral histories reveal that significant transformational processes were already underway among the communities of the Pilanesberg/Magaliesberg region.

Indeed, a great deal of historical detail about sub-Saharan African communities is rooted in their oral traditions or histories, and our examination of the historical context of Marothodi draws heavily from such sources. In this chapter, we first discuss the wider regional historical climate from the 17th century, and then focus on the specific oral traditions of the Tlokwa of Marothodi.

Regional historical climate

Oral histories are silent with regard to the earliest ancestral Sotho-Tswana groups who entered areas south of the Limpopo. The only records are origin stories centred on legendary founders (for a summary see Walker 1997). Where vague references start to emerge in the traditions, they still represent "faint memories of an era in which social formations were fluid and political boundaries remained blurred" (Boeyens 2003: 68). Archaeological sites associated with the Madikwe and Olifantspoort ceramic styles of the 15th and 16th centuries reveal a pattern of small and dispersed settlements (Boeyens 2003; Huffman 2007).

The earliest traditions of historical value describe a recurring pattern of community 'fission', whereby rulers' senior sons or brothers occasionally left their original group and established their own chiefdoms. Many such splinterings were prompted by succession disputes arising from the sometimes confusing and ambiguous kinship systems that determined the rightful heirs to the chieftainship (Legassick 1969; Kuper 1982; Manson 1995). It is also possible that increasing populations, environmental concerns and stirring competition over resources (e.g. avoiding drought or seeking uncontested pasture) may have provoked migrations or influenced sections of a community to hive off and resettle elsewhere (Legassick 1969; Parsons 1995).

From the early 16th century, these seem to have been the primary dynamics behind the dispersal of 'clusters' from the dominant ancestral Tswana lineages. The process eventually resulted in off-shoot groups occupying most of the Highveld by the end of the 17th century, intermingling with and absorbing elements of other communities, including groups of Fokeng already living in the region (Legassick 1969; Maggs 1976a).

However, this pattern of dispersal could only continue for as long as there were relatively uncontested lands to move into and plentiful resources to commandeer. By the 17th century, pressures on the landscape had started to increase as a result of the population growth caused by a period of good rainfall (Hall 1976; Tyson & Lindesay 1992), as well as the continuing movement onto the Highveld of Nguni peoples from beyond the Drakensberg, known as the 'Trans-Vaal Ndebele' (Parsons 1995, Huffman 2007).

Furthermore, from the mid-18th century an increasing demand from the east coast and the Cape colony for commodities like ivory, furs, metals, cattle and feathers, led to a growing interest among Tswana chiefdoms in acquiring trade goods to exchange, which in turn led to an even greater demand for land (Manson 1995; Parsons 1995). This demand was checked by the southern Kalahari in the west and the tsetse fly belt to the north-east. The distributions of Type V and Z stone walled sites defined by Maggs reflect the ecological limits of farming (Maggs 1976a), and when these limits had been reached, competition for resources intensified further.

Tswana chiefdoms turned increasingly to the raiding of cattle, the basis for exchange in Tswana society and the means to security, power and wealth. Cattle could be exchanged not only for trade goods to compete for dominance of the burgeoning market forces, but also for women with their "productive and reproductive power", and the valuable networks of allegiance that intermarriage facilitated (Hall 1998: 258). As described in the early travellers' journals, cattle raiding characterised this period of escalating inter-chiefdom conflict from the later 18th century (Manson 1995).

Accompanying the climate of growing hostility was a trend towards the aggregation of communities from geographically dispersed units into condensed centres of substantial population, wherein all inhabitants pledged allegiance to the resident chief. This 'fusion' of Tswana lineages may have occurred gradually, or as a rapid and sudden response to the regional dynamics. While the quest for ecological advantages may have influenced the process (Hammond-Tooke 1993: 34), it was mainly prompted by the need for rulers to exert greater control over the resources of their chiefdoms, and by the need for insecure communities to obtain an element of protection by attaching themselves to a larger group (Legassick 1969; Manson 1995). The 'ward system' synonymous with Tswana socio-political structure, facilitated the smooth incorporation of foreigners (Schapera 1955; Tlou 1974; Legassick 1969).

By the early 19th century, the aggregation process had created the large Tswana towns like Kaditshwene and Dithakong that we recognise from the early travellers' journals, comprised of thousands of inhabitants living in densely congregated, ethnically diverse wards around the homestead of their resident chief. Kuper suggests that the increased socio-political complexity that accompanied a transition of this scale was reflected in the development of new settlement spatial characteristics, like the separate court or *kgotla* to accommodate a "larger scale decision-making unit" (Kuper 1982: 151), while Hall points to the elaborated "spatial segmentation" that emerged within domestic living areas (Hall 1998: 257). These spatial elements are observed archaeologically at contemporary Tswana sites like Kaditshwene (Boeyens 2000), Molokwane (Pistorius 1992, 1996) and Olifantspoort (Mason 1986).

Parallel to these changes was an increase in political centralisation. Although individual wards within chiefdoms retained some administrative and economic independence under their headmen, ruling chiefs now enjoyed the ability to extract tribute from their subjects in the form of labour and military service, and could harness ritual authority over such vital institutions as initiation ceremonies, agricultural cycles, rainmaking and the formation of both male and female age regiments. Chiefs could now position themselves to take advantage of the parallel economic developments that were underway, such as the production of surplus goods for regional and wider trading and the cultivation of monopolies over craft production and trade routes. With authority becoming increasingly centralised, the chiefs became wealthier and more powerful, and attracted more subjects to their chiefdoms (Legassick 1969; Manson 1995; Parsons 1995).

However, having reached the ecological limits of agropastoral expansion by 1700, with some communities possibly having developed a dependency on maize as a staple crop (Huffman 2006, 2007), the onset of serious droughts in the KwaZulu-Natal area towards the end of the 18th century and the early 19th century may have further destabilised the region (Hall 1976; Curtis, Tyson & Dyer 1978; Huffman 1996; Boeyens 2003). This could have encouraged the aggregation process, as weakened or uprooted communities sought the protection and security of larger, more powerful chiefdoms. It is against this regional historical backdrop that we examine the specific experience of the Tlokwa.

The Tlokwa of Marothodi: evaluating oral traditions

The first oral records of this lineage may relate to the mid-16th century, but they are vague and this dating is highly speculative. The histories increase in detail and focus from the second half of the 18th century, and show that the Tlokwa split a number of times into distinct but related 'branches' during their time in the Pilanesberg/Magaliesberg region. Today, four main branches are recognised: the ba ga Sedumedi, now living at Letlhakeng; the ba ga Bogatsu at Kolontwane; the ba ga Kgosi at Molatedi on the edge of the Mankwe Game Reserve; and the ba ga Gaborone, the senior branch living at Tlokweng in Botswana.

There are three available published sources of recorded oral traditions of the Tlokwa of the Pilanesberg/Magaliesberg region. The earliest of them was published in *Short History of the Native Tribes of the Transvaal* (TNAD 1905) by the Transvaal Native Affairs Department, and is referred to in this discussion as the *Short History*. It consists of a brief account of some of the major events of the Tlokwa with a short genealogical tree. Despite its brevity and the ambiguity surrounding its sources and authorship, it has historical value because it is likely to have been gathered directly from Tlokwa oral testimony. Both the transmission and recording were therefore not influenced by previously published histories, which is an advantage that the two later sources, by default, do not share.

Next is an account by Vivien Ellenberger, the District Commissioner of Serowe in what was then the Bechuanaland Protectorate, in his *History of the Batlokwa of Gaborones* (Ellenberger 1939). He draws upon the contemporary knowledge of the "old men of the tribe" who were living with the senior line of the Tlokwa at Gaborones in the early 20th century. He occasionally uses material from his grandfather's *History of the Basuto* (D. F.

Ellenberger 1912) to supplement the earlier historical detail, and was probably familiar with the *Short History* although no direct reference is made to it.

Lastly, and perhaps more widely known, is a survey by the state ethnologist Paul-Lenert Breutz published in *The Tribes of the Rustenburg and Pilansberg Districts* (Breutz 1953a). His chapters on the Tlokwa groups draw partially upon the *Short History*, on Ellenberger's earlier material, and on an account written by the Tlokwa chief Sedumedi (Native Affairs Department Ms. No. 168). He combined these sources with information gathered from informants at the Kolontwane and Letlakeng settlements.

Assessing the historical reliability of oral traditions can be problematic, and as with all historical sources they must be used with care. The histories related by the Tlokwa, in common with most sub-Saharan African oral traditions, record the selective genealogies and movements of ruling lineages. They reflect shifts in the centre of power that were sometimes, but not always, accompanied by actual population or settlement movements, and are essentially 'official' narratives taught to each generation through chains of transmission. As such, they have the advantage that the formalised nature of their cultivation and transmission within Tswana society involved regular "controlled recital" (Vansina 1961: 23), for example during initiation schools (Mönnig 1967: 119), which generally assists faithful continuity. Furthermore, reference in the Tlokwa traditions to settlement locations in terms of present day farm names provides an invaluable spatial anchor, and enables the tentative plotting of an 'oral geography' to accompany the historical sequence.

Official traditions are, however, vulnerable to manipulation in defence of a variety of social, political or economic interests (which may themselves change from generation to generation), tending to emphasise "events and deeds which promote continuity within the centralised structure of the polity" (Reid & Lane 2004: 9). In the context of early 20th century South Africa when the Tlokwa traditions were recorded, social pressures may have influenced the character of official histories in the telling as Tswana groups responded to the colonial presence with varying combinations of subtle resistance and expedient cooperation (Vansina 1971; Comaroff 1985). We can only speculate about the precise circumstances of the Tlokwa transmissions, but within the milieu of a chief and his council being formally interviewed by European government officials, a guarded or 'intentional' account may have been elicited, and "as soon as a testimony is intentional, it is influenced by the informant" (Vansina 1961: 49). Answers were sometimes 'controlled' by informants, as illustrated in Breutz's account of his interviews with the Fokeng, during which "the earlier history of this tribe would have been described better if the man who knows it best, Ruben Mokgatle, aged about 90, had been allowed to talk" (Breutz 1953a: 77).

Nevertheless, although there may be "no such thing as a testimony that is exclusively aimed at recording history" (Vansina 1961: 48) it is felt that, when handled with the necessary caution, the Tlokwa oral traditions provide a reasonably accurate historical framework within which we can begin to understand Marothodi as a 'snapshot' within the Tlokwa settlement sequence.

The Tlokwa experience from the 18th century

The traditions recorded by Ellenberger only begin to gain focus from around the mid-18th century, when they describe the Tlokwa chiefdom emerging through the Magaliesberg mountains into the Rustenburg area from the south east, under the leadership of Mosima. Although vague, this reference to a south-eastern origin gives us an early indication that the Tlokwa may have had Nguni roots.

Pilanesberg

Upon arriving in the Pilanesberg area, the Tlokwa settled at a place called Bôte, where they remained from about 1740 to 1760 (Fig 3.1). The commentaries in all three sources indicate that this settlement was located on the farm Houwater 496 (later 54JQ) in what is now the Pilanesberg National Park (TNAD 1905: 40; Ellenberger 1939: 170; Breutz 1953a: 201). Mosima died during their 20 year occupation here, and was succeeded by Monaheng, who was in turn succeeded by Matlabane (Ellenberger 1939; Breutz 1953a).

Archaeological excavations in this area have revealed ceramics from the *Ntsuanatsatsi/Uitkomst* sequence together with Type N stone walling. These pottery and walling styles are associated with early Fokeng groups who, according to Huffman's reasoning, originated among Northern Nguni people (Huffman 2007). Thus, assuming the site can be firmly identified as Bôte, it links the Tlokwa with Nguni material culture at this stage in their settlement sequence, and seems to support an Nguni origin (Coetzee 2005; Huffman 2007).

It was at this time that the first recorded phase of the "twenty year hostility" with the Fokeng began (Manson 1996: 352). Breutz's accounts of the Tlokwa ba ga Sedumedi and Tlokwa ba ga Bogatsu show that aggression from the Fokeng was encountered at this early stage in the regional settlement sequence. While the traditions of the ba ga Bogatsu give the impression that the Fokeng threat was evaded (Breutz 1953a: 201), those of the ba ga Sedumedi more explicitly agree with the *Short History* statement that "at Houwater they fought and were defeated by the Bakwena-Ba-Fokeng" (TNAD 1905: 40; Breutz 1953a: 361). In response to this climate of aggression, Matlabane "crossed the Kgetleng (Elands River) and settled on its western bank at Itlholanoga" (Ellenberger 1939: 170), where they lived from about 1760 to 1770 (Fig. 3.1).

Breutz (1953a: 201), in agreement with the *Short History* (TNAD 1905: 40), suggests that the farm Doornhoek 134 (later 91JQ) in the Pilanesberg may have been where Itlholanoga was situated. The site excavated in this area by Revil Mason that he refers to as 'Sun City' may have been the historical Itlholanoga (Mason 1986), and the *Ntsuanatsatsi/Uitkomst* ceramics found here would seem to corroborate the findings from Bôte that point to Nguni origins (Huffman 2007).

This oral and archaeological evidence from the Tlokwa sequence in the Pilanesberg is important to our understanding of the later settlement at Marothodi. Although the Tlokwa seem to have been almost fully 'Tswana-ised' by the early 19th century, their Nguni roots distinguish them from the western Tswana lineages living in the other aggregated capitals in the region, and we might anticipate that Marothodi was not a 'typical' Tswana town.

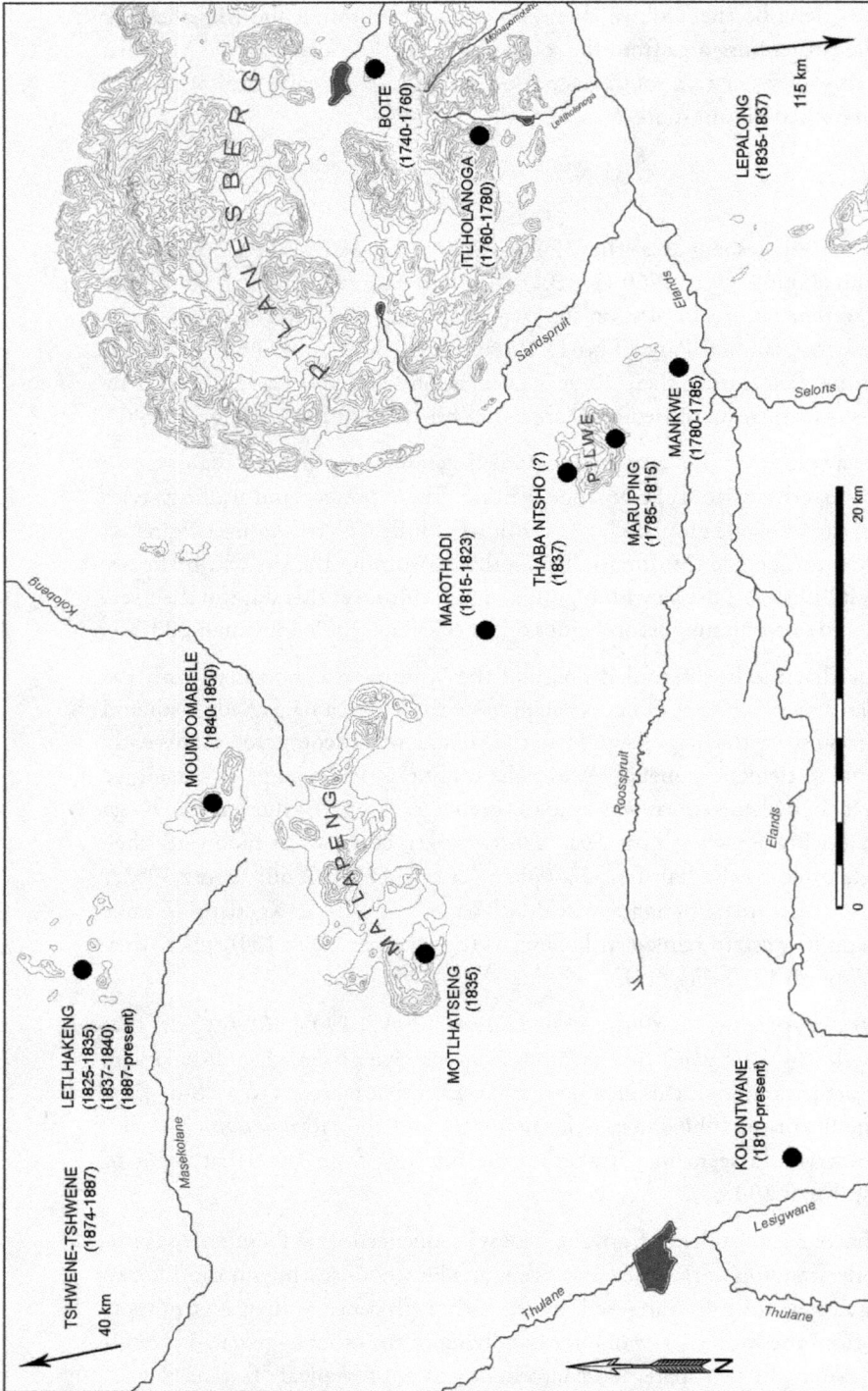

Figure 3.1

Map of the Matlapeng region, showing the locations of the main Tlokwa capitals mentioned in the text. All dates are approximate.

Pilwe

Ellenberger and Breutz agree that from Itlholanoga the chiefdom moved to Mankwe (Fig. 3.1) in about 1780 (Breutz 1953a: 198; Ellenberger 1939: 170).

Taukobong was chief throughout the occupation of Mankwe, and he later led the chiefdom to Maruping in the Pilwe hills a short distance to the north (Fig. 3.1). Ellenberger (171) mistakenly suggests that Maruping was located on the farm Zwaarverdiend 502 (now 234JP) which, as discussed above, was the location of Mankwe further south. Breutz (361) more convincingly asserts the farm Zwartkoppies 116 (now 212JP) as the location of Maruping, which would put the settlement somewhere on the southern half of the Pilwe hills. Aerial photographs of Pilwe show a number of stone ruins on the northern side of the hills, although none are immediately evident on the southern side. Ground survey would be needed to confirm the presence or absence of archaeological settlement evidence here.

Kolontwane

When Taukobong died, Molefe, one of his sons from a junior wife, acted as regent for the young heir, Bogatsu. A dispute arose when Phiri, one of Bogatsu's brothers, urged Bogatsu to take over the chieftainship. Bogatsu refused, preferring to wait for Molefe to die, so Phiri made an attempt on Molefe's life during a hunting trip. In response to this attack, Molefe fled around 35 km westward to a place called Kolontwane on the farm Grootfontein 301 (now 225JP) with some loyal members of the chiefdom (Fig. 3.1). Phiri pursued Molefe, but was defeated. This episode heralds a split in the Tlokwa community, as Phiri then went back to Pilwe with his followers and continued to lead a separate chiefdom there. Molefe settled at Kolontwane from about 1810 and started a new chiefdom, known thenceforth as the Tlokwa ba ga Bogatsu. This branch of the Tlokwa now own the Grootfontein farm and are still resident there, at a settlement called Tlokweng, "the place of the Tlokwa".

It is not clear whether Bogatsu went with Molefe to Kolontwane, or whether he stayed at Pilwe. The accounts of this period in Ellenberger and Breutz are confused due to the fact that Molefe had a great-grandson also called Bogatsu, who later became chief of the Kolontwane branch. In this case, the *Short History* provides some guidance by indicating that the Tlokwa capital or "Main Section" was still at Pilwe after the split, which suggests that Bogatsu, being heir to the chieftainship, continued to live here also. Significantly, it is at Pilwe that the Tlokwa metallurgical expertise first surfaces in the historical records. While living here they "became known as bracelet-makers" (TNAD 1905: 40).

Marothodi

The next major change occurred when Bogatsu came of age and succeeded to the chieftainship in about 1815, whereupon he established a new capital at Marothodi (Fig 3.1), "a big treeless flat about a mile from Pilwe" (Ellenberger 1939: 166, 172). Although remembered in association with the farm Bultfontein 712 (now 204JP) the extant stone walls of the town actually stretch eastward from Bultfontein across two adjacent farms, Diamant (206JP) and Vlakfontein (207JP) where most of the homesteads are located.

Breutz' account initially agrees that Bogatsu "lived at Marothodi", although his some-what vague time scale for the event, "about the end of the 18th century", suggests a slightly earlier occurrence (Breutz 1953a: 362). It is confusing that Breutz evidently contradicts both Ellenberger and himself in the following paragraphs by still referring to Pilwe as "the home of the Tlokwa" (362; quoting Schapera 1942), and by suggesting that "Bogatsu died at Pilwe" (363) and that his son Kgosi "moved to Marothodi" (363), after having already established that the Tlokwa capital was at Marothodi under Bogatsu. It seems that Breutz is mixing different sources here at the expense of continuity. The confusion is caused by the fact, although the capital has moved to Marothodi under Bogatsu, a significant part of the Tlokwa group are still living at Pilwe at this time. Indeed, it seems possible that Bogatsu's son Kgosi may have remained at Pilwe until he took over the chieftainship from his father and "moved to Marothodi" in around 1820 (Breutz 1953a: 363), and it is likely that the two settlements had a close relationship.

Ellenberger and Breutz describe further conflict with the Fokeng while the Tlokwa were under Bogatsu's rule, and recount a dispute over one of Bogatsu's wives as being the main cause of the skirmish. According to Ellenberger, the Fokeng marched on the Tlokwa from their capital at Phokeng, approaching from behind the Pilwe hills. Upon hearing of their approach the Tlokwa ran out to meet them, and battle was engaged on the "Mampoto side of the village" (Ellenberger 1939: 172), somewhere "near Pilwe" (Breutz 1953a: 362). It seems likely that Tlokwa from both Marothodi and Pilwe took part in this battle, as reflected in the version of these events reported by the Kwena ba Modimosana Bammatau (Breutz 1953a: 111). The conclusion recorded in all accounts was that Moseletsana, the chief of the Fokeng (who was also known as Sekete) was captured and executed, and the Fokeng retreated to Phokeng (Ellenberger 1939: 172; Breutz 1953a: 362).

Apart from a brief remark about seizing Tlokwa crops (Breutz 1953a: 62), the Fokeng traditions are relatively silent about conflict with the Tlokwa in this period, despite the histories of the Kwena ba Modimosana ba Mmatau and the Kgatla ba ga Kgafela firmly attesting to Tlokwa involvement in these events (Breutz 1953a: 111, 254). Although the Fokeng version agrees that Pilwe was the scene of Sekete's capture, the pivotal role of the Tlokwa in his capture and death is blurred to the extent that only the Kwena and Kgatla are explicitly mentioned, and the story involving Bogatsu's wife does not feature at all. It is possible that Fokeng sensitivity over the humbling circumstances of the death of their chief may have resulted in a case of "structural amnesia" with regard to the main perpe-trators (Henige 1974: 27). As Vansina reminds us, "a chiefdom whose traditions acknowl-edge that it lost a battle is a rare thing" and "inconvenient traditions are simply forgotten" (Vansina 1971: 447, 457).

Bogatsu died in about 1820 and was buried at Marothodi (Ellenberger 1939: 173). He was succeeded by his senior son Kgosi, who chose to live at Marothodi during his short and turbulent reign. Kgosi became embroiled in more fighting with the Fokeng, which seems to have been motivated by cattle-raiding. At the request of the Ngwaketse he entered into a skirmish with the Kwena, and it was while fighting them that Kgosi was killed and the Tlokwa defeated in about 1823, with lack of support from his own people evidently being a key factor in his capture and execution (Ellenberger 1939: 173; Breutz 1953a: 363).

The Northward Trek

At the time of Kgosi's death, his heir Matlapeng had not yet come of age so one of his minor sons, Leshage, acted as chief. During Lesage's regency, the young Fokeng chief Sebetuane of the Patsa branch consolidated all the Fokeng people, and with a number of separate chiefdoms incorporated under his authority, he initiated a major northward migration of some 30,000 Sotho-Tswana from the Vaal area in 1823 to escape the turbulence of the Ndebele invasions (Ellenberger 1939: 175; Breutz 1953a: 59).

The Tlokwa under Leshage became swept up in this movement. It is not clear whether the Tlokwa were willing participants in the migration, with different sources suggesting that either the Fokeng "drove them north into the country of the Bangwato" (Ellenberger 1939: 176) or that "Lesage joined Sebetwane and travelled north with him with a number of followers" (Breutz 1953a: 364). An earlier reference to this event by D. F. Ellenberger (1912: 309) gives the impression that the Tlokwa were initially driven northward, but after evidently establishing a truce with the Fokeng along the way, decided to stay with them to continue their wanderings. Either way, the Tlokwa had travelled beyond Serowe in present-day Botswana before another split in the chiefdom occurred.

Letlhakeng

While they were in the Serowe region engaging in numerous wars, Bashe (or Baše), a brother of the regent Lesage, secretly returned southward with Matlapeng, the true heir to the Tlokwa chieftainship, with his mother and the portion of the chiefdom that no longer wished to follow Lesage. While Breutz records that they "returned to the old home at Marothodi" (1953a: 364), it seems more likely that they returned to the Marothodi area and not the site itself. Ellenberger records that they went to a place called Letlhakeng, which was "near Marothodi" (1939: 179) on the farm Putfontein 559. Breutz, in an evident self-contradiction, also states that when Matlapeng became chief after Bashe's death (at the hands of Mzilikazi's Ndebele in 1835) he "remained … at Letlhakeng", lending credence to the interpretation that this was where Bashe and his group had settled upon their return to the area from the north (Breutz 1953a: 364). Indeed, with Bashe taking over as a new chief it may, according to custom, have been inappropriate for him to reoccupy the *kgosing* of a previous ruler. When considered against the geographical scale of their recent movements across the landscape, Letlhakeng may have seemed close enough to the old capital for their journey to be remembered as a return to Marothodi.

Breutz (1953a: 364) describes the location of Letlhakeng on the farms Elandsdoorns 547 and Putfontein 559, at least partially affirming Ellenberger's position. The Elandsdoorn farm (now 144JP) is situated in a small group of hills some 12 kilometres north of the Matlapeng hills, and joins the farm Putsfontein (now 159JP) on its south-east boundary. Today there is still a settlement here called Letlhakeng (Fig. 3.1), and it would seem reasonable to assume that this is where Bashe's Tlokwa settled in about 1825, where Matlapeng's son, the future chief Gaborone, was born in the same year (Fig. 3.2), and where Matlapeng succeeded to the chieftainship some ten years later. Given the relative length of the community's occupation at this site, and its chronological proximity to the settlement at Marothodi, it would be very interesting to explore whatever archaeological evidence has survived from the 1825-35 period of occupation at Letlhakeng.

Under Matlapeng, who feared further attacks from the Ndebele, the Tlokwa moved a short distance from Letlhakeng in about 1835 to a place in "another part of the mountains" which Ellenberger calls Motlhatseng (179) and which Breutz locates on the farm Rietfontein 927 (Breutz 1953a: 364). Rietfontein (now 179JP) is situated some 12 km south of Letlhakeng and, in accordance with Breutz (380) would place Motlhatseng somewhere on the southern hills of the Matlapeng range, which are, of course, named after this Tlokwa chief.

Flight from Mzilikazi and return to Letlhakeng

According to Ellenberger, some of the Tlokwa (probably the lineage core and their followers) then moved southward in a temporary retreat from the Ndebele to the Potchefstroom district, and resided for a short time at Lepalong (Ellenberger 1939: 179), the underground cavern refuge of the Kwena Bamodimosana Bammatau who were also hiding from the Ndebele (Breutz 1953a; Pistorius 1992; Hall 1995a). It was during this period that the first European settlers, led by Hendrik Potgieter, moved into the region and waged war against Mzilikazi, subduing the Ndebele in 1837.

Figure 3.2
Chief Gaborone of the Tlokwa, the great-grandson of Bogatsu, photographed by Duggan-Cronin in the early 1900s. The modern capital of Botswana is named after him.

In the same year, as part of their ongoing effort to escape the hostilities, the Tlokwa moved northward again to a place that Ellenberger calls Thaba Ntsho (180) at a location "near Pilwe" (1939: 167), where they remained for less than a year. Breutz makes no reference to either Lepalong or Thaba Ntsho, and no further information about the location of Thaba Ntsho is offered by Ellenberger. Interestingly, Breutz records that the Tlokwa ba Bogatsu (the branch of the chiefdom that had settled at Kolontwane) fled in around 1828 to Thaba Nchu in the present-day Free State, where they took refuge from the Ndebele for several years before returning to Kolontwane (Breutz 1953a: 202).

The temporal proximity of these two events, combined with the similarity of the place names, the shared historical context, the intimate connection between the two communities involved, and the fact that each event is recorded exclusively in one account or the other, raises the possibility that this may have been a single event that became confused in either the chain of transmission, the informing or the recording.

However, as this is unlikely to be resolved on the current evidence and there is no direct contradiction from Breutz, we will tentatively accept Ellenberger's account that the rulers of the senior Tlokwa branch did move southward to Lepalong but were back in the Pilwe area at a place called Thaba Ntsho (Fig. 3.1) by about 1837, from where they returned to their capital at Letlhakeng later in the same year (Ellenberger 1939: 167, 180).

Into Botswana and return to the Transvaal

Breutz and Ellenberger concur that in about 1840 Matlapeng resettled his Tlokwa about 5 km to the south-east at a place called Moumoomabele (Fig. 3.1) on the present-day farm Maabieskraal (161JP), but that the escalating threat of conflict with European settlers in the area prompted them to move north-westward out of the recently established Transvaal Republic and into what would later become the Bechuanaland Protectorate—a strategy adopted by a number of Tswana groups seeking to evade the encroaching Boer Republic in the 19th century (Breutz 1953a: 365; Ellenberger 1939: 180; Boeyens 2004). The Tlokwa settled with the Kwena at Dithêjwane, 13 km from Molepolole, where chief Sechele welcomed them under his jurisdiction.

Subsequent tensions that arose between the younger members of the Tlokwa and Kwena communities during their occasional attacks on the Ngwato prompted Matlapeng to leave Sechele, and resettle with his Tlokwa at Tshwene-Tshwene in the present-day Madikwe Game Reserve (TNAD 1905: 40; Ellenberger 1939: 181; Breutz 1953a: 365; Boeyens 2004). While living here, they became embroiled in a battle between Sechele's Kwena and the Kgatla under chief Lentswe, during which Matlapeng died and was succeeded by his son Gaborone (Fig. 3.2). Because the Tlokwa supported the Kgatla in this battle, their previously friendly relations with the Kwena turned sour. After the war, Lentswe resided among the Tlokwa, who remained at Tshwene-Tshwene for about 12 years.

Division of the Tlokwa

The final major split of the Tlokwa, which was evidently a peaceful one, occurred in around 1886 or 1887 when chief Gaborone moved with his followers back into Kwena territory, settling at a place called Moshaweng close to the modern border between South Africa and Botswana. He repaired the strained relationship with the Kwena chief with an offer of money, and goodwill was re-established with a reciprocal gift of cattle and the allocation of part of the land to Gaborone's Tlokwa. The settlement at Moshaweng became known as Gaborones after him, and the name has since been passed on to the nearby capital of modern Botswana. Another name for Moshaweng is Tlokweng ("the place of the Tlokwa") by which their settlement here—still the residence of the Paramount Tlokwa chief—continues to be known today (Schapera 1955: 9).

When Gaborone moved away, his younger brother Sedumedi took his section of the chiefdom from Tshwene-Tshwene back to Letlakeng where the Tlokwa capital had been over 50 years previously under his father Matlapeng, and where Sedumedi and Gaborone had been born (Fig. 3.1). This branch became known as the Tlokwa ba ga Sedumedi, and they have remained at Letlakeng to the present day. Before he died in 1923 Sedumedi produced a manuscript giving his account of the Tlokwa history (Native Affairs Department Ms. No. 168) which Breutz incorporated into his published account, along with information from interviews with Sedumedi's grandson, Chief Hunt Joseph Montlafi Kalafi Sedumedi (Breutz 1953a).

The section of the Tlokwa who remained at Tshwene-Tshwene themselves departed soon afterward under a son of Matlapeng's 'third house', that is to say, a son from the wife who ranked third in seniority among Matlapeng's wives (Schapera 1955; Tlou 1974; Kuper 1982). There were three brothers of the third house; Kgosi, Mokwena and Sebolao. Ellenberger records that it was Sebolao who became the first chief of this group and led them away from Tshwene-Tshwene to Molatedi, a settlement some 55 km from Moshaweng on the eastern border of the present-day Mankwe Game Reserve (Ellenberger 1939: 185). Breutz, while admitting there was some contradiction among his informants on this matter, advocates that it was Kgosi who took over initially, and led them first to a place called Mudungwane on the farm Rietfontein (179JP) in the southern Matlapeng hills, presumably very close to Motlhatseng where the Tlokwa temporarily settled under Matlapeng in about 1835-6. Only when Kgosi died, he asserts, did Sebolao become regent of the chiefdom and lead them to Molatedi, where the Tlokwa ba Kgosi still reside today (Breutz 1953a: 380).

Tlokwa territory

The Tlokwa oral traditions and their connection to identifiable places on the landscape make it possible to discern two 'scales of movement' of the chiefdom, which correlate with two 'scales of event' in their experience during this period.

The smaller-scale movement is characterised by local readjustments to nearby points on the surrounding terrain. Movements at this scale seem to have been prompted by comparatively 'routine' events such as skirmishes with neighbouring Tswana communities, fission caused by disputes within the chiefdom, or voluntary relocation of the capital upon the succession of a new chief. Their responses to events of this scale seem to have been localised.

By contrast, the larger-scale migrations were prompted by more dramatic and intrusive events, such as the northward movement with the Fokeng confederation led by Sebetuane in 1823, the military turbulence of the Ndebele from whom they fled south to Lepalong in about 1836, and ultimately the arrival of the European settlers that pushed them into Botswana after 1840 (Ellenberger 1939; Breutz 1953a).

Nevertheless, after each of these periods of major dislocation, a substantial proportion of the Tlokwa always found their way back to resettle in this area (with the exception of the senior branch who, as we have seen, eventually settled near modern Gaborone). On the whole, the Tlokwa seem to have preferred to stay within the Matlapeng/Pilwe area since they first arrived in the region.

This pattern might suggest that the Tlokwa had a special bond with this area, and that they were not prepared to relinquish it lightly. In the following chapter we begin to explore the potential dynamics of their relationship with the landscape through an examination of the biophysical context of Marothodi and the surrounding region.

Chapter Four
Biophysical Context

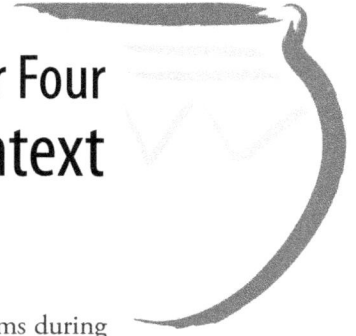

All of the known stone walled Tswana capitals occupied by aggregated chiefdoms during the 18th and early 19th centuries were situated within what could be described as a premium biophysical landscape for agropastoralists. Stretching from the Botswana border in the west, to present-day Gauteng in the east, a fertile strip of mixed bushveld occupies the ecological interface between the Savanna Biome to the north, and the Grassland Biome to the south, offering access to a combination of environmental advantages that was unique within the wider summer rainfall region. This territory has been described elsewhere as the 'Bankenfeld' (Maggs, 1976a; Mason 1986; Hall 2007). However, Bankenfeld is a term that has been given to a specific vegetation type that does not correlate geographically with the area here under discussion (Acocks 1988), and to avoid confusion the term 'Premium Biophysical Landscape' or 'PBL' will be used here to describe this ecological zone in the Pilanesberg/Magaliesberg region.

The resources offered by the PBL were critical to the successful rise of large aggregated centres, with their extensive herds of cattle and unprecedented subsistence requirements. In this chapter we examine the biophysical factors that underpinned the rise of Tswana towns, and perhaps contributed to their demise.

Topography

Marothodi occupies a wide, flat plain that gently slopes down toward the south-east, broken occasionally by low outcrops of bronzite. From within the town walls the Pilanesberg hills can be seen 8.5 kilometres to the north-east, rising up to around 540 metres above the level of the settlement. To the north-west the Matlapeng hills dominate the horizon. The nearest peak is 7.2 kilometres away and climbs to around 340 metres above Marothodi. The Pilwe hills, 8.6 kilometres to the south-east, ascend 250 metres above the surrounding flats (see topographic map, Fig. 3.1 in the previous chapter).

As we have seen, the oral traditions indicate that the Tlokwa group had typically preferred to position their capitals on the hilltops of the Pilanesberg, Matlapeng and Pilwe during their movements across the landscape (Breutz 1953a; Ellenberger 1939). The low, open topography on which Marothodi was situated in the midst of the Tlokwa settlement sequence contrasts sharply with these earlier and later hilltop locations, and indeed, with the elevated positions of other contemporary Tswana towns like Kaditshwene (Boeyens 2000, 2003). Therefore, the rationale for situating Marothodi at this flat point on the landscape, being overlooked by hills, could not have been primarily influenced by a concern for physical defence. Instead the topographic context of the town suggests that the

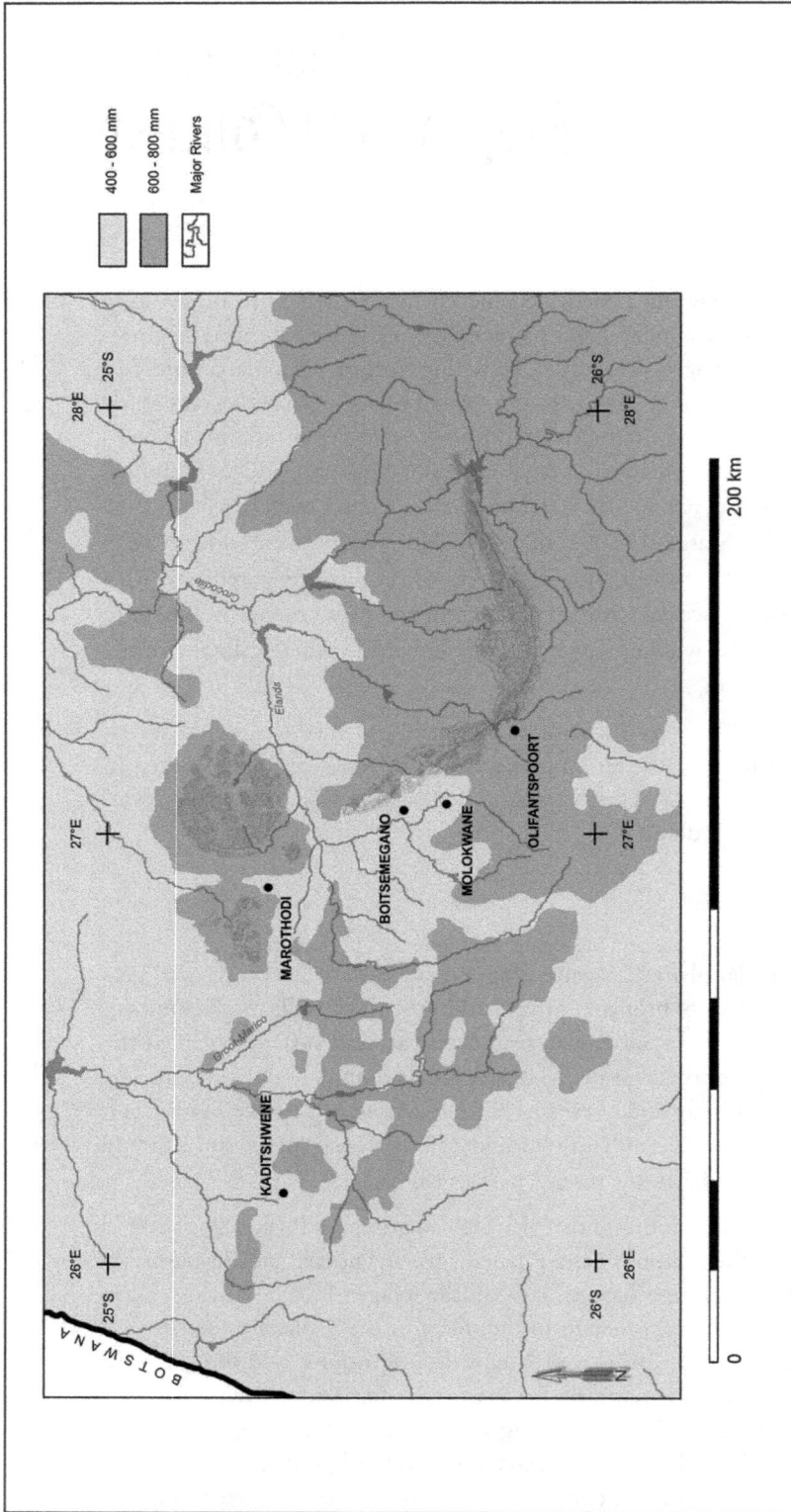

Figure 4.1
Map of the Pilanesberg/Magaliesberg region, showing mean annual rainfall (after Schulze 1997).

Tlokwa enjoyed a level of political and economic confidence and regional security during their occupation here, and that the potential risk of attack was therefore outweighed by other advantages afforded by their location.

Climate

All of the terminal phase Tswana capitals are situated within the mid-summer rainfall area where most of the region's rain falls between October and April, and average summer temperatures range from 18° to 26° C (Schulze 1997). Recent statistics indicate that the region receives a mean annual precipitation of between 400 mm and 600 mm, with slightly higher levels of 600 mm to 800 mm falling in local patches to the south and east, and on the elevated topography of the Matlapeng, Pilanesberg and Magaliesberg hills (Fig. 4.1). Annual rainfall statistics collected by Breutz from 1915 to 1935 at rain stations in the local vicinity of Marothodi show precipitation levels between 480 mm and 705 mm with an average of 591 mm, which seems relatively consistent with the regional data (Breutz 1953a).

Regional distribution studies of pre-colonial agropastoral settlements on the southern Highveld show that most communities were located in areas where tsetse fly were absent, and mean precipitation levels were between 550 mm and 800 mm (Maggs 1976a). The cultivation of sorghum and millet, the staple crops prior to the introduction of maize, requires a minimum annual precipitation of around 500 mm (Huffman 1996), so it would seem that rainfall in the Marothodi region, though sometimes unpredictable and erratic, was generally sufficient for the success of contemporary agropastoral systems.

A period of higher and more consistent rainfall towards the end of the 18th century (Hall 1976; Huffman 1996) would have enhanced opportunities for agricultural success in the region, and there are no hints of drought or famine in the Tlokwa oral traditions during this time (Breutz 1953a; Ellenberger 1939).

Geology

The Marothodi landscape is situated on the western lobe of the Bushveld Igneous Complex, a geological event that intruded the Transvaal Sequence around 2 billion years ago. The Complex forms a batholithic layered basin of some 66,000 square kilometres, with varying thicknesses of up to 9000 metres. It contains the Rustenburg Layered Suite, the Lebowa Granite Suite, varieties of the Rashoop Granophyre Suite, and includes the Merensky and UG-2 Reefs which yield around 75% of the world's platinum and other valuable minerals (Willems 1964; Viljoen & Reimold 1999).

The Rustenburg Layered Suite, a mafic intrusive phase of the Complex, exerts the dominant geological influence on the Marothodi area (Fig. 4.2). The 'norite zone' of the Suite (Wagner 1924) occurs in a globular limb running westward from the Pilanesberg intrusion, bestowing a wide band of sedimentary geology between Marothodi and the Botswana border. Clinopyroxenite dominates the immediate surroundings of Marothodi itself, with Arenite and Norite also occurring in the vicinity. To the north-east of Marothodi, the Bushveld Igneous Complex is itself intruded by the 1.3 billion year old Pilanesberg

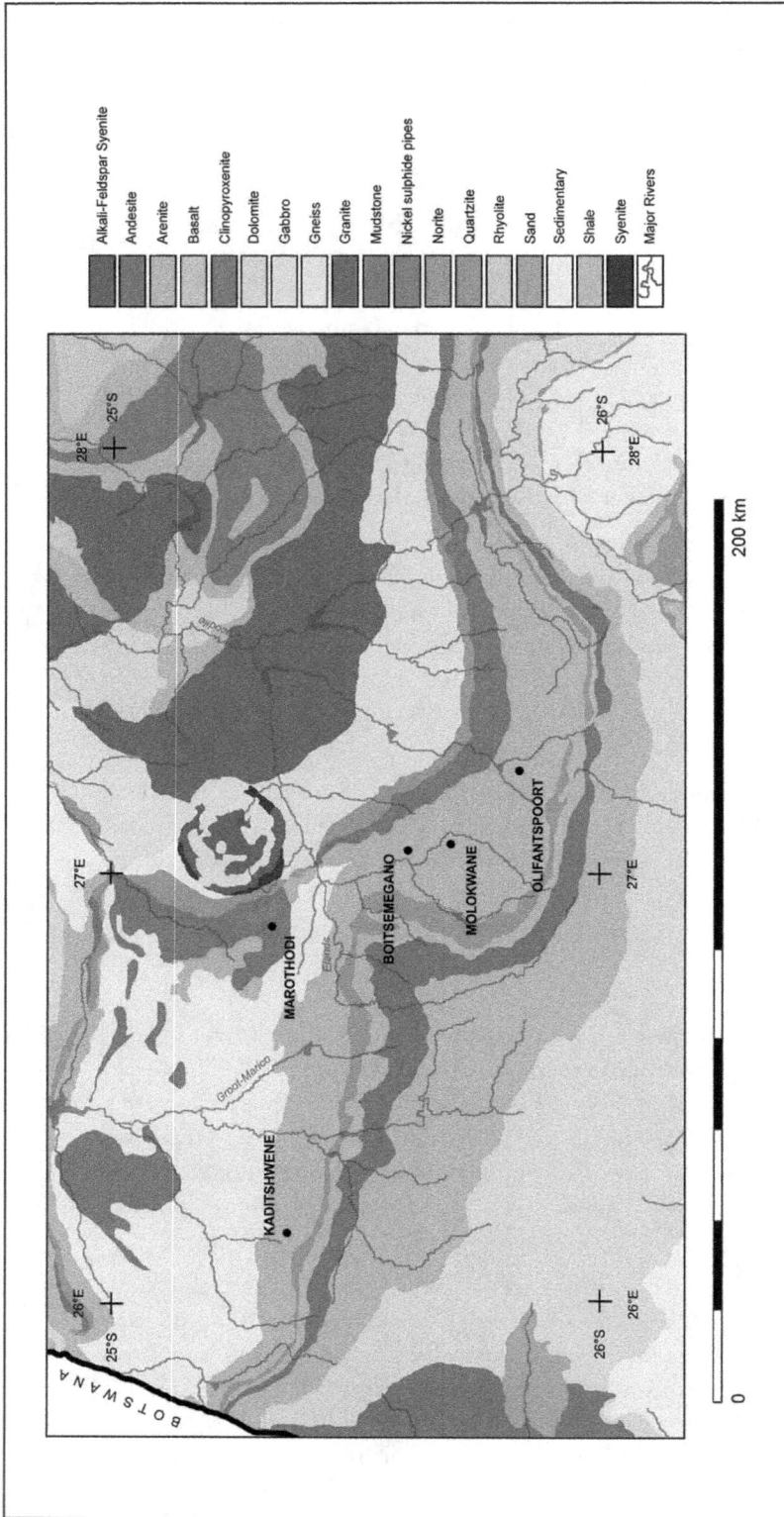

Figure 4.2
Map of the Pilanesberg/Magaliesberg region, showing dominant geology (after DEAT 2000).

Complex, an alkaline ring formation of concentric hills created by a combination of plutonic magma activity followed by processes of erosion (Du Toit 1954; Willems 1964).

Within the modern boundaries of the Vlakfontein farm (207JP) small lenses of outcropping serpentinized harsburgite have been noted, but the geology is dominated by a dark brown pyroxenite, composed of more than 50% bronzite with streaks of anorthosite (plagioclase feldspar with minor clinopyroxene) (Wagner 1924; Schwellnus 1935; Hall *et al.* 2006).

The clinopyroxene bronzite is exposed in occasional small outcrops across the farm, creating the only topographic variation on the local landscape. The highest part of the Marothodi settlement is draped over one of these slight rises. Upon weathering, the angular pseudo-stratification of the bronzite causes it to break up into reddish-brown sub-rectangular blocks, and it is from this readily-available building material that most of the Marothodi stone walling is constructed. The bronzite gradually disintegrates into coarse sand, and eventually forms the dark turf soil that characterises the area (Wagner 1924; Du Toit 1954).

Approximately 2.3 kilometres north-east from the centre of Marothodi, a crescent-shaped belt of nickel and copper rich sulphide pipes curves southward and eastward, almost echoing the nearby perimeter of the Pilanesberg Complex (Fig. 4.2). The ore-rich pipes fill vertical fractures in the pyroxenite country rock, and are capped with a brown weathered opaline gossan which can be collected from outcrops on the surface. This iron-rich gossan occasionally contains veins of hydrated copper oxide minerals, giving the rock a distinctive green streaked colouration (Wagner 1924; Schwellnus 1935; Hall *et al.* 2006). As we will see, the presence of the pipes here was of great significance to the Tlokwa of Marothodi.

Soils

Marothodi and its surrounds are situated on a large patch of deep, dark-coloured clay loam, popularly known as 'cotton soil' or 'black turf' (Division of Economics and Markets 1948; Breutz 1953; Department of Agriculture 1957; Acocks 1988) and classified as "black montmorillonitic clay" in the Schematic Soil Map of Southern Africa (Harmse 1978). The soil classification system currently used in South Africa is the Taxonomic System (Soil Classification Working Group 1991) which is derived from the earlier Binomial System (MacVicar *et al.* 1977). The Taxonomic System describes soils as belonging to a "form" and a "family", and defines the black turf as Arcadia (form) Lonehill 1100 (family) (see Soil Classification Working Group 1991: 64-65).

According to the internationally recognised classification systems of the United States Department of Agriculture (Soil Survey Staff 1998) and the United Nations World Reference Base (FAO, ISRIC and ISSS 1998) the black turf at Marothodi can be identified as an Ustert Vertisol.

Vertisols are characterised by their dark colour and high levels of montmorillonite clay and other smectite minerals that swell and shrink as they become wet and dry. They usually occur in warm climates with distinct alternating wet and dry seasons, and are associated with poorly-drained, flat low-lying areas. The parent material is often a weathered basic or ultra-basic igneous rock, and its occurrence in the Marothodi area is associated with the

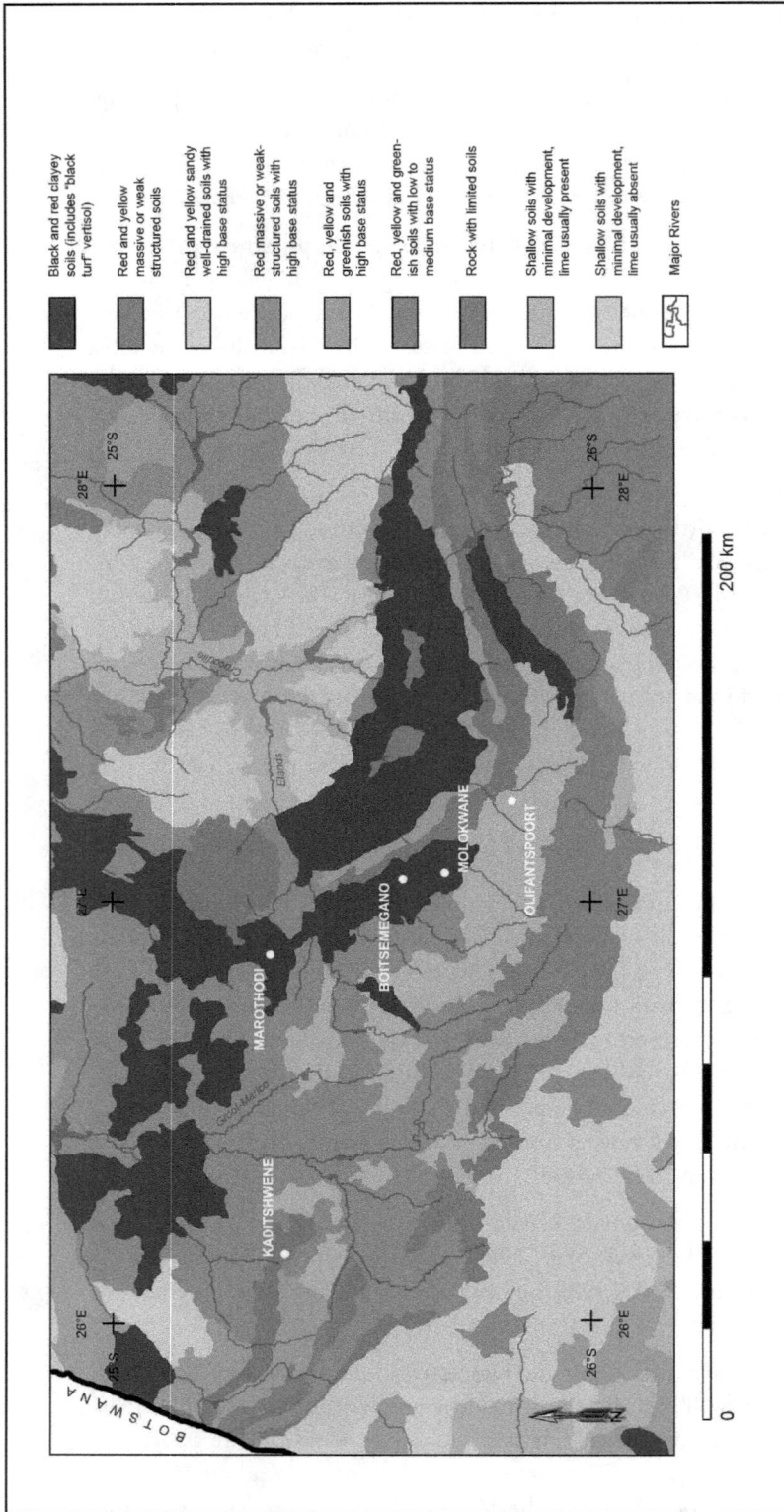

Figure 4.3
Map of the Pilanesberg/Magaliesberg region, showing dominant soil types (after DEAT 2000).

norite zone of the Bushveld Igneous Complex (Blokhuis 2002). The geographical extent of this vertisol body conforms loosely to the rim of the Complex, with patches extending as far west as the present Botswana border, and northward to approximately 75 kilometres north-west of Pietersburg (Fig. 4.3).

Despite the dark colour, vertisols tend to have low levels of organic matter. The regular expansion and shrinking of the soil creates large cracks during the dry season that can extend from 60 cm to 100 cm below the soil surface, or directly onto the underlying bedrock. Cracks may be visible on the surface, but are sometimes obscured by mulch—a self-generated granular or crumby surface horizon that can be between 2 cm and 50 cm deep. The only vegetation vertisols can support is grassland or savanna, and slow-growing deep-rooting trees such as Acacia (Schaetzl & Anderson 2005).

Agriculturally, vertisols are labelled a 'problem soil'. Once wetted they tend to retain water due to typically poor drainage abilities, becoming plastic and impermeable. When dry the soil can become extremely hard. Both wet and dry conditions make tillage costly and difficult, even with machinery. To permit tilling by hand the moisture levels need to be somewhere between these two extremes, and farmers must be flexible enough to respond immediately after the first rains of the summer. The optimal water status occurs only briefly and unpredictably in the erratic rainfall areas in which vertisols usually occur (Ellis & Mellor 1995; Schaetzl & Anderson 2005).

However, where surface mulch is sufficiently developed it forms a natural seedbed, and pedoturbation continuously brings subsoil to the surface to keep the soil chemically rich and capable of sustaining continuous cropping without a fallow period (Ellis & Mellor 1995; Blokhuis 2002). Unfortunately the constant movement of the soil is highly disruptive to surface construction, as can be seen at Marothodi where pedoturbation is gradually causing parts of the archaeological stone walling to be 'swallowed' by the earth.

Prior to the development of soil classification systems in South Africa, the vertisol of the Marothodi region was defined qualitatively in terms of its agricultural properties, being renowned both for its high fertility and its problematic relationship with moisture:

> This soil has very misleading properties and is difficult to cultivate. It cannot be ploughed when soaked and if it is too dry it breaks up into clods. With the right moisture content, however, it has an excellent crumbly structure. The soil is very fertile and sweet, with a subsoil rich in lime, but its water requirements are high and the rainfall is too irregular to ensure good maize crops. (Division of Economics and Markets 1948: 66)

Historically, these properties were well appreciated by Tswana farmers. To the Tswana, the soil is known as *selôkô*. A simplified soil distribution map of the Bopedi region to the north-east of Pretoria (Mönnig 1967: 6), shows that the Tswana communities living in this area encountered the same body of vertisol (associated with the northern rim of the Bushveld Igneous Complex) that the Tlokwa of Marothodi cultivated further west. Within the context of his observation of Pedi agricultural practices, Mönnig describes the soil thus:

> Seloko – a black heavy soil. It is good for all crops, except melons and beans. It tends to crack when hot, but has the advantage that when it rains the water enters deep into the soil through the cracks, and thus it holds the rain and contains moisture for a long time. It

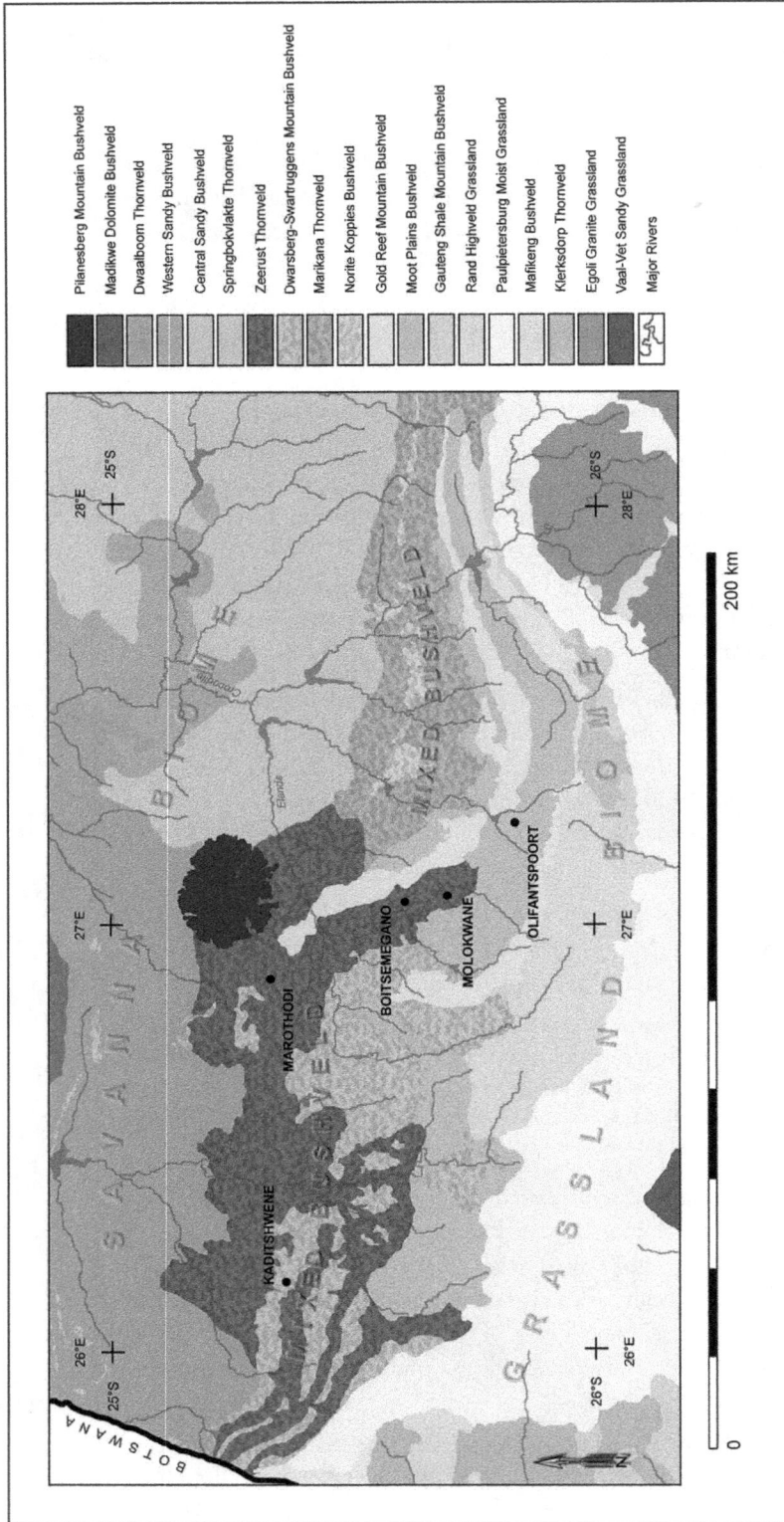

Figure 4.4
Map of the Pilanesberg/Magaliesberg region, showing dominant vegetation types (after Mucina *et al.* 2005).

is considered to be one of the best soils, and sorghum, which grows equally well on poorer soils, is not usually sown on it. (Mönnig 1967: 152)

Despite its problems then, the *selôkô* seems to have been successfully utilised where its cultivation by Tswana agropastoralists was observed, including communities of Kgatla, Ngwato and Rolong (Schapera 1955: 199-200; Comaroff 1985: 63). To compensate for fluctuations in rainfall, each woman would sow on a variety of different soils and may be allocated patches of land dispersed around the agricultural territory of the chiefdom (Comaroff 1985). In the words of Mönnig, "a woman should have a piece of sehlaba as well as a piece of seloko or mašu" (1967: 153). *Sehlaba* is a red soil, good for millet, sorghum, melons, beans and pumpkins. *Mašu* is a grey soil on which all crops grow quickly, but which can suffer from scorching (Mönnig 1967). The patchy occurrences of reddish soil within the Marothodi *selôkô* are a localised variation of the vertisol, with the advantage of greater oxidisation from quartz grain inclusions. These occur particularly on the flats around the fringes of local hills, and may have provided some of the needed variety for the Marothodi farmers (Wagner 1924).

Vegetation

There is a close relationship between the geology and soils of this region and the dominant vegetation groups. Considering the geological and pedological complexity of the southern and western rims of the Bushveld Igneous Complex it is no surprise that this area is characterised by mixed and variable flora.

As mentioned above, all of the archaeological Tswana capitals occur within a zone of mixed bushveld to the north of the Highveld escarpment (Fig. 4.4), along the ecological interface between the Grassland Biome to the south and the Savanna Biome to the north (Acocks 1988; Low & Rebelo 1996; Mucina *et al.* 2005). The precise geographical definition of the bushveld zone differs slightly according to variations in classificatory and mapping criteria, but it can be described as an irregular strip, in places up to 80 kilometres wide, extending from the Botswana border in the west and encompassing the Pilanesberg and Magaliesberg complexes before stretching eastward to present day Gauteng. This bushveld zone occurs at the core of the Premium Biophysical Landscape, which provided the variety of environmental resources necessary to sustain the aggregated populations of the Tswana towns situated here.

The predominant vegetation types surrounding the towns have been classified as Zeerust Thornveld, Dwarsberg-Swartruggens Mountain Bushveld, Marikana Thornveld, Gold Reef Mountain Bushveld, and Moot Plains Bushveld (Mucina *et al.* 2005). The area is characterised by a variety of Acacia species, particularly *A. caffra*, *A. karroo* and *A. robusta*, with *Combretum apiculatum* dominating on shallower soils. Grasses include *Cymbopogon plurinodis*, *Digitaria eriantha*, *Schmidtia pappophoroides* and *Anthephora pubescens*, providing primarily sweet (perennially nutritious) grazing on shallow sandy soils (Acocks 1988; Low & Rebelo 1996).

The southern boundary of the bushveld zone is defined by the Highveld escarpment, as it gives way to the Grassland Biome to the south (Low & Rebelo 1996; Mucina *et al.* 2005).

The change in vegetation here is dramatic, as it becomes dominated by Rand Highveld Grassland and Paulpietersburg Moist Grassland (Mucina *et al.* 2005). Here the gently undulating sandy plains are almost devoid of trees, hosting strongly-tufted grasses including *Eragrostis racemosa, Digitaria tricholaenoides, Cymbopogon plurinodis* and *Setaria flabellata* among others. While erratic rainfall, winds and frosts may have made agriculture problematic here (Huffman 1996; Schulze 1997) the sour and mixed grasses on the northern edge of the Highveld provided adequate spring and summer grazing (Low & Rebelo 1996; Tainton 1999).

To the north of the mixed bushveld zone is a wide area of relatively open savanna, characterised by occurrences of *Acacia karroo* and *robusta* within grasses dominated by *Cymbopogon plurinodis* and *Ischaemum afrum* (Acocks 1988). This vegetation is closely related to the area's fertile dark clay soils overlying norite bedrock (vertisols), and has been referred to variously as Norite Black Turfveld, Clay Thornveld or Dwaalboom Thornveld (Acocks 1988; Low & Rebelo 1996; Mucina *et al.* 2005). As we have seen, it provided fertile soil and sweet grazing, and would have been accessible to many of the Tswana towns to the south.

The flats around Marothodi are characterised by generally sparse vegetation. A higher number of trees can be seen growing on some of the surrounding hills, but local informants say that this is a relatively recent development. These are an important source of fuel for the community living at nearby Bapong today, and it seems likely that any local tree growth would have held a similar, if not greater, value as fuel for the occupants of Marothodi. Thus, the depletion of vegetation in the Marothodi area today might, at least partly, be a consequence over over-exploitation from as far back as the early 19th century.

Tswana capitals within a Premium Biophysical Landscape

In summary, it is evident that the bushveld zone on the interface between the Grassland and Savanna Biomes was the core of a PBL that offered rich, fertile soils and access to the kind of environmental variety that would have been highly valued by agropastoralist communities at different times of the year, or during periods of erratic rainfall. The sweet grazing of the Savanna Biome to the north would have retained its nutritional value perennially, but would also have been susceptible to overgrazing and depletion. The mixed and sour grazing on the Grassland Biome to the south was more reliable in terms of quantity and sustainability, but would have provided limited nutritional value during the winter (Department of Agriculture 1957; Tainton 1999).

Considering the substantial cattle herds in Tswana towns, it may have become vital to extend grazing southward onto the grassland during the spring and early summer, saving the sweet and mixed grazing of the local mixed bushveld and the northerly savanna for winter. In terms of crop yields, the local soils certainly seem to have been agriculturally productive.

Consequently, it is likely that Tswana chiefdoms were powerfully attracted to PBL territory from the 18th century, and this is indeed where the aggregated capitals are converged. This landscape was inevitably contested, and rulers who could confidently occupy this terrain would have attracted allegiance from more vulnerable 'foreigners' (Legassick 1969; Manson 1996). Furthermore, communities situated within the PBL, especially when utilising Sotho-Tswana 'bulk' grain reserve storage technologies (Mönnig 1967: 163; Hammond-Tooke 1981: 8; Comaroff 1985: 64; Pistorius 1996: 67), may have been spared the effects of the 1789-1810 drought felt so keenly among the Nguni peoples of the KwaZulu-Natal region (Hall 1976; Huffman 1996a).

The subsistence requirements of these growing communities continued to expand as populations clustered around the more powerful rulers. It seems likely that the survival of the sizeable Tswana towns eventually became completely dependant upon the mixed resources of the PBL, accounting for the exclusive presence of the capitals here in the terminal phase of the early 19th century. Given the valuable and coveted nature of PBL resources, it is no surprise that escalating inter-chiefdom warfare and cattle raiding dominates the 18th and early 19th century oral histories of this political landscape (Breutz 1953a; Ellenberger 1939; Manson 1996).

Tlokwa copper

Although most of the PBL would have offered similar advantages to agropastoral communities, the distribution of Tlokwa capitals across the landscape reveals a distinct preference for the region around the Matlapeng and Pilwe hills. As discussed in Chapter Three, long distance migrations seem to have been the exception rather than the rule for the Tlokwa, and their movements were generally localised (see Fig. 3.1).

In attempting to understand the Tlokwa preference for this area, our attention is drawn to the one resource that was unique to the Matlapeng/Pilwe locale—the nickel sulphide pipes and their copper ore-rich gossan capping (Fig. 4.2). Preliminary XRF analysis has indicated that the gossan was suitable for smelting and would have been capable of producing prills of copper (Hall *et al.* 2006). These results are concordant with early 20th century prospectors' reports of "a considerable ancient working" discovered on one of the gossan outcrops close to Marothodi:

> Copper was clearly the metal sought and worked, as pieces of copper ore are to be seen among the debris occupying the upper parts of the working. At a depth of about 40 feet there was actually found a copper armlet presumably made from copper smelted from the ore… There is nothing to show, however, that it was smelted on the spot; no slags, tuyeres or furnace remains having hitherto been found. (Wagner 1924: 11)

We have seen in the *Short History* that the Tlokwa were renowned for making jewellery by the time they were living at nearby Pilwe (TNAD 1905: 40). In addition, the 1866 journal of Elizabeth Price, wife of the missionary Roger Price, recounts a conversation with chief Matlapeng that reveals the continuation of Tlokwa mining and metallurgical expertise during their later years in the region (Long 1956: 200; Jan Boeyens pers. com. 2003).

Thus, a picture emerges in which the Tlokwa held a firmly established political and economic relationship with the ore resource, and had been accessing it for a long time. That they were able to maintain their claim over this territory, even after returning from tumultuous long-distance treks to the north and south to escape the Ndebele, suggests that they enjoyed what seems to have been an almost proprietary relationship with the Matlapeng/Pilwe area and the copper ore it provided.

However, the site of Marothodi was not without its problems. The poor and inconsistent supply of water (Wagner 1924; Breutz 1953a) and the structural instability caused by pedo-turbation of the underlying vertisol which, even today, continues to 'swallow' its stone walls, meant that the choice for the location of the capital was clearly a compromise. As parts of the town are literally on top of the ore, it seems likely that its position was influenced by an increasingly disruptive political climate that compelled the Tlokwa to move as close as possible to the pipes in order to secure unrestricted access to this resource. In light of such sacrifices, there can be little doubt that copper was of extreme importance to the Tlokwa.

Indeed, the evidence for metal production that Wagner noted as absent from the vicinity of the gossan outcrops can be seen in abundance around the Marothodi ruins. We explore these ruins in the following chapter, as we are introduced to the archaeological context of the Tlokwa capital.

Figure 4.5
A satellite image of the Matlapeng/Pilwe area, with the site of Marothodi circled. The coordinates refer to the white cross, which is marked approximately in the centre of the stone walled area.

Chapter Five
Archaeological Context

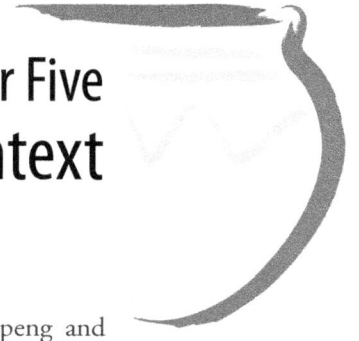

The site of Marothodi is situated almost halfway between the Matlapeng and Pilwe hills, and about 3 km south-east of the present day semi-rural settlement of Bapong. As described in Chapter Three, the majority of Marothodi's homesteads occur on the farm Vlakfontein (207JP), and stretch westwards across the neighbouring farm Diamant (206JP), and onto Bultfontein (204JP). The stone walls extend approximately 3.4 km from east to west, and 2.5 km north to south (Figs. 5.1 and 5.2). As we learned from the oral traditions, the town was occupied for a relatively short period, leaving us with a 'snapshot' of Tlokwa expression—a single component site without multiple occupation phases or major reorganisation. This was one of the primary factors that made Marothodi such a valuable study for this research.

Figure 5.1
Oblique aerial photograph of part of Marothodi from the south-east. The Matlapeng hills are visible in the background.

Figure 5.2
Map of the farm Vlakfontein (207JP) showing the location of the Marothodi stone walling and nickel sulphide pipes.

Macro settlement structure

Viewed in plan, Marothodi consists of three 'zones' of clustered settlement units or home-steads (Figs. 5.2 and 5.3). The density of stone walling, and the size, complexity and quan-tity of identifiable homesteads is much greater in the central zone ('Marothodi Central'), and we can be confident that this area was occupied by the ruling elite of the Tlokwa chief-dom. To the south, a string of at least 16 homesteads stretches away in a south-easterly direction forming a spatially distinct section of the site ('Marothodi South'). To the east of Marothodi Central, a third zone ('Marothodi East') is formed by a row of 12 homesteads arranged in an inverted 'L' shape (Fig. 5.3).

Although it has not yet been proven archaeologically that Marothodi South and Marothodi East are contemporary with Marothodi Central, ethnography suggests that a threefold di-vision was a typical feature in the settlement organisation of most Tswana towns, at least by the early 20th century;

> In most tribes, three local divisions are recognized: central (*fa gare*), upper (*ntlha ya godimo*) and lower (*ntlha ya tlase*). The names are said to be derived from the days when villages were habitually built on the banks of rivers, *godimo* being "up stream" and *tlase* "down stream," with the chief's division in the centre. The divisions were formally of little social importance, except that they ranked in the order given above, and that all the wards in each constituted a single section of the tribal army. (Schapera 1953: 47)

As we have seen from our discussion of oral traditions, allegiance to a particular chief-dom was relatively fluid among Tswana polities in this period, and 'foreigners' from other Tswana lineages were frequently absorbed into a capital (Breutz 1953a). Outsiders who attached themselves to a community in this way were often located in the *ntlha ya godimo* and the *ntlha ya tlase* (Schapera 1955).

At Kaditshwene, the contemporary Hurutshe capital visited by the missionary John Campbell in 1820, archaeological evidence shows that the settlement layout is comprised of three divisions; a central core, which Boeyens refers to collectively as the *kgosing* or "chief's place", flanked by upper and lower divisions to the north and south (Boeyens 2000, 2003). Pistorius (1992, 1994) demonstrates that Molokwane, the contemporary capital of the Kwena Bamodimosana, is also divided into three "clustered zones" with the ruling lineages occupying the central zone.

Given the political control that the Tlokwa evidently enjoyed over the important resources around Marothodi, and the relative confidence and security this provided, we would ex-pect smaller or more vulnerable groups in the region to seek an affiliation with them and to take advantage of the relative ease with which the Tswana ward system could facilitate their incorporation within the chiefdom.

Although Marothodi East and Marothodi South represent a different scale of settlement to the comparable components of Kaditshwene and Molokwane, it seems reasonable to suggest that they were at least a developing expression of *ntlha ya godimo* and *ntlha ya tlase* at the Tlokwa capital. Considering the relatively short period of occupation on such an unpredictable political landscape, they may not have had a chance to fully integrate themselves with the community or extend their physical presence before the chiefdom

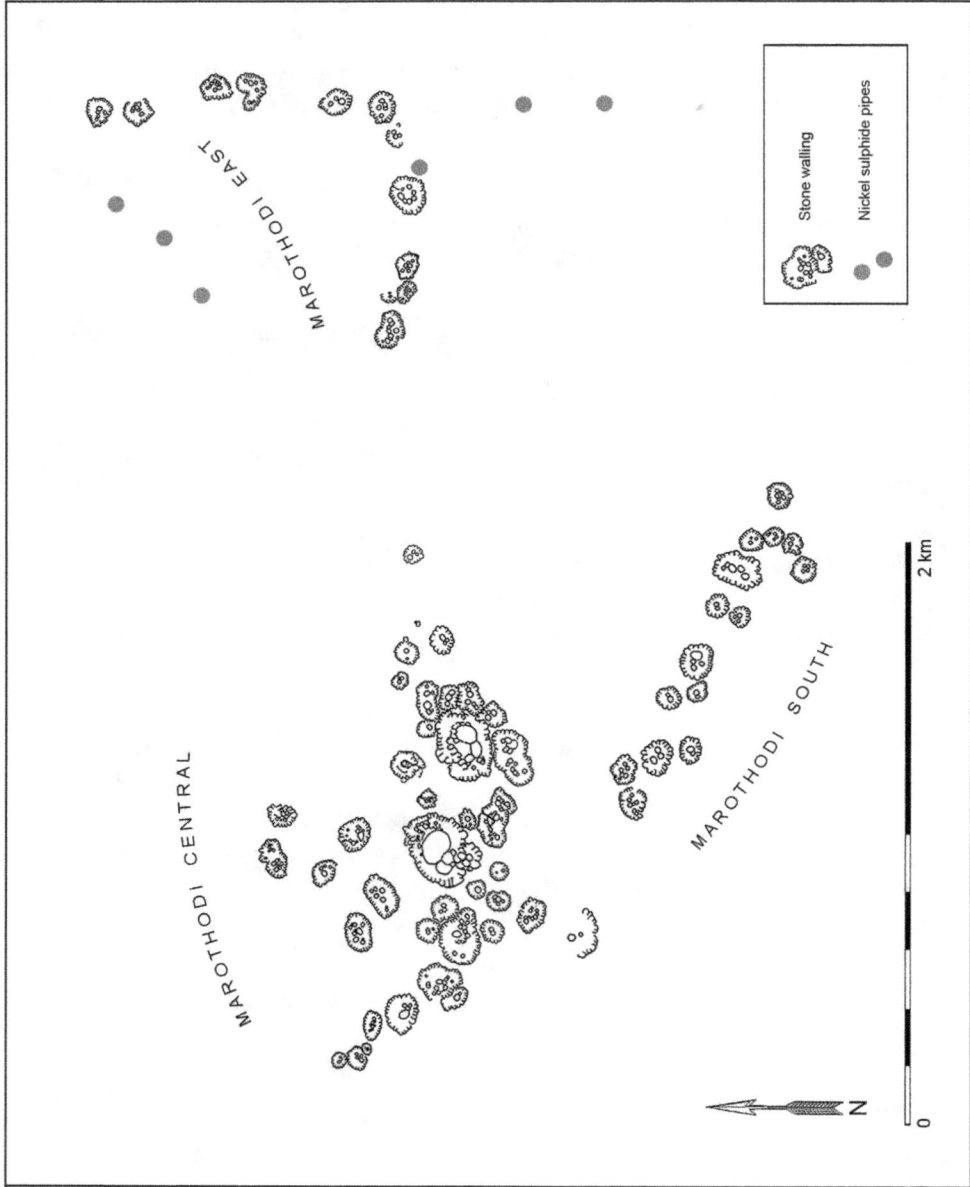

Figure 5.3

Map of the three sections of Marothodi, showing their spatial relationships to each other and to the nearest nickel sulphide pipes.

shifted to Letlhakeng (Breutz 1953a; Ellenberger 1939). This continuous process of ex-pansion meant that Tswana towns were always 'works in progress', and it is tempting to speculate that the *ntlha ya godimo* and *ntlha ya tlase* may have appeared more similar to the Molokwane and Kaditshwene expressions if they could have been observed at a slightly later Tlokwa capital like Letlhakeng. At the time of its abandonment, the population of Marothodi might conservatively be estimated at between 3000 and 5000 strong.

While bearing in mind that "the process of the amalgamation was uneven and incomplete" among some of the frequently-shifting chiefdoms of the early 19th century (Manson 1996: 359), the comparatively large distances between the three sections of Marothodi may also reflect agricultural convenience, enabling women to live within daily walking distance of the fields they were allocated upon joining the chiefdom. The influence this could have upon the layout of densely-populated settlements has been observed among the Pedi:

> To enable all women to have reasonable access to their lands, Pedi villages are usually built in a fairly extensive, sprawling manner, and homesteads on opposite extremes of a village can be as far as five miles apart, and may even be separated from one another by one or more hills or valleys. (Mönnig 1967: 154)

However, a glance at Figures 5.2 and 5.3 raises the suspicion that Marothodi East was de-liberately located among the nickel sulphide pipes, while the *kgosing* in Marothodi Central would still have needed to occupy the highest point in the local landscape. These spa-tial necessities probably exerted the greatest influence over the macro arrangement of the capital.

The Marothodi South and East sections have only been cursorily mapped to provide a working reference, and have not received any archaeological attention. The current research has focussed on Marothodi Central, which is comprised of 36 homesteads extending 1.66 kilometres from east to west, and 0.92 kilometres from north to south (Fig. 5.4).

The map of Marothodi Central shows a physically dominant homestead in the centre of the settlement, which for the purposes of the current study has conveniently been termed the 'Primary' *Kgosing* (Fig. 5.4, PK). It is distinguished not only by its large over-all size but also by the size of its inner central enclosure, which is the single largest cattle kraal at Marothodi. The pioneer archaeologist Revil Mason, after flying over Marothodi in a helicopter in the 1980s, stated that "Vlakfontein (Marothodi) has the largest cattle enclosures registered in the Transvaal" and that they probably represented "some of the largest cattle enclosures known in the African Iron Age" (Mason 1986: 3, 57; Boeyens 2004). Considering the direct relationship between wealth (expressed in cattle) and po-litical power in Tswana societies, we can confidently interpret this homestead as being the focus of the greatest wealth in the community, and consequently the centre of political authority. This homestead was the *kgosing* or "chief's place" at Marothodi—the political, ceremonial and judicial core of the entire chiefdom.

Approximately 120 metres to the east of the 'Primary' *Kgosing* is another dominant home-stead that also contains comparatively large central cattle enclosures and which, according to the same principles, must also represent a centre of political seniority. For convenience, this homestead has been termed the 'Secondary' *Kgosing* (Fig 5.4, SK). Tswana chiefdoms

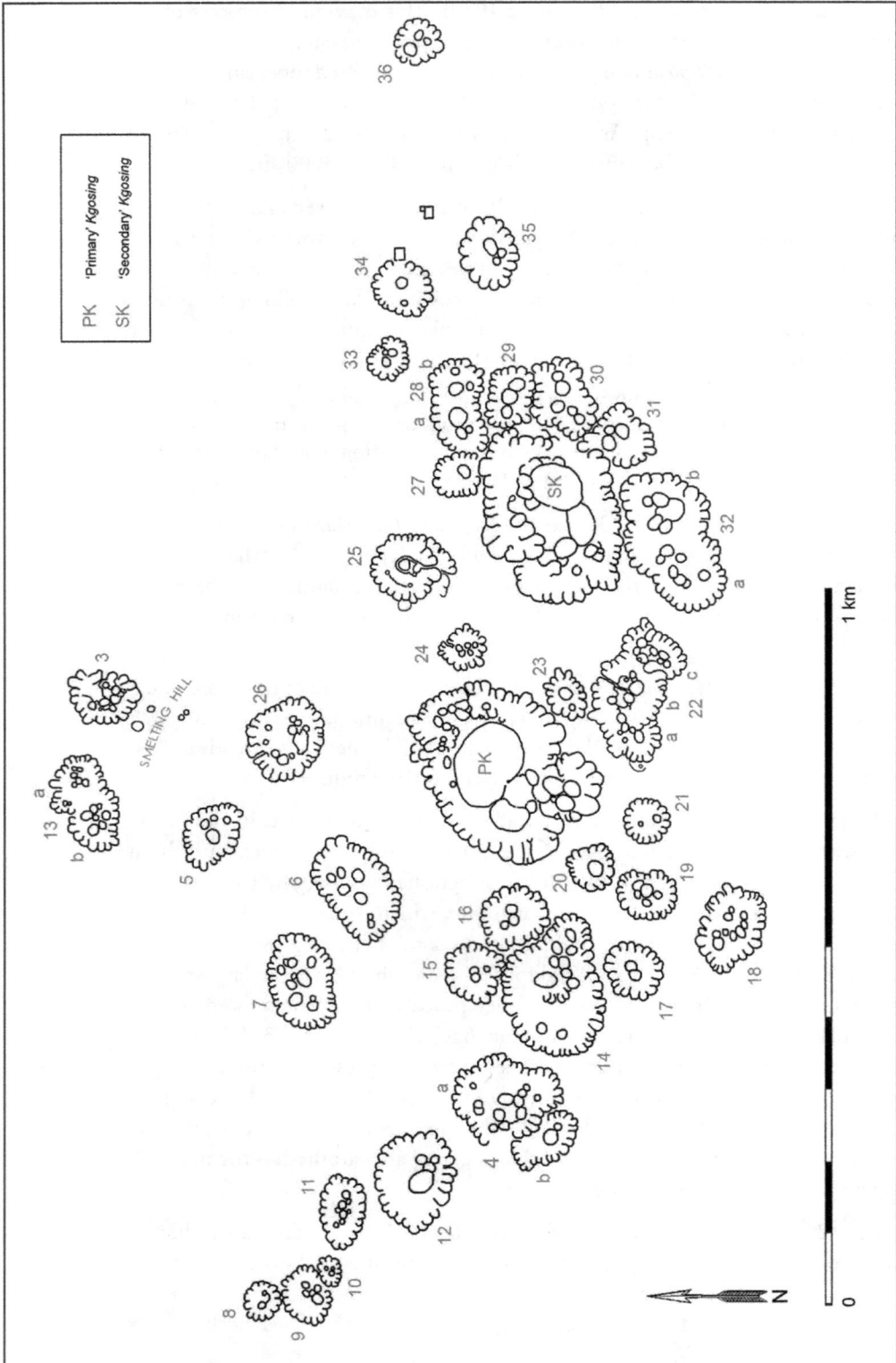

Figure 5.4
Map of Marothodi Central, showing the numbers allocated to individual homesteads.

in this period are essentially two-tier hierarchies, comprising the 'royal' or elite authority of the chief, under whom local headmen administer the 'commoner' or non-elite residents in their smaller homesteads. According to the general African principle that there can be no equals within political and social hierarchies (Comaroff 1985) the existence of two royal homesteads would seem unusual if considered in isolation. As we have seen however, the oral traditions of the Tlokwa at Marothodi provide an historical context that resolves this anomaly by describing how the founder of this capital, Bogatsu, died some time around 1820 and was succeeded as chief by his son, Kgosi (Boeyens 2004; Breutz 1953a; Ellenberger 1939).

The two *kgosing* visible on the settlement plan therefore represent an historical sequence during the occupation of the site. A new chief would be required by custom to establish a new *kgosing* physically distinct from his predecessor's homestead, which in this case would still have been occupied by the members of Bogatsu's ward. Indeed, this taboo was probably one of the motivating factors behind the common practice of new chiefs to start a new capital upon their succession, as exemplified in the Tlokwa oral traditions when Bogatsu moved to Marothodi in about 1815. The later decision of Kgosi to establish his new *kgosing* so close to that of his father possibly represented a compromise between tradition and the economic interests that required them to stay near the copper ore source.

The chronology of the two *kgosing* at Marothodi has not yet been archaeologically resolved beyond doubt, although we can suggest that the 'Primary' *Kgosing* was most likely the one that belonged to Bogatsu in light of its position on the only piece of elevated topography in the town. As Tswana attitudes towards status are frequently expressed through elevation (Kuper 1982; Huffman 1986b; Hall 1996) the highest point in the settlement would have been reserved for the elite residence, and the first chief to occupy this spot in the landscape would have established himself on this slightly raised outcrop.

As in all contemporary Tswana towns, the spatial relationship and proximity of individual homesteads to the central *kgosing* is determined by the relative status of each homestead. The homesteads governed by headmen who are directly descended from chiefs are either ranked according to how recently the related chief was in power, or according to seniority of birth among the headmen. Among commoner homesteads belonging to the ruling community by birth, relative status is based on the length of time the homestead has been established as a ward. Commoner homesteads of foreigners are ranked according to the length of time they have been incorporated into the chiefdom, but are nevertheless inferior to those of the ruling community. As the lowest-status members of the chiefdom, they are usually located furthest away from the *kgosing* (Schapera 1955; Tlou 1974).

The position of each homestead in relation to the *kgosing* is predetermined in accordance with this system, and is replicated each time the chiefdom is moved to a new location (Schapera 1953). Mönnig describes this procedure among the Pedi:

> In moving a village, once a new site has been chosen by an advance group, the whole tribe moves to the new site in one single migration, and has to carry all its possessions and move all its stock with it. ...the sites are chosen for the different *kgoros* (homesteads), and each unit will plant the entrance poles for its group on its appointed site. ...the *kgoros* are placed according to rank, alternatively to the left and to the right of the chief's *kgoro*. (Mönnig 1967: 247)

Micro settlement structure

Archaeologically, the homesteads at Marothodi appear comparable in their design and features to homesteads recorded at other contemporary Tswana archaeological sites (e.g. Boeyens 2000; Pistorius 1992, 1994; Mason 1986). The stone walling itself is constructed in a style common to Sotho-Tswana sites of the period, being composed of two parallel outer dry-stone walls with the space between them filled with rubble to create a single wall, usually about a metre thick (see Walton 1958). It is likely that at least some of the rubble fill was extracted from the numerous open quarries or 'borrow pits' that can be seen in various places around the settlement.

The spatial organisation of each homestead expresses a level of variability around a series of core principles. Within the interior complex of enclosures at the centre of each one it is usually possible to identify the court complex (*kgotla*), the administrative heart of the homestead through which each headman exercised his local authority, and where important meetings were held and cases were tried. Cases which proved to be too serious or complex for the homestead court were referred up to the chief's court in the *kgosing* (Schapera 1953, 1955). Close to the *kgotla,* and sometimes physically attached to it, is the main cattle kraal of the homestead. Its central position is a reflection of the economic, ritual and spiritual significance held by cattle in Tswana society (Schapera 1955; Kuper 1982) as "the main avenue to wives and children and therefore to power, success and status" (Huffman 1986b: 297).

Figure 5.5
A sample of the type of metallurgical debris visible on the ground at Marothodi: various forms of slag, and green coloured gossan containing copper ore from the nearby nickel sulphide pipes.

The outer perimeter of each homestead is defined by 'scalloped' walling; a circular arrangement of connected bays that face inward towards the central complex of kraals and *kgotla*. Each bay defines a household or *lapa* (sing.), the domestic living space of a married woman and her immediate family. Circular mounds formed by the collapsed and burnt dwelling structures or houses are usually visible on the ground surface within the *malapa* (pl.), along with various circular arrangements of upright stones that were foundations for other domestic structures. Other features such as stone granary platforms and grinding stones are also frequently seen on the ground.

This peripheral zone was conceptually female space, "spatially and symbolically distinguished from the male sphere" in the centre of the homestead. Each domestic *lapa* was divided into a front and back courtyard, with the main dwelling structures usually forming the partition between the two. The back courtyard was the "privileged sphere of the woman of the house", and was spiritually associated with the female ancestors. This was considered intensely private space (Comaroff 1985: 48, 58).

Metallurgical evidence

As discussed in Chapter Four, Marothodi is characterised by high quantities of evidence for metal production (Figs. 5.5 and 5.6). A ground survey of the visible metallurgical evidence around the town, and the results of preliminary analyses, have elucidated aspects of the macro spatial patterning of both iron and copper production sites (Fig. 5.7). Where iron smelting sites are identified, the furnaces tend to be located either on the outer edges of the settlement or between groups of homesteads, generally maintaining a degree of separation from the nearest living areas. By contrast, copper production is spatially tied to homesteads, and even more tightly linked with individual households. The distribution of metal production sites provided a convenient framework for our excavation sampling strategy.

In Figure 5.8 overleaf, the homesteads and metal production sites that were investigated archaeologically are indicated. Over the next four chapters we take a closer look at these areas, and present an account of the survey and excavations undertaken within them.

Figure 5.6
An example of an air pipe or 'tuyere' fragment from Marothodi, with slag from inside the smelting furnace sticking to its exterior.

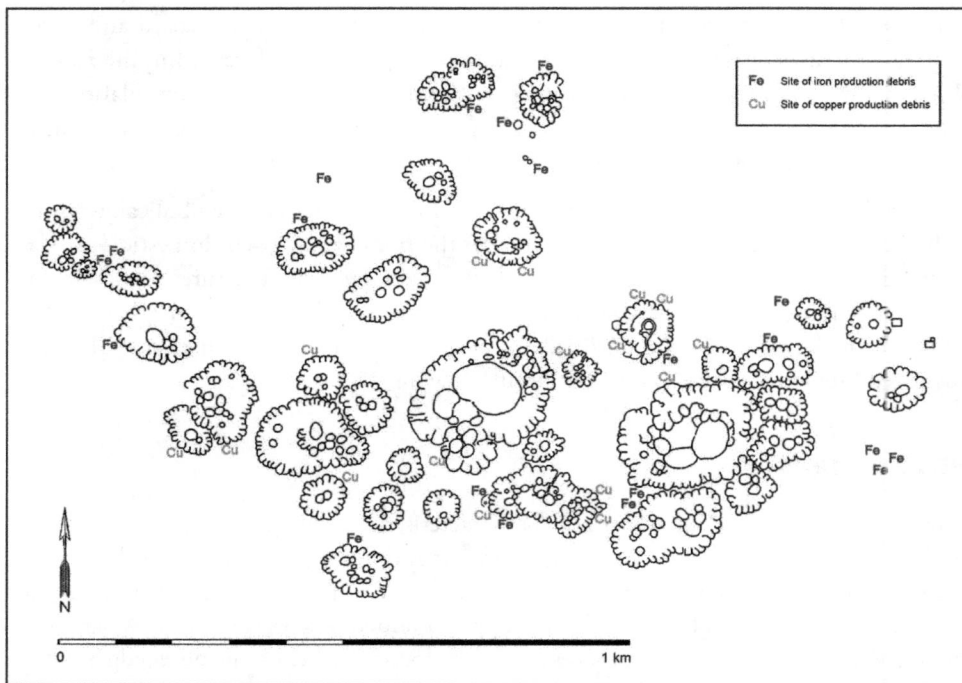

Figure 5.7
Map of Marothodi Central, showing the distribution of metallurgical debris associated with iron and copper production (a conservative representation based on preliminary ground survey and excavation).

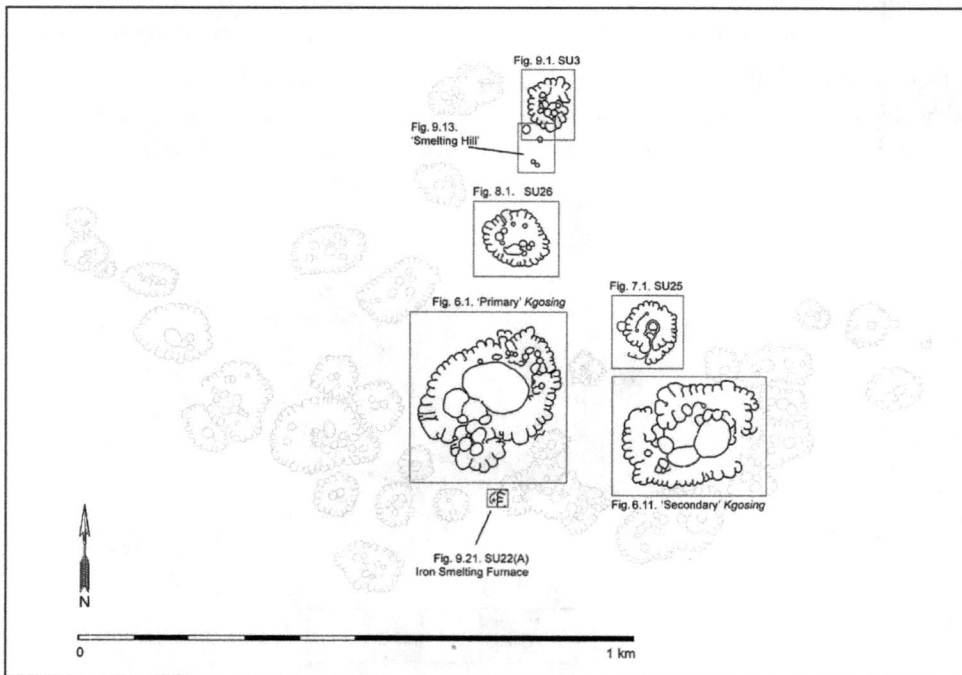

Figure 5.8.
Map of Marothodi Central, showing the location of the larger-scale plans presented in Chapters Six to Nine.

Chapter Six
Royal Residences

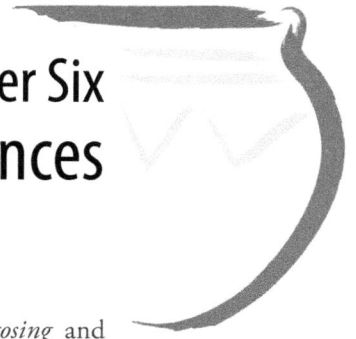

In this chapter we explore the spatial organisation of the 'Primary' *Kgosing* and the 'Secondary' *Kgosing*, the two physically dominant homesteads at the centre of Marothodi, and present the results of the archaeological excavations carried out there. As discussed in Chapter Five, both *kgosing* exhibit the superior size, spatial complexity and central position that reflect the relationship between wealth/cattle and political power in Tswana society (see Kuper 1982; Huffman 1982, 1986b, 2001). They are clearly centres of spiritual and political authority, and residences of the Tlokwa royal families. We discovered in Chapter Three that the occurrence of two royal homesteads at Marothodi reflects an historical event—the succession of the first chief Bogatsu by his son Kgosi in around 1820 (Boeyens 2004; Breutz 1953a; Ellenberger 1939).

Spatial organisation of the 'Primary' *Kgosing*

The fact that a *kgosing* was home to the ruling family of the chiefdom has important implications for understanding its spatial composition and organisation. In addition to its position as the centre of judicial, ceremonial and political power, the royal homestead reflected the worldview and cosmology of the entire chiefdom in microcosm, and elements of this are represented in its spatial layout and the arrangement of social groups within it (Mönnig 1967; Pistorius 1996).

The 'Primary' *Kgosing* is situated in the centre of Marothodi, on a slight rise in an otherwise very flat landscape. An initial glance at the homestead map (Fig. 6.1) shows aspects of the general spatial patterning characteristic of all Tswana homesteads. A perimeter stone wall of scalloped courtyards surrounds a central cluster of circular stone walled enclosures, with the spaces in between containing ash middens, the remains of collapsed structures, and a variety of other features. To move towards a more ethnographically-grounded understanding of how space within the settlement was organised we must acknowledge the principle that each Tswana homestead revolved around its court complex, the centre of administrative and ceremonial power (Mönnig 1967; Comaroff 1985). This centre of power is therefore the first feature to be identified in the 'Primary' *Kgosing*.

The Cattle Kraals and Court Complex

As a reflection of the conceptual link between cattle, men and power, the court complex is usually part of the route used by cattle as they move between the formal entrance to the homestead and the main cattle kraal. Along this thoroughfare the route usually passes near or through the court complex, and close to the senior domestic *malapa*.

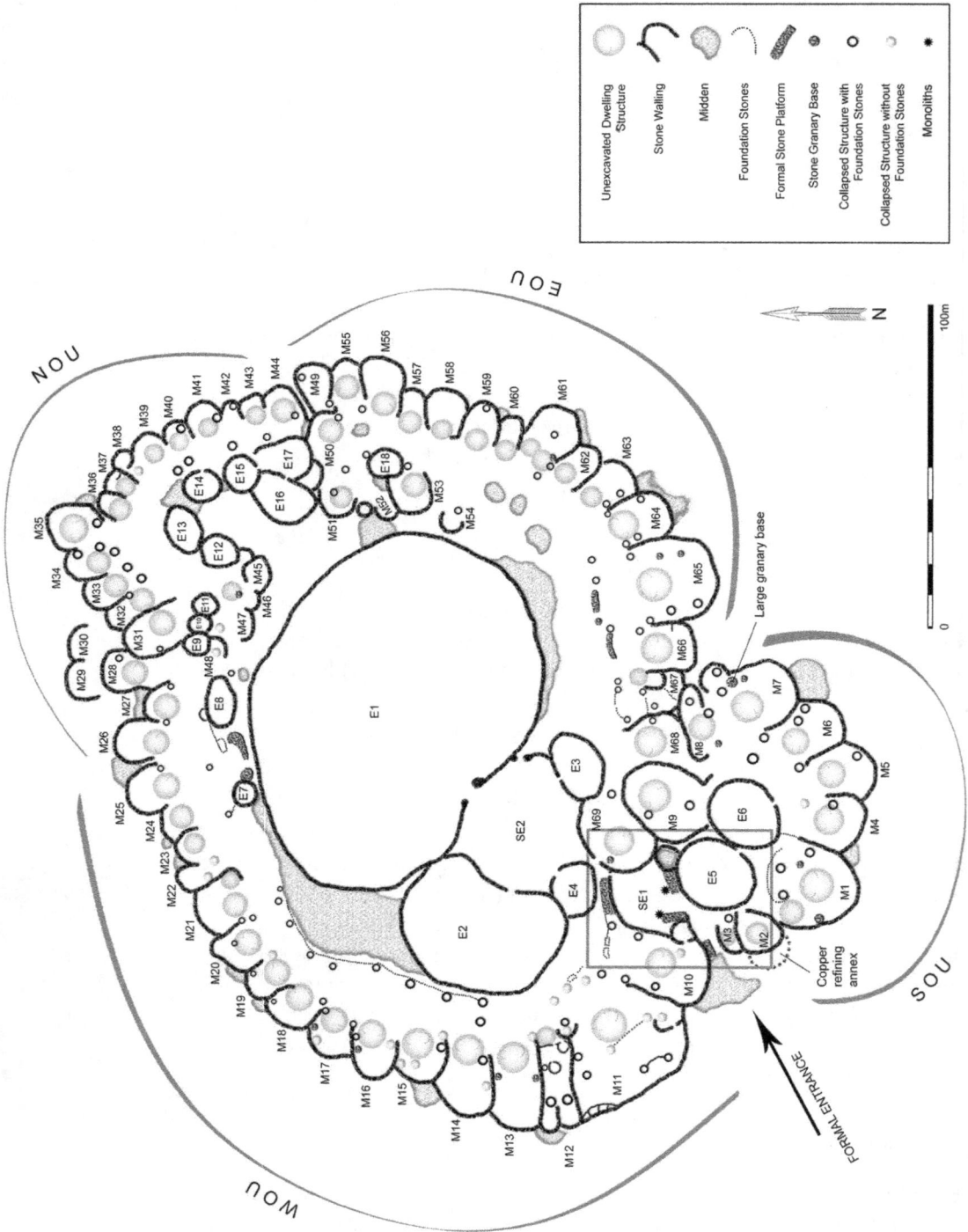

Figure 6.1

Map of the 'Primary' Kgosing at Marothodi. The ribbons indicate the extent of the four occupation units, and the box marks the area of the enlarged plan of the court complex in Fig. 6.5.

The main cattle kraal in the centre of the 'Primary' *Kgosing* is easy to identify, and measures approximately 110 metres across its maximum diameter (Fig. 6.1). Its significant size, and the cattle numbers implied, reflect either significant military success or, in light of the evidence for commodity production at Marothodi, a particularly robust economic status in the region. Dung found in random auger samples collected from the interior of the enclosure certainly attests to the keeping of cattle here, but it would be difficult to ascertain the density of the herd from dung deposits alone, especially if the practice of periodically removing dung from the floor of kraal enclosures for use as fuel is taken into account (see Maggs 1976a: 133). But at face value, a kraal of this size makes a powerful statement about prosperity, wealth and regional status.

The entrance into the main kraal, here referred to as E1, is well defined. The wall termini are formalised with wide rounded ends (Fig. 6.1). This opening leads into the kraal from SE2, which is one of the 'secondary enclosures' that are a common feature in the walling arrangements at Marothodi and at other Tswana sites (see Maggs 1976a; Pistorius 1996). They often occur near the centre of a homestead, between the main kraals and the court complex, and by definition are created between the walls of other enclosures. Many secondary enclosures seem to have served as 'cattle management' spaces, from which livestock could be sorted and directed into particular kraals. Indeed, here in the 'Primary' *Kgosing*, SE2 is an area from which access can be gained directly into all four of the main central kraals of the homestead, E1 to E4. The reddish-brown soil in SE2 forms a significant contrast to the thick blue-grey dung inside the surrounding kraals. This area may also have been used to accommodate gatherings of people. Being surrounded by kraals this was conceptually 'male' space (Comaroff 1985) and gatherings in such areas may have been restricted to initiated men, with women perhaps attending on special occassions (Pitje 1950a; Pistorius 1996).

In the south-west corner of SE2, a narrow opening leads into another secondary enclosure, SE1. Like SE2, SE1 is formed primarily from the walls of other adjacent enclosures, but there are a number of features here that imbue this space with special significance. There are three large 'formal stone platforms' associated with SE1, two of them on the southern side of the enclosure, and one on the northern side, close to the narrow opening between SE1 and SE2. These platforms differ from stone granary bases in that they are sub-rectangular in shape, and made with large stone blocks to create a flat elevated surface some 0.5 metres above ground level. Similar platforms have been observed at other contemporary Tswana sites (see Pistorius 1994; 1996). They occur at points along the main cattle thoroughfare, where they probably assisted with cattle driving, or close to the court complex where they are found in association with the *kgotla*, and may have performed a ceremonial role. The platforms in SE1 are 'court platforms' of this type, and their ceremonial significance is symbolically emphasised by the presence of collapsed bronzite monoliths associated with each one (Fig. 6.1). It seems likely that SE1 was the supreme *kgotla* of Marothodi.

An enclosed midden adjacent to the south-eastern platform is identified as the court midden. Court middens are identified primarily by their spatial context as they always occur in close proximity to the *kgotla*. They receive ash from the court fire, and other debris from court activities, and are consequently characterised by 'male' refuse (see Huffman 1996b). The ash of court middens has conceptual significance, its whiteness representing 'coolness', and by extension peace, justice and stability (Hammond-Tooke 1981; Comaroff 1985).

The court middens at Marothodi often have a distinctive structure. The ash is deposited within a low enclosing stone wall, and develops a flat surface as it accumulates inside. In a sense, it eventually becomes a sort of platform. The frequent association of such middens with formal stone platforms and the *kgotla* emphasises their significance as controlled repositories of waste material generated during judicial or ceremonial activities in the court complex.

A narrow opening leads from the southern end of SE1 into a passageway dominated by another formal stone platform, and this marks the formal entrance/exit to the 'Primary' *Kgosing*. The ground surface in the entranceway is covered with midden ash (Figs. 6.1 and 6.5). In keeping with Tswana custom, it was common for cattle to be directed across middens as they entered a homestead, to provide a conceptually 'cooling' or cleansing effect that counteracts the 'heat' with which they may have become polluted during their sojourn in the outside world (Hammond-Tooke 1981: 145). The practice may also have had an added practical advantage in helping to remove ticks and other parasites picked up in the veld (Huffman 1986b: 296).

The midden blankets a slight rise in the terrain at this point, which forms the single highest point at Marothodi (as indicated by the presence of a modern survey beacon here). As suggested earlier, this slight elevation was probably a key factor in the decision to establish the centre of Marothodi's political power at this specific point on the landscape. In light of the Tswana principle of elevation as an expression of rank (Huffman 1986b: 301; Hall 1996: 317) we can be confident that SE1 and its associated features represent the political and ritual core of the town, and consequently of the entire chiefdom. It is therefore appropriate that this is the vicinity in which the largest and most senior domestic *malapa* occur (Fig 6.1), and it is to the domestic sphere that we now turn our attention.

The Domestic Sphere

Approximately 69 domestic *malapa,* of various sizes, together form the perimeter walling around the 'Primary' *Kgosing*. An analysis of the map of the homestead (Fig. 6.1) shows that the *malapa* are arranged in distinct groups that can be defined by their physical relationships to one another. A deliberate gap between the wall of one *lapa* and the next suggests a conceptual boundary between *malapa* belonging to one particular family or *masika*, and those belonging to another. In this way, it becomes evident that the 'Primary' *Kgosing* is composed of four individual 'occupation units'. If these units have their own cattle kraals, each can be recognised as a semi-independent socio-political entity. To aid clarity, these distinct occupation units have been identified and labelled on the homestead map, and are described here.

Southern Occupation Unit (SOU)

The SOU is unique in that its *malapa* form an almost completely separate circle around two oval enclosures, serving to emphasise its distinction from the other occupation units (Fig. 6.1, E5 and E6). Having identified the primary centre of political power at the court complex, we would expect the core of the royal residence—the dwelling of the chief and his wives—to be located in close proximity to this area. The SOU, being on the highest ground and conceptually at the 'back' of the homestead, seems most likely to represent this elite residency (see Huffman 1986b; Hall 1995).

Lapa M1, as the largest of the SOU *malapa*, was probably the household of the chief's senior wife. Here it is possible to discern the separation of front and back courtyards—spatial features of the Tswana household described historically by early travellers such as William Burchell (1824). Without exception, this is the basic structure of all household space at Marothodi, with the central dwelling structure/s usually marking the boundary between front and back courtyard space. *Lapa* M1 contains three dwelling structures, two 'utility structures' or 'kitchens' (for preparing/cooking food) and a large stone granary base.

Another demonstration of status can be seen in *lapa* M7, where an exceptionally large circular stone platform represents the base of a huge granary, measuring 0.80 metres in height and 5.0 metres in diameter (Fig. 6.2). This may have been the chief's grain store (see Huffman 1986b: 299; Taylor 1984: 250). Stone granary bases are a common feature in domestic areas around Marothodi and other Tswana settlements. They kept the grain basket or container (*sefalana*) separated from the damp ground (see Figs. 1.2, 1.9 and 6.3) (Larsson & Larsson 1984; Mason 1986; Pistorius 1992). The exceptionally large size of the example in M7 makes an unambiguous—and highly visible—statement about the wealth and status of the ruling family, and by extension of the whole chiefdom. Such a demonstration of prosperity would also have served to reinforce the authority and popularity of the chief, whose success as a ruler was largely dependant upon his rainmaking abilities, and the harvest he could provide for his people (Schapera 1953; Comaroff 1985).

Attached to the back courtyard wall of *lapa* M2, a semi-circular double row of stones defines an activity space or 'annex'. This was examined by a visiting team from the University of South Africa (UNISA), and was identified as a copper refining site, where smelted copper was re-melted to remove impurities (see Hall *et al.* 2006). We discuss the archaeology of copper refining in more detail later in this chapter.

Of the two circular enclosures in the centre of the SOU, E6 contains dung, which identifies it as a small cattle kraal. It was possibly in here that the chief's own animals were corralled. This enclosure may also have doubled as an 'ancestral graveyard' where royal men were buried (see Huffman 1986b: 299; Pistorius 1996: 157).

The other enclosure, E5, does not contain dung, and the offset angles of the walls at the entrance create a deliberate sense of seclusion in the interior by restricting visibility from outside (see Walton 1958: 138). In addition, E5 is built with some of the highest and most carefully constructed stone walling anywhere at Marothodi, which serves to heighten this effect. The privacy of this entrance is further protected by a fence across the front of *lapa* M1 that screens it from inside the senior domestic courtyard. These factors support the identification of this enclosure as the chief's *kamore* or chamber—the private meeting place where he received counsel from his closest advisors.

Figure 6.2
The large stone granary
base in *Lapa* M7 of the
SOU, in the 'Primary'
Kgosing of Marothodi.

Figure 6.3
Tswana granaries at 'Old
Palapye', an Ngwato capital
in Botswana, circa 1898.
(W. C. Willoughby)

The only visible domestic middens associated exclusively with the SOU are those around the southern edge, between the back walls of *malapa* M1 and M4, and M6 and M7. *Malapa* M2 and M3 may also have contributed to the midden at the main entranceway into the *Kgosing*, sharing it with M10 (Fig. 6.1).

Parts of the SOU walling arrangement suggest a degree of reorganisation or expansion (see Huffman 1986b). It seems reasonable to suggest that the SOU, as the chief's residence, was the first homestead to be established on this spot, and that the other occupation units were added later. With this in mind, it seems possible that *lapa* M9 may originally have been a kraal and was 'recycled' as a household at a later stage, although the presence of dung here has not been tested. *Lapa* M69 may have originated as a household of the SOU, and was perhaps later reoriented to become part of the adjacent unit, the EOU.

Western Occupation Unit (WOU)

The WOU includes *malapa* M10 to M25, and extends northward from the court complex before curving around the north-west perimeter of the homestead. It terminates at a narrow gap between M25 and M26 that separates the WOU from the NOU. The high status of the WOU is expressed by its physical relationship with the court complex, and by the absence of any kraals of its own. The implication of this is that men of the WOU kept their cattle in the central kraal complex.

The high status of the WOU is also indicated by what appears to be a direct access route from the rear of *lapa* M10 into SE1, and from the front of the same *lapa,* past a formal stone platform, into SE2 (Fig 6.5). In addition, the sheer size of the immediately adjacent *lapa* M11 leaves no doubt about the seniority of this household. As the largest domestic household at Marothodi, M11 seems likely to have been the residence of the chief's mother—considered in Tswana society to be "the most powerful woman in the chiefdom" (Pistorius 1996: 152).

The open area in front of *malapa* M15 to M23 is dominated by a large midden that abuts the exterior edge of the two largest cattle kraals, E1 and E2 (Fig. 6.1). Judging by the extensive spread of this deposit, it seems likely that it received material from most, if not all, of the WOU *malapa.* Its use as a communal depository emphasises the domestic cohesion of the WOU households. The north-west edge of this midden is lined with a row of 9 circular structures, each approximately 3 metres in diameter, visible above the ground surface as rings of protruding foundation stones. These structures are all linked by a single line of upright stones, which possibly supported some kind of fence or palisade. Although none of the structures have been excavated, they were probably associated with food preparation.

A repeated feature at Marothodi is the placement of large communal middens in front of domestic courtyards, abutting the outside of the central kraal walls. Smaller middens do occur outside some back courtyard walls, as at M12, M14/15, M1/19, M20, M23 and M24, which were presumably used by those specific *malapa.* But the larger forward middens are the product of multiple households.

This pattern invites speculation that the forward deposition of middens "in public view at the front of the settlement" may have been a reaction to living in a high density town environment, prompted by anxieties about the disposal of intimate ash outside where it was exposed to neighbouring homesteads (Huffman & Steel 1996: 54). Concerns about 'witches' stealing ash and using it against the household that produced it were a feature of Nguni perceptions of ash as a potentially dangerous substance (Raum 1973), which contrast with the Sotho-Tswana concept of ash as cooling and healing (Hamond-Tooke 1981). This practice at Marothodi may therefore reflect some residual habit from the Tlokwa's Nguni roots. The enclosing of court middens with their characteristic stone walls may also be related to these principles.

At the northern end of the WOU, two formal stone platforms occupy the open space in front of *lapa* M25 (Fig. 6.1). Being situated firmly in the 'female' sphere, areas like this may have acted as gathering places for ceremonial events that involved women, perhaps including totemic dances and *bojale,* female initiation rituals (see Mönnig 1967; Schapera 1953; Comaroff 1985; Pistorius 1996).

Northern Occupation Unit (NOU)

The NOU incorporates *malapa* M26 to M48, and occupies the north-eastern perimeter of the homestead (Fig. 6.1). The *malapa* surround a group of 10 small circular enclosures, numbered E8 to E17. The position of the NOU at the opposite end to the elite residence and the small size of its *malapa* and kraals reflect the lower status of its occupants (see Huffman 1986b). Access into the NOU can be gained via the gap on the western edge of M26, through the space between M35 and M36, or through the narrow alleyway on the southern edge of M44. It is notable that at all of these openings there are ash middens. Additional small patches of domestic midden are visible outside the back walls of M27, and also between enclosures E13 and E14, and between E8 and E1. The fact that the NOU has its own kraals (E12 to E17) indicates that this unit was semi-autonomous, and possibly had its own court complex.

Eastern Occupation Unit (EOU)

The EOU is physically joined to the NOU, but the arrangement of the walling between the two occupation units clearly indicates their separation (Fig. 6.1). The EOU includes *malapa* M49 to M69, and those at the northern end are arranged in a circular formation around a small enclosure, E18. This appears to be the only enclosure exclusive to the EOU. At the south-western end, a gap in the wall between kraals E1 and E3 provided pedestrian access from the EOU into SE2, reinforcing the expectation that SE2 was a space for people as well as for cattle management. Their access to this important area suggests that the occupants of the EOU held relatively high status within the 'Primary' *Kgosing*.

Domestic middens are highly visible within the EOU, with deposits occurring between M52 and E1, along the front of *malapa* M60 to M63, behind *malapa* M59/60, M61/62 and M63/64, and a notably large forward midden abutting the outside wall of kraal E1 in the large open space in front of M65. *Lapa* M65 is the largest in the EOU, and the open area in front of it is dominated by two formal stone platforms. Platforms of this nature sometimes define the entrances to the front courtyards of elite households at Marothodi.

Spatial comparison with Molokwane

At this point it might be valuable to compare the 'Primary' *Kgosing* at Marothodi with that of another contemporary Tswana settlement. In particular, the *kgosing* of Molokwane, the Kwena Modimosana capital some 33 kilometres to the south-east, exhibits both similarities and differences in spatial organisation (Fig. 6.4) (Pistorius 1996).

There are seven kraals in the centre of the *kgosing* at Molokwane, which, while greater in number, collectively represent a similar area of kraal space to those in the 'Primary' *Kgosing* at Marothodi. They surround a large secondary enclosure which Pistorius has labelled 'TKC' (Third Kraal Complex). This space is conceptually equivalent to SE2 at Marothodi.

An opening on the west side of the TKC leads into another secondary enclosure called the 'SKC' (Second Kraal Complex), which is dominated by a number of stone platforms and a court midden, described as the location of a 'holy fire' (Pistorius, 1996: 160). This ceremonially significant space is equivalent to SE1 at Marothodi, and represents the *kgotla* of Molokwane. A narrow opening flanked by two stone platforms on the southern side of the SKC leads to an area referred to as the FKC (First Kraal Complex), containing a 'private chamber' with a notably high, well-built wall, a small kraal which acted as an 'ancestral graveyard', and an 'inner sanctum' in which ritual sacrifices were made (Fig. 6.4). There are strong parallels here with some of the features in the SOU at Marothodi, where E5, with its impressive walling, has been identified as the chief's private *kamore*, and the small kraal E6 presents itself as an equivalent to Molokwane's 'ancestral graveyard'. It is noteworthy that the senior *lapa* at Molokwane, referred to as 'FRHSM01' (Front Right Hand Side Malapa 01) faces directly into the private chamber and the ancestral graveyard (Fig. 6.4), an arrangement reflected at Marothodi in the way that *lapa* M1, which we have identified as the senior dwelling, faces directly towards enclosures E5 and E6 (Fig. 6.1).

Another point of comparison is that the elite dwelling area at Molokwane, which Pistorius labels FRHSM 01-7, is situated on the highest point on the landscape, affording a view over much of the rest of the town (Pistorius 1996: 151), and is significantly located in the western portion of the *kgosing*. Pistorius places considerable emphasis on the importance of an east/west right/left dichotomy in Tswana worldview as it is reflected in settlement layout, and it is worthwhile briefly exploring these ideas in relation to Marothodi.

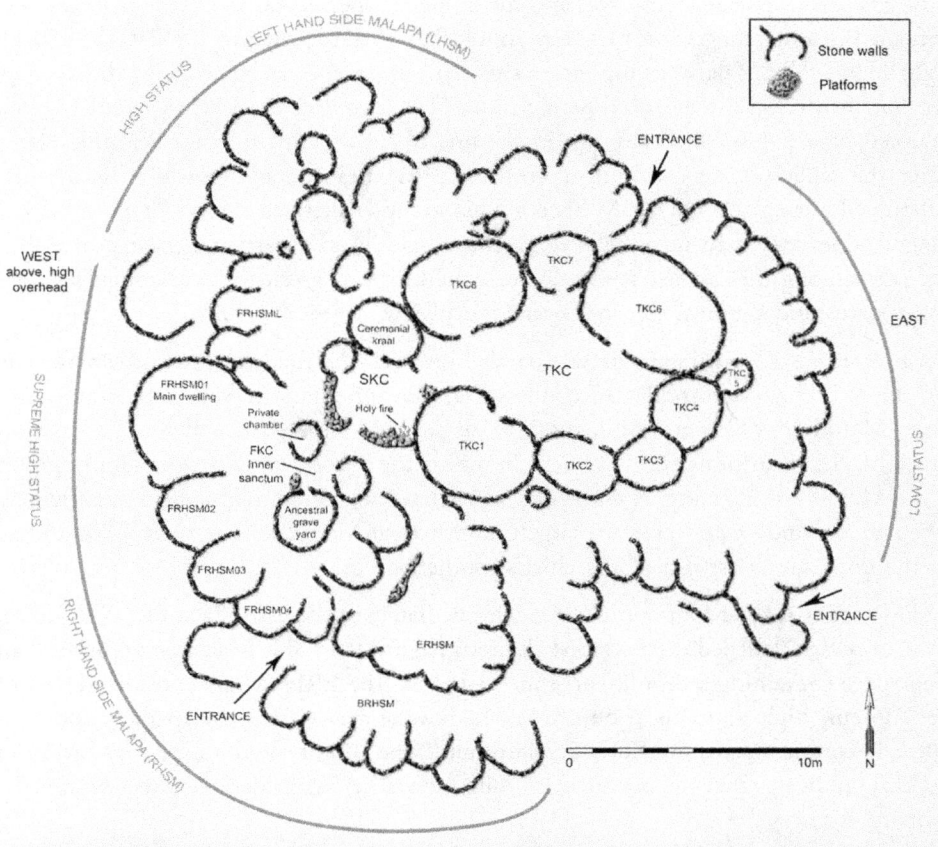

Figure 6.4
Plan of the *Kgosing* at Molokwane (after Pistorius 1996).

According to Tswana worldview, the western side of a settlement is generally associated with high status and the east with low status, as represented at Molokwane by the positioning of the elite dwelling area and the senior court on the west side of the *kgosing*. At Marothodi, the elite dwelling area (SOU) with its senior court also occupies a western portion of the *kgosing*, although relatively speaking, it is positioned further south than the example at Molokwane. This may be because the Tlokwa at Marothodi had little topography to work with, and had to ensure above all else that the senior *malapa* of the SOU occupied this minor elevation on the landscape. It may have been necessary to compromise elements of an 'ideal' settlement orientation in order to achieve this.

Pistorius identifies a number of distinct clusters of *malapa* in the Molokwane *kgosing* that might be comparable to the occupation units recognised in the 'Primary' *Kgosing* at Marothodi. His spatial analysis, based largely on Pedi ethnography (Mönnig 1967) in combination with an ethnographically-derived "hypothetical explanatory model", is orientated from the viewpoint of the opening from the SKC, facing into the FKC and toward the south-western edge of the site. From this position, the 'FRHSM' group of *malapa* occupy a position to the left, and the LHSM '(Left Hand Side Malapa) group are located to the right, and in accordance with the explanatory model should therefore represent the most senior and second most senior family groups respectively (Fig. 6.4).

As he has identified the chief's son and his family as the second most senior in the settlement, Pistorius' suggestion that they should have been located in the BRHSM (Back Right Hand Side Malapa) component, situated out on the far left edge of the *kgosing*, and not in the LHSM group, is perhaps unexpected (unless the LHSM could only be occupied by a family who were not in the line of succession). Instead, Pistorius places either the chief's uncle or younger brother in the LHSM, and possibly his mother. Although locating the Queen Mother in this group makes sense ethnographically, her presence does not seem to be reflected archaeologically in a particularly large or elaborate *lapa* among the LHSM group, as we would expect, given the conceptual link between status and physical size in Tswana worldview.

However, it is still possible to draw a parallel between the LHSM group at Molokwane and the WOU at Marothodi. If we follow Pistorius' orientation, from the entrance between Marothodi's SE1 and SE2, the SOU is situated on the left and the WOU is on the right. This positions the WOU as home to the second most senior family group in the Marothodi 'Primary' *Kgosing* and, as we have suggested, highlights the extremely large and elaborate *lapa* M11 (the largest anywhere at Marothodi) as a strong candidate for the domestic courtyard of the chief's mother.

Looking again at the Molokwane *kgosing*, immediately to the east of the FRHSM group, a row of *malapa* labelled the ERHSM (Eastern Right Hand Side Malapa) curl around an open space containing a prominent stone platform. The ERHSM are considered part of the "supreme high status" portion of the Molokwane *kgosing*, and are spatially and conceptually comparable to the EOU at Marothodi. The size of the dominant *lapa* M65 in the EOU indicates that the occupying family indeed held considerable status within the 'Primary' *Kgosing*.

Another Tswana homestead that can be compared to the 'Primary' *Kgosing* is the contemporary site at Olifantspoort (see Mason 1986: 374), approximately 60 kilometres southeast of Marothodi on the southern side of the Magaliesberg hills (Fig. 1.2). Although this is a smaller settlement, the position of the homestead known as Site 20/71 on a prominent rise in the landscape suggests that it held senior status. Here, an east-west dichotomy is again evident, with 'Enclosures VI and VII' identified as senior *malapa* on the west/south-west edge. The clusters of *malapa* to which they belong may, in addition, represent the equivalents of the SOU and WOU of Marothodi respectively, with 'Enclosure VII' perhaps representing the chief's mother's dwelling at Olifantspoort.

By contrast, the *kgosing* of the contemporary Hurutshe capital Kaditshwene, situated some 75 kilometres west of Marothodi (Fig. 1.2), presents a departure from some of the spatial similarities shared by the other Tswana towns discussed hitherto (Boeyens 2000: 9, 2003: 72). The peripheral *malapa*, for example, do not join together to create the impression of a continuous circular perimeter as they do at Marothodi and Molokwane, and the main cattle kraals are not linked. The spatiality of Kaditshwene is discussed in more detail later in this chapter, when we explore the 'Secondary' *Kgosing* at Marothodi.

Excavations at the 'Primary' *Kgosing*

A small excavation was undertaken in the court midden, in the court complex of the 'Primary' *Kgosing*. This midden is situated in the south-east corner of SE1 (see Figs. 6.5, 6.6 and 6.7). The purpose was to gather data that would contribute to a comparison between material from elite, ceremonial court middens, and domestic middens elsewhere at Marothodi.

The Court Midden

As described in the previous chapter, court middens are identified as such on the basis of their consistent association with court complexes (Huffman 1996b). The court midden here in the 'Primary' *Kgosing* shares structural similarities with other court middens at Marothodi, in that it is surrounded by a formal stone wall that controls the deposit within. Inside the wall, the surface of the midden rises approximately 0.50 m above the ground level of SE1, and is level with the surface of the abutting stone platform on its western edge.

A sample trench of 5.0 square metres was excavated into the centre of the midden, oriented to avoid the outcrops of protruding bedrock that were revealed during grass clearance and trowelling of the midden surface. Approximately 1.65 cubic metres of deposit were excavated, which consisted of up to six layers of ashy soil capped by 0.10 m of humic weathered topsoil. The midden has a maximum depth of 0.54 m. The ashy layers were similar in consistency and colour, ranging from a grayish-brown to light brownish-grey. Some large naturally occuring rocks provided solid flat surfaces beneath the ash, and it seems that the midden wall was deliberately constructed around them.

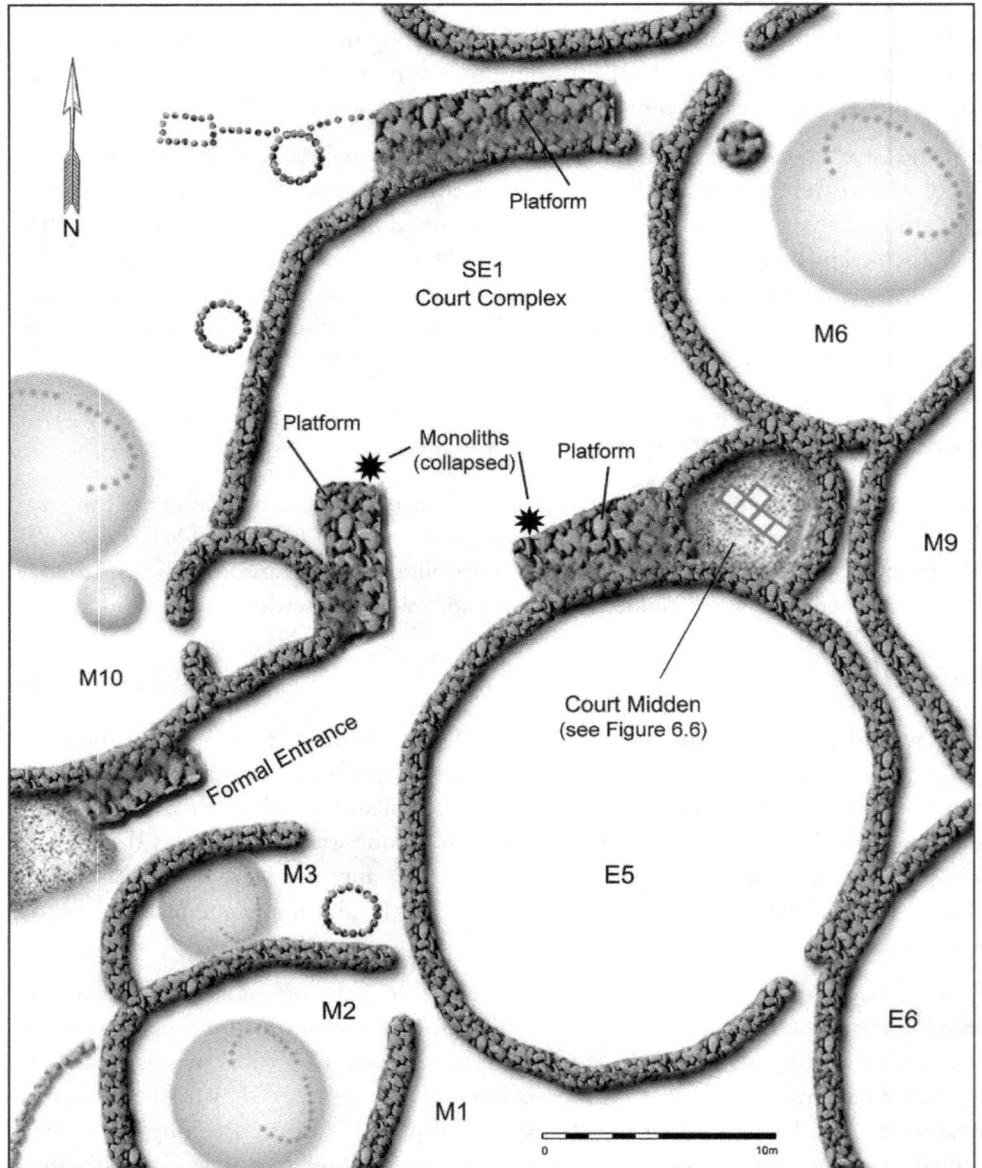

Figure 6.5
Plan of the court complex in the 'Primary' *Kgosing*, showing the location of the court midden and the position of the excavation trench (see Fig. 6.1 for orientation).

Figure 6.6
Plan of the excavated
trench in the court midden
of the 'Primary' *Kgosing*.
Blocks of underlying
bedrock are shown at the
base of the trench.

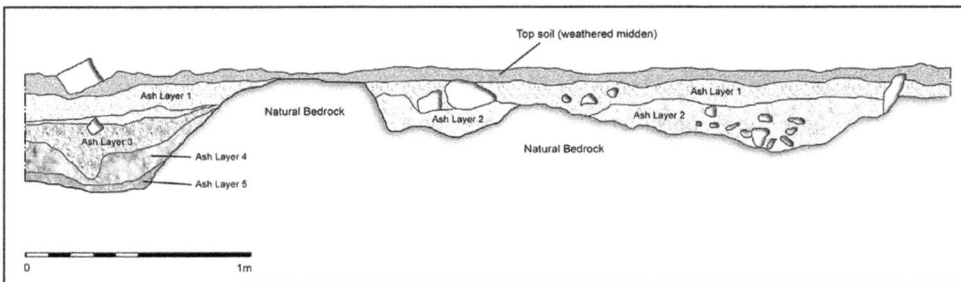

Figure 6.7
North-east facing section
of the trench in the court
midden.

Figure 6.8
Rim sherds from the court
midden of the 'Primary'
Kgosing.

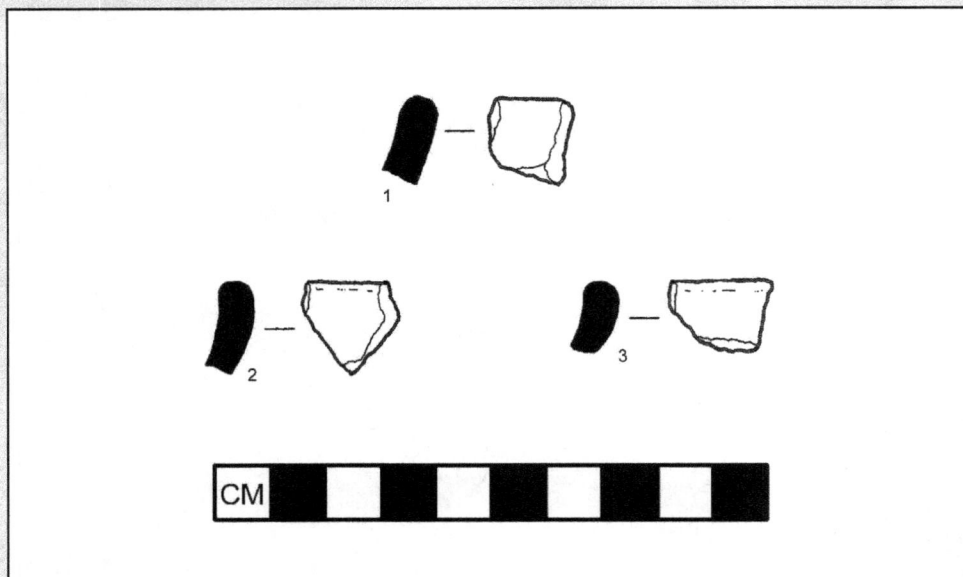

Figure 6.8 Ceramic Descriptions

1. Smooth-necked jar, plain. Profile Mode: 1A. Provenance: 'Primary' *Kgosing*, Court Midden, Square E, Level 4. Cat. No. V654.

2. Smooth-necked jar, plain. Profile Mode: 1A. Provenance: 'Primary' *Kgosing*, Court Midden, Square A, Level 3. Cat. No. V655.

3. Smooth-necked jar, plain. Profile Mode: 1A. Provenance: 'Primary' *Kgosing*, Court Midden, Square A, Level 3. Cat. No. V656.

Artefacts from the Court Midden

Ceramics

A total of 82 sherds (1412.1g) were retrieved from the court midden, of which only 3 were diagnostic (Table 6.1). The overall density was 855.7g of ceramic sherds per cubic metre of excavated material. None of the sherds recovered were suitable for multi-dimensional analysis (Fig. 6.8).

		Sherds	Mass (g)	Mass (g) per m³	% of total sherds
Layer 1	Diagnostic	0	0	0	0
	Adiagnostic	29	857.7	519.8	35.4
Layer 2	Diagnostic	0	0	0	0
	Adiagnostic	26	422.3	255.9	31.7
Layer 3	Diagnostic	2	3.8	2.3	2.4
	Adiagnostic	23	125.3	75.9	28.1
Layer 4	Diagnostic	1	1.8	1.1	1.2
	Adiagnostic	1	1.2	0.7	1.2
Subtotals	Diagnostic	3	5.6	3.4	3.6
	Adiagnostic	79	1406.5	852.3	96.4
Totals		82	1412.1	855.7	100

Table 6.1
Quantities of ceramic sherds from the court midden of the 'Primary' *Kgosing*.

Figure 6.9
Tim Hitchens lays a measuring tape across the court midden of the 'Primary' *Kgosing* in preparation for planning.

Metallurgy

A small quantity of metallurgical debris was recovered from the court midden, including 48.3g of slag and a few small pieces of magnetite (Table 6.2). No finished metal artefacts were found.

Other Artefacts

The court midden yielded a single ostrich eggshell bead (#MAR303), a small clay horn detached from the head of a cattle figurine (#MAR307), and a smoothed upper grindstone (#MAR306) (Fig. 6.10).

Table 6.2
Quantities of metallurgical debris from the court midden of the 'Primary' *Kgosing*.

Material Type	Mass (g)	Mass (g) per m³	% of total
Smelting/flow Slag	48.3	29.3	24.3
Magnetite	150.7	91.3	75.7
Totals	199.0	120.6	100

Figure 6.10
Artefacts retrieved from the court midden of the 'Primary' *Kgosing*.

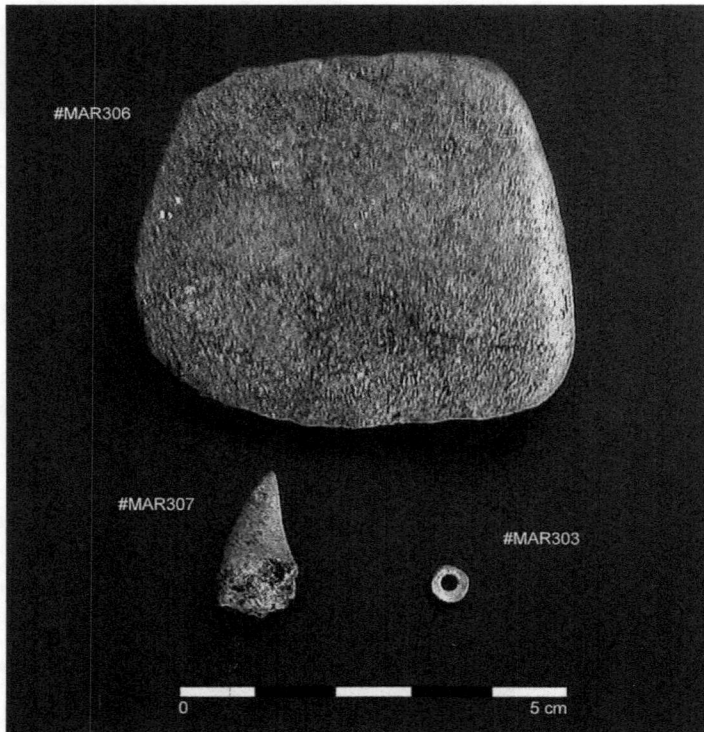

Spatial organisation of the 'Secondary' *Kgosing*

Situated some 120 metres to the east of the 'Primary' *Kgosing*, the 'Secondary' *Kgosing* extends approximately 190 metres from east to west, and about 150 metres north to south (see Figs. 5.4 and 6.11). With a total of 57 identified *malapa*, this homestead seems to have accommodated a slightly smaller population than its counterpart to the west. If the occupation of Marothodi had not been disrupted by Kgosi's death and the subsequent movement northward, it is quite possible that the 'Secondary' *Kgosing* would have expanded to accommodate the natural growth of the community (see Sanderson 1981: 249; Huffman 1986b: 301). As with the 'Primary' *Kgosing*, our exploration of the 'Secondary' *Kgosing* begins by identifying the core of political authority.

The Cattle Kraals and Court Complex

The comparatively large size of the main kraal in the 'Secondary' *Kgosing*, leaves no doubt about its status as an elite homestead, and makes an unambiguous statement about the prosperity, power and status of the residents (Fig. 6.11). As the primary kraal, it is to enclosure E1 that the main cattle avenue can be expected to lead, so it is from here that we develop our orientation. Unfortunately, the stone walling of the kraal is in a state of collapse along much of its length, to the extent that any definite indication of an entranceway into the enclosure has been lost. The precise location of the opening might be revealed by further careful fieldwork, but its predicted position as marked on the map seems reasonable in light of other organisational indicators. There is a small opening in the kraal wall on the northern side, but as this leads directly into domestic courtyard space it is unlikely to have been used as an entrance/exit for cattle.

The formal route from outside the homestead to this point at E1 is most likely to have been through Entrance A on the east side (Fig. 6.11). It is possible that Entrance A was not originally as wide as it now appears to be, but that perishable materials were used to control this opening. Wooden post fences or palisades frequently adorned important entrances in Tswana settlements, as exemplified ethnographically at the Ntšhabeleng settlement at Mothopong (Bothma 1962: Plate 1-1). Once through this entrance, the cattle turned northward and passed between the domestic dwellings and, notably, between two formal stone platforms. As seen in the 'Primary' *Kgosing*, such stone platforms are often observed along the main cattle thoroughfare in Tswana homesteads, and may have assisted with driving livestock.

The cattle then veered westward over a midden for 'cooling' before entering through the narrow opening into a secondary enclosure, SE4. This entranceway is flanked on the northern side by an elevated 'platform midden' similar to that described in SE1 of the 'Primary' *Kgosing*. The pairing of this feature with the formal stone platform on the other side of the entrance emphasises its ceremonial significance, and together they help to identify this area as the court complex, and the midden as a court midden (Fig. 6.11). SE4 can be recognised as a space conceptually equivalent to SE1 in the court complex of the 'Primary' *Kgosing*. This was probably the location of the *kgotla*, and it is therefore appropriate that it is close to the largest kraal, E1, here in the 'Secondary' *Kgosing*.

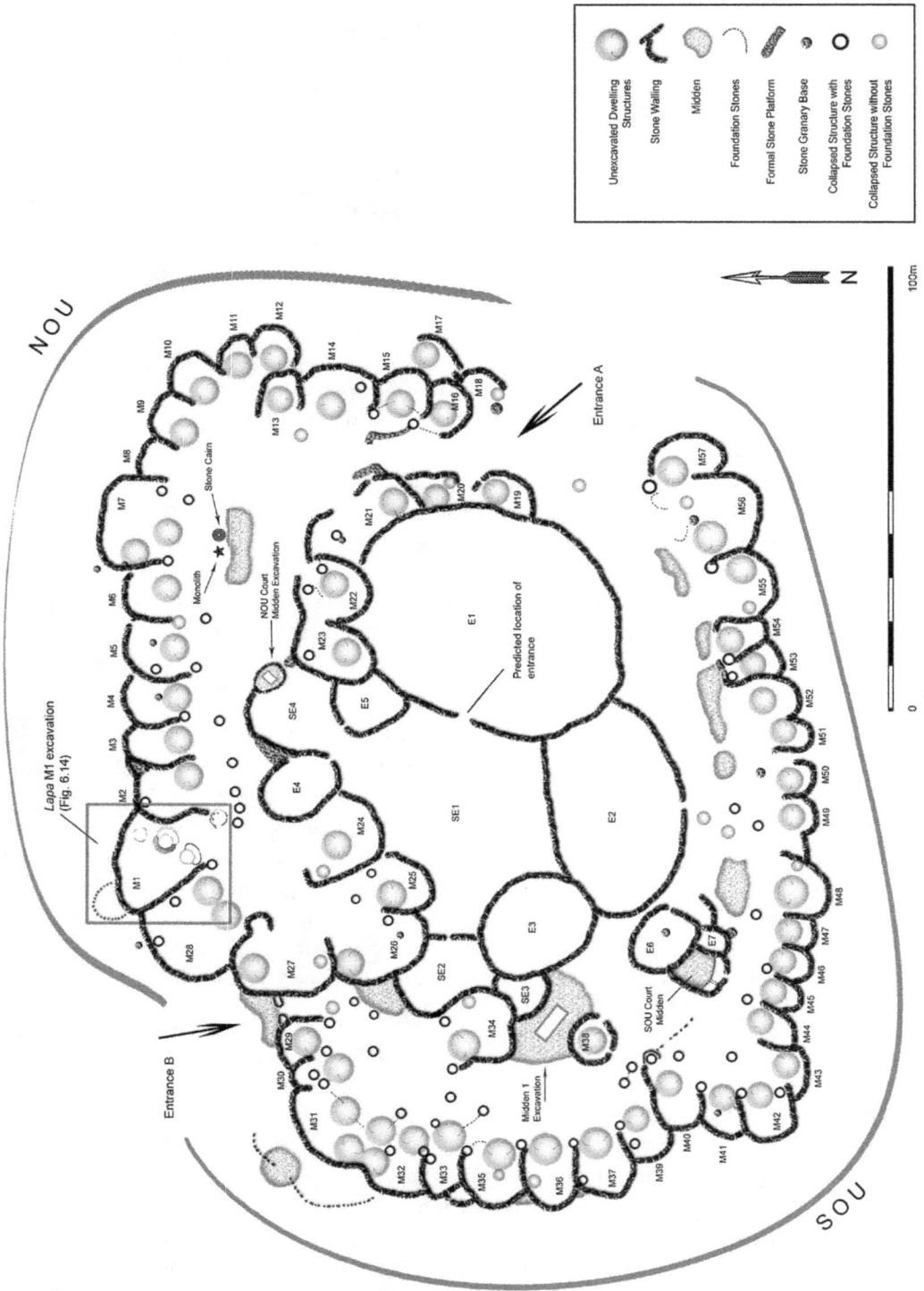

Figure 6.11
Map of the 'Secondary' Kgosing at Marothodi, showing the two occupation units.

A second formal stone platform connects the western wall of SE4 with the enclosure E4, emphasising the conceptual unity of these features. E4 and the opposite enclosure E5 must be interpreted as part of the court complex. E5 contained no dung, and might therefore be identified as the chief's private *kamore*. Enclosure E4 did contain dung, and was probably a small kraal. Consequently, these two enclosures are interpreted as equivalent to E5 and E6 respectively in the 'Primary' *Kgosing*.

The Domestic Sphere

Having determined the location of the political centre of power it is possible to interpret the organisation of the surrounding *malapa*, and it becomes clear that the 'Secondary' *Kgosing* is composed of two occupation units: a Northern Occupation Unit (NOU) and a Southern Occupation Unit (SOU) (Fig. 6.11).

Northern Occupation Unit (NOU)

The spatial relationship between the NOU and the court complex indicates that the NOU was the senior of the two occupation units, and the residence of the royal family. The *malapa* belonging to the NOU occupy the northern and north-eastern perimeter of the homestead, and include numbers M1 to M28 (Fig. 6.11). Their arrangement is an almost complete elongated circle, and is thus reminiscent of the royal occupation unit (SOU) of the 'Primary' *Kgosing* (Fig. 6.1). This 'curling' pattern of households facing each other in a loop seems to be a recurring spatial expression of kinship ties among elite sections of a community, and may reflect high status.

Figure 6.12
The stone cairn (left) and domed monolith (right) in front of *lapa* M7 in the 'Secondary' *Kgosing* at Marothodi, viewed from the north.

The NOU includes the largest *malapa* in the 'Secondary' *Kgosing*, namely M1, M28 and M7. In front of M7, a domed monolith and a stone cairn (slightly disturbed by an intrusive tree) are positioned next to each other, approximately 1.50 m apart (Fig. 6.12). The cairn is 0.70 m high, with a diameter of 1.50 m. The monolith is 0.40 m high and 0.35 m in diameter. These features mark the entrance to the front courtyard of the high status *lapa* M7, and thus occur in a similar context to the stone platforms observed in front of M65 in the 'Primary' Kgosing (Fig. 6.1).

The interpretation of a possibly deeper significance for the pairing remains speculative, although Ntšhabeleng (Pedi) ethnography describes how young girls would place round stones at the entrance to the senior dwelling at the completion of their initiation course (Bothma 1962: 12).

The relative proximity of *lapa* M7 to the opening of the court complex further strengthens the interpretation of this household as the residence of the chief's senior wife—equivalent to *lapa* M1 in the 'Primary' *Kgosing*.

Southern Occupation Unit (SOU)

The SOU on the south-west side of the 'Secondary' *Kgosing* also has its own court complex. This incorporates enclosures E6 and E7, and has a formal stone platform with a court midden enclosed by a low stone wall, although both of these features are less physically imposing than their counterparts in the NOU (Fig. 6.11). The presence of a separate court complex, however, serves to emphasise the administrative semi-independence of the SOU.

Entrance B on the north-west perimeter, provides access into the SOU (Fig. 6.11). At face value, we might assume that SOU cattle entered here, and were herded southward towards the SOU court complex, and then eastward into enclosure E2. Indeed, the midden deposit in the entranceway would repeat the concept of 'cooling' cattle as they entered the homestead from the outside, and leading them past the SOU court complex would express the association between cattle and political and ritual power.

However, Entrance B leads directly into a 'busy' domestic area, with structures and features here that would clearly have presented obstacles to cattle. Instead, it would seem logical to interpret Entrance B as a pedestrian entrance, and to suggest that SOU cattle also entered the homestead from Entrance A.

In contrast to the looping formation of the *malapa* in the NOU, the 27 domestic courtyards of the SOU, which include numbers M29 to M57, are arranged in an open arc around the south-western perimeter of the homestead. The only exceptions are *malapa* M34 and M38, which do face back towards the others. Indeed, M38 looks like it may originally have been a small cattle kraal, which suggests a degree of expansion or rearrangement here. The comparatively smaller size of the SOU *malapa* serves to emphasise their inferior status to those in the NOU. Although none were excavated, most SOU *malapa* contain the familiar traces of a variety of collapsed structures on the ground.

Domestic middens are generally more visible in the SOU than in the NOU. The largest of these is located approximately 30 metres to the north of the court complex. This midden was sampled by excavation, and is referred to here as Midden 1.

Spatial comparison with Kaditshwene

The east-west/low-high status dichotomy that characterises the 'Primary' *Kgosing* at Marothodi, and which is also evident at Molokwane and Olifantspoort, is not as explicit at the 'Secondary' *Kgosing*. In this regard the spatial organisation more closely resembles that of the *kgosing* at Kaditshwene (Fig. 6.13), and some of the spatial similarities between the two sites are worthy of discussion here (Boeyens 2000, 2003).

The senior residential unit of Kaditshwene is situated to the north of its main *kgotla*, and features a central open space partly surrounded by *malapa*. The looping formation of the Kaditshwene *malapa* reflects the high status of their occupants, and is similar to the arrangement we have observed at the NOU of the 'Secondary' *Kgosing*. At Kaditshwene there is a midden in the centre of this space, and formal stone platforms with monoliths flank the *kgotla* entrance to the south (Fig. 6.13). This is similar to the arrangement in the NOU of the 'Secondary' *Kgosing* at Marothodi. The open space in front of *lapa* M7

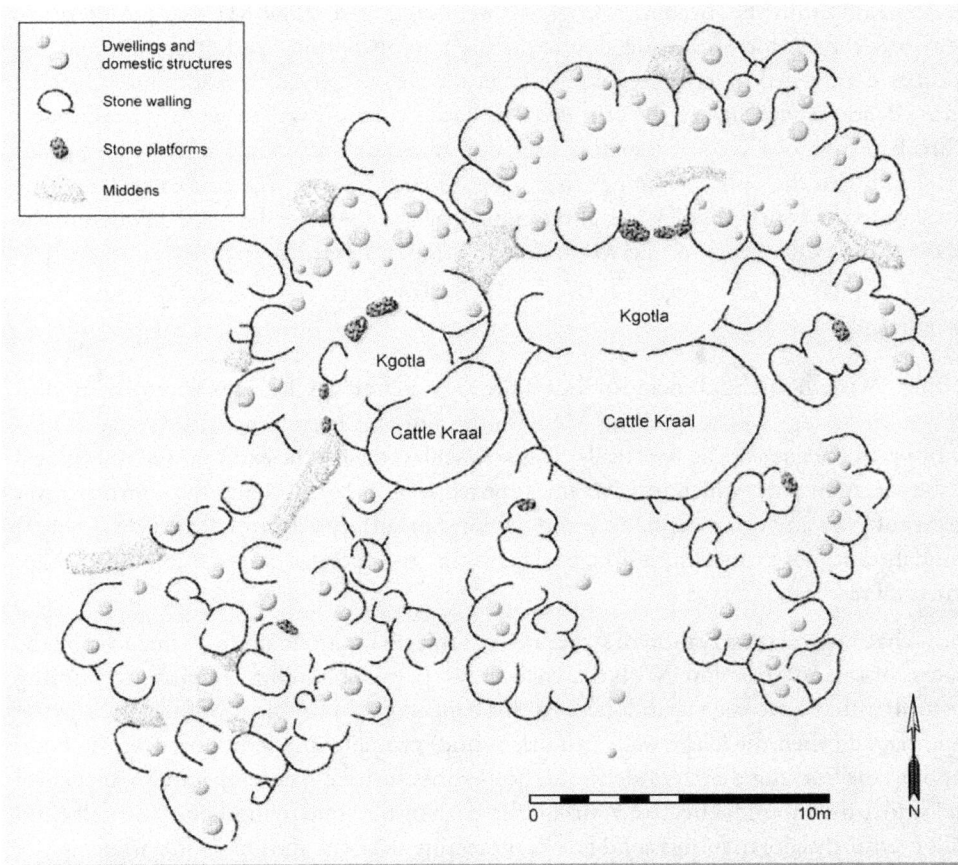

Figure 6.13
Plan of the main ward in the *kgosing* of Kaditshwene (after Boeyens 2003).

(marked by the stone cairn and monolith) also contains a midden, and the entrance to the court complex is flanked by the court midden and a stone platform. At both sites, the court complex is entered from the north side, and from there access is gained south-ward to the main cattle kraal. It might also be noteworthy that the two homesteads have entrances between *malapa* in similar places: one on the eastern side (where one could enter the residential area through a prominent north-westerly oriented passageway on both sites); and one on the northern side through a gap between the two main clusters of *malapa*.

As we saw in Chapter Two, major differences in settlement style or organisation are some-times considered to be a reflection of distinct identities or lineages (Maggs 1976a; Boeyens 2003; Huffman 2007), and considering the relative ease with which families from differ-ent groups could be absorbed into Tswana towns we might expect to see a degree of vari-ety in homestead layout within an aggregated capital. In terms of the cultural principles underlying the spatial organisation of the 'Secondary' *Kgosing* at Marothodi, however, it is clear that the differences in layout compared to the 'Primary' *Kgosing* are essentially varia-tions on a set of shared themes, and should not be over-emphasised.

Excavations at the 'Secondary' *Kgosing*

Three areas within the 'Secondary' *Kgosing* were excavated. *Lapa* M1 was the domestic courtyard chosen for excavation due to its high status within the homestead, and the fact that it appeared to have been archaeologically well preserved. In addition, M1 had a screened 'annex' attached to the outside of its back courtyard wall in which metallurgical debris had been observed. It therefore provided an opportunity to sample the household associated with the only such annex in the 'Secondary' *Kgosing*. The court midden at the entrance to the court complex was also sampled, as was the large domestic midden in the centre of the SOU, which is referred to here as Midden 1 (see Fig. 6.11).

Domestic *lapa* M1

As the Tswana household includes the whole *lapa* and all the features within it, an area excavation strategy was adopted for M1 with the aim of exposing the entire courtyard in-terior up to the ends of the *lapa* walls. This was achieved with the exception of one 'block' in the southern part, which was left unexcavated (Fig. 6.14). Initially the courtyard was cleared of grass and other vegetation, and the interior surface was trowelled clean. Upright foundation stones protruding through the covering soil revealed the position of the main structural features.

The archaeological preservation of structures is, somewhat parodoxically, influenced by the process of their destruction. With thatched roofs, Tswana buildings are prone to burning down after they have been abandoned. As this happens, the burning roof first falls into the building, and then the 'daga' walls (sundried mud) crumble into a mound over the floor, trapping the burning thatch underneath. Sometimes furnace-like temperatures are gener-ated under the mound, effectively 'firing' the daga of the underlying floor. The collapsed walls eventually cool to form a solid dome, protecting the floor and any *in situ* artefacts.

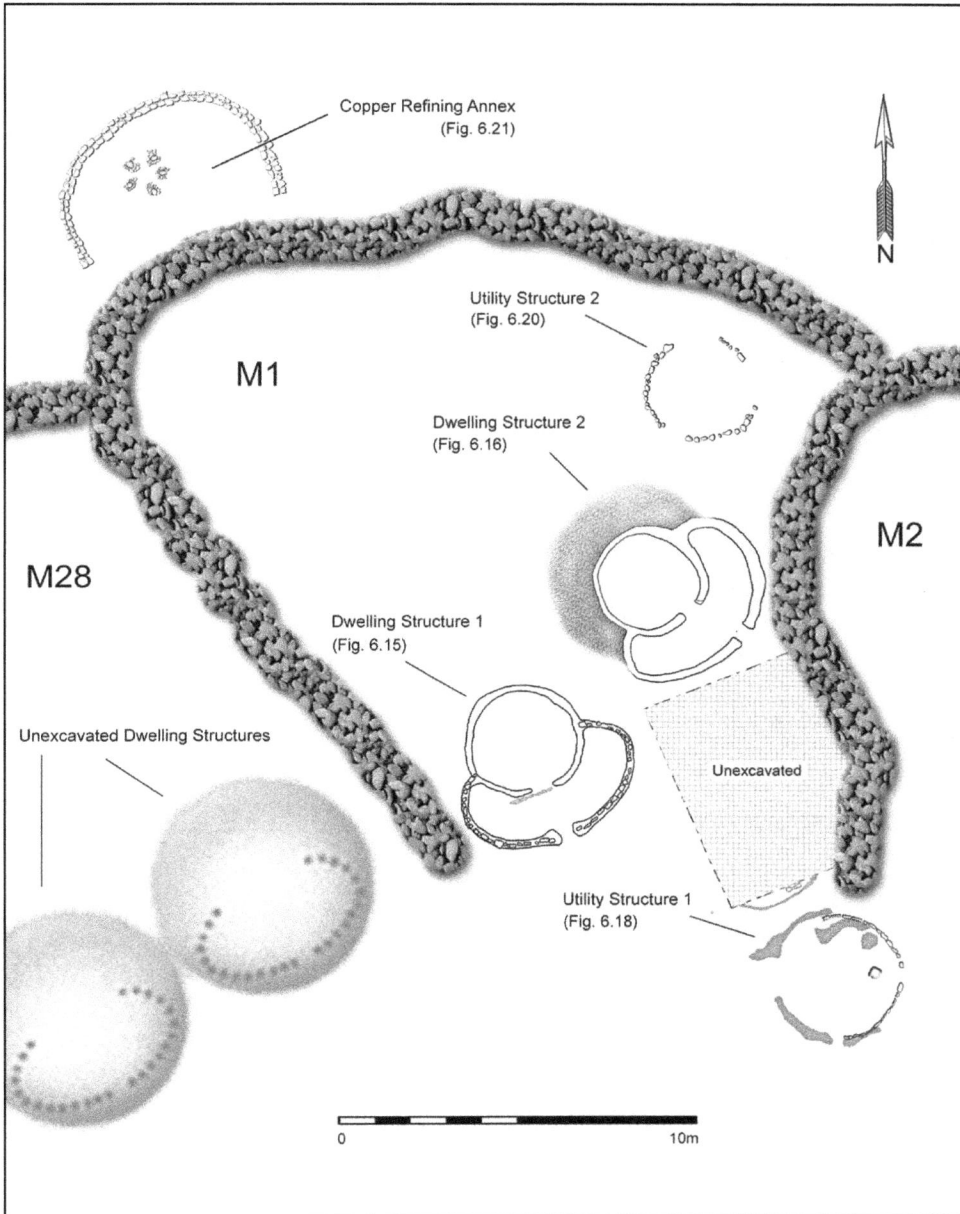

Figure 6.14
Plan of *lapa* M1 in the 'Secondary' *Kgosing* showing the positions of the excavated features discussed in the text.

Four structures were excavated. The two main domestic dwelling structures, with their entrances facing forward, mark the boundary between front and back courtyards. A large 'utility structure', probably used for preparing and cooking food, was situated in the front courtyard, and in the eastern corner of the back courtyard there was a smaller circular structure. As described above, the annex on the outside of the back courtyard wall was also excavated. We begin by describing these features, and then present all of the finds from *lapa* M1 together.

Dwelling Structure 1

The floors of Dwelling Structure 1 were well-preserved. Most of the wall foundations survived up to 0.10 m high, and much of the interior floor plaster was intact (Fig. 6.15). The circular inner room, which had been slightly disturbed by a tree root, measured 3.0 m in diameter. At the entrance a line of door-slide base stones, 1.25 m in length, had survived *in situ*. A deep groove was worn along the length of these stones from the friction of the wooden sliding door, of which there was no archaeological trace. As with all recorded door slides at Tswana sites, it opened to the left as one faces it from the outside (see Mason 1986; Maggs 1993a).

In the front veranda space, a worn lower grindstone was positioned just to the south of the door-slide base stones, on the left-hand side as one enters the veranda from outside the structure. The daga floor of the front veranda was slightly better preserved than that of the inner room. The floor daga of both the inner room and the front veranda had been smeared up at the junction of floor and wall to create a smooth join between the two.

Outside the front veranda wall, on the north side of the structure, a sub-circular patch of stone cobbling with a few loose ceramic sherds suggested the presence of a 'pot stand' here. Similar features are often identified at contemporary Tswana sites, usually in this position outside the house where the front veranda connects to the main house wall (Mason 1986). They were used to support a large semi-permanent storage vessel which may have contained water, grain or beer (Larsson & Larsson 1984). Being under the eaves of the roof, the pot would have been afforded some shade during the heat of the day.

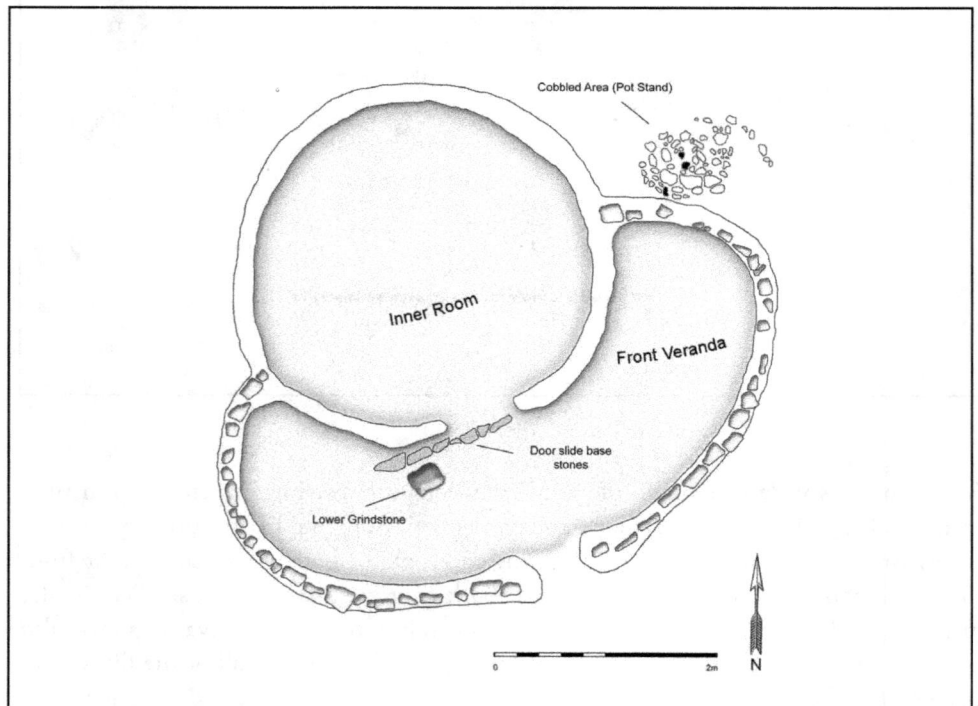

Figure 6.15
Plan of the excavated floor and foundations of Dwelling Structure 1, in *lapa* M1 of the 'Secondary' *Kgosing*.

Small patches of rough stone 'cobbling' were noted around the northern exterior (rear) of the structure, but this was very ephemeral and difficult to define. There was no evidence that this space had been walled in to form a rear veranda, so it was probably an open storage area under the eaves of the roof. If parts of the ground needed to be reinforced in this way, it is possible that waterlogging was a problem for the residents of *lapa* M1.

In summary, the foundations of Dwelling Structure 1 represent a 'cone-on-cylinder' type structure similar in form to other historically, archaeologically and ethnographically observed Tswana dwellings (e.g. Burchell 1824; Kay 1833; Mason 1986; Larsson & Larsson 1984). The exact form of the front veranda component is difficult to reconstruct from the foundations alone, but it probably had a low wall at the front, and was open up to the eaves of the thatched roof. The basic form of Dwelling Structure 1 is repeated at all other excavated houses at Marothodi.

Dwelling Structure 2

Dwelling Structure 2 is located 3.0 m to the north-east of Dwelling Structure 1 (see Fig. 6.14) It was not visible prior to excavation due to the lack of orthostatic foundation stones and the low profile of the overlying wall rubble mound. After initial surface clearance, the reddish colouration of the soil in this location suggested the presence of fired daga, and further excavation exposed the floor and wall foundations of the structure (Fig. 6.16).

Much of the floor was well preserved, and had been coloured red when the structure burnt down. Up to 0.25 m of vertical plastered walling survived close to the adjacent *lapa* stone wall, and in places the charred remains of the pole and stick framework could be seen inside the wall cross-section (Fig. 6.17).

The diameter of the circular inner room was 2.45 m. The roots of a nearby tree had intruded through the daga flooring, but this had not disturbed the rest of the feature. Although no trace of a door slide could be seen between the inner room and the front veranda, a fragment of door slide base stone with a linear groove worn into one surface was recovered from the wall rubble. A patch of ash on the front veranda floor indicated the presence of a hearth here.

At the back of the structure, a crescent-shaped area of densely packed stone cobbles abutted the exterior wall in the area where we might have expected a rear veranda to be. Although this surface was much more obvious that the small patches of reinforcement behind Dwelling Structure 1, no traces of a wall enclosing the cobbled area were identified. Once again, this may have been an open storage space. The remains of two charred wooden posts set into the cobbled surface were exposed, which presumably helped to support the overhanging eave of the thatched roof.

On the northern edge of the cobbled surface, an area of compact clay-like deposit was exposed, characterised by inclusions of densely-packed bone flecks. The interpretation of this deposit remains uncertain but it may represent a space where small domestic animals, such as chickens, were slaughtered, or where bone was worked into ornaments. A sample was collected, and faunal analysis might reveal more information.

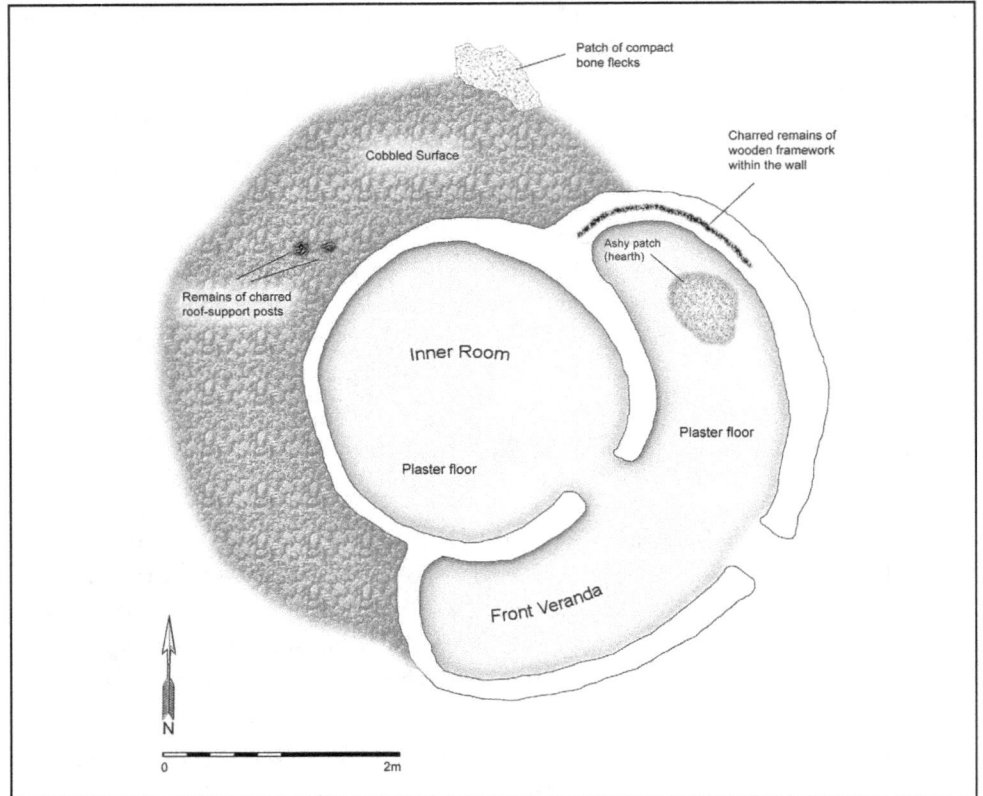

Figure 6.16
Plan of the excavated
floor and foundations of
Dwelling Structure 2,
in *lapa* M1 of the
'Secondary' *Kgosing*.

Figure 6.17
A view of the front veranda
of Dwelling Structure
2 during excavation,
showing the patch of white
ash where a hearth was
situated, and the well-
preserved plaster on the
surviving wall foundations.

Utility Structure 1

Near the end of the eastern *lapa* wall that separates M1 from M2, a semi-circular arrange-ment of upright foundation stones indicated the presence of a collapsed structure (see Fig. 6.14). As it was clearly not a dwelling structure, we called it Utility Structure 1. Excavation revealed a circular foundation with a diameter of 3.50 m (Fig. 6.18). The only surviving foundation stones were those on the eastern side of the structure that were visible prior to excavation. On the western side, the wall base was indicated by ephemeral traces of daga. The interior floor surface was not as well preserved as those in the nearby dwelling struc-tures, but was characterised by patches of compact stone cobbling. Similar areas of cob-bling were also found outside the structure, on the north- and south-west exterior surfaces. A worn lower grindstone was situated on the interior floor surface towards the rear of the building, helping to identify this as a food preparation structure or 'kitchen'.

Figure 6.18
Plan of the excavated floor and foundations of Utility Structure 1, in *lapa* M1 of the 'Secondary' *Kgosing*.

Although no *in situ* evidence for a sliding door was observed, the position of five flat 'paving stones' on the western exterior of the structure indicated that the door was situated on this side. In addition, two fragments of door slide base stone were recovered from the wall rubble. One had a narrow groove worn into one flat surface, and the other had wide grooves worn into both upper and lower surfaces, indicating its reuse. The fact that the structure had a sliding door indicates that it was a full cone-on-cylinder structure, serving to distinguish Utility Structure 1 from other ethnographically described Tswana 'kitchens', which usually seem to have had only a low wall with the roof resting on poles, (Larsson & Larsson 1984: 68; Huffman 1986: 300).

An unusual feature associated with Utility Structure 1 might be described as floor 'tiling'. The surfaces outside the foundations on the west and north sides were covered in purposefully laid ceramic sherds to create mosaic-like surfaces (Fig. 6.19). In some places the tiling was two or three layers deep, which indicated periodic attempts to repair or preserve it. This seems to have been an elaborately designed walkway or path constructed to compensate for ground instability or waterlogging. This discovery supports the probablility that the underlying turf soil was particularly problematic in this part of the 'Secondary' *Kgosing*, and that a variety of measures were employed to address the issue.

Figure 6.19
Ross Porter records a linear stretch of 'mosaic' floor tiling on the north-west side of Utility Structure 1.

To the north of the building, an ephemeral curved line of daga appears to follow the arc of the path as it disappears into the unexcavated area. It is possible that this may be part of another structure as yet unexposed, and that the tiled path provided a walkway between this and Utility Structure 1 (Fig. 6.18).

Utility Structure 2

In the north-east corner of *lapa* M1, in the area behind Dwelling Structure 2 at the rear of the courtyard (see Fig. 6.14), a circular arrangement of foundation stones belonging to another structure were examined (Fig. 6.20). The foundations had a maximum diameter of 4.0 m, with a number of gaps around the circumference so they did not form a complete circle. Some of the stones were firmly embedded in the courtyard surface, but others were loosely set in position. On the eastern perimeter, a line of embedded ceramic sherds and a long flat stone were used in combination as a door slide base, clearly indicating that this structure had a sliding door, and most probably a full wall up to the roof.

Although no formal floor surface could be identified in the interior of the structure, a number of ceramic sherds lying uniformly flat on the ground at the base of the wall rubble gave an indication of the inner floor horizon. The doorway of this structure opens into the extreme north-east corner of the *lapa*. This is a secluded entrance when compared to the doors of the dwelling structures and Utility Structure 1, which are oriented towards the front of the courtyard.

The overall impression is of a relatively 'informal' structure of low status that may have accommodated "servants" (see Lichtenstein 1928: 378). Indeed, this structure occupies a conceptually similar position to the "servant's house" in the *lapa* described by Burchell (1824) in his plan of a senior Tlhaping courtyard (see Fig. 1.5 in Chapter One). Alternatively, Utility Structure 2 could have been used for storage.

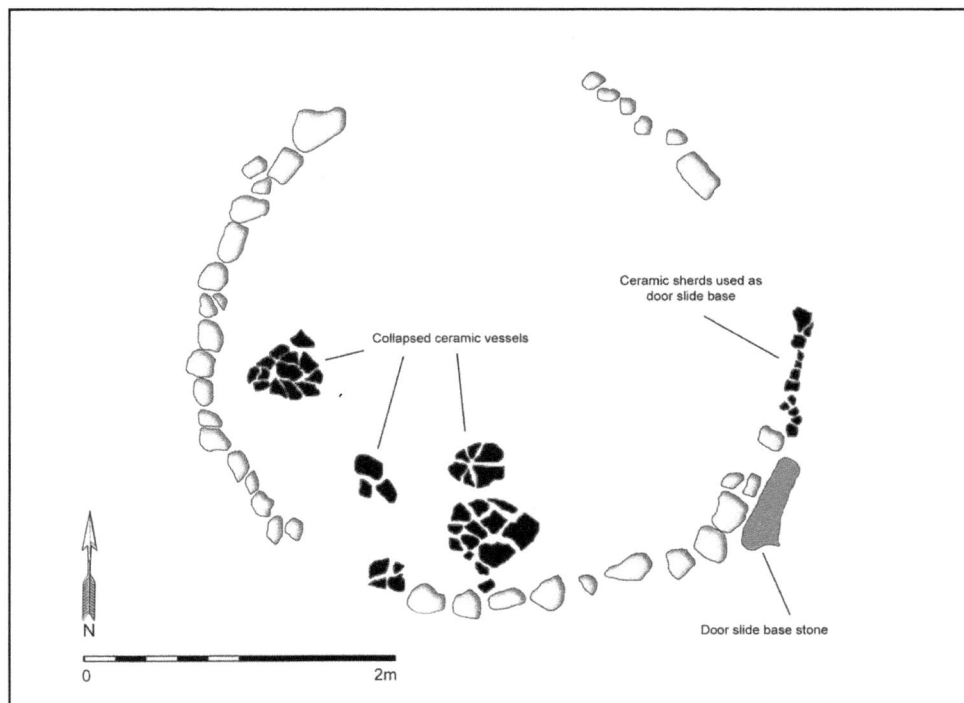

Figure 6.20
Plan of the excavated floor and foundations of Utility Structure 2, in *lapa* M1 of the 'Secondary' *Kgosing*.

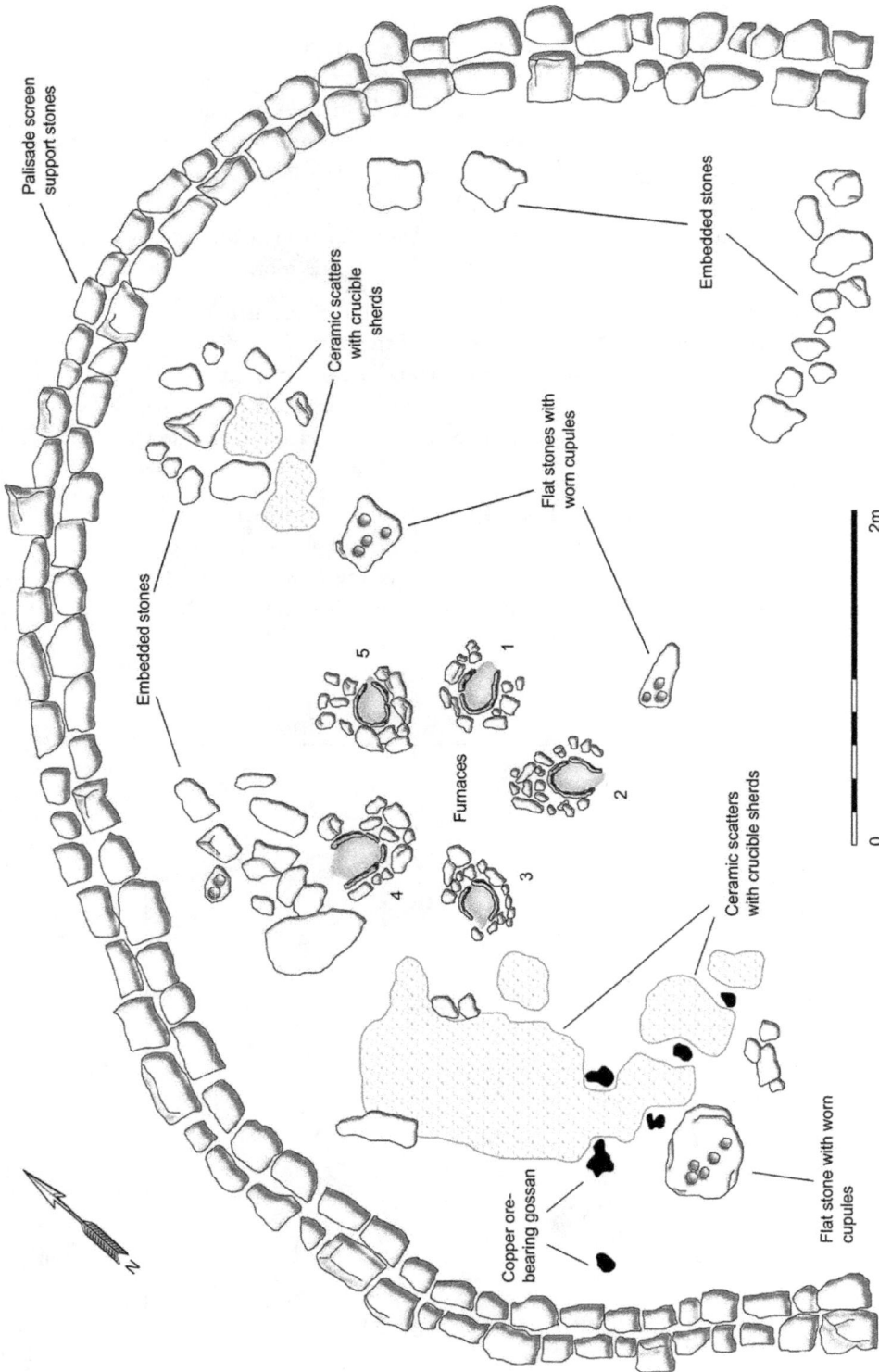

Figure 6.21
Plan of the Copper Refining Annex, behind *lapa* M1 of the 'Secondary' *Kgosing* at Marothodi.

Copper Refining Annex

In Chapter Five the high quantity of metallurgical debris at Marothodi was described. A concentration of this material had been observed on the northern edge of *lapa* M1, which identified this area specifically as a place of copper production.

Here, a double row of large upright stone blocks are arranged in a semi-circle to define an activity space or 'annex' immediately outside the back courtyard wall (see Fig. 6.14). This type of stone arrangement is interpreted as a support for a wooden palisade fence or screen, which would have been secured within the central space between the stones (for an ethnographic reference for palisade support stones, see Bothma 1962: Plate 1-1). Palisade supports like these occur at many locations around Marothodi.

The screen enclosed an area approximately 8.0 m in diameter (Fig. 6.21). A gap of about 1.0 m at each end of the screen provided two points of access into the annex from either side. Significantly, there was no access directly from the back courtyard of *lapa* M1. Instead, the most direct route from inside the 'Secondary' *Kgosing* to the annex would have been through Entrance B, some 45 metres to the south-west (see Fig. 6.11).

Figure 6.22
Furnaces inside the
Copper Refining Annex
under excavation.

Figure 6.23
Copper refining furnace
No.1 (see Fig. 6.21)
showing the shallow
inner daga dish forming
a chute for the tuyere at
the opening between
the support stones.

Initial surface clearance inside the annex revealed several clusters of ceramic sherds that were vitrified on one or more surface. These are identified as crucible sherds (see Stayt 1931: 64; Hall *et al.* 2006: 23). They were accompanied by pieces of green coloured pieces of rock resembling the ore-bearing gossan described by Wagner (1924), along with scatters of slag. This material was concentrated within the annex interior, although small quantities were found immediately outside the perimeter screen.

Further excavation revealed a cluster of five small furnaces in the centre of the annex (Fig. 6.22). The furnaces were elliptical in shape, and were arranged radially to face each other. They were all similar in size, measuring 0.50 to 0.80 m long, by 0.40 to 0.50 m wide and 0.10 to 0.20 m in depth. Each consisted of a supporting superstructure of stones partially sunk into the ground, with smooth daga lining on the inner surface forming an elliptical bowl. A single opening at the outer end of each furnace indicated the possible position of a tuyere port, and where the daga was sufficiently preserved it curved upward towards the aperture to form a smooth chute (Fig. 6.23). Each furnace had at least two layers of daga lining, suggesting that they may been used more than once.

The lack of daga debris in the vicinity of the furnaces seemed to suggest that they had little, if any, superstructure above the ground, and that the furnaces as excavated are almost complete. They must, therefore, have been able to perform their function with only the limited insulation these structures would have provided. This observation, in combination with the large quantity of crucible sherds here, supports the interpretation of these furnaces as being for the secondary re-melting or 'refining' of previously smelted copper. The large flat stones near the furnaces, some with small cupules worn into the surface, may have been used as 'anvils' for the crushing of previously smelted slag to obtain embedded copper prills for re-melting (see Stayt 1931; Hall *et al.* 2006). The scatters of broken up slag around the furnace interior seem to support this interpretation (Fig. 6.21).

It is noteworthy that the 'Secondary' *Kgosing* has only one refining annex associated with it. This is also the case at the 'Primary' *Kgosing* where, as described earlier, a similar copper refining annex was identified. This was attached to the back courtyard wall of *lapa* M2, immediately adjacent to the senior dwelling, M1 (see Fig. 6.1). At both *kgosing*, the annex is linked to high status households, giving the impression that copper refining was a controlled process, and that this activity was restricted to certain people in the community. We return to a discussion of the technology and organisation of copper production in Chapter Ten.

Artefacts from *lapa* M1 of the 'Secondary' *Kgosing*

Ceramics

A total of 3395 sherds (83,657.5g) were recovered from *lapa* M1, not including those that were part of the tiled pathways or door slide bases. Only 185 of the total (5.45%) were diagnostic (Fig. 6.24). The majority of sherds from the structures were found mixed up in collapsed wall rubble, except for 3 sherds found on the 'pot stand' behind Dwelling Structure 1, another 9 resting on the interior floor surface of Utility Structure 1, and 43 on the floor of Utility Structure 2 (Tables 6.3 to 6.6).

The Copper Refining Annex yielded 823 sherds, most of which came from the interior surface of the annex (Table 6.7). Those with any trace of vitrification or slag were counted as crucible sherds, and included with the metallurgical debris.

In total, two sherds from M1 were suitable for multi-dimensional analysis. Vessel #V17 from Dwelling Structure 2 was classified as 'Class 1' (*Uitkomst* facies): a smooth-necked jar with a horizontal band of comb-stamping on the rim, another horizontal band of comb-stamping on the shoulder, and below this a horizontal row of pendant triangles with black graphite infill. The black colouring has turned to white, possibly a consequence of exposure to high temperatures during the terminal burning of the structure. Vessel #V74 was recovered during the initial trowelling of the courtyard surface and was classified as 'Class 3' (*Buispoort* facies): a short-necked jar with a single horizontal band of nicking on the rim (Fig. 6.24, 1 and 2).

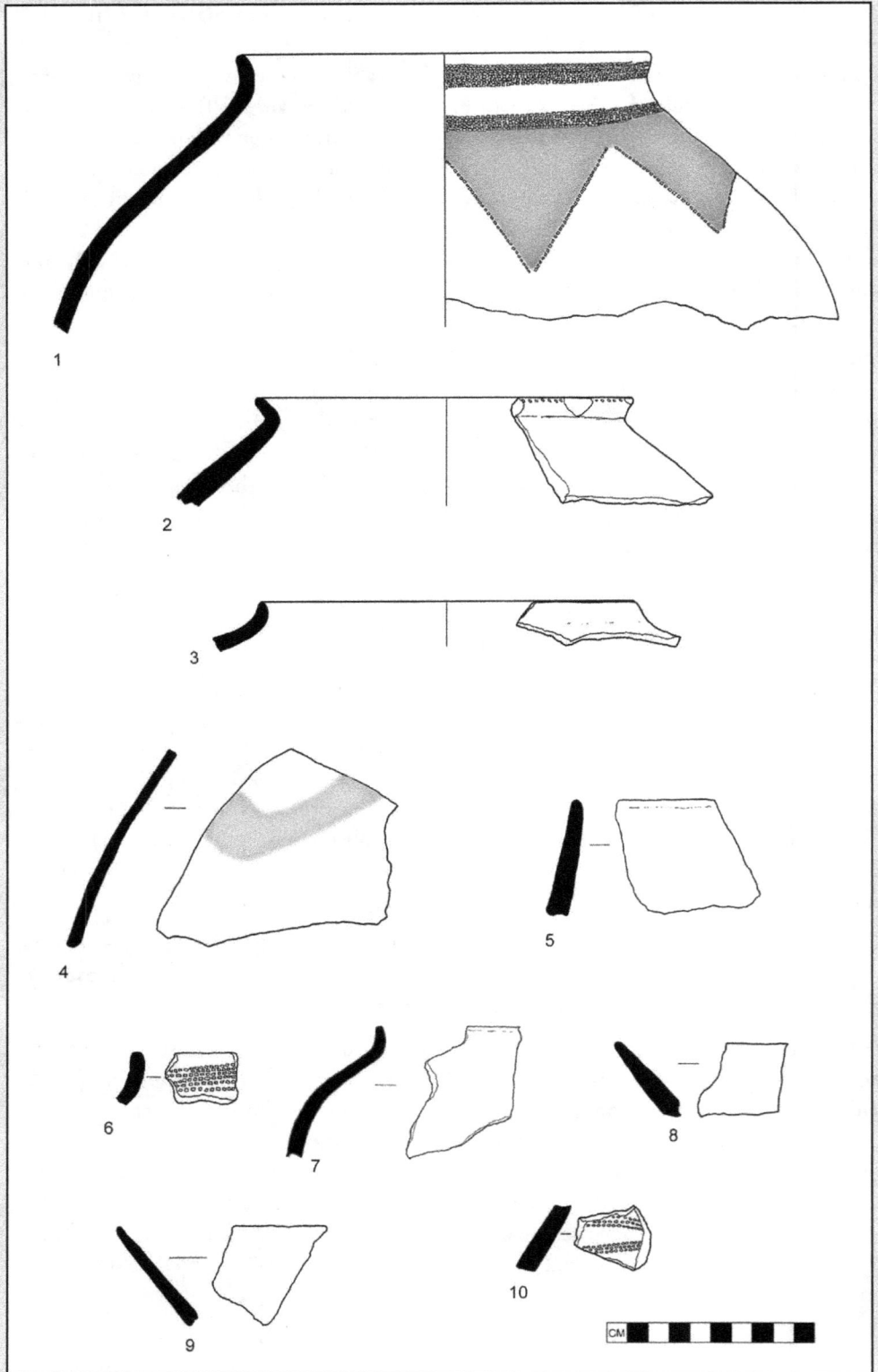

Figure 6.24
Decorated sherds and representative profile types from *lapa* M1 of the 'Secondary' *Kgosing*.

Figure 6.24 Ceramic Descriptions

1. Smooth-necked jar with two horizontal bands of comb-stamping above pendant triangles with black graphite infill and comb-stamped outlines. Profile Mode: 1A. Layout Mode: 1. Decoration Mode: 1. Multi-dimensional Class: 1. Provenance: 'Secondary' *Kgosing*, M1, Dwelling Structure 2, wall rubble. Cat. No. V17.

2. Short-necked jar with nicking on the rim. Profile Mode: 1B. Layout Mode: 2. Decoration Mode: 2. Multi-dimensional Class: 3. Provenance: 'Secondary' *Kgosing*, M1, courtyard floor. Cat. No. V74.

3. Smooth-necked jar, plain. Profile Mode: 1A. Provenance: 'Secondary' *Kgosing*, M1, Utility Structure 1, wall rubble. Cat. No. V61.

4. Body sherd, no profile information. Coloured band in approximate chevron design. Provenance: 'Secondary' *Kgosing*, M1, Dwelling Structure 2, wall rubble. Cat. No. V32.

5. Straight-necked jar, plain. Profile Mode: 1C. Provenance: 'Secondary' *Kgosing*, M1, Utility Structure 1, wall rubble. Cat. No. V68.

6. Smooth-necked jar rim, with horizontal band of comb-stamping. Profile Mode: 1A. Layout Mode: 2. Decoration Mode: 2. Multi-dimensional Class: 2. Provenance: 'Secondary' *Kgosing*, M1, Utility Structure 1, wall rubble. Cat. No. V63.

7. Smooth-necked jar, plain. Profile Mode: 1A. Provenance: 'Secondary' *Kgosing*, M1, Dwelling Structure 1, wall rubble. Cat. No. V46.

8. Simple bowl, plain. Profile Mode: 2B. Provenance: 'Secondary' *Kgosing*, M1, Dwelling Structure 1, wall rubble. Cat. No. V48.

9. Simple bowl, plain. Profile Mode: 2B. Provenance: 'Secondary' *Kgosing*, M1, Utility Structure 1, wall rubble. Cat. No. V66.

10. Decorated sherd, no profile information. Two horizontal bands of comb-stamping, not parallel. Provenance: 'Secondary' *Kgosing*, M1, Dwelling Structure 1, wall rubble. Cat. No. V42.

Table 6.3
Quantities of ceramic sherds
from Dwelling Structure 1
of *lapa* M1 in the
'Secondary' *Kgosing*.

		Sherds	Mass (g)	% of total sherds
Wall Rubble	Diagnostic	24	274.2	5.0
	Adiagnostic	456	5981.3	94.4
Pot Stand	Diagnostic	0	0	0
	Adiagnostic	3	63.4	0.6
Subtotals	Diagnostic	24	274.2	5.0
	Adiagnostic	459	6044.7	95.0
Totals		483	6318.9	100

Table 6.4
Quantities of ceramic sherds
from Dwelling Structure 2.

		Sherds	Mass (g)	% of total sherds
Wall Rubble	Diagnostic	68	4926.5	8.3
	Adiagnostic	748	27064.4	91.7
Totals		816	41843.9	100

Table 6.5
Quantities of ceramic sherds
from Utility Structure 1.

		Sherds	Mass (g)	% of total sherds
Wall Rubble	Diagnostic	54	979.1	6.7
	Adiagnostic	747	13097.0	92.2
Interior Floor	Diagnostic	0	0	0
	Adiagnostic	9	170.4	1.1
Subtotals	Diagnostic	54	979.1	6.7
	Adiagnostic	756	13267.4	93.3
Totals		810	14246.5	100

Table 6.6
Quantities of ceramic sherds
from Utility Structure 2.

		Sherds	Mass (g)	% of total sherds
Wall Rubble	Diagnostic	4	27.4	0.9
	Adiagnostic	416	5220.8	89.8
Interior Floor	Diagnostic	0	0	0
	Adiagnostic	43	823.9	9.3
Subtotals	Diagnostic	4	27.4	0.9
	Adiagnostic	459	6044.7	99.1
Totals		463	6072.1	100

Table 6.7
Quantities of ceramic
sherds from the Copper
Refining Annex.

		Sherds	Mass (g)	% of total sherds
Annex Interior Surface	Diagnostic	35	365.8	4.3
	Adiagnostic	763	14317.7	92.7
Annex Exterior Scatter	Diagnostic	0	0	0
	Adiagnostic	25	492.6	3.0
Subtotals	Diagnostic	35	365.8	4.3
	Adiagnostic	788	14810.3	95.7
Totals		823	15176.1	100

Metallurgy

With the exception of one small piece of slag (8.1g) from the wall rubble of Dwelling Structure 1, the domestic interior of *lapa* M1 was devoid of metallurgical debris. This was surprising, given its proximity to, and evident association with, the Copper Refining Annex outside the back wall.

The 6868.1g of metallurgical debris from the annex itself consisted primarily of pieces of copper ore-bearing gossan (44.6%), crucible sherds (42.8%) and scatters of broken up smelting/flow slag (10.2%) (Table 6.8 and Fig. 6.25).

Material Type	Mass (g)	% of total mass
Copper ore-bearing gossan	3048.6	44.6
Crucible sherds	2931.5	42.8
Smelting/flow slag	694.9	10.2
Tuyere fragments	153.3	2.2
Totals	6868.1	100

Table 6.8
Quantities of metallurgical debris from the Copper Refining Annex.

Figure 6.25
A sample of the metallurgical debris recovered from the Copper Refining Annex behind *lapa* M1, including pieces of ore-bearing gossan and some slag.

Figure 6.26
Stone artefacts from
Dwelling Structure 1 of
lapa M1 of the 'Secondary'
Kgosing.

Figure 6.27
Artefacts from Dwelling
Structure 2 of *lapa* M1.

Stone

A rounded floor smoother (#MAR25) was recovered from the interior floor of Dwelling Structure 1, with worn edges on all sides. One of the flatter surfaces was particularly well worn. The wall rubble yielded another small smoothing stone (#MAR24), a flat oval-shaped upper grindstone (#MAR37), a partial upper grindstone with wear on three sides (#MAR47) and a piece of door slide base (#MAR46) with a visible door groove (Fig. 6.26).

From Dwelling Structure 2, an upper grindstone (#MAR10) worn smooth on both flat surfaces was recovered from the wall rubble, along with a length of door slide base stone (#MAR9) with a very prominent door groove (Fig. 6.27).

A long, narrow stone (#MAR35) was retrieved from the rubble of Utility Structure 1, with highly abrasive edges. It had both longitudinal abrasions and 'cut marks' on the edges and corners, and may have been used as a whet stone (Fig. 6.28).

Metal Objects

An iron spear head with a tang (#MAR155) was found in the wall rubble of Dwelling Structure 2, measuring 178 mm in length and with a maximum width of 24 mm (Fig. 6.27). The wall rubble of Utility Structure 1 yielded a long iron 'pin' or needle with a flat end, 210 mm long (#MAR153), and an iron adze 90 mm long and 35 mm wide at the flat end (#MAR154) (Fig. 6.28).

Scraping Tools

Three abraded bone scrapers were retrieved from the wall rubble of Dwelling Structure 1. The rubble of Dwelling Structure 2 yielded three scrapers, one of bone and two ceramic. One ceramic and four bone scrapers were found in the rubble of Utility Structure 1, and a single ceramic scraper came from the interior fill of copper refining furnace No. 2.

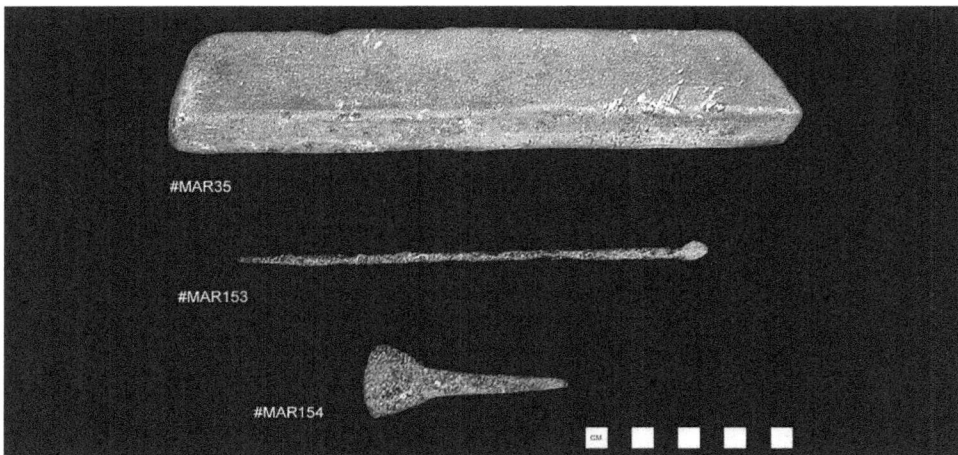

Figure 6.28
Artefacts from
Utility Structure 1
of *lapa* M1.

NOU Court Midden

The court midden is situated approximately 40 metres to the south-east of *lapa* M1 in the centre of the NOU, the senior division of the 'Secondary' *Kgosing* at Marothodi (Fig. 6.11). The ceremonial significance of the court midden, and its association with the political and spiritual heart of the *kgosing*, and therefore of the chiefdom, was discussed earlier in this chapter. It flanks the formal opening into the NOU court complex and is enclosed by a low oval wall some 6.0 m in maximum diameter, within which the ash has gradually accumulated. With the aim of learning more about the material composition of an elite court midden and to facilitate comparison with domestic middens, a sample trench measuring 2.0 x 3.0 m was excavated in the centre of the deposit (Fig. 6.29).

Excavation was carried out in arbitrary horizontal spits 0.10 m thick. Beneath a shallow crust of weathered ash, the fine, light-grey ashy deposit appeared to be largely homogenous. There was no trace of any horizontal stratigraphy, until at a depth of 0.54 m a slightly more compact horizon was reached, upon which a number of large rocks had been placed (Fig. 6.29). Approximately 0.05 m above this horizon, on the north-west side of the trench, a piece of woven fabric was observed protruding from the section.

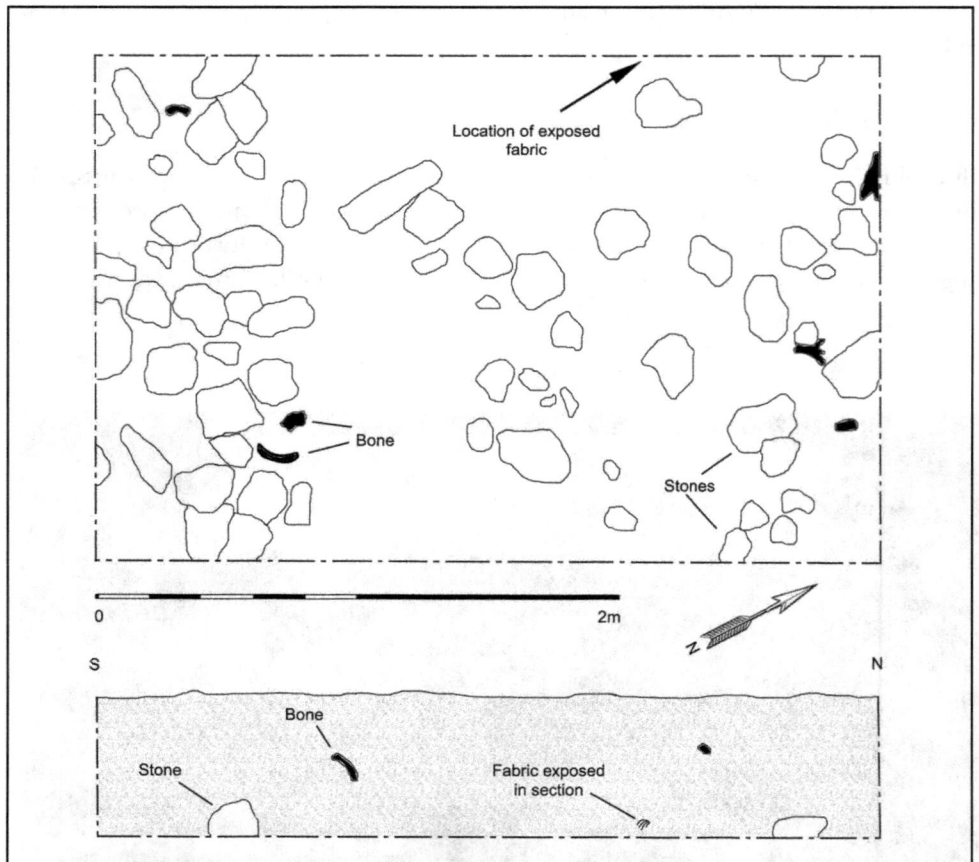

Figure 6.29
Plan (top) and south-east facing section (below) of the sample trench excavated into the court midden in the NOU of the 'Secondary' *Kgosing*. The plan shows the horizon at 0.54 m deep, and the location of the fabric exposed in the section wall is indicated (see Fig. 6.36).

This evidence was a cause for concern. Studies of archaeological Sotho-Tswana sites suggest that the placing of large stones over human inhumations was a common burial practice (Maggs 1976a; Walton 1958), and this has also been observed historically (Casalis 1889: 145). Ethnographic studies of other Bantu-speaking groups describe the placing of stones over burials "to keep the spirit confined, making it more difficult for it to escape to bring evil to its relatives" (Stayt 1968: 162). The appearance of the fabric reminded us that the dead were sometimes wrapped in burial shrouds (Mönnig 1967: 139; Stayt 1968: 162).

Consequently, at this point in the excavation the possibility was considered that one or more human inhumations might exist within the unexcavated portions of the midden, and that the fabric might have been part of such a shroud. Although this has not been established beyond doubt, I was unwilling to risk disturbing a human burial prematurely, and made a decision to discontinue the excavation of the court midden until appropriate dialogue with local and descendent communities could occur. A small piece of the fabric exposed in the section had become detached during the process of excavation, and this was collected as a sample for analysis. The following account presents all the archaeological material retrieved down to the 0.54 m horizon, the depth to which excavation was limited. A total of 3.24 cubic metres of midden deposit were excavated.

Figure 6.30
Ash from the court midden is sieved to retrieve small archaeological materials.

Artefacts from the NOU Court Midden

Ceramics

A total of 320 sherds (3552.2g) were retrieved from the court midden, of which 34 (10.6%) were diagnostic (Table 6.9). None of the sherds recovered were suitable for multi-dimensional analysis (Fig. 6.31).

Metallurgy

Metallurgical debris from the court midden was minimal, with a total of only 72.1g of slag retrieved, along with a single tuyere fragment. One piece of magnetite was also recovered (Table 6.10). The only metal artefact was a corroded iron 'needle' (#MAR152), which was 69 mm in length (Fig. 6.32).

Scraping Tools

A total of 108 scrapers were recovered from the court midden, of which 10 were abraded sherds, and 98 were recycled bone.

Stone

There were four upper grindstones recovered from the court midden (#MAR19, #MAR17, #MAR22 and #MAR39). In addition, a wall/floor polishing stone was retrieved (#MAR27) which was originally part of a door slide base stone. The linear groove worn into one of the flat surfaces reveals the artefact's original use (Fig. 6.33).

Clay Figurines

Three fragments of moulded clay were recovered from the court midden. All seemed fairly amorphous, but they are likely to be pieces of cattle figurines. One (#MAR136) may be part of an animal head, while (#MAR133) has a pinched protrusion which might represent part of an animal leg or horn. The other fragment (#MAR135) has no defining characteristics apart from evidently having been moulded on one surface (Fig. 6.34).

Beads

The court midden yielded 6 beads. Three of these (#MAR93, 95 and 107) were ostrich eggshell. Another (#MAR106) looks like it might be ivory. Of the other two beads, one seems to be copper (#MAR105), and the other looks like a piece of smoothed bone (#MAR99). It is cylindrical in shape, tapered slightly at one end, and unpierced (Fig. 6.35).

Fabric

The piece of fabric from the south-east facing section has the appearance of brown wool. The fine fibres are knitted into 'tubes' or ribs, giving it a soft, stringy texture (Fig. 6.36).

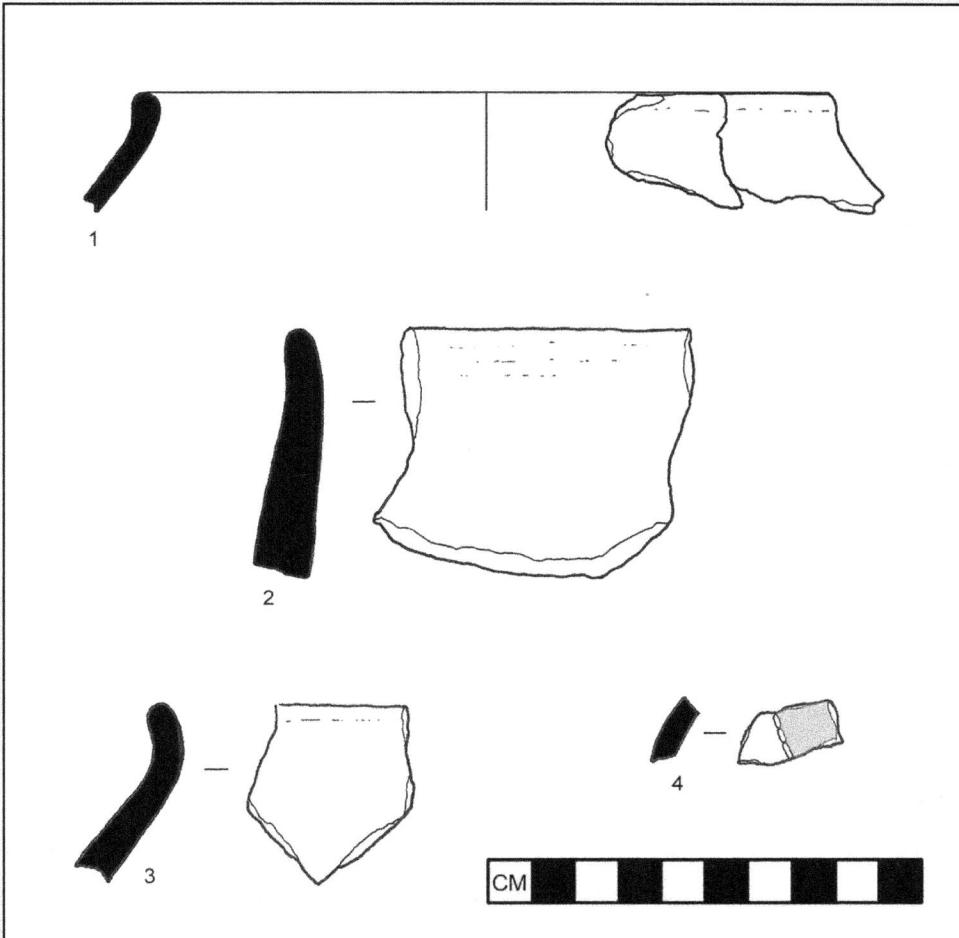

Figure 6.31
Decorated sherds and representative profiles from the NOU court midden.

Figure 6.31 Ceramic Descriptions

1. Smooth-necked jar, plain. Profile Mode: 1A. Provenance: 'Secondary' *Kgosing*, Court Midden, Square F, Level 3. Cat. No. V112.

2. Smooth-necked jar, plain. Profile Mode: 1A. Provenance: 'Secondary' *Kgosing*, Court Midden, Square D, Level 4. Cat. No. V109.

3. Smooth-necked jar, plain. Profile Mode: 1A. Provenance: 'Secondary' *Kgosing*, Court Midden, Square C, Level 3. Cat. No. V104.

4. Decorated sherd, no profile information. Comb-stamped line with black graphite, possibly a pendant triangle. Provenance: 'Secondary' *Kgosing*, Court Midden, Square C, Level 3. Cat. No. V105.

Table 6.9
Quantities of ceramic
sherds from the NOU
court midden.

	Sherds	Mass (g)	Mass (g) per m³	% of total sherds
Diagnostic	34	482.0	148.8	10.6
Adiagnostic	286	3070.2	947.6	89.4
Total	320	3552.2	1096.4	100

Table 6.10
Quantities of metallurgical
debris from the NOU
court midden.

Material Type	Mass (g)	Mass (g) per m³	% of total
Smelting/flow slag	41.4	12.7	24.5
Tabular slag	30.7	9.4	18.2
Tuyere fragments	8.2	2.4	4.8
Magnetite	88.7	27.4	52.5
Total	169.0	52.2	100

#MAR152

Figure 6.32
Iron 'needle' from the NOU
court midden.

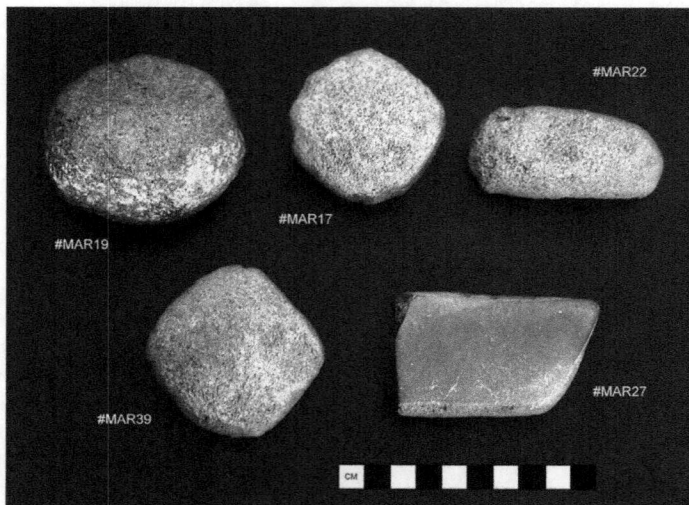

Figure 6.33
Stone artefacts from the
NOU court midden.

Figure 6.34
Moulded clay fragments
from the NOU court
midden.

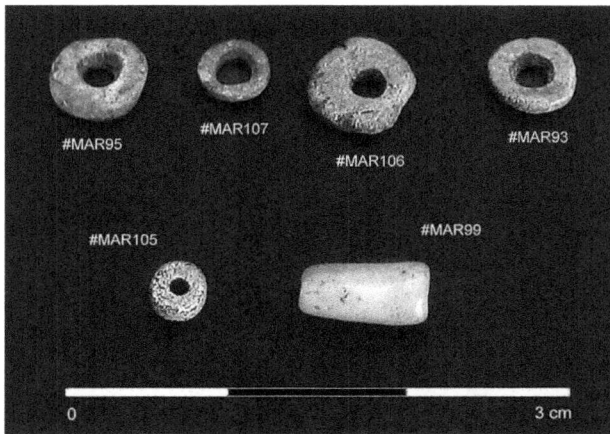

Figure 6.35
Beads from the NOU court
midden.

Figure 6.36
The wool sample retrieved
from the south-east
facing section of the NOU
court midden, with an
enlargement (far left).

Midden 1

Midden 1 was the largest and deepest domestic midden identified in the 'Secondary' *Kgosing*. Occupying a central position in the SOU, it directly abuts the walls of M34, M38 and SE3, but in light of its location it is likely to have received material from any or all of the *malapa* from M29 to M39, and possibly beyond (see Fig. 6.11). Because of its large size and potentially broad domestic representation it was deemed a valuable target to sample, and importantly, would provide material for comparison with the NOU court midden.

The excavation tactic employed maximized the horizontal area sampled, and also obtained a complete vertical section of the midden at its deepest point. A 3.0 x 7.0 m trench was excavated in arbitrary spits of 0.10 m each, to a depth of 0.30 m. Then within this area, at what was perceived to be the highest point on the surface of the midden, a 1.0 square metre sondage was further excavated down to the natural soil at the base of the deposit (Fig. 6.37). Thus, a total of 6.6 cubic metres of deposit were excavated.

The maximum depth of the midden was 0.50 m. Its size seems more likely to be a result of the high number of households contributing to it, rather than an indication of the length of time it was in use. Aside from a shallow weathered crust on the surface, no stratigraphy was observed in any of the sections. The deposit was an homogenous light grey ash. There was no vertical or horizontal change in artefact density, and despite the size of the midden, the overall density of material other than bone was low.

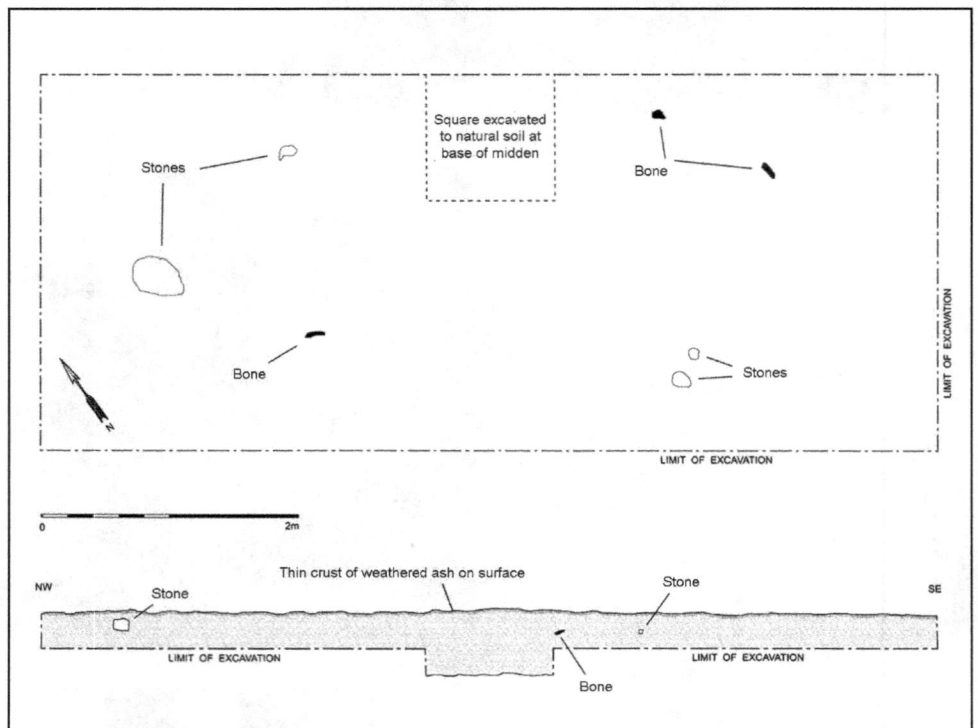

Figure 6.37
Plan (top) and south-west facing section (below) of the sample trench excavated into Midden 1 in the SOU of the 'Secondary' *Kgosing*. The plan shows the horizon at 0.30 m deep, and the position of the square that was excavated to the base of the midden (see Fig. 6.11 for the location of the trench).

Artefacts from Midden 1

Ceramics

A total of 4115 sherds (40200.2g) were retrieved from Midden 1, of which 356 were diagnostic (Table 6.11). The average density of ceramic sherds was 6090.9g per cubic metre of excavated deposit.

One of the diagnostic sherds was suitable for multi-dimensional analysis. Vessel #V130 was tentatively identified as 'Class 4' (*Buispoort* facies): a 'straight' open bowl with a horizontal band of nicking on the rim. It should be noted that this sherd is very small and incomplete, and its profile is difficult to identify with certainty (Fig. 6.38, 7).

Metallurgy

Despite the proximity of Midden 1 to the Copper Refining Annex, very little metallurgical debris was found (Table 6.12). The presence of magnetite suggests some association with iron smelting processes, although this cannot be inferred from a single piece of ore.

Two iron objects were retrieved from the Midden 1 sample: a tapered length of a 'pin' (#MAR150) and a thin, amorphous, flat piece of iron that was broken into two fragments (#MAR151). In addition, a hook-shaped piece of copper wire, possibly part of an earring, was also recovered (#MAR149) (Fig. 6.39).

Scraping Tools

Midden 1 yielded 566 scrapers, of which 127 were abraded ceramic sherds, and 439 were recycled bone.

Stone

Three stone artefacts were recovered from Midden 1: a reddish-coloured upper grindstone with a highly worn 'domed' surface (#MAR41); an angular-shaped stone, worn very smooth, that might have been used as a smoothing stone for interior walls and floors of structures (#MAR13); and a fragment of an abrasive flat stone, possibly a piece of a whet stone or perhaps a door slide base (#MAR36).

Beads

A total of 19 disc-shaped ostrich eggshell beads were recovered from Midden 1, of which 9 were broken fragments. The beads ranged from 4.5 to 8 mm in diameter (Fig. 6.40).

Clay Figurines

Seven pieces of moulded clay were recovered from the Midden 1 sample, all of which were incomplete fragments. These were probably pieces of cattle figurine, or may have included some wild species (Fig. 6.41).

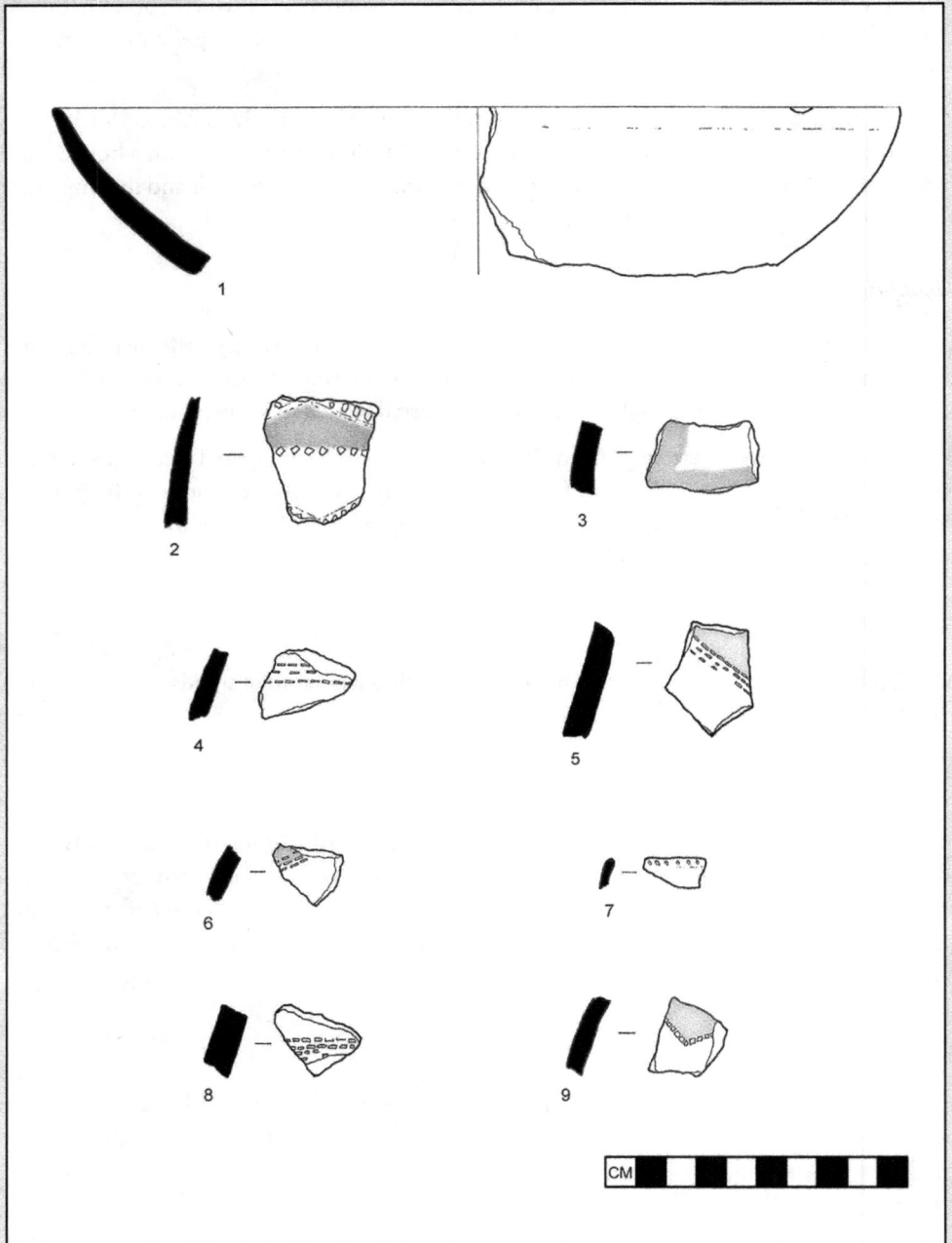

Figure 6.38
This page and opposite:
Decorated sherds and
representative profiles
from Midden 1 in the
'Secondary' *Kgosing*
(descriptions on page 116).

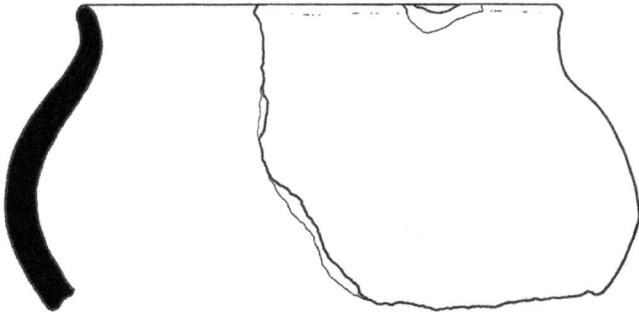

10

11

12

13

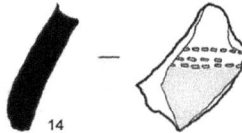

14

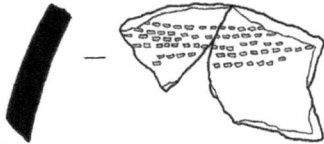

15

16

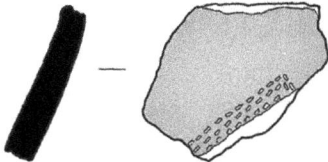

17

18

CM

Figure 6.38 Ceramic Descriptions

1. Simple bowl, plain. Profile Mode: 2B. Provenance: 'Secondary' *Kgosing*, Midden 1, Square H, Level 4. Cat. No. V304.

2. Decorated sherd, no profile information. Upturned triangle with black graphite infill, upper and lower boundaries lined with punctates. Below, a pendant triangle lined on the lower edge with punctates. Provenance: 'Secondary' *Kgosing*, Midden 1, Square C, Level 3. Cat. No. V161.

3. Body sherd with angled black graphite band. No profile information. Provenance: 'Secondary' *Kgosing*, Midden 1, Square C, Level 3. Cat. No. V162.

4. Decorated sherd, no profile information. Horizontal band of comb-stamping (incisions?). Provenance: 'Secondary' *Kgosing*, Midden 1, Square C, Level 2. Cat. No. V167.

5. Decorated sherd, no profile information. Pendant triangle with black graphite infill and comb-stamped outline. Provenance: 'Secondary' *Kgosing*, Midden 1, Square D, Level 2. Cat. No. V186.

6. Decorated sherd, no profile information. Pendant triangle (?) with black graphite infill and comb-stamped outline. Provenance: 'Secondary' *Kgosing*, Midden 1, Square B, Level 3. Cat. No. V132.

7. Rim of 'straight' open bowl (?) with nicking. Profile Mode: 2B (?). Layout Mode: 2. Decoration Mode: 2. Multi-dimensional Class: 4 (tentative). Provenance: 'Secondary' *Kgosing*, Midden 1, Square A, Level 1. Cat. No. V130.

8. Decorated sherd, no profile information. Horizontal band of comb-stamping. Provenance: 'Secondary' *Kgosing*, Midden 1, Square B, Level 2. Cat. No. V155.

9. Decorated sherd, no profile information. Pendant triangle with black graphite infill, outlined with comb-stamping. Provenance: 'Secondary' *Kgosing*, Midden 1, Square D, Level 2. Cat. No. V188.

10. Smooth-necked jar, plain. Profile Mode: 1A. Provenance: 'Secondary' *Kgosing*, Midden 1, Square L, Level 4. Cat. No. V422.

11. Decorated sherd, no profile information. Pendant triangle with black graphite infill, lined with comb-stamping. Provenance: 'Secondary' *Kgosing*, Midden 1, Square F, Level 3. Cat. No. V253.

12. Decorated body/neck sherd, incomplete profile. Horizontal band of comb-stamping, above upturned triangles with black graphite infill and comb-stamped outline, above a horizontal band of comb-stamping. Provenance: 'Secondary' *Kgosing*, Midden 1, Square G, Level 3. Cat. No. V256.

13. Decorated sherd, no profile information. Comb-stamping, design undetermined. Provenance: 'Secondary' *Kgosing*, Midden 1, Square H, Level 2. Cat. No. V297.

14. Decorated sherd, no profile information. Horizontal band of comb-stamping with black graphite beneath. Provenance: 'Secondary' *Kgosing*, Midden 1, Square I, Level 1. Cat. No. V344.

15. Decorated sherd, no profile information. Horizontal band of comb-stamping. Provenance: 'Secondary' *Kgosing*, Midden 1, Square K, Level 3. Cat. No. V378.

16. Decorated sherd, no profile information. Horizontal band of comb-stamping. Provenance: 'Secondary' *Kgosing*, Midden 1, Square L, Level 2. Cat. No. V413.

17. Decorated sherd, no profile information. Angled line of comb-stamping against black graphite – possible pendant triangle. Provenance: 'Secondary' *Kgosing*, Midden 1, Square K, Level 1. Cat. No. V389.

18. Decorated sherd, no profile information. Pendant triangle with black graphite infill and comb-stamped outline. Provenance: 'Secondary' *Kgosing*, Midden 1, Square C, Level 2. Cat. No. V174.

	Sherds	Mass (g)	Mass (g) per m³	% of total sherds
Diagnostic	356	4093.2	620.2	8.7
Adiagnostic	3759	36107.0	5470.8	91.3
Total	4115	40200.2	6090.9	100

Table 6.11
Quantities of ceramic sherds from Midden 1.

Material Type	Mass (g)	Mass (g) per m³	% of total mass
Smelting/flow slag	344.0	52.1	71.6
Magnetite	136.3	20.7	28.4
Total	480.3	72.8	100

Table 6.12
Quantities of metallurgical debris from Midden 1.

Figure 6.39
Metal objects from Midden 1.

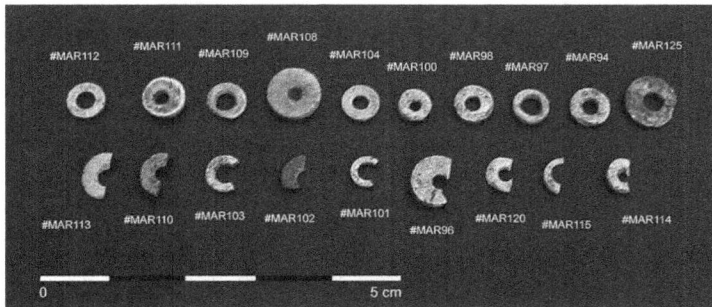

Figure 6.40
Beads from Midden 1.

Figure 6.41
Fragments of moulded clay from Midden 1.

Discussion

The distinction of court middens as repositories of material generated by male activities in the court complex is suggested by historical and ethnographic evidence (Burchell 1824; Campbell 1822; Schapera 1953; Mönnig 1967). This is where men spent a significant amount of time engaged in practices such as hide working, and where they drank beer and roasted meat. The court complex is also where certain ceremonial activities, such as the ritual slaughtering of animals, took place.

The nature of these activities leads to the assumption that the material deposited in court middens should be archaeologically distinguishable from that in domestic middens, which would have received a wider range of general household debris. Thus, we might expect to see higher quantities of burnt bone in court middens, scorched during the roasting of meat, with perhaps a higher number of wild species represented in the faunal assemblages. A higher density of scraping tools associated with hide working might also be expected. The ceremonial significance of court middens might encourage the deposition of high-status or valuable goods, and the absence of general household activities like cooking might result in a narrower range of ceramic profiles. Although the sample sizes are small and the faunal data is not yet available, certain conclusions might be tentatively drawn from a comparison of the ceramic assemblages.

Firstly, the excavations demonstrated a significant difference in general ceramic density per excavated cubic metre between the two midden contexts. The court middens of the 'Primary' *Kgosing* and the 'Secondary' *Kgosing* yielded only 855.7g and 1154.0g, respectively, of ceramic material per excavated cubic metre. By contrast, the domestic Midden 1 of the 'Secondary' *Kgosing* contained 6090.9g of ceramic sherds per cubic metre—over 6 times greater than the average density of the two court middens. This comparison offers a preliminary indication that court middens were somehow distinguished from their domestic counterparts in terms of the overall quantity of materials that were deposited in them.

However, these results may be influenced by uneven archaeological preservation. It is perhaps likely that more ceramic vessels and pots were circulating in domestic contexts, where food was prepared and cooked. By contrast, wooden vessels may have featured more prominently in the court complex. The men would have drunk beer out of wooden calabashes, and perhaps eaten out of wooden bowls as well as ceramic vessels, and wood is less likely to have survived.

Nevertheless, a comparison of the range of ceramic profiles from each midden also hinted at a more restricted range in the court middens (Tables 6.13 and 6.14). Although the presence of smooth-necked jars were dominant in all samples, this type of vessel formed 100% of the identifiable profiles in the court midden of the 'Primary' *Kgosing*, and 95.8% of those from the court midden in the 'Secondary' *Kgosing*. The 'Secondary' *Kgosing* court midden also contained 4.2% necked bowls. The greatest profile variety, however, was seen in the domestic Midden 1, which was composed of 80.6% smooth-necked jars, 16.7% straight open bowls, 0.9% necked bowls and 1.8% pot lids (Fig. 6.42). The pot lids in particular are related to cooking, and as anticipated, are completely absent in court middens.

Thus, although the samples are small, these results do hint at a subtle contrast between the material content of domestic middens and court middens, and indicate that court middens were recipients of a more restricted pattern of deposition. Overall, however, it is still primarily the spatial setting and style of construction that serves to distinguish court middens from their domestic counterparts.

	Smooth-necked jar (1A)	Short-necked jar (1B)	Straight open bowl (2B)	Necked bowl (2A)	Pot Lid (3)	Undetermined
Court Midden	3	0	0	0	0	0

Table 6.13
Ceramic profile types from the 'Primary' *Kgosing*.

	Smooth-necked jar (1A)	Short-necked jar (1B)	Straight-necked jar (1C)	Straight open bowl (2B)	Necked bowl (2A)	Pot lid (3)	Undetermined
Midden 1	266	0	0	55	3	6	26
Court Midden	23	0	0	0	1	0	10
M1 surface clearance	1	1	0	0	0	0	0
M1 Dwelling Structure 1	9	0	0	6	0	0	1
M1 Dwelling Structure 2	11	0	0	0	0	0	1
M1 Utility Structure 1	19	0	1	0	0	0	1
M1 Utility Structure 2	4	0	0	0	0	0	0
M1 Copper Refining Annex	7	1	0	0	0	0	0
Totals	340	2	1	61	4	6	39

Table 6.14
Ceramic profile types from the 'Secondary' *Kgosing*.

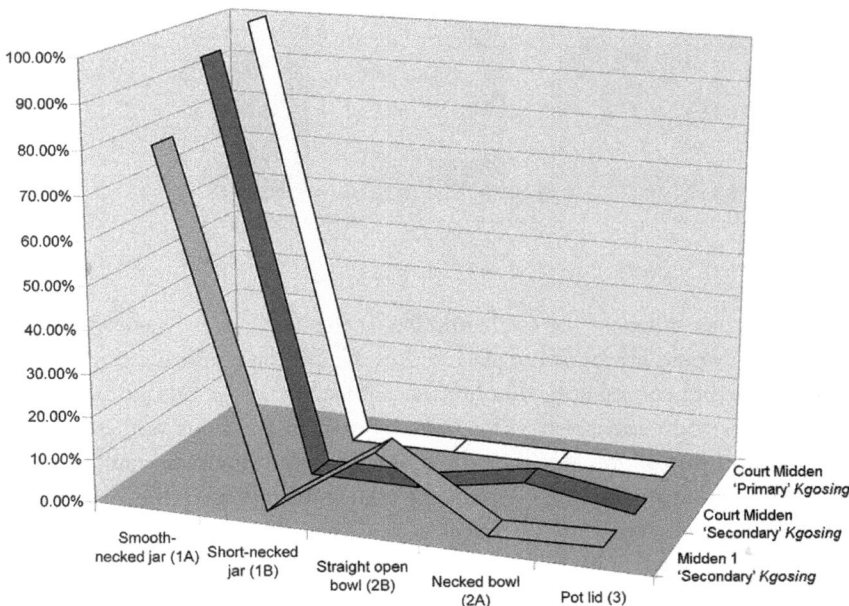

Figure 6. 42
Graph showing the percentages of different ceramic profile types from the three royal middens.

Another expectation based on historical and ethnographic evidence was that the court middens, being situated in the court complex where men practiced hide working, would contain a higher density of bone or ceramic scraping tools than domestic middens. This distinction was demonstrated at the contemporary Tswana town at Olifantspoort, where an excavation in 'Ash Heap I' (the elite court midden) yielded a relatively high concentration of scraping tools, particularly abraded stone flakes (Mason 1986).

At Marothodi, however, the opposite trend was observed. The court midden in the 'Primary' *Kgosing* did not yield any scrapers at all. The court midden in the 'Secondary' *Kgosing* had a scraper density of 33.3 per cubic metre of excavated deposit, but the domestic Midden 1 had a much higher density of 85.8 scrapers per cubic metre (Fig. 6.43). These surprising results indicate that relatively little hide working occurred in the royal court complexes, and that it seems to have been focused in other central parts of these homesteads. The position of Midden 1 in the 'Secondary' *Kgosing* suggests that this activity may have been practiced in areas such as SE2 or SE3 (see Fig. 6.11). Bone was the preferred material, forming 79.9% of all scrapers from the two *kgosing*. The other 20.3% were ceramic sherds. No stone scrapers were recovered.

Figure 6.43
Bar chart showing the density of bone and ceramic scrapers from the three royal middens.

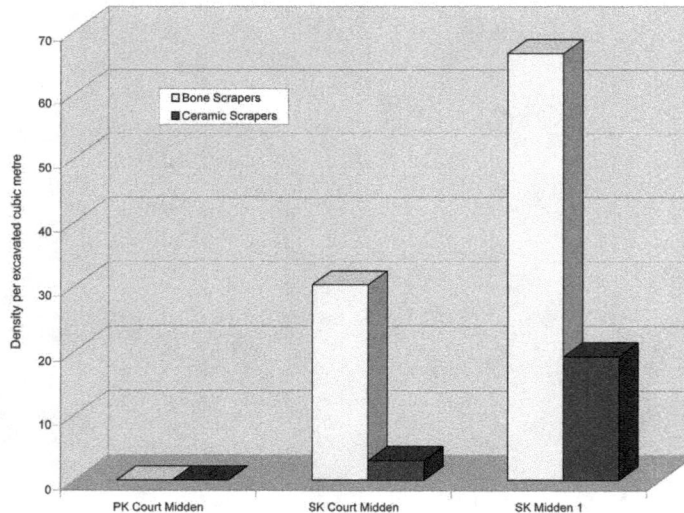

The presence of a human burial in the court midden of the 'Secondary' *Kgosing* has not been confirmed, but it would not be out of place. Ethnographic data indicates that men of status were often buried in central areas of a homestead, usually in the central cattle byre adjoining the *kgotla* or court (Schapera 1955: 59). A burial in the court midden would be a slight variation on this theme, but the underlying guiding principles would remain intact. This midden is connected to the *kgotla* of the high-status NOU in the 'Secondary' *Kgosing*, and flanks the main avenue to the central cattle byres. The ash of the midden may also have performed a conceptually cooling and cleansing role (Hammond-Tooke 1981: 145), addressing the "ritual impurity (*ditshila*) which contaminates everyone who comes into contact with the body" (Mönnig 1967: 139). Indeed, several human burials were found in ash middens at the contemporary Tswana site of Olifantspoort (Mason 1986), but the only other archaeological examples of human burial in a court midden are those at K2, the early 13th century Leopard's Kopje capital on the southern banks of the Limpopo River. Most of these burials were later than the occupation of the capital (Wood 2000) and may have been people who died 'hot' or abnormal deaths, and therefore needed a special burial (Fouche 1937; Huffman & Murimbika 2003; Huffman 2007).

In practical terms, a well-managed ash deposit may have been preferable to the underlying turf soil for burying the dead, considering its instability. Until the presence of an inhumation here is confirmed however, this discussion is largely conjectural.

Preliminary analysis of the fabric from the court midden (Fig. 6.36) has indicated that it is likely to be fine machine-knitted Merino wool (Sam Dymond, pers. com. 2008). Merino sheep were introduced to South Africa in 1789, with small flocks bred in the Western Cape from 1810 (Hanekom 1960). However, it was in the Eastern Cape that Merino farming and the wool trade really developed during the 1820s and 30s in the hands of the 1820 English settlers around Grahamstown (Hockley 1948). With skilled spinners and frame knitters among them (Nash 1987) this type of material may have been in limited circulation in the Eastern Cape before Marothodi was abandoned in about 1823, as the first fruits of a fledgling industry.

At face value, the paucity of glass trade beads at Marothodi does not suggest a high volume of regular trade contact with European suppliers, and trade between the Grahamstown settlers and communities of the interior was illegal until the mid-1820s (Butler 1974). But in response to the harsh economic realities of life on the fringes of the colony, some of the more intrepid settler merchants were known to have ventured northward to trade illicitly with African people (Rivett-Carnac 1963). Through their endeavours it is possible that woollen garments of the kind found at Marothodi were made available to Tswana rulers in exchange for cattle, ivory or other commodities. If so, it would almost certainly have been regarded as a prestige item by its owner, and its deposition in a high status court midden, perhaps with a human burial, would have been appropriate.

The exploration of *lapa* M1 in the 'Secondary' *Kgosing* offered a view of a senior household within a 'royal' homestead. The 'mosaic' tiled floor surfaces or pathways were an unusual and elaborate feature of this *lapa*. As suggested earlier, considering the other evidence for floor reinforcement techniques around this household, such as the cobbled surfaces behind each of the dwelling structures and the floors in and around Utility Structure 1, it seems likely that the tiling was primarily a practical solution to an environmental problem. It was obviously a challenge to keep the ground firm and dry in this part of the homestead. Nevertheless, the fact that the tiles had to be re-set frequently, forming multiple layers, suggests that this was a fragile solution, and that there were more effective ways to stabilise a floor surface if functionality was the only consideration. Thus, the carefully laid tiles may also have had some artistic or symbolic value.

While few ceramic sherds were suitable for multi-dimensional analysis, the decorated pieces were predominantly characterised by comb-stamped horizontal bands and pendant triangles (Tables 6.15 and 6.16). These decorative traits are associated with the *Uitkomst* ceramic facies and, in anticipation of a larger sample size, would seem to support our understanding of Tlokwa ancestral identity as stemming from Nguni roots (Huffman 2007).

Table 6.15
Decorative techniques on diagnostic sherds from the 'Secondary' *Kgosing*.

	Comb-stamping	Rim-nicking	Punctates	Coloured bands	Appliqué	Total
Midden 1	20	1	3	1	0	25
Court Midden	1	0	0	0	0	1
M1 Dwelling Structure 1	1	0	0	0	0	1
M1 Dwelling Structure 2	1	0	0	0	0	2
M1 Utility Structure 1	1	0	0	0	0	1
Total	24	1	3	2	0	30
% of total	80%	3.3%	10%	6.7%	0%	100%

Table 6.16
Multi-dimensional analysis of ceramics from the 'Secondary' *Kgosing*.

Vessel No.	Context	Class	Vessel shape	Decoration position	Decoration motif	Description
17	M1 Dwelling Structure 2	1	1A	1	1	Smooth-necked jar with a horizontal band of comb-stamping on the rim, another horizontal band of comb-stamping on the shoulder, and below this a horizontal row of pendant triangles with black graphite infill and comb-stamped outline.
74	M1 surface clearance	3	1B	2	2	Short-necked jar with a single horizontal band of nicking on the rim
130	Midden 1	4	2B	2	2	Straight open bowl with a single horizontal band of punctates on the lip.

Two copper refining annexes were identified at the royal homesteads. One was situated behind *lapa* M2 in the 'Primary' *Kgosing*, and the other was attached to *lapa* M1 of the 'Secondary' *Kgosing*. The annex at the 'Secondary' *Kgosing* was examined in detail by the author, and served to clarify the archaeological distinction between this copper refining stage, and the primary smelting stage of copper production.

Two key observations are made from this analysis. Firstly, the two annexes are, in each case, the only sites of copper production at the royal homesteads. Nowhere else, in either the 'Primary' or 'Secondary' *Kgosing*, is there any evidence for primary smelting or refining, which suggests that production here was restricted in terms of quantity, and that it was limited to copper refining.

Secondly, both refining annexes are closely associated with the highest status components of each *kgosing*, indicating that copper production was not only limited here, but that it was controlled by the elite. This provides an important point of comparison for the following chapter, in which we examine the archaeology of a non-elite or 'commoner' homestead at which there was a particularly high density of metallurgical material.

Chapter Seven
Copper Specialists

S ettlement Unit 25 is situated close to the centre of Marothodi (see Fig. 5.4). Its relative proximity to the elite centre of power suggests, at face value, that the occupants
may have been of the ruling Tlokwa community by birth, and that their headman held
a certain level of seniority (see Schapera 1955; Mönnig 1967; Tlou 1974). Nevertheless, its
smaller scale, and particularly its small cattle kraal, identifies SU25 as a non-elite or 'commoner' homestead, and it therefore provides a comparison with the royal residences. As we
will see, however, SU25 turned out to be far from typical. In this chapter we explore the
spatial organisation of the homestead, and then report on the excavations.

Spatial organisation of Settlement Unit 25

SU25 is located approximately 200 metres to the north-east of the 'Primary' *Kgosing*, and
about 100 metres north-west from the 'Secondary' *Kgosing* (Fig. 5.4). It has an east-west
diameter of about 75 metres and a slightly greater north-south diameter of 85 metres
(Figs. 7.1 and 7.2).

The Cattle Kraal and Court Complex

As with the two *kgosing*, we begin our spatial exploration of SU25 at its political centre.
In contrast to the royal homesteads, SU25 has only one cattle kraal, which is located in the
middle of the homestead (Fig. 7.1, E1). There is one opening in the south-west perimeter of
the kraal, which leads into a small secondary enclosure, SE1. This space is identified as the
kgotla, and the eastern portion contains a raised court midden. The small enclosure on the
south-west edge of SE1, directly opposite the kraal entrance, may have been the headman's
private *kamore* (Fig. 7.1, E2).

Access to and from the central kraal and *kgotla* is via a narrow passage formed between two
parallel stone walls. This passage or 'cattle track' curls around the perimeter of the kraal,
and extends some 35 metres to the southern perimeter of the homestead (Fig. 7.3). This is
unusual, as walled cattle tracks are more commonly found on the outside of Tswana homesteads, leading up to the perimeter wall (see Huffman 1986b: 298; Mason 1986: 374;
Pistorius 1999: 121). They were designed to control the movement of cattle, keeping them
off of the cultivated fields as they were herded in and out of the settlement.

The 18th century stone walled site at Boschoek, in Suikerbosrand near Johannesburg,
provides an example of an 'external' cattle track (Huffman 1986b; Hall 1996). The formal entrance to the Boschoek homestead is clearly defined on its southern side by a linear

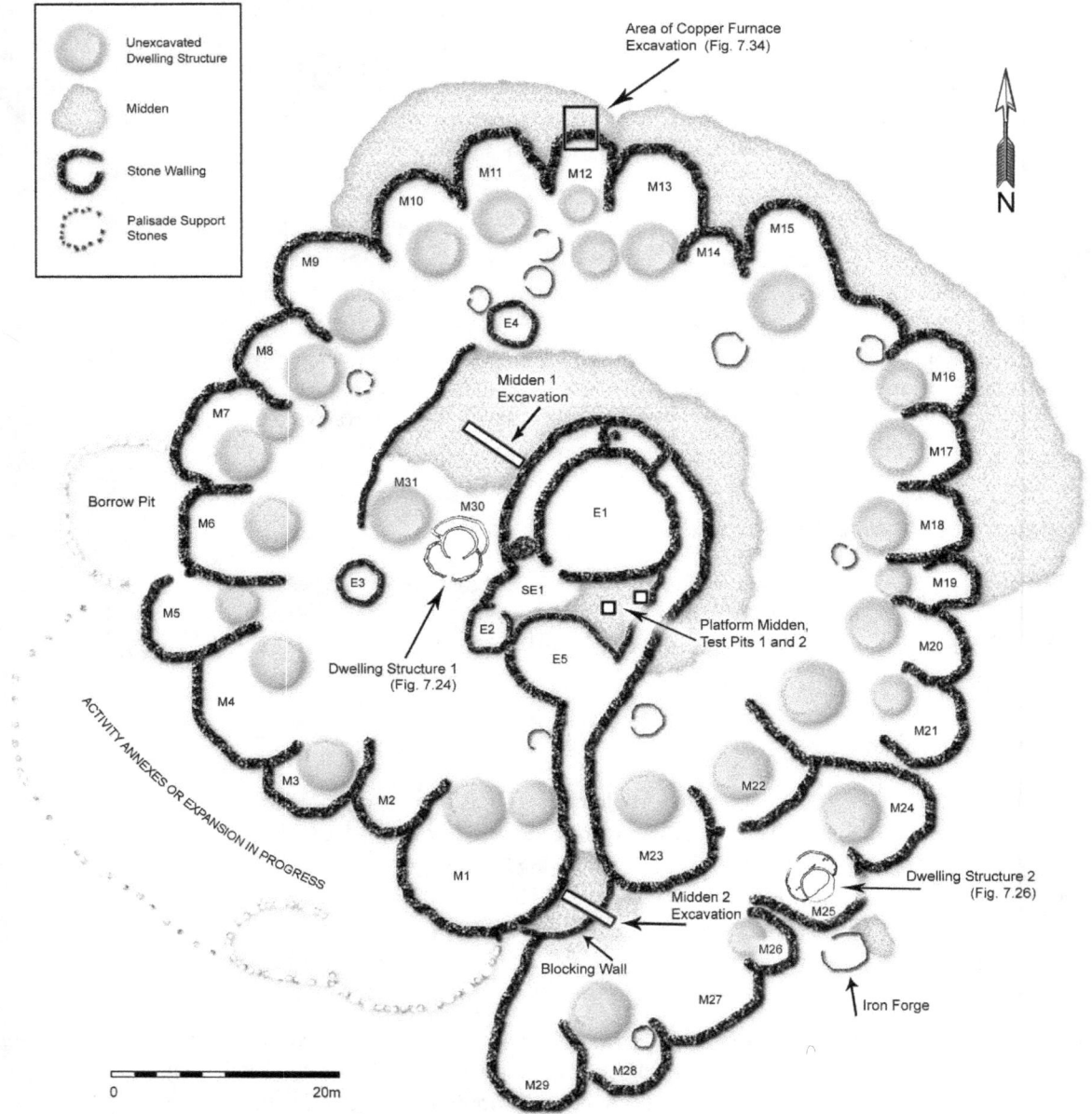

Figure 7.1
Map of Settlement Unit 25 showing the main features under discussion in this chapter.

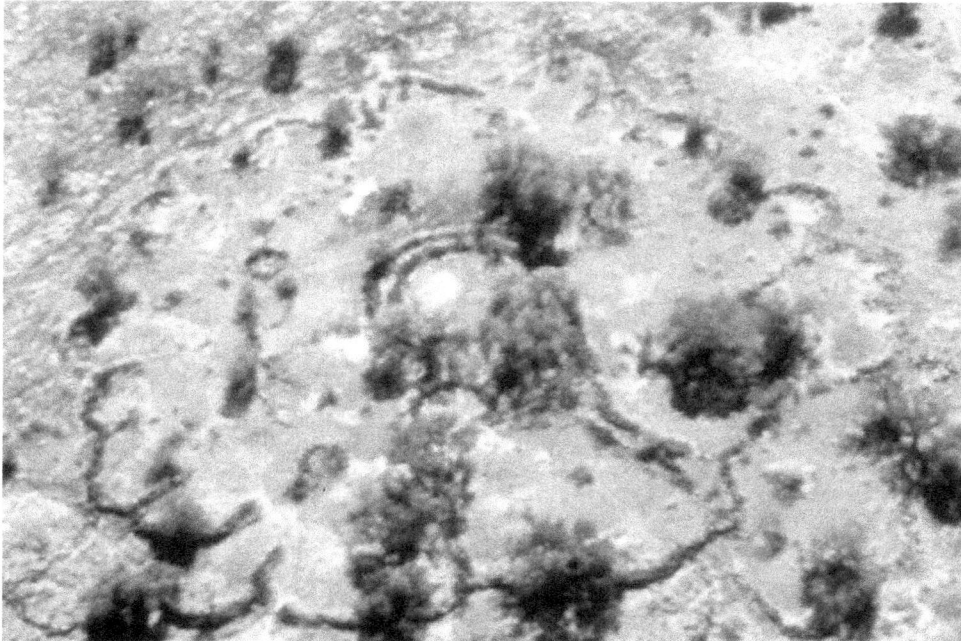

Figure 7.2
Oblique aerial photograph
of SU25, viewed from
the south-west.

Figure 7.3
View of the circular cattle
track from the east, as it
curves around the northern
edge of the central kraal.
The arrow points to the
location of Midden 1
excavation trench.

stone passageway leading from the exterior to an opening or 'gate' in the perimeter wall (Fig. 7.4). To reach the entrance to the kraals inside, the Boschoek cattle then moved either clockwise or anti-clockwise around the kraal complex, guided by "stone lanes" to the northern side (Huffman 1986b: 296).

The movement of livestock (and possibly people) in SU25 seems to have been even more tightly controlled. Here, as we have seen, the cattle track occurs inside the homestead and loops completely around the perimeter of the kraal before entering the court complex—an arrangement that seems to be unparalleled among recorded Tswana settlements in the region (Fig. 7.1). It is some 300 kilometres to the north-east that we find a hint of a possibly related form of spatial expression, in the Pietersburg area of today's Limpopo Province (Loubser 1994). Here, stone settlements built by Ndebele or Koni people (evidently 'Sotho-ised' Nguni) seem to be characterised by an internal cattle track that leads to a small enclosure, which is interpreted as a 'milking and slaughter' area. From here, stone passageways lead to the main kraals. The whole central complex is surrounded by a sub-circular wall (Fig. 7.5). This settlement type has been termed 'Badfontein' after similar sites identified further south (Huffman 2007; Delius & Schoeman 2008).

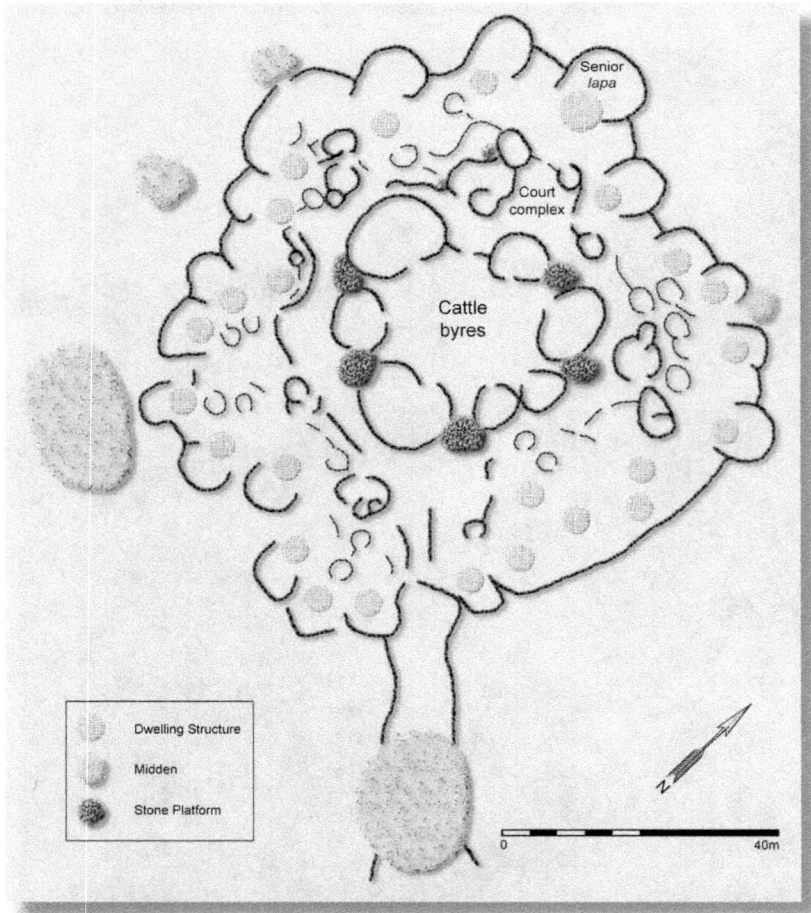

Figure 7.4
Map of the 18th century homestead at Boschoek in Gauteng (after Huffman 1986b).

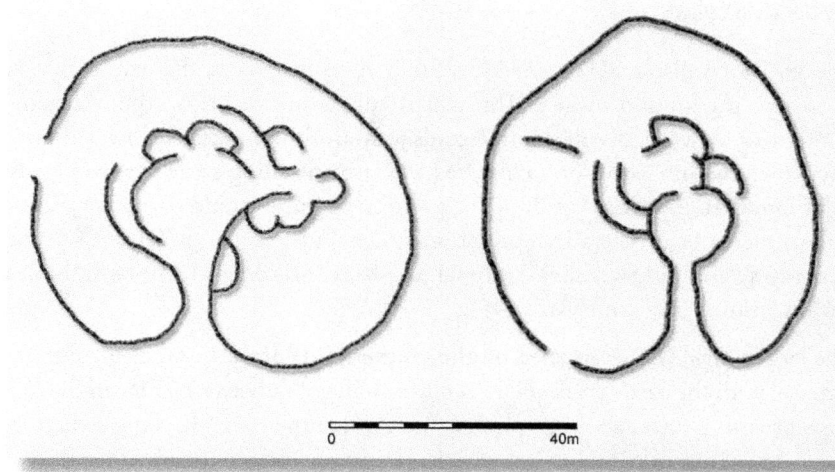

Figure 7.5
Examples of Badfontein
type walling arrangements
(after Loubser 2004).

At face value, despite the limited spatial detail in the Badfontein maps (Fig. 7.5), general similarities can perhaps be recognised between this walling style and the internal walling arrangement of SU25 (Fig. 7.1).

While we should, of course, be wary of attaching too much significance to a single example, a comparison with an Nguni-derived settlement pattern raises the possibility of a recently non-Tswana origin for the original inhabitants of SU25. They may have been incorporated into the Tlokwa community during the occupation of Marothodi, or at a slightly earlier point in the settlement sequence. It is clear, as we have seen, that the fluidity of political allegiance in this period and the high tolerance of foreigners in Tswana towns would have facilitated such an inclusion. The perimeter 'scallops' that define individual *malapa* at SU25 are notably absent from the Badfontein examples, but scalloping is a Tswana feature that could have been adopted by the SU25 occupants after they became attached to the Tlokwa chiefdom.

The placement of a midden inside the southern end of the SU25 cattle track (Fig. 7.1, Midden 2) perfomed a similar function to the middens previously noted in formal entranceways to the 'Primary' *Kgosing* and 'Secondary' *Kgosing*, and continues the theme of white ash 'cooling' the livestock on their way into the homestead from outside (see Hammond-Tooke 1981; Huffman 1986b). The enclosure approximately halfway along the cattle track (Fig. 7.1, E5) may have been for managing livestock before they entered the kraal (see Huffman 2007; Jannie Loubser, pers. com. 2008).

A number of small transverse walls block the interior passage of the cattle track on the northern and western sides of the kraal. Additionally, the formal entrance to the homestead at the southern end of the cattle track has been deliberately blocked by a wall (Fig. 7.1). The stratigraphic relationships between walling and midden in this area indicate that a degree of remodelling and expansion had occurred within the homestead, particularly in the south-eastern area where a row of 6 *malapa*, M24 to M29, appear to have been attached to the homestead after the cattle track had been blocked off (Fig. 7.1). Clarifying the stratigraphic sequence in this area was one of the key research aims at SU25.

The Domestic Sphere

The *malapa* walls at SU25 have sunk into the turf soil to the extent that some barely rise above the ground surface. This is particularly noticeable on the northern side of the homestead. As with all other homesteads at Marothodi, most *malapa* contain at least one circular dome indicative of a collapsed or burnt dwelling structure. Many also have upright foundation stones that show the position of front veranda walls. In addition, circular arrangements of orthostatic foundation stones indicate the presence of domestic 'utility structures', and artefacts such as upper and lower grindstones can be seen on the ground within a number of courtyards.

The largest *lapa*, M1, is situated on the southern side of the homestead, and shares its eastern wall with the cattle track (Fig. 7.1). M1 is one of only two *malapa* in SU25 that, on the basis of visible traces above ground, contain more than one dwelling structure. The other one is M7. This, in combination with its large size, leads to the identification of M1 as the primary *lapa*, the household of the headman's senior wife. It is significant that access to the court complex from M1 is through an entrance to E5. From here one could step across the low containing wall of the court midden into SE1 and E2 (it is only around 0.45 m high). Alternatively, protocol may have required people to walk from E5 along the cattle track, anti-clockwise around the kraal, to reach the court complex.

On the western side of the kraal and court complex, two dwelling structures are positioned next to each other, and face south-west towards *malapa* M3 and M4 (Fig. 7.1, M30 and M31). Their central position seems at odds with the general spatial organisation in the rest of SU25 because their back courtyard boundaries, which are on the northern side of the structures, are not visible. Instead of the usual stone walling, they are likely to have been constructed of wooden poles and thatch. Nevertheless, these structures and their courtyards can be recognised as integral with *malapa* M1 to M5. Their 'reverse' orientation is suggestive of the inward-looking house arrangement sometimes seen among high status families. We observed this pattern in the SOU and the EOU in the 'Primary' *Kgosing* (Fig. 6.1) and in the NOU of the 'Secondary' *Kgosing* (Fig. 6.11), where some *malapa* are spatially opposed to others in the same group.

Domestic ash middens are highly visible at SU25, and although they are generally shallow, they occupy large areas relative to the size of the homestead. At the centre of the homestead, a large domestic midden abuts the outside wall of the cattle kraal around much of its perimeter (Fig. 7.1, Midden 1). Midden 1 is widest on the north-west side, where it is bounded by a relatively straight wall that may have been built to control it. The position of Midden 1 behind *malapa* M30 and M31 suggests that these households contributed to the deposit. Furthermore, the southern edge of the midden appears to respect their back courtyard space (Fig. 7.1). Indeed, it is likely that most, if not all, households at SU25 contributed to this midden to some degree.

Shallow midden deposits were also discernable around the north-east perimeter of the homestead, where ash was tipped over the back courtyard walls of *malapa* M9 to M19 (Fig. 7.1). The deposition of midden over back courtyard walls is more noticeable at SU25 than at the 'Primary' *Kgosing* and 'Secondary' *Kgosing*. As discussed in Chapter Six, although back courtyard middens do occur at the royal homesteads, the dominant trend there was to take ash forward, towards the central kraal walls. Preliminary survey of SU25 revealed a significant degree of metal working debris on the surface of the perimeter middens, particularly scatters of slag, small fragments of furnace daga, and pieces of the copper ore-bearing gossan. This material was also noted, to a lesser extent, on the central midden, and particularly on the eastern side of the cattle kraal.

On the outside of the homestead on the south and west sides, curvilinear rows of large stones define an intermittent series of 'back annex' spaces behind *malapa* M1 to M6 (Fig. 7.1). These may have been activity spaces, or may represent an incomplete process of expansion in this part of the homestead. On the western perimeter of SU25, a deep, crescent-shaped depression containing large naturally outcropping blocks of norite is surrounded by stone blocks. This seems likely to have been a 'borrow pit' from which the builders of this homestead retrieved stone for the construction of the walling (Fig. 7.1).

Excavations at Settlement Unit 25

Having observed during ground survey that there was a significant amount of metal production occuring at SU25, the rationale for excavation was to sample different aspects of a settlement that was intensively engaged in metallurgy, as well as to expose some of the actual metal working areas themselves. Excavations were also geared towards understanding the stratigraphic sequence of the homestead because, as noted earlier, a degree of re-modelling seems to have occurred here, particularly in the south-eastern area. Finally, to contribute to 'elite versus commoner' comparisons within the town, it was important to record household organisation and to retrieve samples from both the court midden and domestic middens.

In pursuit of these aims, excavations were undertaken in Midden 1 on the north-west side of the kraal, in Midden 2 inside the southern terminus of the cattle track, and in the court midden. Two dwelling structures were also excavated: Dwelling Structure 1, in *lapa* M30 on the west side of the kraal; and Dwelling Structure 2, in *lapa* M25 on the south-eastern periphery of the homestead. In addition, an area of concentrated metallurgical debris on the northern edge of the homestead behind *lapa* M12 was examined (Fig. 7.1).

Midden 1

The trench in Midden 1 was situated on the north-west side of the kraal, perpendicular to the external wall of the surrounding cattle track (see Figs. 7.1 and 7.3). The trench measured 1.0 x 6.0 m, and was excavated in spits of 0.05 m thick to the midden base at 0.36 m. The total volume excavated was approximately 1.6 cubic metres.

Stratigraphy in Midden 1 was simple, consisting of a 0.10 m thick surface crust of dark grey weathered ash, which blended into the main light-grey ash underneath (Fig. 7.6). As the light grey ash continued right down to the black turf soil at the base, the midden was treated as a single deposit.

Artefacts from Midden 1

Ceramics

A total of 1619 sherds (9857.6g) were retrieved from Midden 1, of which 134 were diagnostic (Table 7.1). The overall density was 6161.0g of sherds per cubic metre of excavated deposit. One sherd from Midden 1 (#V900), although fragmentory, had just enough profile for multi-dimensional analysis. It was identified as 'Class 2' (*Uitkomst* facies): a smooth-necked jar with a single horizontal band of comb-stamping on the rim (Fig. 7.8, 13).

Metallurgy

As could be expected from the density of metallurgical evidence on the surface of SU25, Midden 1 also contained a large amount. In total, 13596.1g of debris were recovered from Midden 1—a density of 8497.6g per cubic metre of excavated deposit (Table 7.2). The material was dominated by smelting/flow slag. Some large plano-convex 'cakes' formed by slag puddling at the base of a furnace were also found, along with fragments of clay tuyere (2089.8g) and a number of crucible sherds (845.9g). In addition, nodules of copper ore (gossan) and potential iron ore (magnetite) were also found. A small unidentified wedge-shaped iron object with a rounded point (#MAR312) was the only finished metal artefact retrieved from Midden 1 (Fig. 7.9). Results of a preliminary analysis of these materials are published in Hall *et al.* 2006.

Scraping Tools

A total of 394 scrapers were recovered from Midden 1. This included 64 made from abraded ceramic sherds and 330 pieces of recycled bone.

Beads

A total of 23 beads were recovered from Midden 1. Eighteen of these were disc-shaped ostrich eggshell beads, of which 14 were fully intact. Two cylindrical-shaped copper beads were found (#MAR62 and 52), an iron bead (#MAR317), and two broken cylindrical blue-green glass beads (#MAR66 and 65) (Fig. 7.10).

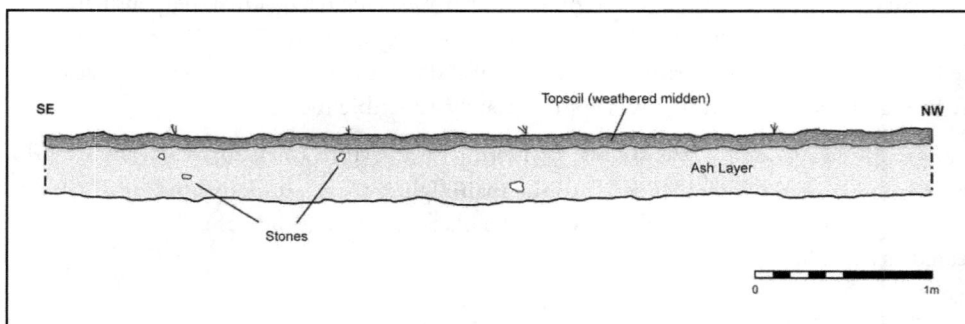

Figure 7.6
North facing section of the trench excavated into Midden 1 of SU25.

Stone

Two stone artefacts were recovered from Midden 1: a piece of a door slide base stone, made from the local norite rock with a prominently worn 'door groove' on one surface (#MAR6); and a polished smoothing stone (#MAR43) that may have been used to smooth the walls and floor of structure interiors (Fig. 7.11).

Clay Figurines

A small figurine of a cow (#MAR84) was the most complete clay figurine found at Marothodi (Fig. 7.12). Although quite eroded in places and without horns, the characteristic form is relatively easy to identify. The only other clay fragment retrieved from this midden was a small cylindrical piece, 'pinched' at one end, which remains uninterpreted (not pictured).

Ivory

A curved band of ivory with broken ends (#MAR79) was retrieved from Midden 1, which probably formed part of a bracelet (Fig. 7.13).

Figure 7.7
(a) Field team members proceed with the excavation of Midden 1 and the sorting of finds. (b) A view of the excavated trench from the south-east end.

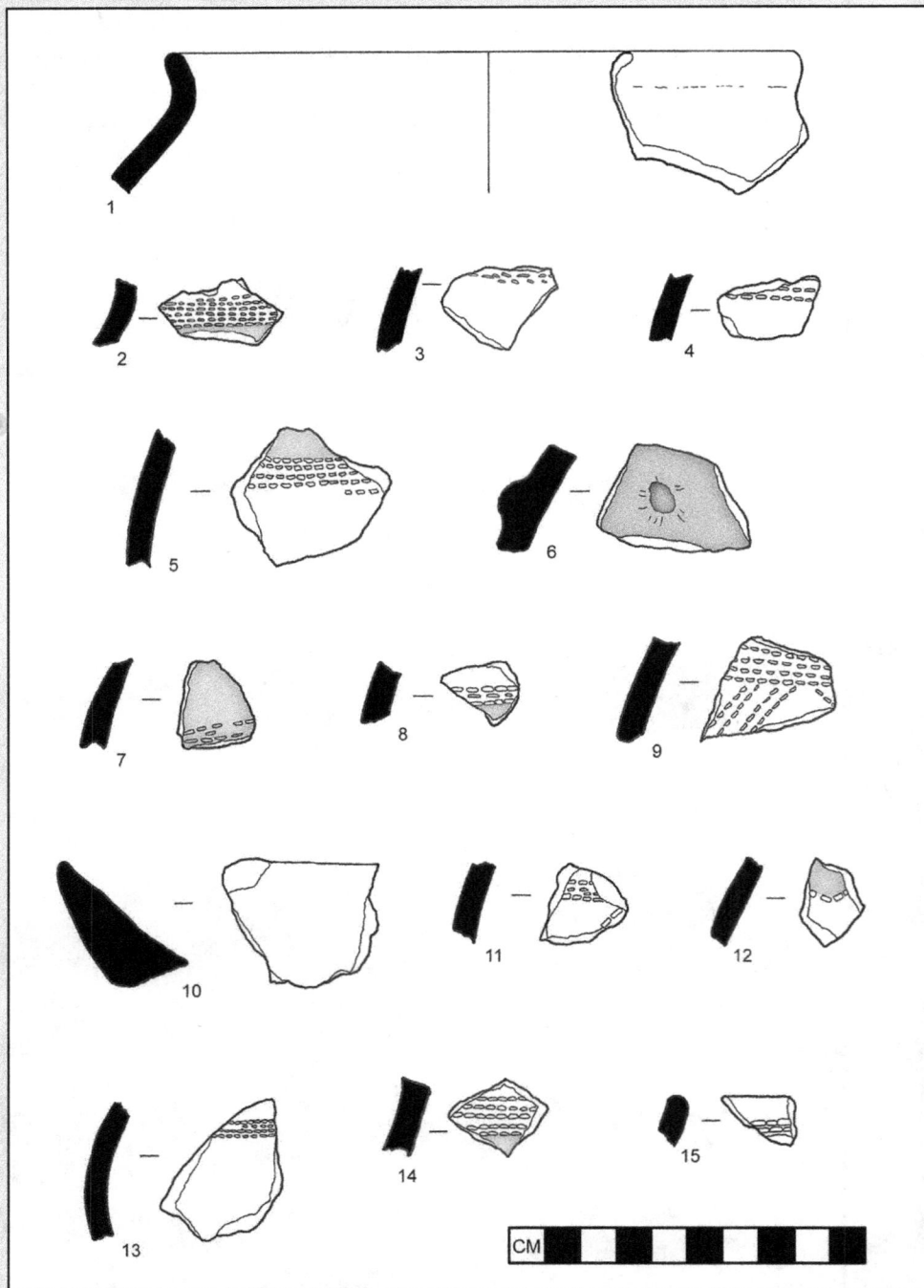

Figure 7.8
Decorated sherds and
representative profiles from
Midden 1 of SU25.

Figure 7.8 Ceramic Descriptions

1. Smooth-necked jar, plain. Profile Mode: 1A. Provenance: SU25, Midden 1, Square D, Level 3. Cat. No. V913.

2. Decorated sherd, no profile information. Horizontal band of comb-stamping above black graphite. Provenance: SU25, Midden 1, Square C, Level 2. Cat. No. V797.

3. Decorated sherd, no profile information. Horizontal band of comb-stamping. Provenance: SU25, Midden 1, Square B, Level 3. Cat. No. V902.

4. Decorated sherd, no profile information. Horizontal band of comb-stamping. Provenance: SU25, Midden 1, Square C, Level 3. Cat. No. V903.

5. Decorated sherd, no profile information. Horizontal band of comb-stamping below black graphite. Provenance: SU25, Midden 1, Square D, Level 3. Cat. No. V905.

6. Body sherd, no profile information, black (possibly burnt). Appliqué protrusion (broken). Provenance: SU25, Midden 1, Square B, Level 3. Cat. No. V906.

7. Decorated sherd, no profile information. Band of comb-stamping, black (possibly burnt). Provenance: SU25, Midden 1, Square B, Level 1. Cat. No. V782.

8. Decorated sherd, no profile information. Horizontal band of comb-stamping above black graphite. Provenance: SU25, Midden 1, Square D, Level 3. Cat. No. V898.

9. Decorated sherd, no profile information. Horizontal band of comb-stamping above angled lines of comb-stamping – possibly outlining pendant triangles. Provenance: SU25, Midden 1, Square C, Level 3. Cat. No. V899.

10. Simple bowl, plain. Profile Mode: 2B. Provenance: SU25, Midden 1, Square B, Level 3. Cat. No. V908.

11. Decorated sherd, no profile information. Horizontal band of comb-stamping above angled line of comb-stamping – possibly outlining a pendant triangle. Provenance: SU25, Midden 1, Square A, Level 3. Cat, No. V901.

12. Decorated sherd, no profile information. Angled line of comb-stamping beneath black graphite infill – possibly pendant triangle. Provenance: SU25, Midden 1, Square A, Level 1. Cat. No. V731.

13. Smooth-necked jar with a horizontal band of comb-stamping on the rim. Profile Mode: 1A. Layout Mode: 2. Decoration Mode: 2. Multi-dimensional Class: 2. Provenance: SU25, Midden 1, Square D, Level 3. Cat. No. 900.

14. Decorated sherd, no profile information. Horizontal band of comb-stamping above black graphite. Provenance: SU25, Midden 1, Square A, Level 1. Cat. No. V730.

15. Decorated rim sherd, insufficient profile information. Horizontal band of comb-stamping. Provenance: SU25, Midden 1, Square D, Level 3. Cat. No. V904.

Table 7.1
Quantities of ceramics from
Midden 1 of SU25.

	Sherds	Mass (g)	Mass (g) per m³	% of total sherds
Diagnostic	134	728.7	455.4	8.3
Adiagnostic	1485	9128.9	5705.6	91.7
Total	1619	9857.6	6161.0	100

Table 7.2
Quantities of metallurgical
debris from Midden 1 of
SU25.

Material Type	Mass (g)	Mass (g) per m³	% of total mass
Smelting/flow slag	6215.2	3884.5	45.7
Tuyere fragments	2089.8	1306.1	15.4
Tabular slag	1327.0	829.4	9.7
Furnace base slag	959.3	599.6	7.1
Copper ore bearing gossan	878.3	548.9	6.5
Crucible sherds	845.9	528.7	6.2
Frothy glassy slag	697.6	436.0	5.1
Magnetite	409.7	256.1	3.0
Partially reduced ore (iron)	128.9	80.6	1.0
Hollow slag droplets	44.4	27.8	0.3
Total	13596.1	8497.6	100

Figure 7.9
Iron object from Midden 1
of SU25.

#MAR312

Figure 7.10
Beads from Midden 1 of
SU25.

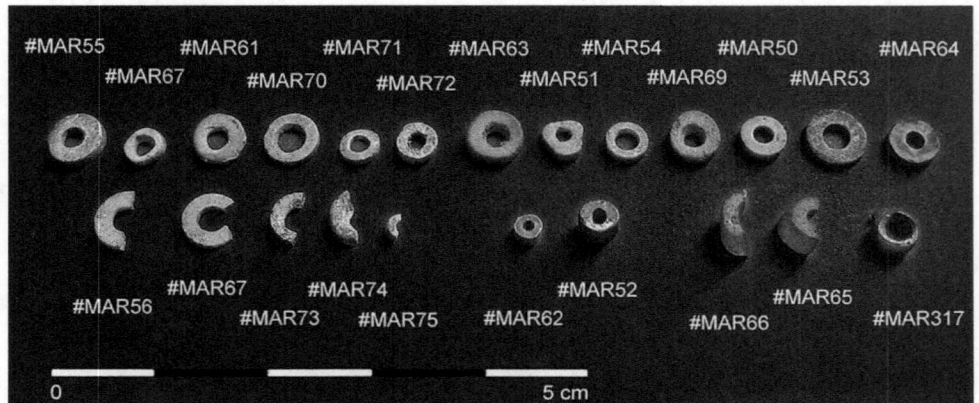

Figure 7.11
Stone artefacts from
Midden 1 of SU25.

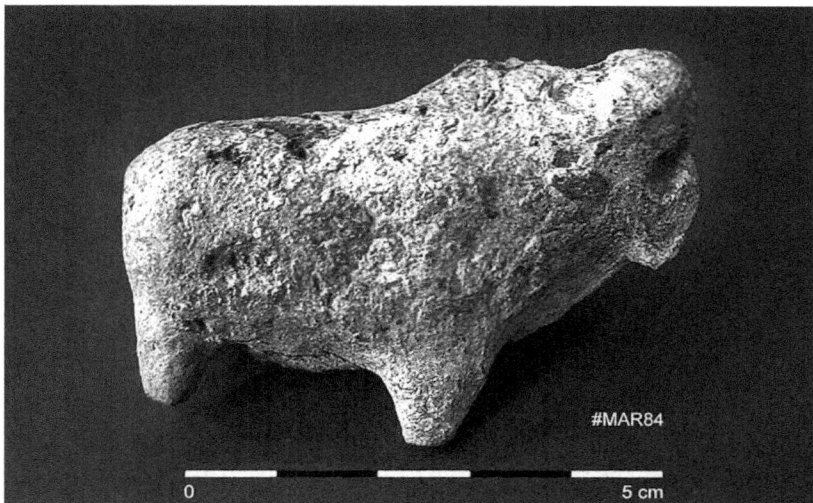

Figure 7.12
Clay cattle figurine from
Midden 1 of SU25.

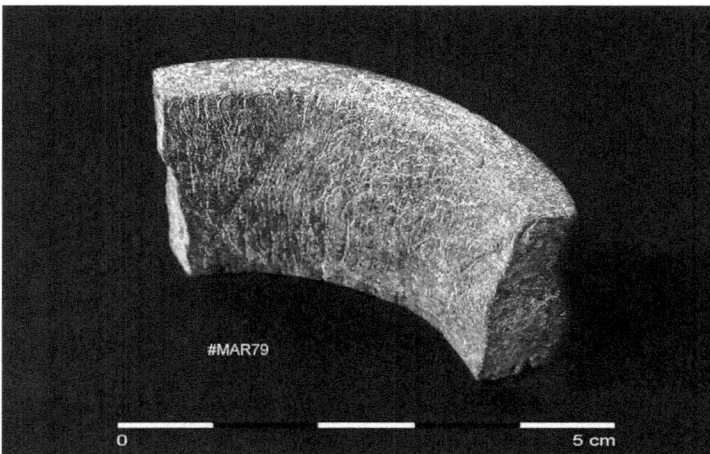

Figure 7.13
Fragment of an ivory
bracelet from Midden 1 of
SU25.

Midden 2

The excavation of Midden 2 was directed to elucidate the sequence of remodelling associated with the blocking of the original cattle track entrance, and the building of the row of 6 peripheral *malapa*, M24 to M29 (Fig. 7.1). The excavation also generated a material sample for comparison with other middens.

Access into the row of peripheral *malapa* from outside the homestead is through a narrow passageway between M25 and M26 (Fig. 7.1). This entrance is situated opposite a feature outside the homestead that is identified as an iron forge. Although it was not excavated, this interpretation is based on the associated slag scatters, the hammered surfaces of the large flat stones that form part of its structure, and a small iron hammer head observed on the ground in the immediate vicinity. The spatial relationship between the forge, the entranceway, and *malapa* M24 to M29 suggests that the occupants of these households had some association with iron forging activity. It was therefore important to understand their relationship with the rest of SU25.

Prior to excavation it was noted that Midden 2 appeared to lie beneath the blocking wall, but abutted against the back courtyard wall of *lapa* M23, hinting that excavation of the midden might serve to clarify the sequence of walling in this part of the homestead.

A trench measuring 1.5 x 5.0 m was positioned across the widest section of Midden 2, stretching from inside the cattle track and across the 'blocking' wall (Fig. 7.1). Excavation initially proceeded in horizontal spits of 0.05 m deep, but continued according to archaeological stratigraphy after the first distinct layer was identified. The maximum depth of the midden was revealed to be 0.32 m, and 1.44 cubic meters of deposit were excavated in total.

The stratigraphy of Midden 2 was more complex than that of Midden 1 (Fig. 7.14). At its base, the foundation stones of an earlier wall terminus were discovered, sunk into the underlying turf soil. The position of this earlier wall suggested that it was the original end of the western wall of the cattle track (Fig. 7.14). Above this, four separate layers of ash were identified in the south-facing trench section. The earliest (Layer 4) was deposited directly onto the underlying turf soil, and was capped by a thin layer of culturally sterile soil which was probably an attempt to control the spread of the ash. Layer 3 had built up on top of this 'capping layer', and was itself sealed by another capping layer. The reddish-brown soil of the capping layers appears to have been derived from weathered anorthosite, and not the black turf soil that occurs naturally at the base of the midden. Significantly, Layers 3 and 4 seem to respect the same boundaries at both ends, and at the western end they stop abruptly next to the position of the earlier wall terminus. This suggests that Layers 3 and 4 were contemporary with the earlier wall, and built up against it (Fig. 7.14).

The most extensive layer, Layer 2, occurred on top of the uppermost soil capping deposit, and spread beyond the boundaries that confined the lower layers (Fig. 7.14). Consequently, it seems reasonable to suggest that Layer 2 built up after the original wall terminus had been removed, subsequently expanding up to its present position against the back courtyard wall of *lapa* M1. The latest ash layer, Layer 1, was a localised accumulation on the uppermost surface around the blocking wall. This deposit had a looser consistency than the main ash layers, and considering the lack of archaeological material in it, may represent a more recent accumulation (either windblown or disturbed by modern cattle) which had settled against the blocking wall. Most importantly, the western courtyard wall of *lapa* M29 abuts the blocking wall, indicating that this row of *malapa* were later elements of the archaeological sequence in this part of SU25. With this established, it seems possible that the ephemeral walling behind *malapa* M1 to M5 represents the beginning of further expansion on the south-west side of the homestead (Fig. 7.1).

Artefacts from Midden 2

Ceramics

A total of 3329 sherds (21935.5g) were recovered from Midden 2 (Table 7.3). This included 132 diagnostic sherds, representing 4% of the total (Fig. 7.15). The overall density of sherds was 15233.0g per cubic metre, with Layer 2 having the highest density. No sherds from this midden were suitable for multi-dimensional analysis.

Metallurgy

The deposit yielded 3121.8g of metallurgical debris, which is a density of 2168.0g per cubic metre of excavated deposit (Table 7.4). Smelting/flow slag made up over 42% of

Figure 7.14
Plan (top) and south facing section (below) of the trench excavated into Midden 2 in SU25.

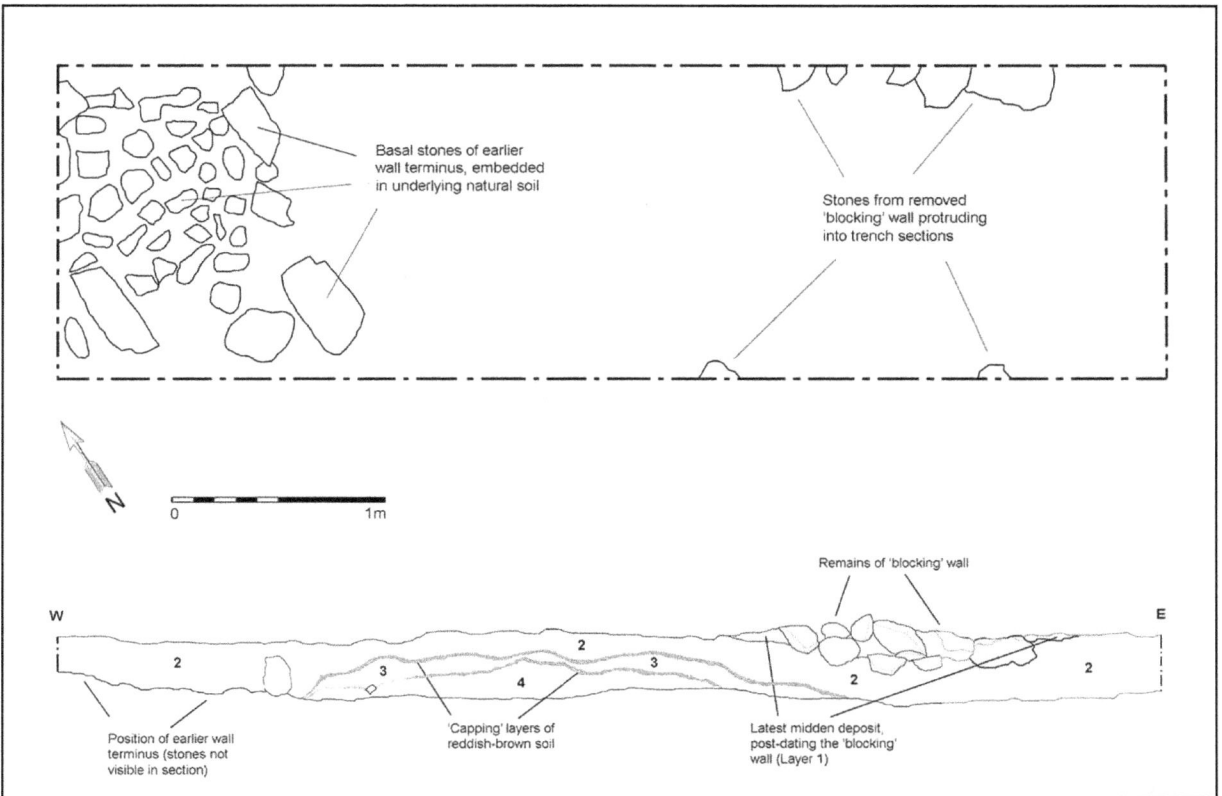

Basal stones of earlier wall terminus, embedded in underlying natural soil

Stones from removed 'blocking' wall protruding into trench sections

N

0   1m

Remains of 'blocking' wall

W

2

2

3

4

3

2

2

E

Position of earlier wall terminus (stones not visible in section)

'Capping' layers of reddish-brown soil

Latest midden deposit, post-dating the 'blocking' wall (Layer 1)

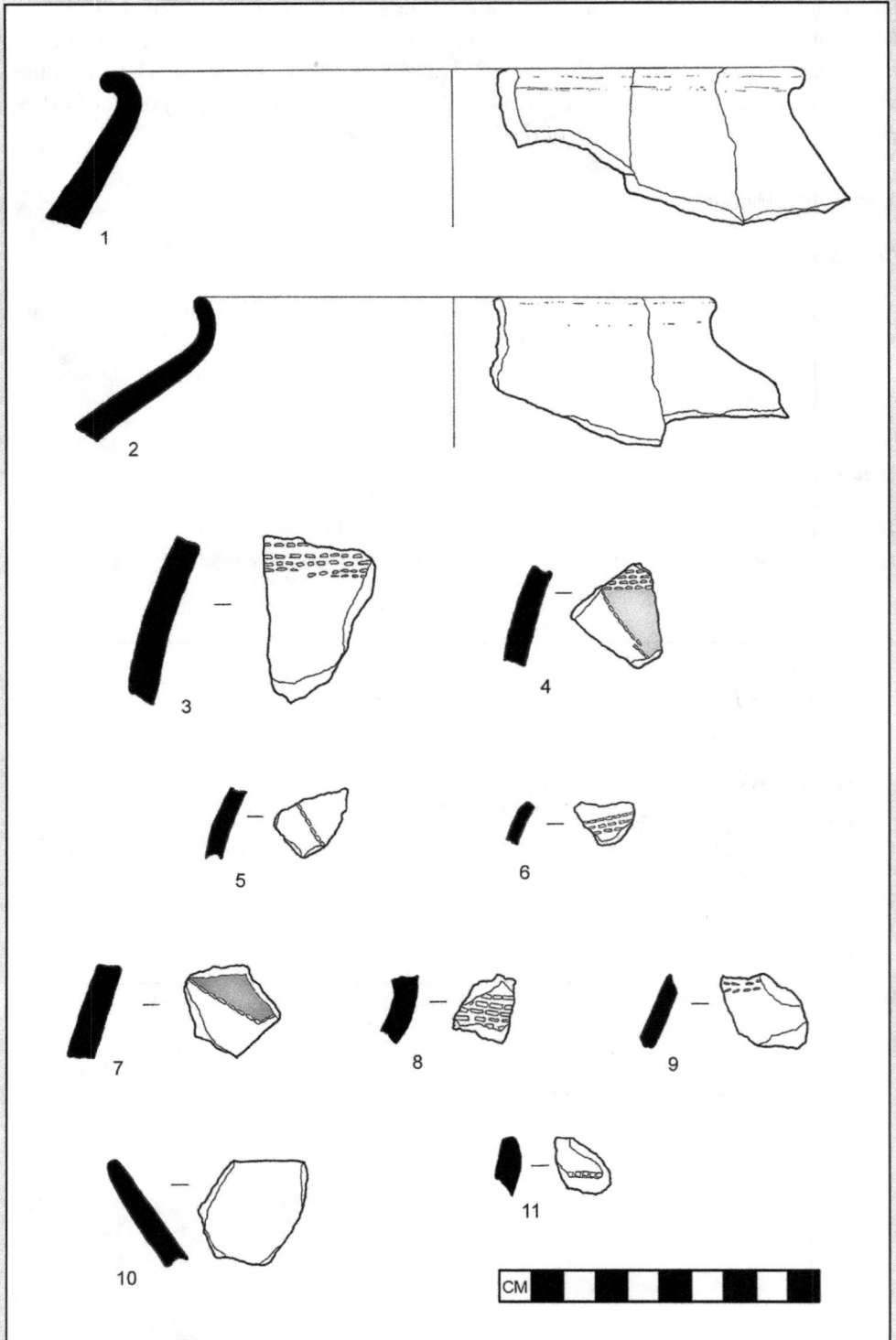

Figure 7.15
Decorated sherds and representative profiles from Midden 2 of SU25.

Figure 7.15 Ceramic Descriptions

1. Smooth-necked jar, plain. Profile Mode: 1A. Provenance: SU25, Midden 2, Square A, Level 1. Cat. No. V845.

2. Smooth-necked jar, plain. Profile Mode: 1A. Provenance: SU25, Midden 2, Square B, Level 2. Cat. No. V810.

3. Decorated sherd, no profile information. Horizontal band of comb-stamping. Provenance: SU25, Midden 2, Square B, Level 1. Cat. No. V807a. Same vessel as V807b (4).

4. Decorated sherd, no profile information. Horizontal band of comb-stamping above pendant triangle with black graphite infill and comb-stamped outline. Provenance: SU25, Midden 2, Square B, Level 1. Cat. No. V807b. Same vessel as V807a (3).

5. Decorated sherd, no profile information. Angled line of comb-stamping, possibly outlining a pendant triangle. Provenance: SU25, Midden 2, Square C, Level 2. Cat. No. V854.

6. Decorated sherd, no profile information. Horizontal band of comb-stamping. Provenance: SU25, Midden 2, Square A, Level 2. Cat. No. V855.

7. Decorated sherd, no profile information. Angled lines of comb-stamping outlining a pendant triangle with black graphite infill. Provenance: SU25, Midden 2, Square A, Level 1. Cat. No. V846.

8. Decorated sherd, no profile information. Horizontal band of comb-stamping. Provenance: SU25, Midden 2, Square B, Level 2. Cat. No. V811.

9. Decorated sherd, no profile information. Horizontal band of comb-stamping. Provenance: SU25, Midden 2, Square C, Level 1. Cat. No. V806.

10. Simple bowl, plain. Provenance: SU25, Midden 2, Square D, Level 2. Cat. No. V856.

11. Decorated rim sherd, insufficient profile information. Horizontal band of comb-stamping. Provenance: SU25, Midden 2, Square B, Level 1. Cat. No. V861.

the assemblage. Furnace base slag and tabular slag (which is often vitrified furnace wall) were also well represented, suggesting an emphasis on primary smelting contexts. Other elements included crucible sherds and tuyere fragments, iron ore (magnetite) and copper ore.

Three iron objects were recovered from Midden 2: an adze (#MAR310), a short fragment of heavily corroded pin (#MAR314) and a 36 mm long iron 'point' (#MAR315) (Fig. 7.16).

Scraping tools

A total of 217 scrapers were found in Midden 2, of which 40 were abraded ceramic sherds, and 177 were recycled pieces of bone.

Beads

Four beads were recovered from Midden 2. Three of these were disc-shaped ostrich egg-shell beads, of which only one (#MAR57) was fully intact. One cylindrical copper bead (#MAR58) was also retrieved (Fig. 7.17).

Stone

The only stone artefact from Midden 2 was a reddish-coloured polishing stone (Fig. 7.18).

Table 7.3
Quantities of ceramic sherds from Midden 2.

		Sherds	Mass (g)	Mass (g) per m³	% of total sherds
Layer 2	Diagnostic	73	827.8	574.9	2.2
	Adiagnostic	1977	13869.0	9631.1	59.4
Layer 3	Diagnostic	0	0	0	0
	Adiagnostic	406	1974.3	1371.0	12.2
Layer 4	Diagnostic	59	339.4	235.7	1.8
	Adiagnostic	814	4925.0	3420.1	24.4
Subtotals	Diagnostic	132	1167.2	810.6	4.0
	Adiagnostic	3197	20768.3	14422.4	96.0
Totals		3329	21935.5	15233.0	100

Table 7.4
Quantities of metallurgical debris from Midden 2.

Material Type	Mass (g)	Mass (g) per m³	% of total mass
Smelting/flow slag	1316.6	914.3	42.2
Furnace base slag	489.2	339.7	15.7
Tabular slag	397.8	276.2	12.7
Crucible sherds	362.1	251.5	11.6
Tuyere fragments	307.8	213.7	9.9
Copper ore bearing gossan	96.7	67.1	3.1
Vitrified furnace lining	93.0	64.6	3.0
Froth glassy slag	45.3	31.5	1.4
Iron ore (magnetite)	13.4	9.3	0.4
Total	3121.8	2168.0	100

Figure 7.16
Iron artefacts retrieved
from Midden 2 of SU25.

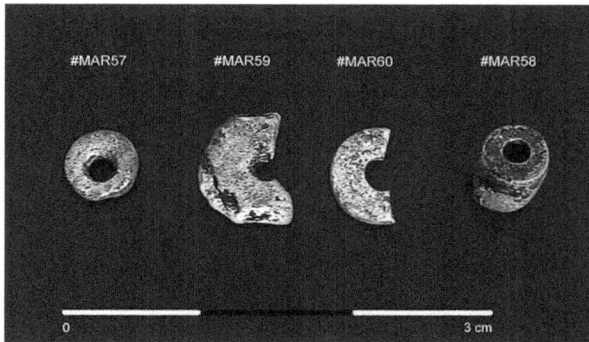

Figure 7.17
Beads from Midden 2.

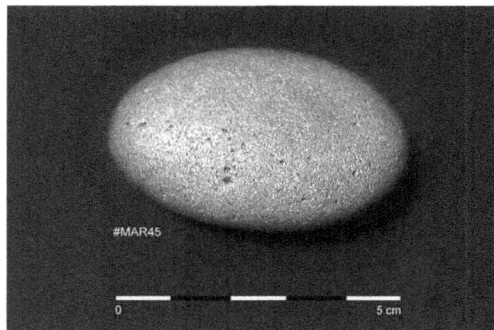

Figure 7.18
Polishing stone from
Midden 2 of SU25.

Court Midden

The court midden in SU25 is situated within SE1, the court complex, immediately to the south of the kraal. The deposit has accumulated between the kraal wall, the western wall of the cattle track and the northern wall of E5.

Two 1 x 1 m sondages were excavated in the midden. Test Pit 1 was situated approximately in the centre of the deposit, and Test Pit 2 was positioned against the cattle track wall that forms the eastern boundary of the midden (Fig. 7.1).

The excavations revealed the midden deposit to be, on average, 0.40 – 0.45 m deep, with a relatively complex stratigraphy. Two of the clearest sections in each test pit were recorded: the west and north facing sections of Test Pit 1; and the north and east facing sections of Test Pit 2 (Fig. 7.19). The latter section shows that the eastern boundary wall of the midden was two courses high (0.40 m at this point), and was constructed directly on the sterile surface of the underlying turf soil, thus sharing this surface with the earliest ash layer (Fig. 7.19).

Beneath the dark grey humic topsoil, both pits revealed a series of ashy layers separated by bands of reddish-brown layers of culturally sterile soil. These may have been deliberate capping layers of the kind observed in Midden 2. The artefactual material was concentrated in the three intervening ashy layers. The similarity of the excavated deposits in each test pit clearly demonstrated that the midden was a single entity, and therefore the materials from both pits are combined for analysis.

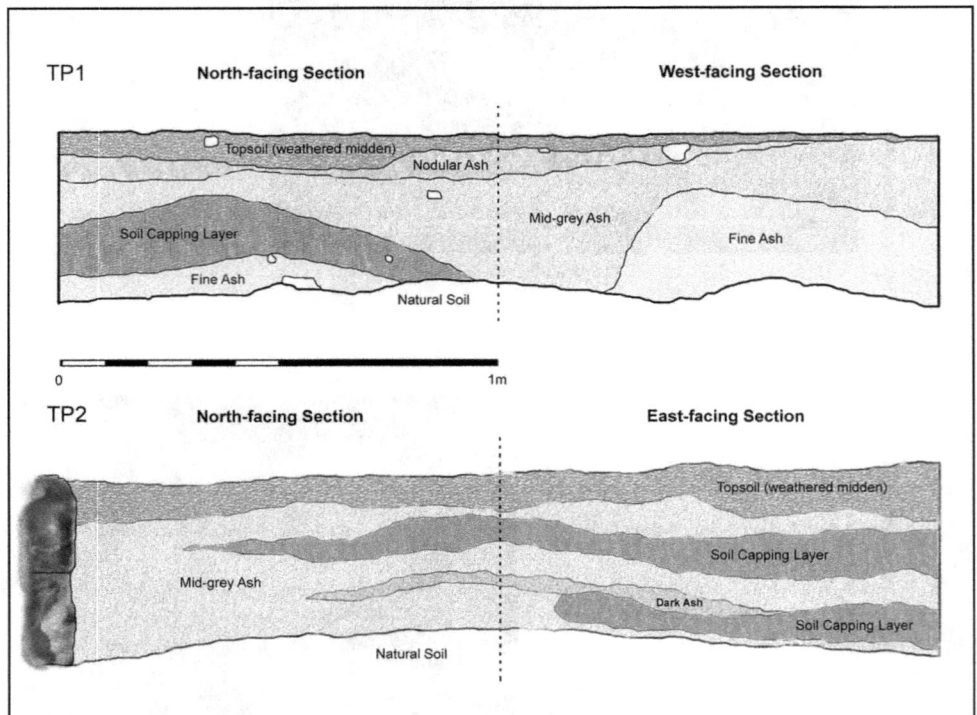

Figure 7.19
North and west facing sections of Test Pit 1 (top) and north and east facing sections of Test Pit 2 (below) in the court midden of SU25.

Artefacts from the Court Midden

Ceramics

The court midden had a low ceramic density, averaging 3164.5g per excavated cubic metre (Table 7.5). Of the 272 (2721.5g) sherds recovered, 30 were diagnostic (Fig. 7.21). None were suitable for multi-dimensional analysis.

Metallurgy

As with Middens 1 and 2, the court midden at SU25 revealed plenty of evidence for copper production, with an emphasis on smelting/flow slag (59.9%) and slag associated with furnace structures (29.4%) (Table 7.6). In terms of finished metal artefacts, the midden yielded what appears to be a heavily corroded piece of an iron needle or pin (#MAR80) (Fig. 7.22).

Scraping Tools

A total of 47 scrapers were recovered from the court midden. Of these, 12 were abraded ceramic sherds and 35 were recycled bone.

Clay Figurines

A curved, pointed piece of moulded clay that looks like a horn from a cattle figurine (#MAR85) was retrieved from the court midden (Fig. 7.23).

Figure 7.20
The excavation of Test Pit 1 begins, in the court midden of SU25.

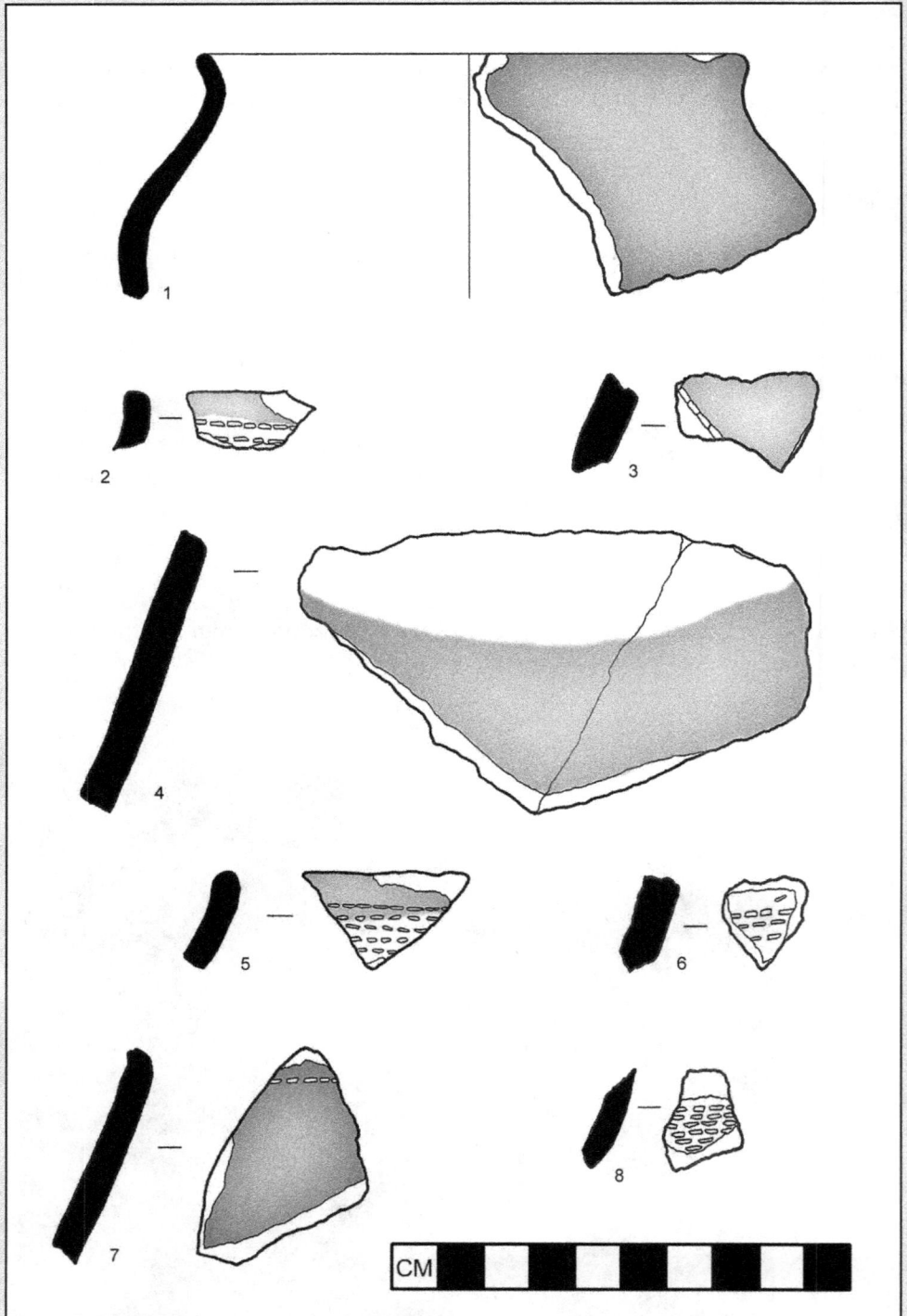

Figure 7.21
Decorated sherds and
representative profiles from
the court midden of SU25.

Figure 7.21 Ceramic Descriptions

1. Smooth-necked jar, plain. Profile Mode: 1A. Provenance: SU25, Court Midden, Test Pit 2, Level 2. Cat. No. V586.

2. Decorated sherd, no profile information. Horizontal band of comb-stamping below black graphite. Provenance: SU25, Court Midden, Test Pit 1, Layer 2. Cat. No. V560.

3. Decorated sherd, no profile information. Angled line of comb-stamping with black graphite infill – possibly pendant triangle. Provenance: SU25, Court Midden, Test Pit 2, Level 1. Cat. No. V580.

4. Body sherd, no profile information. Dark colouration on lower portion (possibly scorched). Provenance: SU25, Court Midden, Test Pit 2, Level 1. Cat. No. V579.

5. Decorated rim sherd, insufficient profile information. Horizontal band of comb-stamping below black graphite. Provenance: SU25, Court Midden, Test Pit 2, Level 2. Cat. No. V588.

6. Decorated sherd, no profile information. Horizontal band of comb-stamping. Provenance: SU25, Court Midden, Test Pit 2, Level 1. Cat. No. V583.

7. Decorated sherd, no profile information. Horizontal band of comb-stamping with black colouration (possibly burnt). Provenance: SU25, Court Midden, Test Pit 1, Layer 1. Cat. No. V651.

8. Decorated sherd, no profile information. Horizontal band of comb-stamping. Provenance: SU25, Court Midden, Test Pit 2, Level 3. Cat. No. V587.

Table 7.5
Quantities of ceramic
sherds from the court
midden of SU25.

		Sherds	Mass (g)	Mass (g) per m³	% of total sherds
Nodular ash	Diagnostic	3	48.3	56.2	1.1
	Adiagnostic	32	497.4	578.4	11.8
Mid-grey ash	Diagnostic	22	161.7	188.0	8.1
	Adiagnostic	146	1188.2	1381.6	53.7
Fine ash	Diagnostic	5	101.3	117.8	1.8
	Adiagnostic	64	724.6	842.5	23.5
Subtotals	Diagnostic	30	311.3	362.0	11.0
	Adiagnostic	242	2410.2	2802.5	89.0
Totals		272	2721.5	3164.5	100

Table 7.6
Quantities of metallurgical
debris from the court
midden of SU25.

Material Type	Mass (g)	Mass (g) per m³	% of total mass
Smelting/flow slag	1744.3	2028.2	59.9
Furnace base slag	428.4	498.1	14.7
Vitrified furnace lining	427.0	496.5	14.7
Crucible sherds	189.1	219.9	6.5
Tabular slag	85.8	99.8	2.9
Tuyere fragments	26.2	30.5	0.9
Copper ore bearing gossan	12.3	14.3	0.4
Total	2913.1	3387.3	100

#MAR80

0   5 cm

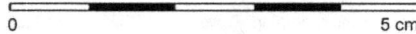

Figure 7.22
Corroded iron 'pin' from the
court midden of SU25.

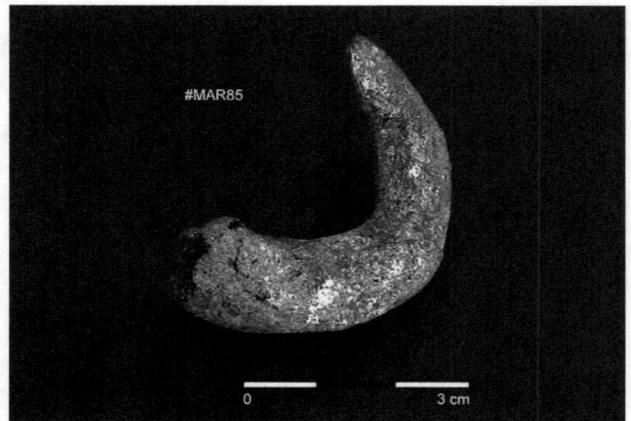

#MAR85

0   3 cm

Figure 7.23
Clay horn of a cow figurine
from the court midden of
SU25.

Dwelling Structure 1

Dwelling Structure 1 in *lapa* M30 is one of two domestic structures excavated at SU25. It is situated on the west side of the kraal (Fig. 7.1). It was chosen for excavation because of its unusual position and orientation, and because the mound of wall rubble covering its buried floor was higher than that of the adjacent dwelling structure. This is usually a result of higher temperatures when the structure burnt down, and tends to predict the favourable preservation of the 'baked' floor underneath.

The surviving wall foundations revealed the basic shape of the house, with its circular inner room and a doorway connecting it to the front veranda (Fig. 7.24). There was a faint suggestion of a rear veranda wall, but this part of the structure was disturbed by tree roots so it has been indicated tentatively on the structure plan. Although the floor was not perfectly preserved, it was possible to see a thin layer of smoothed surface plaster in various places, particularly on the front veranda. Six carbonised post stubs were identified around the perimeter of the inner room, which probably helped to support the eaves of the thatched roof. The slate base-stone of the door slide had evidently been removed from beneath the doorway. Although speculative, the overall impression was that this house had stood unoccupied for some time before the rest of the homestead was finally abandoned, and that most objects that were considered useful had been taken. A row of upright stones marked a lateral wall extending towards the adjacent dwelling structure to the west. If it was continuous, access from Dwelling Structure 1 to the midden behind it would have been between the house and the western edge of the cattle kraal/court complex (Fig. 7.24).

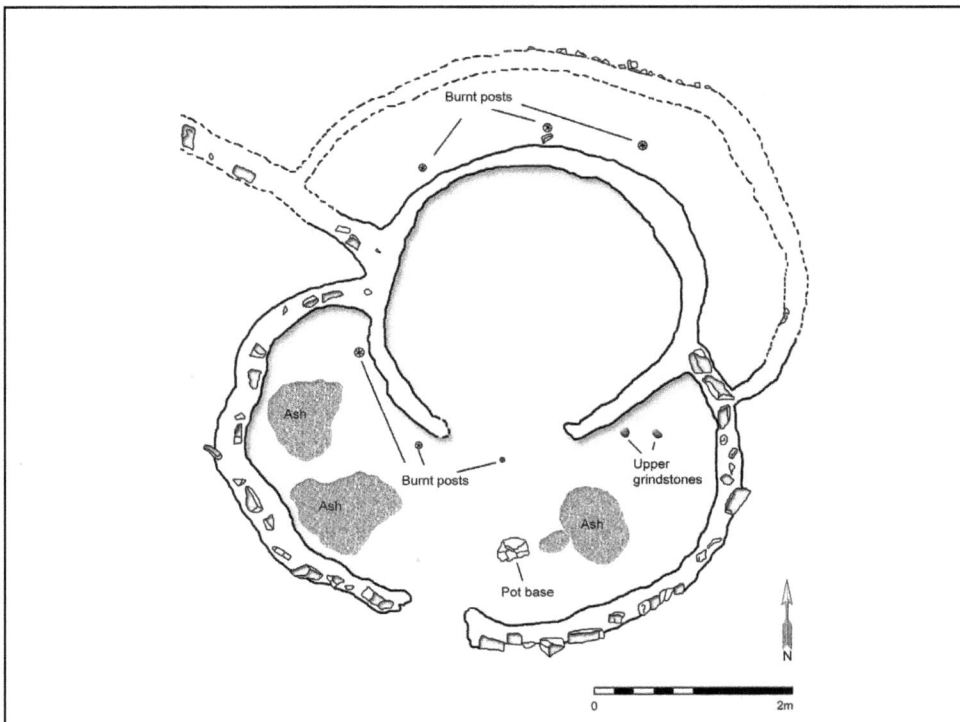

Figure 7.24
Plan of the floor and wall foundations of Dwelling Structure 1 in SU25 (see Fig. 7.1 for location).

Figure 7.25
Dwelling Structure 1 after
excavation, viewed from
the south-east with the
Matlapeng Hills in the
background.

Figure 7.25
Dwelling Structure 1 after excavation, viewed from the south-east with the Matlapeng Hills in the background.

Dwelling Structure 2

Dwelling Structure 2 is situated in *lapa* M25 on the south-eastern edge of the homestead (Fig. 7.1). As we have discussed, the excavation in Midden 2 indicated that this row of *malapa* were a later addition to SU25, and their association with the iron forge just outside the perimeter walling raised the possibility that the occupants of this household may have been involved in the forging activity. Excavation of Dwelling Structure 2 was intended to investigate this possibility and, it was hoped, shed further light on the organisation of metal production at SU25.

As initial clearance progressed and the outline of the structure became more apparent, it was noted that there was comparatively little room between the rear of the house and the *lapa* wall behind it (Fig. 7.1). As we have discussed, this back courtyard area is both practically and conceptually an important space in the Tswana household. It seemed, however, that the position of the back wall of M25 was restricted by the presence of the iron forge on the other side. As the forge incorporated large, naturally outcropping stones within its structure, we can assume that its position was not negotiable, and that that the builders of M25 compromised their back courtyard space in return for proximity to the forge. Furthermore, there is easy access to this feature through the passageway between M25 and M26, which leads from the front courtyards of both households directly to the forge.

The preservation of Dwelling Structure 2 was slighter better than that of Dwelling Structure 1 further west, a comparison which might support the suggestion that Dwelling Structure 1 was abandoned and allowed to deteriorate for some time before the terminal abandonment of the homestead. The plastered floor surfaces within Dwelling Structure 2 and on its front veranda, while not fully intact, were more complete than those of Dwelling Structure 1, and it was possible to identify burnt ashy patches, some of which may have been small

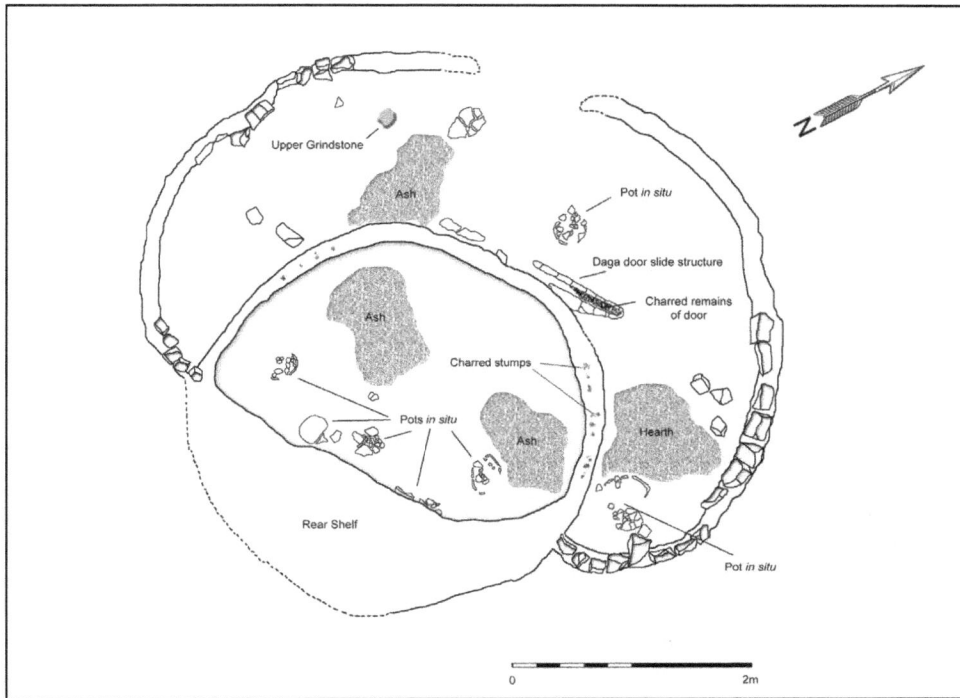

Figure 7.26
Plan of the floor and wall
foundations of Dwelling
Structure 2, in M25 of SU25.

Figure 7.27
Eastern end of the
door slide of Dwelling
Structure 2, showing
in situ charred remains
of the wooden door.

hearths (Fig. 7.26). Charred wooden stumps were exposed within the surviving remains of the inner walls—residues of the reinforcing stick framework onto which the daga of the walls was pressed. In addition, the linear daga structure that supported the sliding door mechanism was largely intact, and contained some charred remains of the door itself (Fig 7.27). The presence of a rear storage shelf at the back of the inner room was suggested by a number of ceramic sherds leaning up against the 'step', although this was difficult to define along the outside edge where the daga became more ephemeral (Fig. 7.26).

Artefacts from Dwelling Structures 1 and 2

Ceramics

In total, the two dwelling structures yielded 1291 sherds (26348.9g), of which 118 were diagnostic (Tables 7.7 and 7.8). In terms of total ceramic mass from the two Dwelling Structures, the majority (66.1%) were retrieved from Dwelling Structure 2. This included a number of nearly complete vessels that were trapped *in situ* on the interior floor, reflecting the superior preservation of this house (see Fig. 7.28). By contrast, no complete pots occurred on the floor of Dwelling Structure 1, where all sherds were found mixed up in the wall rubble—another hint that this structure may have been abandoned some time before the rest of the homestead. No sherds from the dwelling structures were suitable for multi-dimensional analysis (Fig. 7.29).

Table 7.7
Quantities of ceramic sherds from Dwelling Structure 1 of SU25.

		Sherds	Mass (g)	% of total sherds
Surface clearance	Diagnostic	1	1.5	0.2
	Adiagnostic	57	379.0	12.4
Wall rubble	Diagnostic	13	256.9	2.8
	Adiagnostic	391	6034.0	84.6
Subtotals	Diagnostic	14	258.4	3.0
	Adiagnostic	448	6413.0	97.0
Totals		462	6671.4	100

Table 7.8
Quantities of ceramic sherds from Dwelling Structure 2.

		Sherds	Mass (g)	% of total sherds
Surface clearance	Diagnostic	14	33.3	1.7
	Adiagnostic	261	675.2	31.5
Wall rubble	Diagnostic	37	713.2	4.4
	Adiagnostic	125	1459.6	15.1
Floor surface	Diagnostic	53	6369.1	6.4
	Adiagnostic	339	10427.1	40.9
Subtotals	Diagnostic	104	7115.6	12.5
	Adiagnostic	725	12561.9	87.5
Totals		829	19677.5	100

Figure 7.28
An intact drinking vessel retrieved from the interior floor of Dwelling Structure 2 (see Fig. 7.29, 3).

Metallurgy

The two dwelling structures yielded a total of 1437.3g of metallurgical debris (Tables 7.9 and 7.10). At Dwelling Structure 1, smelting/flow slag made up 43.8% of this material, with iron ore (magnetite) comprising 30.4%. Copper production was represented by crucible and tuyere fragments, and a small quantity of copper ore. All of the debris was either on the surface of the mound or mixed up in the wall rubble. Two copper objects were recovered: a fragment of a curved copper rod, evidently incomplete, which may have been part of a bangle (#MAR316); and a copper earring (#MAR318) (Fig. 7.30). The material from Dwelling Structure 2 was also dominated by slag, with crucible and tuyere fragments present as well. The only link to iron working might be the 156.4g of magnetite retrieved from the wall rubble, but its presence here does not offer an obvious link to the forge behind the *lapa*.

Material Type	Mass (g)	% of total mass
Smelting/flow slag	277.8	43.8
Iron ore (magnetite)	193.0	30.4
Crucible sherds	84.0	13.2
Tabular slag	53.4	8.4
Frothy glassy slag	14.0	2.2
Copper ore bearing gossan	7.3	1.2
Tuyere fragments	4.0	0.6
Hollow slag droplets	1.1	0.2
Total	634.6	100

Table 7.9 Quantities of metallurgical debris from Dwelling Structure 1 of SU25.

Material Type	Mass (g)	% of total mass
Smelting/Flow slag	358.8	44.7
Tabular slag	208.4	25.9
Iron ore (magnetite)	156.4	19.5
Crucible sherds	68.0	8.5
Frothy glassy slag	10.4	1.3
Copper ore bearing gossan	0.7	0.1
Total	803.0	100

Table 7.10 Quantities of metallurgical debris from Dwelling Structure 2.

Stone

Dwelling Structure 1 yielded two upper grindstones. The smaller grindstone (#MAR8) had two smoothed surfaces. The other (#MAR11) was more rounded so as to be almost spherical. All parts of its surface were worn, but the two flattest sides also had small 'dimples' or pockmarks in the centre, suggestive of hammering or grinding into these surfaces (Fig. 7.31). Two smoothing stones and three upper grindstones were recovered from Dwelling Structure 2. One of the upper grindstones (#MAR44) was found *in situ* on the floor of the front veranda (Fig 7.32).

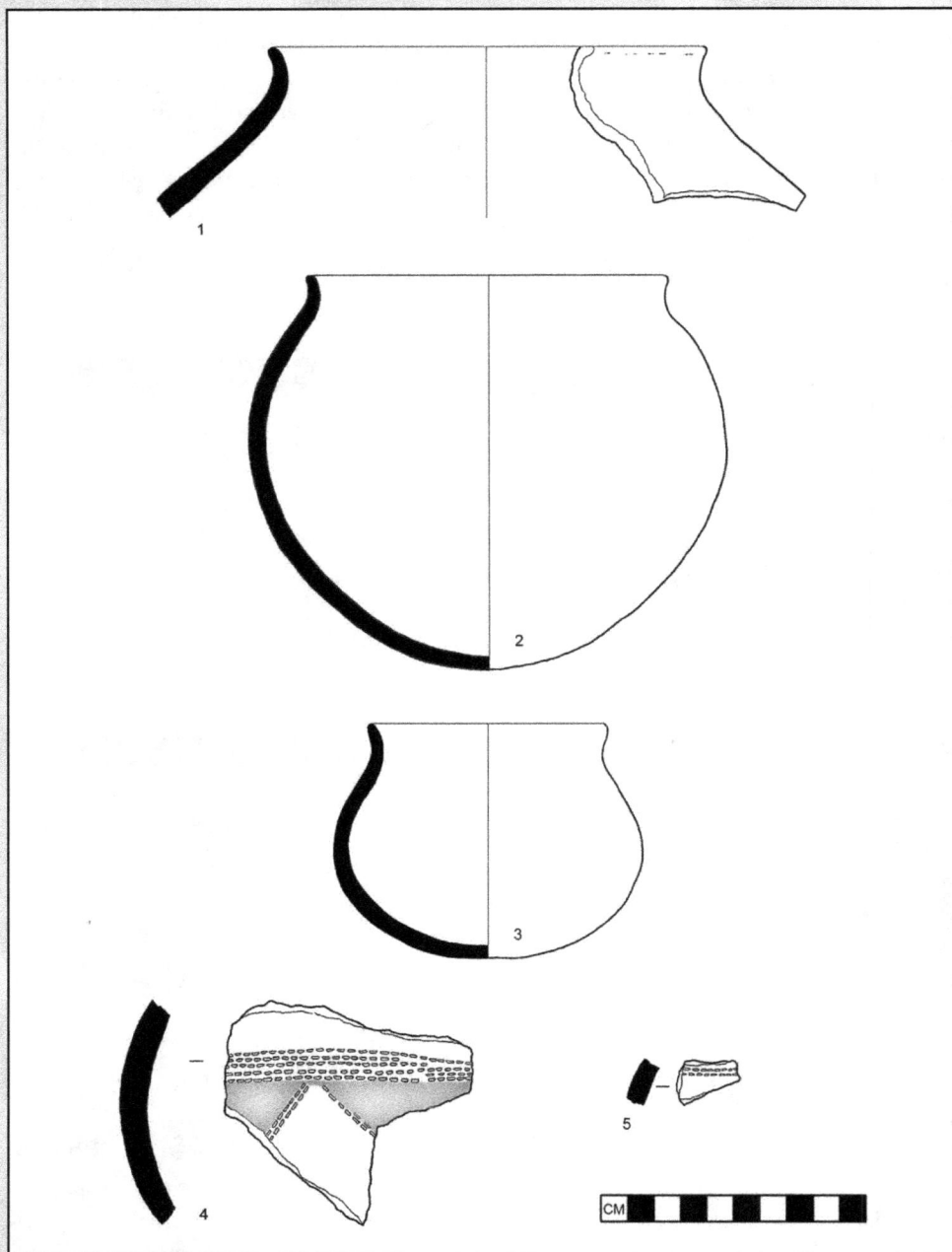

Figure 7.29
Decorated sherds and
representative profiles
from Dwelling Structures
1 and 2 in SU25.

Figure 7.29 Ceramic Descriptions

1. Smooth-necked jar, plain. Profile Mode: 1A. Provenance: SU25, Dwelling Structure 1, structural rubble. Cat. No. V706.

2. Smooth-necked jar, plain. Profile Mode: 1A. Provenance: SU25, M25, Dwelling Structure 2, interior floor surface. Cat. No. V589.

3. Smooth-necked jar, plain. Profile Mode: 1A. Provenance: SU25, M25, Dwelling Structure 2, interior floor surface. Cat. No. V601.

4. Decorated body sherd, insufficient profile. Horizontal band of comb-stamping above pendant triangles with black graphite infill and comb-stamped outline. Provenance: SU25, M25, Dwelling Structure 2, structural rubble. Cat. No. V628.

5. Decorated sherd, no profile information. Horizontal band of comb-stamping. Provenance: SU25, M25, Dwelling Structure 2, structural rubble. Cat. No. V607.

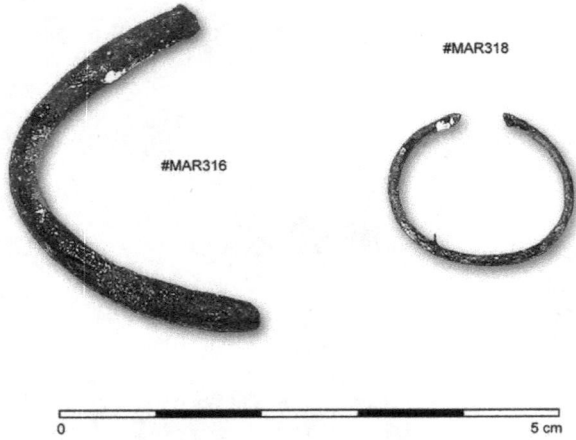

Figure 7.30
Copper objects found in
Dwelling Structure 1 of
SU25.

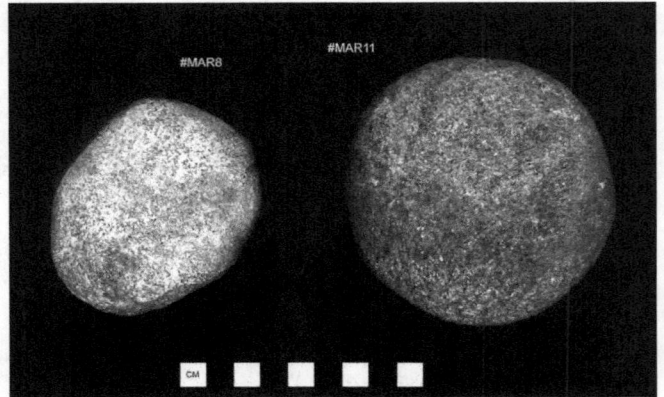

#MAR316

#MAR318

0   5 cm

Figure 7.31
Stone artefacts from
Dwelling Structure 1.

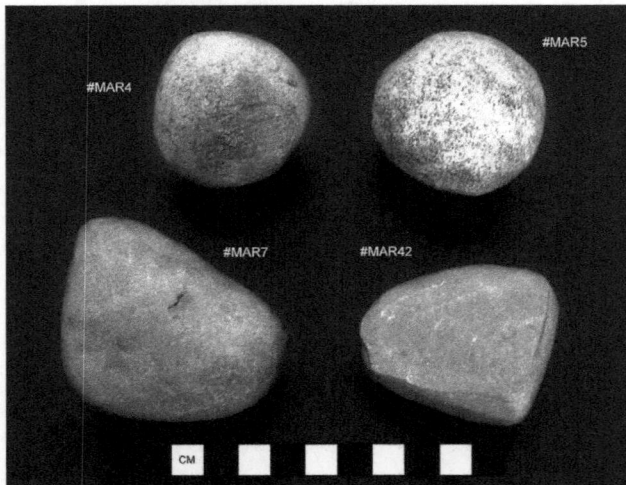

#MAR8   #MAR11

CM

Figure 7.32
Stone artefacts from
Dwelling Structure 2.

#MAR4   #MAR5

#MAR7   #MAR42

CM

Copper Smelting Site

As previously discussed, it was noted during preliminary survey of SU25 that the surface of the shallow midden deposits outside the northern and eastern perimeter walls of the homestead contained significant quantities of metallurgical debris. On closer inspection in the area behind *lapa* M12, scattered lumps of reddish-brown fired daga were found, which indicated that there might have been smelting furnaces in this vicinity. A grid was laid out around the most concentrated daga, incorporating a section of the M12 *lapa* wall. This area was cleared of grass and loose stones, and trowelled clean (Fig. 7.33).

A compact surface of brownish 'gritty' soil was exposed beneath 10 to 20 mm of humic topsoil. This surface contrasted with the natural black turf soil beneath. Much of the slag and copper ore recovered from this area was resting on this horizon, and it was probably the original working surface. Despite the disturbance caused by fallen stones from the back wall of *lapa* M12, it was possible to discern several concentrated patches of furnace daga, three of which were *in situ* furnaces (Fig. 7.34). The other patches may also have represented furnaces, but their preservation was too poor to be certain.

Approximately 1.0 m to the north of the furnaces, a flat rock was embedded in the ground, its surface marked by cupules and pecking (Figs. 7.33 and 7.34). This may have been used as an 'anvil' stone for the breaking up of copper ore prior to being placed in the furnaces (see Stayt 1931: 64). The most intact of the furnaces, named Furnace 1, was chosen for excavation.

Figure 7.33
The author clears the area of the Copper Smelting Site on the northern edge of M12 at SU25. The flat 'anvil' rock is visible near the centre (see Fig. 7.34).

Figure 7.34
Plan of the Copper Smelting
Site on the northern edge
of M12 at SU25.

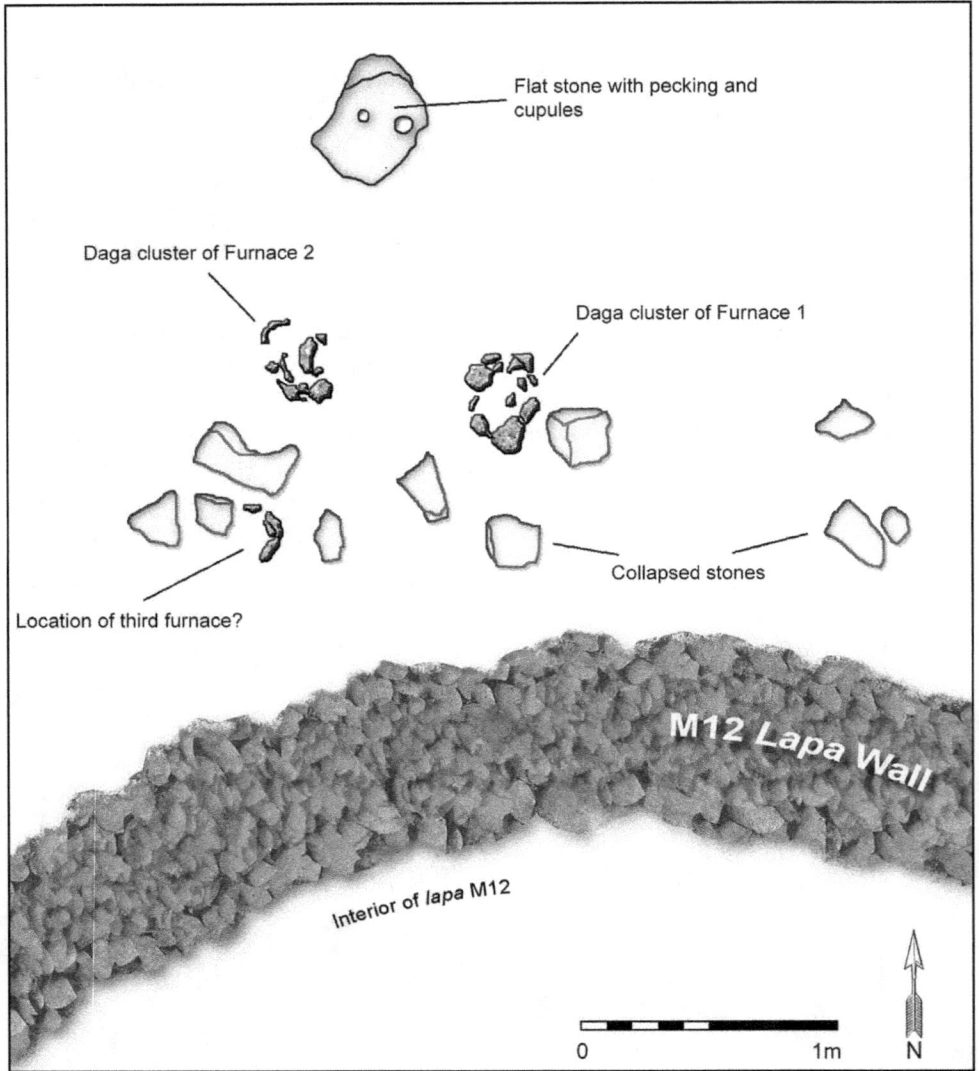

Figure 7.34
Plan of the Copper Smelting
Site on the northern edge
of M12 at SU25.

The furnace was a shallow oval shaped bowl cut into the ground surface, and orientated approximately north-west to south-east (Fig. 7.35). The maximum length of the cut was 0.64 m, and the maximum width at the northern end was 0.33 m, narrowing down to 0.22 m at the southern end. The eastern wall had slumped slightly due to a rock fall nearby. The furnace cavity had a rounded base, and a maximum depth of 0.19 m.

The inner walls of the furnace were lined with multiple layers of reddish-brown fired daga, each between 10 and 20 mm thick. Although the lining at the northern end of the furnace had been dismantled, it was possible to count at least five separate linings in the better-preserved southern half (Fig. 7.36). A plating of slag adhered to the innermost daga lining on the western edge of the furnace. A thin layer of grey, powdery ash was discovered at the base, filling a hole in the daga 'floor' that was presumably created when the smelted copper was removed.

There were not many broken pieces of daga found in the vicinity of the furnace, which suggests that the structure had little, if any, superstructure above the original working surface. Consequently, the furnace was probably a simple pit or bowl-type structure without a daga 'roof' or covering (see Friede & Steel 1988; Collette 1993).

No obvious tuyere port was found, although it is possible that this may have been situated at the northern end where the daga has been removed. A shallow depression in the ground on the edge of the furnace at this end may have been associated with it. If the tuyere was positioned here, it certainly seems likely that the furnace lining would need to have been broken away in order to remove it, along with the copper, after the smelt.

The daga cluster approximately 0.80 m to the west was not fully excavated, but was exposed sufficiently to confirm that this was another furnace similar in size, shape and orientation to Furnace 1. It seems likely that other furnaces, as yet undefined, also occur in the vicinity, and indeed around much of the northern edge of SU25.

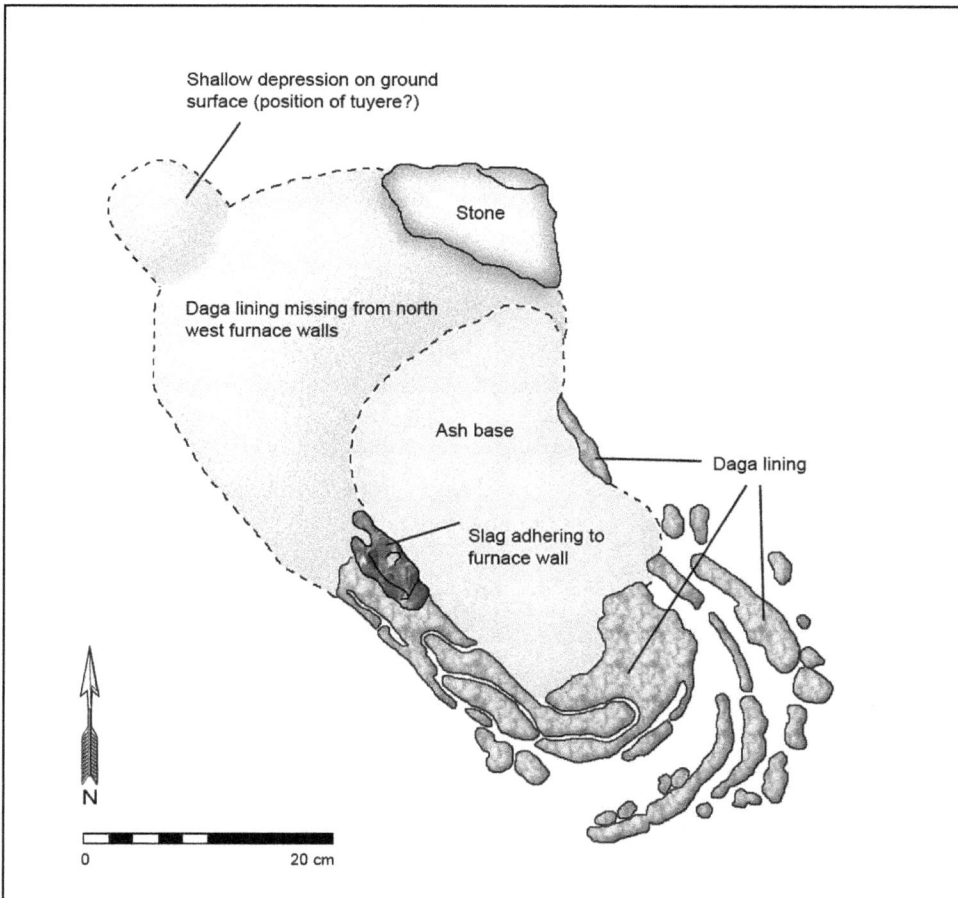

Figure 7.35
Plan of excavated Furnace 1 in the Copper Smelting Site of SU25.

Figure 7.36 (right)
Copper Smelting Furnace 1
showing pieces of displaced
daga lining.

Figure 7.37 (below)
Iron object found close to
Furnaces 1 and 2.

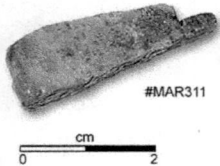

#MAR311

cm
0   2

Metallurgy from the Copper Smelting Site

This discussion excludes the 806.2g of loose vitrified furnace lining found in and around Furnace 1. As this lining is included in the table below, the percentages presented there differ accordingly (Table 7.11).

Not including the lining, a total of 628.1g of metallurgical debris was collected from the fill inside the furnace cavity and the area immediately around the structure. Of this, smelting/flow slag formed a significant 75.1% of the material, indicating that these furnaces represented 'primary' smelting. Crucible sherds represented a comparatively low 2.7%, but their presence here indicates that refining was probably practiced somewhere nearby.

Although only 2 small pieces of ore-bearing gossan were retrieved from within the excavated zone itself, larger quantities of this material were visible on the ground surface in the surrounding area and were likely to have been associated with the smelting activity here. It is perhaps surprising that no tuyere fragments were found here. A small wedge-shaped piece of iron (#MAR311) was retrieved from the working surface between Furnaces 1 and 2, the purpose of which remains undetermined (Fig. 7.37).

Table 7.11

Quantities of metallurgical debris from the Copper Smelting Site at SU25 (percentages incorporate vitrified furnace lining).

Material Type	Mass (g)	% of total mass
Vitrified furnace lining	806.2	56.2
Smelting/flow slag	471.6	32.9
Tabular slag	107.6	7.5
Frothy glassy slag	29.3	2.0
Crucible sherds	16.8	1.2
Hollow slag droplets	1.5	0.1
Copper ore bearing gossan	1.3	0.1
Total	1434.3	100

Discussion

The most significant observations from SU25 are that the scale of metal working going on here was intense, and that the homestead appeared to be going through a process of expansion and remodelling. Part of this remodelling involved blocking off the cattle track, both at its mouth and along its route around the kraal. Although we cannot confirm exactly when the blocking occurred, the important point is that, as demonstrated by the stratigraphy of Midden 2, the homestead was still occupied and continued to function after this had taken place. The deliberate blocking of the cattle track is a clear indication that at some stage during the occupation of SU25, the corralling of cattle inside the homestead had ceased.

Furthermore, the quantity of metallurgical debris, such as slag, crucible sherds and residual pieces of copper ore found in the middens and, to a lesser extent, in the dwelling structures, points to a scale of production that must have far outweighed the needs of this particular homestead alone. The intensity of this production, combined with the remodelling that accompanied it, suggests that the occupants of this homestead had actually become specialist metal producers.

The emphasis at SU25 is clearly on copper. Although working in iron is hinted at with the relatively modest quantities of magnetite retrieved (the iron ore of choice) and the presence of the iron forge behind *lapa* M25, this evidence is overwhelmed by the quantity of copper production debris. Furthermore, no iron smelting furnaces were observed at or around this homestead.

The presence of the copper furnaces behind *lapa* M12 confirmed that the process of primary smelting was being undertaken at SU25 and that, like the copper refining annexes at the two *kgosing*, this process was spatially associated with the back courtyards of households. No copper refining areas were identified at SU25, but as we have seen, the presence of crucible sherds here suggests that refining was going on somewhere at this homestead in addition to primary smelting. The organisation of metal production at Marothodi is a theme we return to in Chapter Ten.

The density of metallurgical debris in the sampled middens seemed relatively consistent throughout the depth of each deposit, indicating that copper production had been undertaken here throughout the whole occupation of SU25. The indication that some domestic structures within the homestead, like Dwelling Structure 1, became abandoned while activity in SU25 clearly continued, lends support to the idea of a significant shift in the functioning of this part of the town prior to its terminal abandonment.

The production of surplus copper raises questions as to the destination of this commodity. The two *kgosing*, which did not engage in primary smelting themselves, may have been among the recipients, either from trade or through tribute. Indeed, there is quite a close spatial relationship between SU25 and the 'Secondary' *Kgosing* in particular. The orientation of the SU25 cattle track/formal entrance towards Entrance B of the 'Secondary' *Kgosing* may reflect a special association between the two homesteads (see Fig. 5.4). The possibility that SU25 was a specialist copper producer for the 'royal Court' is worthy of consideration.

Figure 7.38
Graph showing the
percentages of different
types of metallurgical
debris from the features
excavated in SU25.
All features share a
high occurrence of
smelting/flow slag.

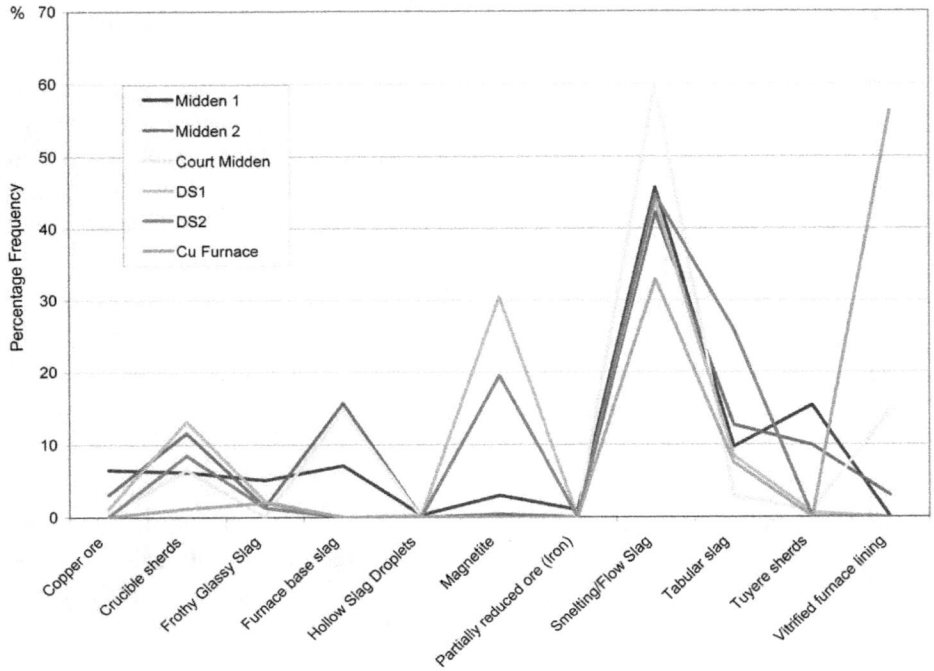

Figure 7.38
Graph showing the
percentages of different
types of metallurgical
debris from the features
excavated in SU25.
All features share a
high occurrence of
smelting/flow slag.

All of the features excavated at SU25 had a similar material profile in terms of the different types of metallurgical debris represented. Most strikingly, but perhaps as we might expect, there was a clear emphasis on smelting/flow slag at all sites (Fig. 7.38). This is a statistical indicator of the general predominance of primary smelting at this homestead.

The presence of bone and ceramic scrapers in the middens indicated that, in addition to metal production, hide working was also practiced at SU25. Continuing the trend observed in the previous chapter at the two *kgosing*, the court midden at SU25 contained the lowest density of scrapers, with only 54.7 per cubic metre. By contrast, Midden 2 at the southern end of the cattle track contained 150.7 scrapers per cubic metre, and Midden 1 had the highest density with 246.3 scrapers per cubic metre. In all middens, bone seems to have been the preferred material. Of all scrapers, 82.4% were bone, and only 17.6% were pot sherds (Fig. 7.39).

The stratigraphy of both Midden 2 and the court midden included periodic 'capping layers' of sterile reddish-brown soil between the layers of ash (Figs. 7.14 and 7.19). While this feature has not been observed at other Sotho-Tswana sites, examples of similar capping layers have been recorded in Ndebele middens in present day Limpopo and Mpumalanga provinces, where the practice is interpreted as a reflection of Nguni fears of ash as a potentially dangerous substance that needed to be monitored (Loubser 1994; Huffman &

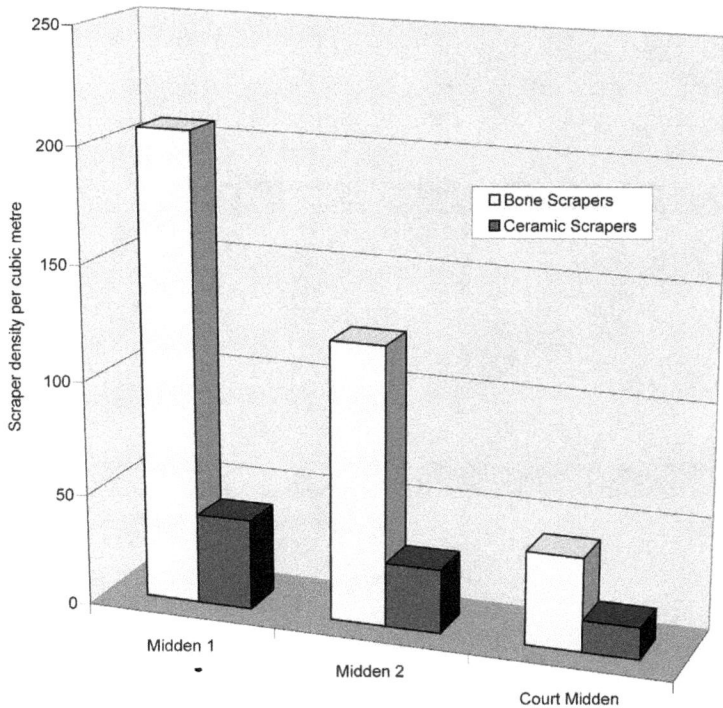

Figure 7.39
Bar chart showing the density of bone and ceramic scrapers in each of the three middens excavated at SU25.

Steel 1996; Schoeman 1998). The capping layers help to prevent the ash from falling into the hands of 'witches' who would use it to harm the households who produced it. Thus, this practice may have similar motivations to the placing of ash middens in the centre of homesteads which, as previously discussed, is a common occurrence at Marothodi.

If the use of capping layers in middens is considered to be "a good indicator of people with a worldview that originated in the Nguni areas of KwaZulu-Natal" (Schoeman 1998: 51), then the evidence for this practice at SU25 may add weight to the suggestion that the occupants of this homestead were of recent Nguni origin. Alternatively, it might simply be a reflection of the deeper Nguni origins of the whole chiefdom.

Certainly, the Marothodi ceramic styles continue to reflect Nguni roots. In common with the decorated sherds from the two *kgosing*, the sherds from SU25 are also dominated by comb-stamping and pendant triangle motifs (Table. 7.12). As noted in the previous chapter, these attributes are characteristic of the *Uitkomst* ceramic facies (Huffman 2007).

In summary, Settlement Unit 25 might be considered 'atypical' in a number of ways, particularly in regard to the intensive copper production going on here, and the influence this seems to have had on the spatial organisation of the homestead. In the following chapter, we try to place SU25 in context by comparing it with another commoner homestead that had not been affected to such a degree by processes of specialist production.

Table 7.12
Decorative techniques on
diagnostic sherds from
SU25.

Context	Comb-stamping	Rim-nicking	Punctates	Coloured bands	Appliqué
Midden 1	12	0	0	0	1
Midden 2	7	0	1	0	0
Court Midden	5	0	1	0	0
Dwelling Structure 2	2	0	0	0	0
Total	26	0	2	0	1

Table 7.13
Ceramic profile types from
SU25.

Context	Smooth-necked jar (1A)	Short-necked jar (1B)	Straight open bowl (2B)	Necked bowl (2A)	Pot Lid (3)	Undetermined
Midden 1	79	2	19	0	1	11
Midden 2	74	0	6	0	1	8
Court Midden	14	0	2	0	0	4
Dwelling Structure 1	11	0	1	0	3	0
Dwelling structure 2	45	0	3	0	3	2
Total	223	2	31	0	8	25

Table 7.14
Multi-dimensional analysis
of ceramics from SU25.

Vessel	Context	Class	Vessel	Decoration	Decoration	Description
900	Midden 1	2	1A	2	2	Smooth-necked jar with a single horizontal band of comb-stamping on the rim

Figure 7.40
The daga floors and wall foundations of dwelling structures can be well preserved beneath
the hard dome of wall rubble that usually covers them. Here, field team members proceed
with the excavation of Dwelling Structure 2, in *lapa* M25 of SU25.

Chapter Eight
Hearth and Home

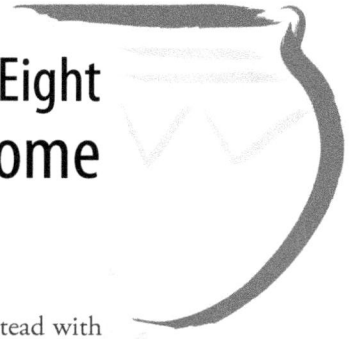

Having explored and sampled SU25, a non-elite or 'commoner' homestead with such a strong emphasis on copper production, it was important to be able to compare it with another homestead of similar size and socio-political status within Marothodi. Settlement Unit 26 seemed most appropriate for such a comparison. It occupies a similar position in the town relative to the royal centres of power (see Fig. 5.4), and given the almost equal number of *malapa* to SU25 it seems to have been roughly equivalent in terms of population. We begin by examining key elements of the spatial organisation of SU26, and then turn to an account of the excavations conducted within the homestead.

Spatial organisation of Settlement Unit 26

The diameter of SU26 is approximately 110 metres east to west, and 95 metres north to south (Fig. 8.1). The complex organisation of SU26 contrasts with the simple layout of SU25, and seems closer in form to the Molokwane type walling associated with western Sotho-Tswana (Huffman 2007), which characterises other towns in the region. Nevertheless, some key concepts in spatial organisation are clearly shared with SU25. As with the other homesteads explored thus far, we start by identifying the centre of political power.

The Cattle Kraals and Court Complex

In the central zone there are 12 identifiable enclosures of various sizes (E1 to E12), four 'secondary enclosures' (SE1 to SE4) and various stretches of walling controlling and subdividing the intervening spaces (Fig. 8.1). The large open space in the centre of the homestead, SE2, is partially subdivided and probably served as cattle management space. It may also have accommodated public gatherings of people.

The formal entrance into the homestead is via a prominent passageway on the north-west side, between *malapa* M15 and M16. This may be comparable to the internal cattle track in SU25, but here it is simply formed by extensions of household walls and is not a separate feature. Once through this entrance, cattle enter a secondary enclosure, SE1, from where they could be herded in either of two directions, 'Route A' or 'Route B'. Route A leads north-east through a stone 'gateway' into a corridor, over a midden (referred to here as 'Midden 1'), past the small enclosure E7 and towards E8, where they enter SE2 from the east side. The wall in front of *malapa* M21 to M23 is for cattle control (Fig. 8.1). The cattle could also continue around to the south and enter the area in which enclosures E9 and E10 are dominant. This area incorporated a court complex. It is significant that along Route A, as we have seen at other homesteads, cattle pass over a midden before going

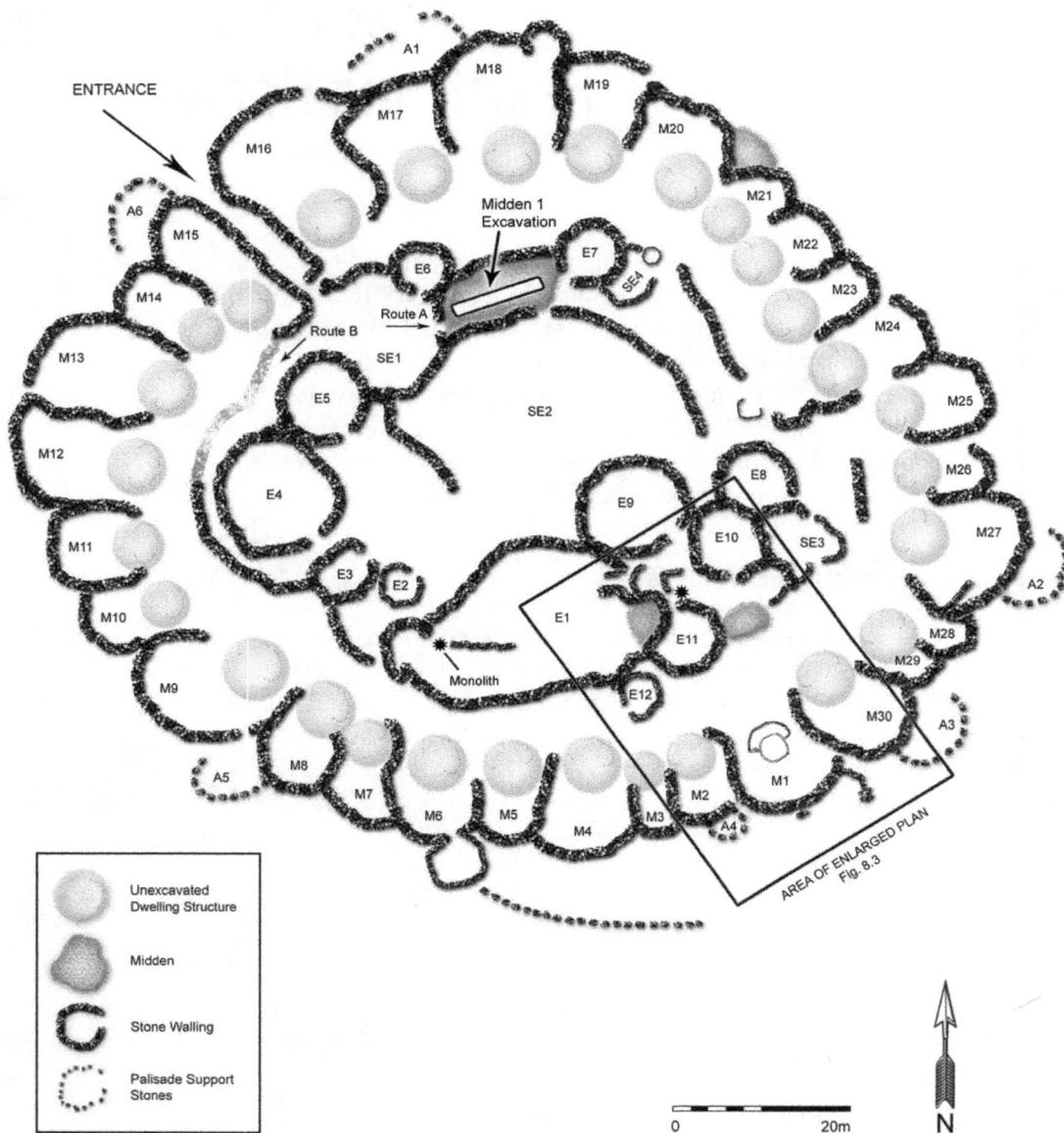

Figure 8.1
Map of Settlement Unit 26 showing the location of the Midden 1 excavation, and the enlarged plan of *lapa* M1 and the court complex in Fig. 8.3.

through the court complex and into the heart of the homestead. The entrance to the court complex is from the south-east, opposite *lapa* M30. The main opening here contains another midden, and a wide passageway leads, via a monolith, past entrances into E10, E11, E9, and ultimately into the largest enclosure, E1. The headman's private *kamore* is likely to have been in either E10 or E11, while E9 may accommodated his personal herd of cattle, and may also have been the site of an 'ancestral graveyard' (see Huffman 1986b; Pistorius 1996). The presence of a monolith at the western end of E1, and a midden at its eastern end near the court, imbues this large enclosure with a degree of ceremonial significance beyond that of a simple kraal, and it may have incorporated the *kgotla* (Fig. 8.1).

It is instructive to compare the spatial organisation of SU26 with SEL1, a slightly smaller homestead at the contemporary Kwena Modimosana capital of Molokwane, some 33 km to the south-east (Pistorius 1992, 1996). There are two main central kraals in SEL1, labelled EKC5 and EKC1, which are entered from a secondary enclosure in the middle of the homestead (Fig. 8.2). The secondary enclosure is only accessible from the east side, through an opening elaborated with a set of four flanking stone platforms and small enclosures, which are collectively identified as the main court complex. One of the small enclosures, EKC3, has "an exceptionally high wall (2,0m) and a small, low entrance covered by a lintel" (Pistorius 1992: 63). While the presence of the low lintel might suggest that this was a small

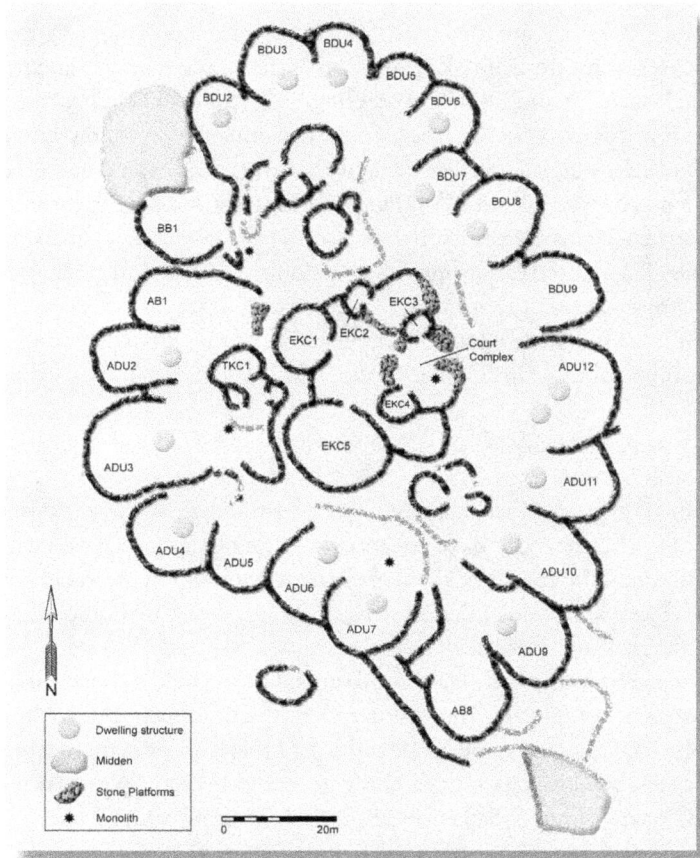

Figure 8.2
Map of SEL1 at Molokwane
(after Pistorius 1992).

stock enclosure, Pistorius identifies this as the *kgotla* of the headman, although he seems to mean a 'private council chamber', or *kamore* as we are calling them at Marothodi.

The ceremonial significance of this area is emphasised by the occurrence of a monolith close to the entrance of EKC3. The senior *lapa* at SEL1, labelled ADU12, is identified by virtue of its size and its position opposite the entrance to the court complex. The low wall in front of *lapa* BDU9 (Fig. 8.2) is similar in position and orientation to the guiding walls in front of *malapa* M21 to M23 and M26 at SU26, and probably had a similar function (Fig. 8.1). They helped to prevent cattle from wandering into households as they were herded past. In the previous chapter we observed similar guiding walls at Boschoek (see Fig. 7.4).

Although the court complex at SU26 does not possess any large formal platforms like those at SEL1, there is a notable similarity in the position and orientation of the two small enclosures E10 and E11, when compared to EKC3 and EKC4 at the Molokwane home-stead (Figs. 8.1 and 8.2). The court complexes of each site also contain a monolith in very similar locations near the headman's *kamore*, symbolising the ceremonial and political sig-nificance of this space.

The midden at the eastern end of E1 may be associated with activities in the *kgotla*, but the main court midden is tentatively identified in the space between the entrances to E1 and E9, where a deeper ash deposit has accumulated between the walls of the adjacent enclo-sures, opposite a monolith (Fig. 8.3).

Route B is an alternative route for cattle to take upon entering the homestead (Fig. 8.1). It turns southward from SE1, and runs along a passageway that curves around the outside of enclosures E5 and E4 before entering SE2, from where it has direct access to enclosures E2 to E5. It is possible that these enclosures include a second court complex, associated with the *malapa* on the western edge of the homestead. Some of the largest *malapa* occur here, such as M9, M12 and M13. Furthermore, M9 and M13 have entrances/exits directly from their back courtyards, a privilege that appears to be associated with high status households (Fig. 8.1). These factors raise the possibility that there may be two distinct 'centres', reflect-ing different kin groups at SU26. But if this is the case, it seems likely that the senior court complex was situated on the eastern side, at the opposite end to the main entrance to the homestead (see Huffman 1986b).

The Domestic Sphere

Thirty individual *malapa* have been identified at SU26, most of which contained the fa-miliar circular mounds of collapsed dwelling structures, along with various other domestic buildings indicated by their orthostatic foundation stones. Having identified the court complex we would anticipate that the senior domestic households were situated close to its entrance, and they are identified at *malapa* M1 and M30 (Figs. 8.1 and 8.3). Both of these *malapa* have relatively large courtyards, but it would be speculative to suggest which of the two was occupied by the senior wife of the headman. The walling arrangements hint that M30 was the first to be built, and might therefore be senior. The construction sequence of Tswana *malapa* was very carefully governed by principles that dictated the precedence of senior dwellings (Mackenzie 1871: 367; Mönnig 1967: 212).

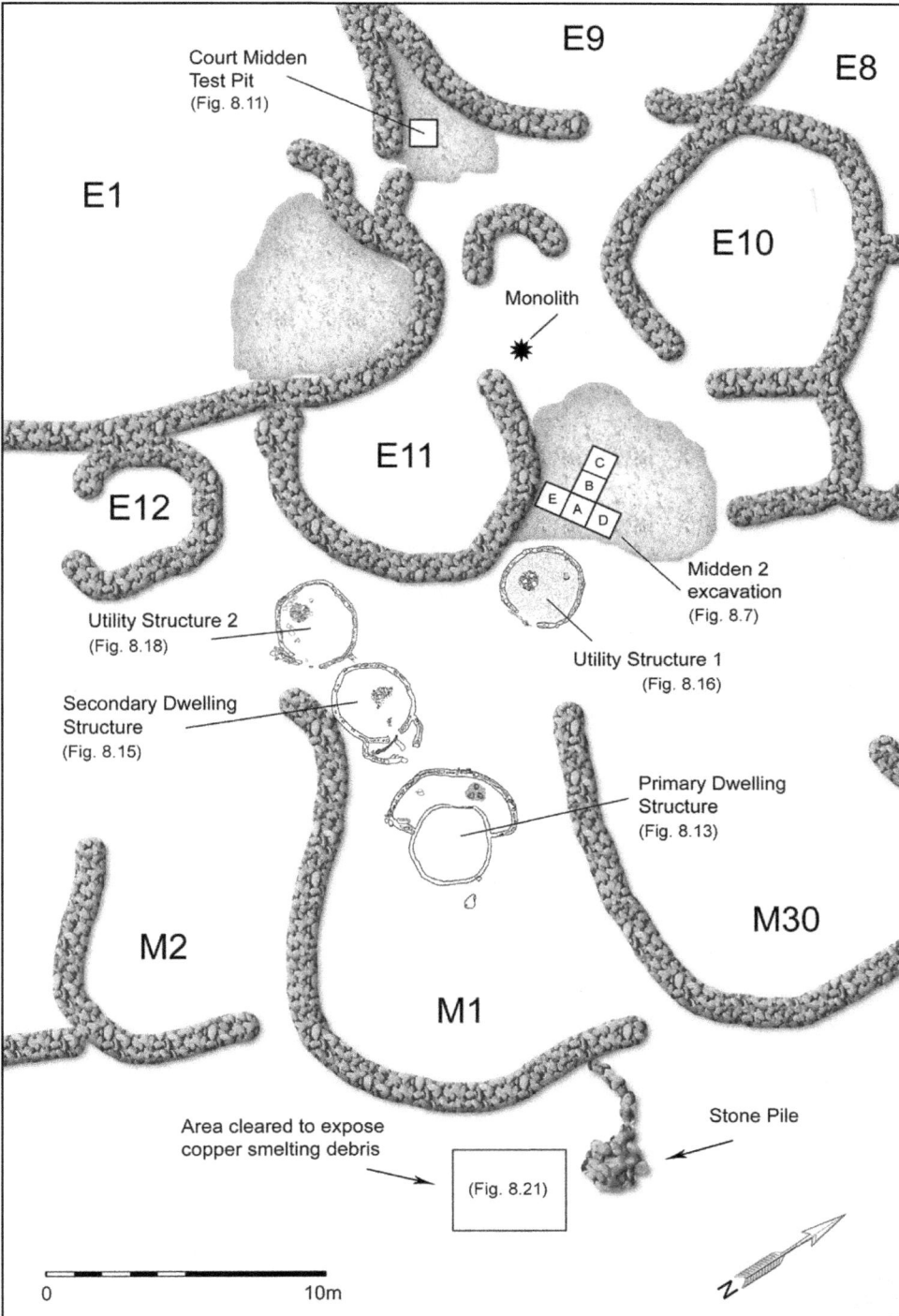

Figure 8.3
Plan of *lapa* M1 and the court complex in SU26, showing the features excavated in M1 and the locations of the trenches excavated into Midden 2 and the court midden (see Fig. 8.1 for orientation).

Whatever the precise ranking order of households, these senior *malapa* are directly oppo-site the formal cattle entrance to the homestead. This reflects one of the spatial concepts of the Central Cattle Pattern model, according to which;

> …the front of a settlement was reserved for public, secular and dangerous activities, while the back was restricted to private, sacred, and life-giving functions… This spatial arrange-ment meant that the most important person lived at the back in the most protected posi-tion. (Huffman 1986b: 300)

This arrangement, however, is not always expressed in homestead layout at Marothodi. We have seen at SU25 that the *lapa* identified as the senior household is situated next to, and not opposite, the formal entrance to the homestead (see Fig. 7.1).

At various locations around the outside of the perimeter walling, a number of 'annexes' can be identified (A1 to A6) behind *malapa* M17, M27, M30, M2, M9 and M15 respectively. These are defined by the double rows of large stones in the style observed at the Copper Refining Annex behind *lapa* M1 of the 'Secondary' *Kgosing* (see Fig. 6.21), which are in-terpreted as supports for wooden palisade fencing.

Excavations at Settlement Unit 26

Excavation targets at SU26 were selected to retrieve data that could be compared both with the commoner homestead SU25, and also with the elite homesteads, the 'Primary' *Kgosing* and the 'Secondary' *Kgosing*. One of the senior *malapa* at SU26 was excavated (M1) and three middens were sampled: domestic Middens 1 and 2, and the court midden (Figs. 8.1 and 8.3).

Midden 1

Midden 1 is located in the Route A corridor through which cattle were herded on their way around the kraal complex, just to the east of the opening from the secondary enclo-sure SE1 (Fig. 8.1). A trench measuring 1.0 x 7.0 m was excavated into the midden in 0.05 m spits, and a total of 1.31 cubic metres of deposit was removed.

The simple stratigraphy consisted of a dark grey root horizon up to 0.10 m thick, over-laying the main body of grey powdery ash. This was deposited directly onto the natural underlying turf soil. The maximum depth of the midden was 0.24 m (Fig. 8.4, a). The ash layer contained occasional flecks of charcoal. As the top layer was not an archaeologically meaningful deposit, the midden was treated as a single unit for analysis.

Artefacts from Midden 1

Ceramics

Of the 665 (7503.6g) sherds recovered from Midden 1 (Table 8.1) 53 were diagnostic. The overall density of ceramic sherds was 5727.9g per cubic metre of excavated soil. None were suitable for multi-dimensional analysis (Fig. 8.5).

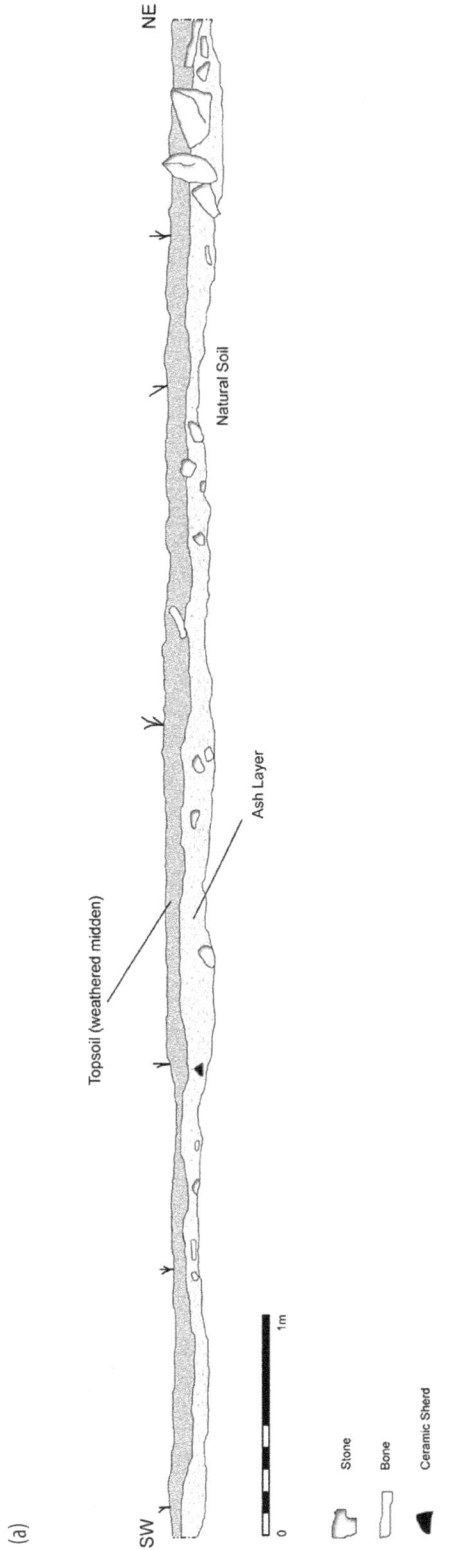

(a)

SW

NE

Topsoil (weathered midden)

Natural Soil

Ash Layer

0 1m

Stone
Bone
Ceramic Sherd

(b)

(c)

Figure 8.4
(a) The south facing section of Midden 1 in SU26.
(b) All Marothodi middens contained faunal remains, like this fragment of a cow skull.
(c) Against the backdrop of the Pilanesberg hills, ash from a Marothodi midden is carefully sieved to retrieve tiny artefacts.

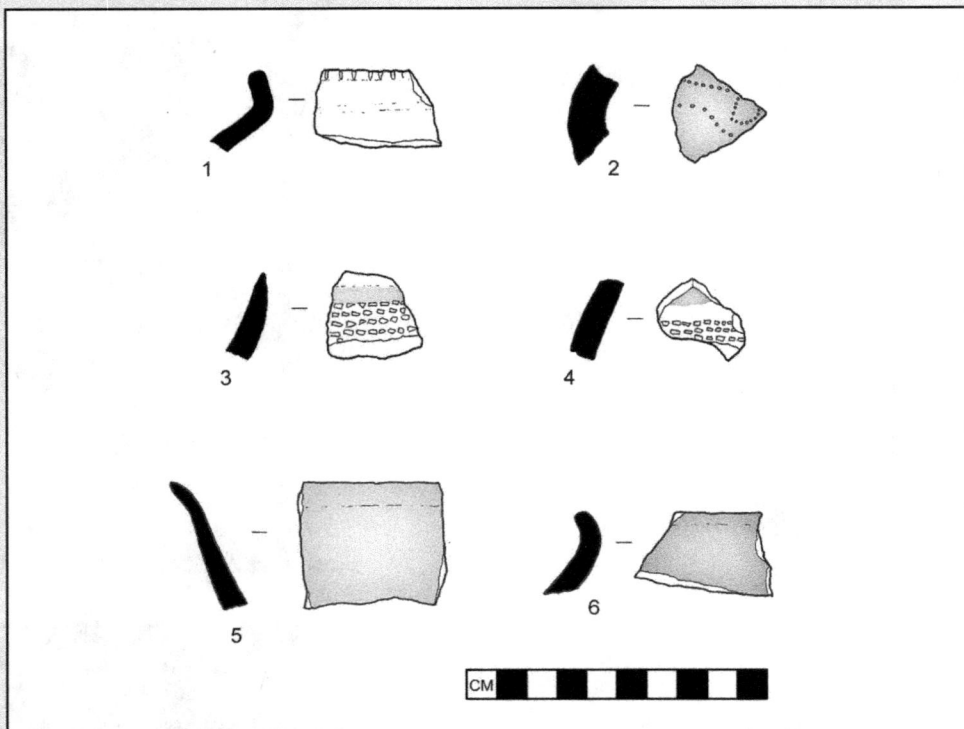

Figure 8.5
Decorated sherds and
representative profiles from
Midden 1.

Figure 8.5 Ceramic Descriptions

1. Rim sherd of short-necked jar with nicking on the rim. Insufficient profile to ascertain the possibility of additional decoration. Profile Mode: 1B. Provenance: SU26, Midden 1, Square D, Level 4. Cat. No. V483.

2. Decorated body sherd, no profile information. Lines or geometric patterns of punctates. Provenance: SU26, Midden 1, Square D, Level 1. Cat. No. V491.

3. Decorated rim sherd, no profile information. Horizontal band of comb-stamping with black graphite above. Rim is abraded to a point. Provenance: SU26, Midden 1, Square G, Level 2. Cat. No. V506.

4. Decorated sherd, no profile information. Horizontal band of comb-stamping with black graphite above. Provenance: SU26, Midden 1, Square G, Level 2. Cat. No. V507.

5. Necked bowl, plain with black colouration (possibly burnt). Profile Mode: 2A. Provenance: SU26, Midden 1, Square E, Level 4. Cat. No. V495.

6. Smooth-necked jar, plain with black colouration (possibly burnt). Profile Mode: 1A. Provenance: SU26, Midden 1, Square D, Level 3. Cat. No. V484.

	Sherds	Mass (g)	Mass (g) per m³	% of total sherds
Diagnostic	53	677.0	516.8	8.0
Adiagnostic	612	6826.6	5211.1	92.0
Total	665	7503.6	5727.9	100

Table 8.1
Quantities of ceramic sherds from Midden 1 of SU26.

Metallurgy

The only metallurgical debris retrieved from Midden 1 was a single piece of smelting/flow slag, with a mass of 195.58g. One finished metal object was retrieved (#MAR83), a flat oar-shaped iron blade with pointed tang (Fig. 8.6).

Scraping tools

Midden 1 yielded 131 scrapers, of which 23 were abraded ceramic sherds and 108 were recycled bone.

Clay Figurines

Three small fragments of moulded clay were recovered from Midden 1, including two amorphous pieces that remain uninterpreted (#MAR87 and #MAR88), and a cylindrical fragment (#MAR90) which could be the broken base of a cow horn (Fig. 8.6).

Stone

A white, spherical upper grindstone was found in Midden 1 (#MAR30) with a diameter of 70 mm (Fig. 8.6).

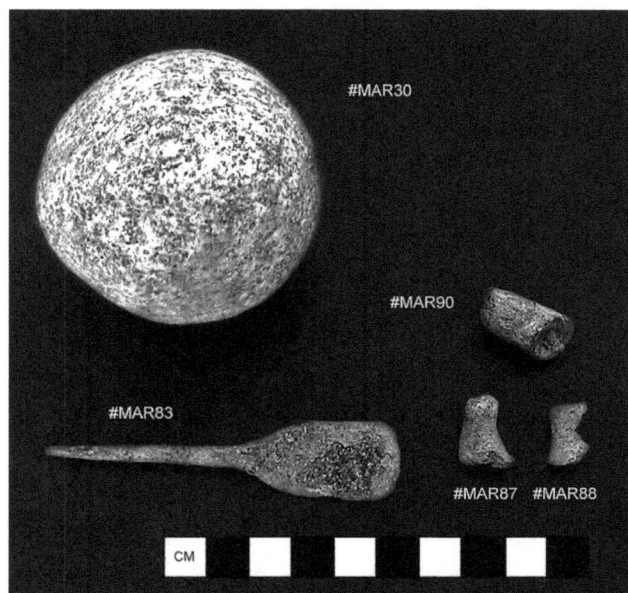

Figure 8.6
Artefacts from Midden 1 of SU25.

Midden 2

This midden is located at the entrance to the court complex in front of *malapa* M1 and M30, immediately to rear of Utility Structure 1 in *lapa* M1 (Fig. 8.3). It had accumulated some 0.30 - 0.35 m above the walking surface of the *malapa* and the nearby enclosures. It was chosen for excavation because of its depth, and because of its domestic context, although its proximity to the court complex was also considered.

Five 1.0 x 1.0 m squares were excavated in the centre of the midden (Fig. 8.3) in arbitrary spits 0.05 m deep. The T-shape of the trench optimised the volume of accessible deposit by avoiding most of the outcropping rocks around which the midden had accumulated.

The maximum depth of the deposit within the excavated trench was 0.36 m at the northern end, becoming shallower towards *lapa* M1 to the south (Fig. 8.7). Approximately 1.7 cubic metres of deposit were excavated in total. The simple stratigraphy consisted of a 0.04 m crust of humic soil and weathered ash overlying the main deposit of grey powdery ash, with occasional flecks of charcoal and small stone inclusions. No additional stratigraphy was evident in any of the excavated sections. The midden had accumulated over a combination of the underlying natural soil and bedrock, and was treated as a single unit for analysis.

Artefacts from Midden 2

Ceramics

A total of 268 sherds (3343.2g) were excavated, of which 26 were diagnostic (Table 8.2). The density of ceramic sherds was a relatively low 1966.6g per excavated cubic metre of deposit. No sherds were suitable for multi-dimensional analysis (Fig. 8.8).

Table 8.2
Quantities of ceramic sherds from Midden 2 of SU26.

	Sherds	Mass (g)	Mass (g) per m³	% of total sherds
Diagnostic	26	410.2	241.3	9.7
Adiagnostic	242	2933.0	1725.3	90.3
Total	268	3343.2	1966.6	100

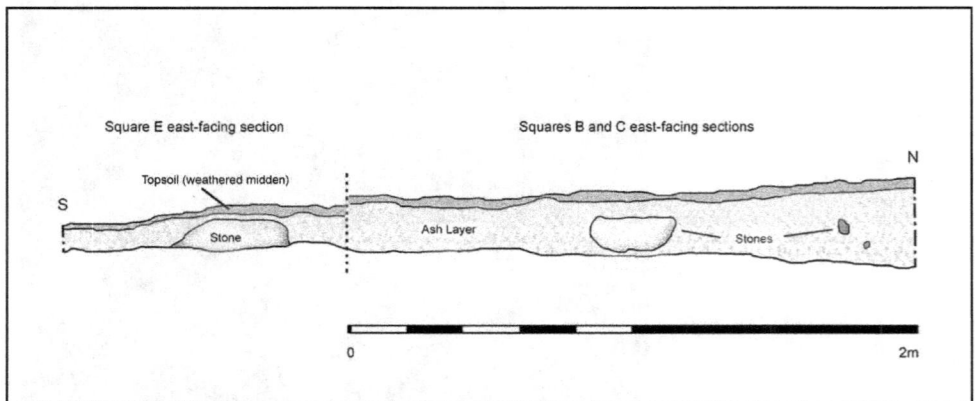

Figure 8.7
East facing sections of squares E, B and C of Midden 2.

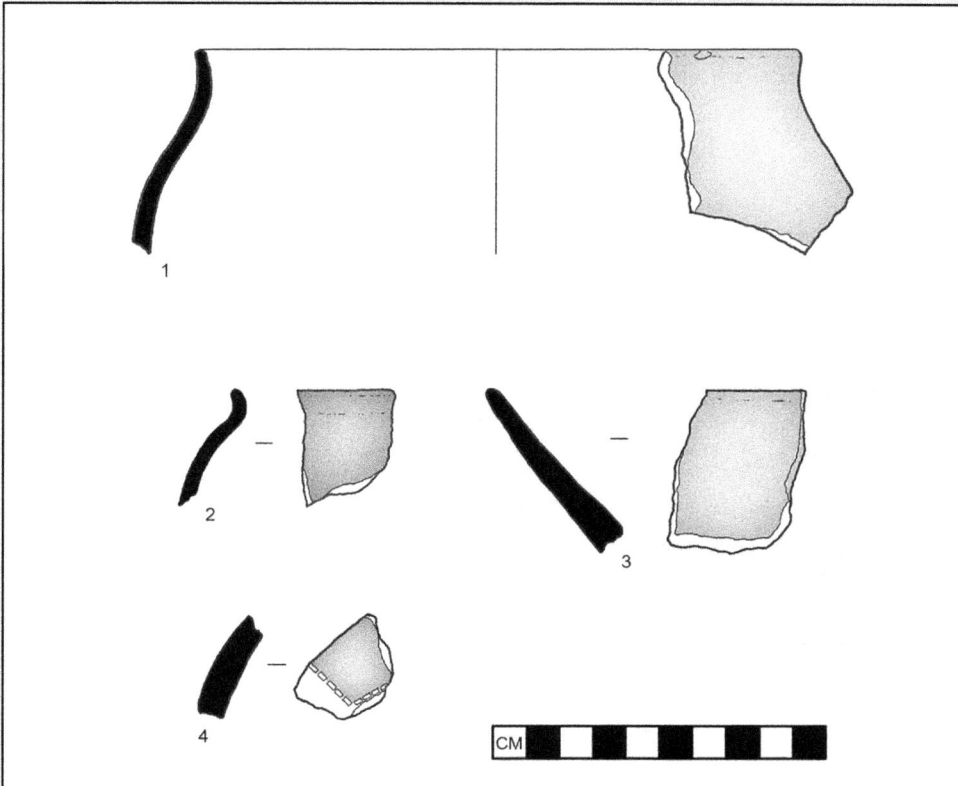

Figure 8.8
Decorated sherds and representative profiles from Midden 2.

Figure 8.8 Ceramic Descriptions

1. Smooth-necked jar, plain with natural black colouration. Profile Mode: 1A. Provenance: SU26, Midden 2, Square C, Level 3. Cat. No. V521.

2. Smooth-necked jar, plain with natural black colouration. Profile Mode: 1A. Provenance: SU26, Midden 2, Square A, Level 3. Cat. No. V516.

3. Simple bowl, plain with natural black colouration. Profile Mode: 2B. Provenance: SU26, Midden 2, Square C, Level 4. Cat. No. V517.

4. Decorated sherd, no profile information. Pendant triangle with black graphite infill and comb-stamped outline. Provenance: SU26, Midden 2, Square C, Level 1. Cat. No. V524.

Scraping tools

There were 97 scrapers from Midden 2. Nine of these were abraded sherds, and 88 were recycled bone.

Beads

Midden 2 yielded two complete disc-shaped ostrich eggshell beads (Fig. 8.9).

No metallurgical debris or any other artefacts were recovered from Midden 2.

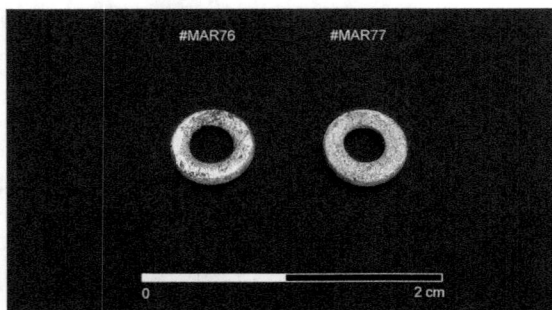

Figure 8.9
Beads from Midden 2 of
SU26.

Figure 8.10
A view of *lapa* M1 from
the north-west. In the
foreground, field team
members proceed with the
excavation of Midden 2.

Court Midden

The deposit that we have interpreted as the court midden does not conform to the usual pattern of being enclosed within its own wall, but instead it has accumulated between the walls of enclosures E1 and E9. It is associated with a raised platform near the entrance to E1. A 1.0 x 1.0 m test pit was excavated into the midden to retrieve data for comparison with domestic middens in SU26, and with middens in other homesteads. The test pit was excavated in arbitrary 0.05 m spits, close to the wall of E1 (see Fig. 8.3).

The stratigraphy of the deposit was very simple. Beneath a 0.05 m humic horizon was homogenous grey ash with occasional charcoal flecks and stones that had tumbled from the adjacent wall. The natural soil at the base of the ash was exposed at a maximum depth of 0.67 m. The total excavated volume was approximately 0.65 cubic metres (Fig. 8.11).

Artefacts from the Court Midden

Ceramics

All ceramics were retrieved from the lower 0.25 m of the ash. From 0.25 m to the surface—including the layer of top soil—the test pit yielded no archaeological artefacts. A total of 162 sherds were recovered (1161.5g), of which 7 were diagnostic (Table 8.3). None were suitable for multi-dimensional analysis (Fig. 8.12).

Scraping Tools

The court midden yielded 30 scrapers, including 5 abraded ceramic sherds and 25 recycled pieces of bone.

No metallurgical debris or any other artefacts were recovered from the court midden.

	Sherds	Mass (g)	Mass (g) per m³	% of total sherds
Diagnostic	7	25.8	39.7	4.3
Adiagnostic	155	1135.7	1747.2	95.7
Total	162	1161.5	1787.0	100

Table 8.3
Quantities of ceramic sherds from the court midden of SU26.

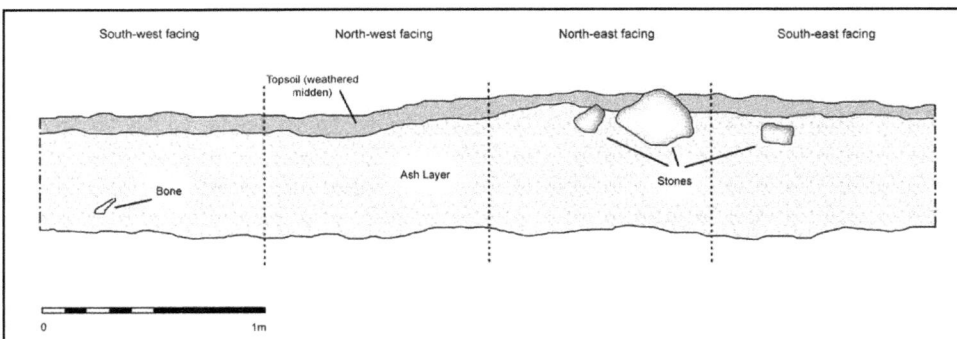

Figure 8.11
The four sections of the test pit excavated into the court midden of SU26.

Figure 8.12
Representative ceramic
profiles from the
court midden.

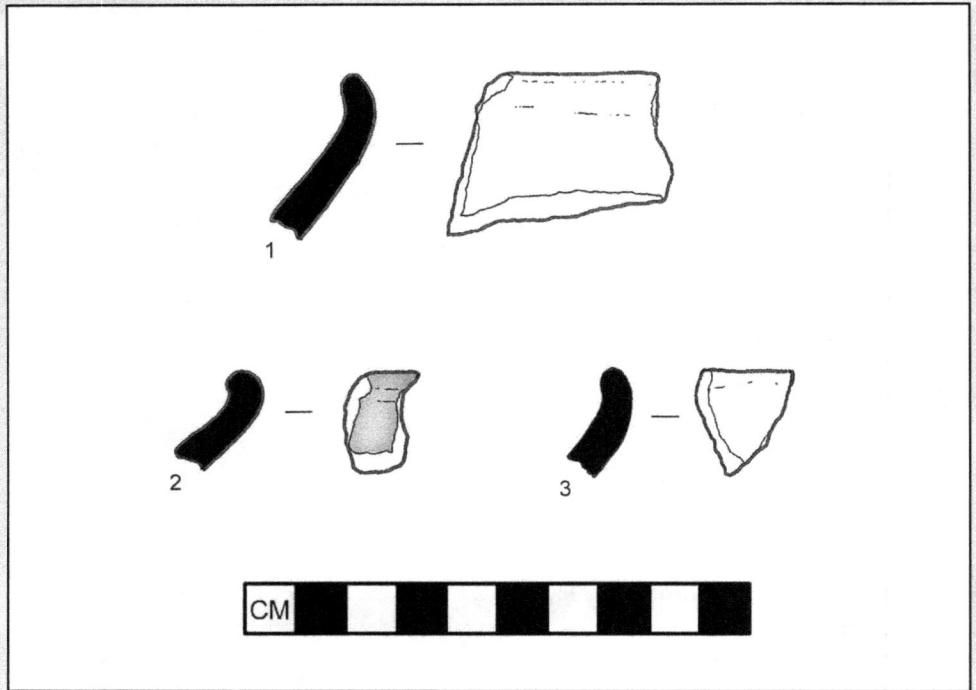

Figure 8.12 Ceramic Descriptions

1. Smooth-necked jar, plain. Profile Mode: 1A. Provenance: SU26, Court Midden, Level 7. Cat. No. V549.

2. Smooth-necked jar, plain with natural black colouration. Profile Mode: 1A. Provenance: SU26, Court Midden, Level 8. Cat. No. V547.

3. Smooth-necked jar, plain. Profile Mode: 1A. Provenance: SU26, Court Midden, Level 8. Cat. No. V546.

Domestic *lapa* M1

As discussed earlier, *lapa* M1 was one of the senior households within SU26. As archaeological features in the courtyard seemed to be relatively well preserved, this *lapa* was chosen for excavation to provide a comparison with other households excavated at Marothodi.

M1 is approximately 18.0 m in length from north to south (if the wall of M11 is taken as its northern edge) and has a maximum width of 11.0 m (Fig. 8.3). There is an entrance/exit at the eastern end of the back courtyard wall. Outside, a line of stones leads southward from the wall in an arc, and connects to a circular stone pile situated some 3.0 m behind the *lapa*. Each excavated feature is described here, and then finds from *lapa* M1 are described together.

Primary Dwelling Structure

The dominant structure in M1 was the Primary Dwelling Structure, which was situated centrally within the *lapa* (see Fig. 8.3). The wall foundations (Fig. 8.13) were similar in plan to those of the dwelling structures excavated in the 'Secondary' *Kgosing* and in SU25.

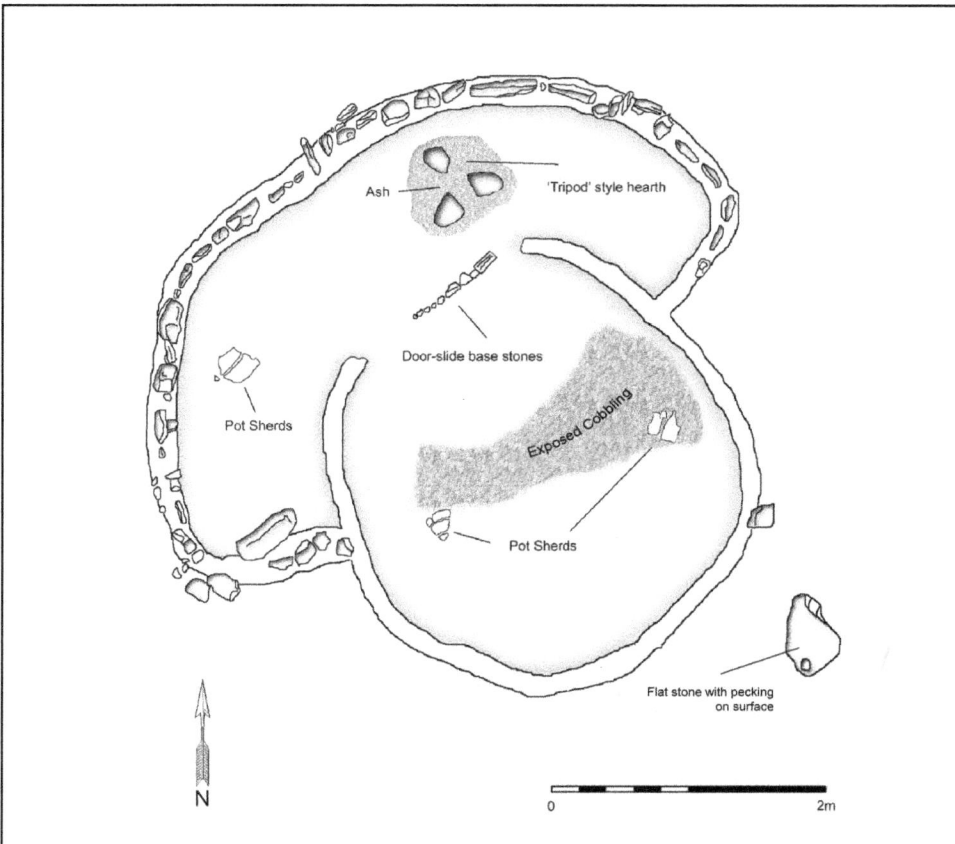

Figure 8.13
Plan of the floor and wall foundations of the Primary Dwelling Structure in *lapa* M1 of SU26.

A circular inner room connected to a crescent-shaped front veranda, which was outlined with orthostatic foundation stones (Fig. 8.13). One notable difference to other dwelling structures was that the wall base and foundation stones at the front were continuous, suggesting that there must have been a raised step across the entrance to the front veranda. The floors, both within the inner room and on the front veranda, were well fired and consequently better preserved than those uncovered at SU25. Cobbled patches of small, densely-packed stones were exposed under parts of the interior floor.

On the floor of the front veranda, a cooking hearth was exposed, situated on the left as one enters the veranda from outside. It was comprised of three stones of even size and height, arranged in a triangular formation. The stones acted as a stand for a cooking pot (see Maggs 1976a: 235-237; Comaroff *et al*. 2007: Plate 2.13). As we will see, this style of hearth was a characteristic feature of other domestic structures in SU26.

Behind the Primary Dwelling Structure, a flat stone with a pecked surface rests on the courtyard floor. It is similar to the 'anvil stone' observed in the Copper Smelting Site at SU25, and a possible link to copper production here at SU26 is discussed below.

Secondary Dwelling Structure

The Secondary Dwelling Structure was found immediately to the north-west of the Primary Dwelling Structure, and adjacent to the end of the western *lapa* wall (see Fig. 8.3). Its doorway faces back towards the Primary Dwelling Structure. The small size of the front veranda clearly limited domestic activity here, and this may be a reflection of who used this building. It contains no hearth, and is instead dominated by the door slide base stones. A large stone lies across the centre of the front veranda floor, and looks as though it may originally have stood upright (Figs. 8.14 and 8.15).

Figure 8.14
A view into the excavated front veranda of the Secondary Dwelling Structure, from the north-east.

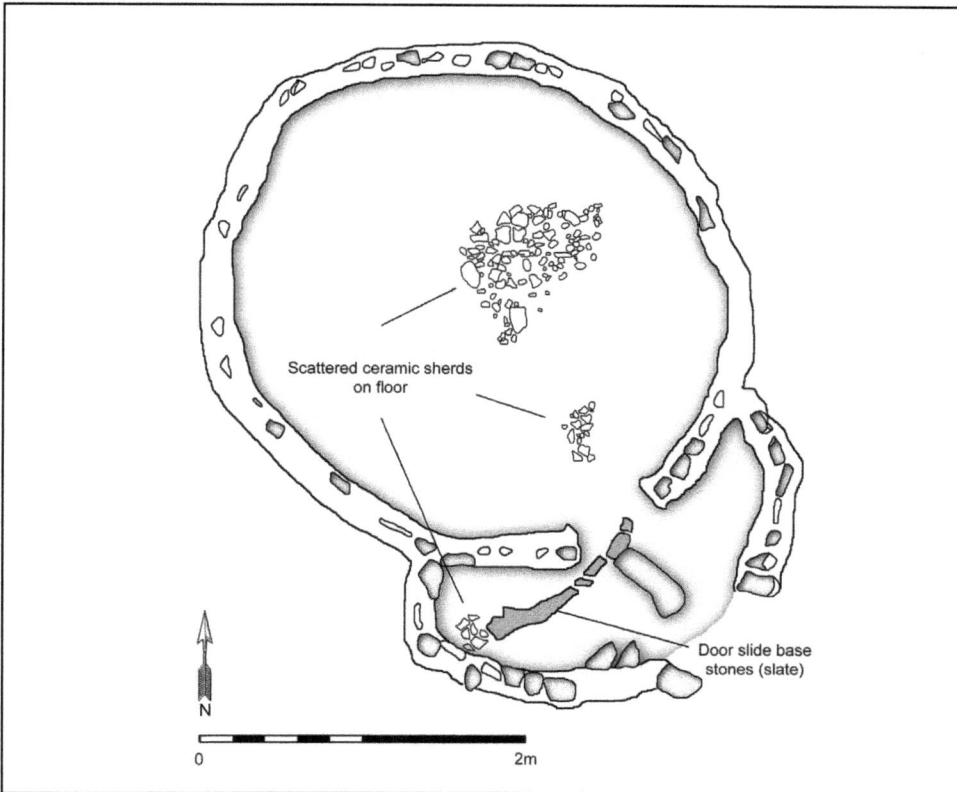

Figure 8.15
Plan of the Secondary
Dwelling Structure in *lapa*
M1 of SU26.

Utility Structure 1

Approximately 8.0 m to the north-east of the Primary Dwelling Structure, Utility Structure 1 (US1) is situated close to enclosure E11 and Midden 2, in the front courtyard area of *lapa* M1 (see Fig. 8.3). As we saw in *lapa* M1 of the 'Secondary' *Kgosing*, this position is commonly where 'kitchens' are found—structures used primarily for preparing food.

Despite its distance to the other structures in M1, the orientation of the doorway of US1, which faces back towards the Primary Dwelling Structure, indicates that the structure was an integral part of M1 and not M30, the adjacent *lapa* to the east.

The maximum diameter of the structure was 3.12 m (Fig. 8.16). The foundation of the daga wall was built upon a circle of orthostatic stones, and had an 0.80 m wide doorway. Instead of a stone door base, the door slid back and forth upon a row of pot sherds into which a visible groove had been worn. The existence of a sliding door indicates a complete cone-on-cylinder kitchen structure, possibly similar in design and function to Utility Structure 1 in *lapa* M1 of the 'Secondary' Kgosing.

Removal of the wall rubble revealed a paved interior floor of smooth, flat and closely laid stones. This floor must have been smeared over with daga, but this is not preserved (see Maggs 1976a: 235). Among the paving stones, a worn lower grindstone had been set deep into the floor towards the rear of the structure, on the right hand side (Fig. 8.16). This was clearly permanently fixed in place. In the centre-left area, a 'tripod' hearth dominated the floor. In a variation of the example in the Primary Dwelling Structure, the three stones of this hearth were placed on a circular 'plate', the surface of which was covered with a mosaic of carefully laid ceramic sherds.

Interestingly, a thin layer of destruction debris, comprised of burnt daga with flecks of charcoal, was identified beneath the tiled surface of the hearth. The debris indicated that US1 had burnt down and been rebuilt at least once during its period of usage, prior to its eventual abandonment and terminal collapse.

A large, deeply worn lower grindstone was situated outside the structure, on the right hand side of the door. It was evidently fixed into the activity surface of the *lapa*, but was broken in two (Figs. 8.16 and 8.17).

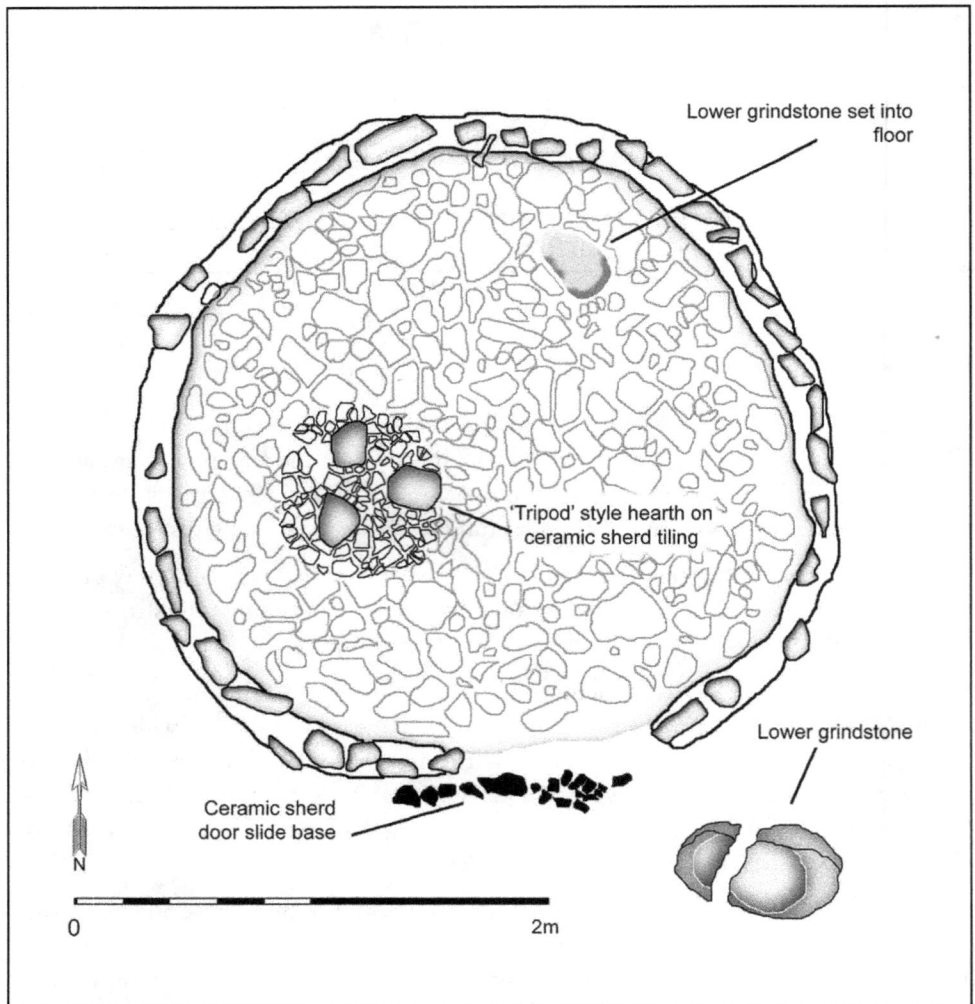

Figure 8.16
Plan of the floor
and foundations of
Utility Structure 1 in
lapa M1 of SU26.

Figure 8.17
Utility Structure 1 viewed
from the south-east
during excavation. The
broken lower grindstone
and associated upper
grindstones are visible in
the foreground.

Utility Structure 2

Before excavation began in SU26, the position of Utility Structure 2 (US2) suggested that it was associated with *lapa* M1 (see Fig. 8.3). As work progressed however, the position and orientation of the structure's doorway indicated that it was probably a part of M2, the adjacent *lapa* to the south-west. This was substantiated with the discovery of a narrow stretch of wall base connecting US2 with the back wall of the Secondary Dwelling Structure, which would have restricted access to the structure from M1. Nevertheless, it was decided that excavation of the structure should continue, as it would potentially provide a useful comparison with US1, and make a contribution to the material sample from SU26.

Excavation of US2 revealed a circular wall base consisting of orthostatic foundation stones lined with traces of the original daga wall (Fig. 8.18). The maximum diameter of the structure was 3.10 m, and the general shape and size was very similar to US1. This was clearly another kitchen. The doorway was a 0.98 m gap in the southern perimeter of the structure. The presence of a sliding door was clearly indicated by two distinct door slide wear grooves in the usual position to the left of the doorway. One groove had been worn into a row of ceramic sherds, similar to the ceramic door slide base of US1. The second groove was worn into a row of flat pieces of slate. The two grooves ran almost parallel to each other, with an angle of 10° between them, indicating that the door had been either replaced or re-set at least once during the structure's use.

A narrow exploratory sondage excavated through the interior floor revealed no evidence for paving in US2 (Fig. 8.18). Traces of compact patches of daga were encountered beneath the wall rubble during excavation, which seem to have represented the remains of an activity surface. US2 also contained a 'tripod' hearth of three stones set on a tiled platform of ceramic sherds on the left hand side (Fig. 8.19). This was very similar to the example in US1.

Several large ceramic sherds belonging to the same vessel were found resting *in situ* between and around the hearth stones, suggesting that this pot was sitting on the hearth at the time of the building's collapse. The level of the hearth tiling probably indicates the most recent interior floor level, and this was 0.07 m lower than the level of the *lapa* surface outside.

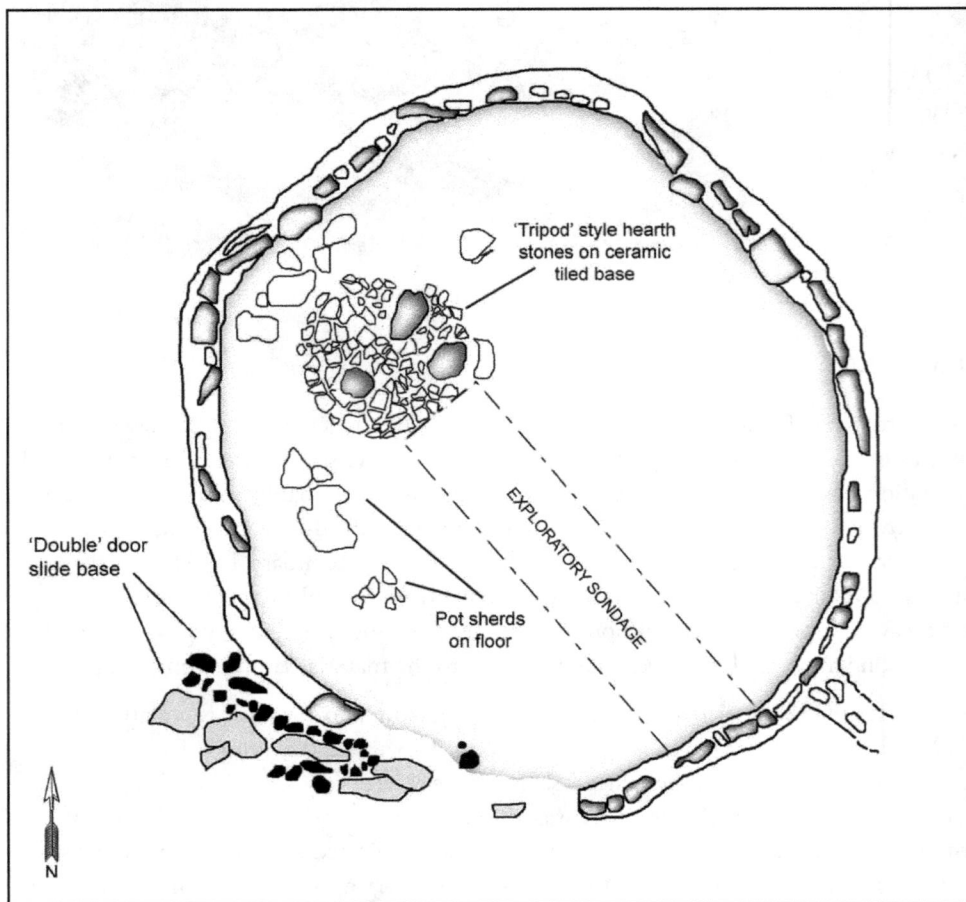

Figure 8.18
Plan of the floor and wall foundations of Utility Structure 2 in *lapa* M1 of SU26.

Figure 8.19
The 'tripod' hearth in
Utility Structure 2 during
excavation, showing the
ceramic tiled surface and *in
situ* ceramic sherds on the
surrounding floor surface.

Figure 8.20
A Tswana woman uses
an early 20th century
version of a 'tripod' hearth
in her *lapa* at Mochudi in
Botswana. (I. Schapera)

Copper Smelting Site

As mentioned earlier, a preliminary survey of the area around *lapa* M1 revealed concentrations of reddish-brown daga in the space immediately behind the back courtyard wall (see Fig. 8.3). The spatial and material parallels to the Copper Smelting Site explored at SU25 (see Figs. 7.33 and 7.34), as well as the presence of a flat stone covered in pecking and cupules behind the Primary Dwelling Structure here in M1 (see Fig. 8.13), led to the expectation that this was a copper smelting site similar to that at SU25.

In order to explore this possibility further, a grid was laid out around the most densely concentrated daga (see Fig. 8.3), and the surface within was carefully trowelled. This procedure revealed significant quantities of scattered furnace daga, along with slag and pieces of green copper ore gossan (Fig. 8.21). It is anticipated that continued exposure would have revealed furnace structures, and therefore this area is confidently identified as a primary copper smelting site similar to that exposed at SU25.

Figure 8.21
Assistant Field Director
Sarah Court trowels the
copper smelting site behind
lapa M1 of SU26, revealing
concentrations of furnace
daga, slag and copper ore
bearing gossan.

Artefacts from *lapa* M1

Ceramics

In total, *lapa* M1 yielded 1449 sherds (26980.0g), of which only 63 were diagnostic (Fig. 8.22).

In the Primary Dwelling Structure, some sherds were found on the interior floor and the floor of the front veranda, but the vast majority of the 395 ceramic sherds (8985.4g) from this structure came from the wall rubble. Three sherds were diagnostic (Table. 8.4).

There was a concentration of sherds covering the inner floor of the Secondary Dwelling Structure. Most of these came from one large plain jar that was on the floor when the building collapsed. These comprised the majority of the 625 sherds recovered from this structure (8823.0g), of which 31 were rims (Table 8.5). No other artefacts were found during the excavation of the Secondary Dwelling Structure.

A total of 118 sherds (1558.2g) were recovered from the wall rubble of Utility Structure 1. This count does not include those incorporated into the door slide base or the hearth tiling, which were considered part of the structure (Table 8.6). Three sherds were diagnostic, and belonged to the same vessel. In addition, a sample of 15 sherds (431.8g) was collected from the hearth tiling. These differed from the other assemblages in that they had a glittery surface sheen indicative of mica inclusions in the fabric (see Rosenstein 2008; Hall *et al.* 2008).

A total of 311 sherds (7613.4g) were recovered during the excavation of Utility Structure 2 (not including those in the tiled hearth or door slide). These came from the floor (109) and the wall rubble (202) (Table 8.7). Twenty-six sherds were diagnostic, of which 2 were suitable for multi-dimensional analysis: one was classified as "Class 2" (*Uitkomst* facies), a smooth-necked jar with a horizontal band of comb-stamping on the rim; and the other a "Class 3" (*Buisport* facies), a short-necked jar with a horizontal band of nicking/punctates on the rim (Fig. 8.22).

Metallurgy

The only metal artefacts from *lapa* M1 were two corroded iron objects recovered from the wall rubble of the Primary Dwelling Structure; a flat, wedge-shaped piece with a rounded tip which may have been a spearhead or a knife (#MAR81); and a spatula-shaped implement, possibly the blade of a small hoe or a chisel (#MAR82). Both objects had suffered corrosion on their exterior surfaces (Fig. 8.23). No material associated with metallurgical production was found in *lapa* M1.

Scraping Tools

Two bone scrapers were recovered from the floor of Utility Structure 2. These were the only artefacts found with this structure, and the only scrapers from *lapa* M1.

Table 8.4
Quantities of ceramic
sherds from the Primary
Dwelling Structure in *lapa*
M1 of SU26.

		Sherds	Mass (g)	% of total sherds
Front veranda floor	Diagnostic	3	814.7	0.8
	Adiagnostic	0	0	0
Interior floor	Diagnostic	0	0	0
	Adiagnostic	70	2198.2	17.7
Wall rubble	Diagnostic	0	0	0
	Adiagnostic	322	5972.5	81.5
Subtotals	Diagnostic	3	814.7	0.8
	Adiagnostic	392	8170.7	99.2
Totals		395	8985.4	100

Table 8.5
Quantities of ceramic
sherds from the Secondary
Dwelling Structure.

		Sherds	Mass (g)	% of total sherds
Wall rubble	Diagnostic	29	812.7	4.6
	Adiagnostic	517	7014.4	82.7
Front veranda floor	Diagnostic	0	0	0
	Adiagnostic	7	150.3	1.1
Interior floor	Diagnostic	2	102.4	0.3
	Adiagnostic	70	743.2	11.2
Subtotals	Diagnostic	31	915.1	5.0
	Adiagnostic	594	7907.9	95.0
Totals		625	8823.0	100

Table 8.6
Quantities of ceramic sherds
from Utility Structure 1.

		Sherds	Mass (g)	% of total sherds
Wall rubble	Diagnostic	3	13.6	2.5
	Adiagnostic	115	1544.6	97.5
Total		118	1558.2	100

Table 8.7
Quantities of ceramic sherds
from Utility Structure 2.

		Sherds	Mass (g)	% of total sherds
Wall rubble	Diagnostic	17	500.6	5.5
	Adiagnostic	185	1582.3	59.5
Interior floor	Diagnostic	9	1576.8	2.9
	Adiagnostic	100	3953.7	32.1
Subtotals	Diagnostic	26	2077.4	8.4
	Adiagnostic	285	5536.0	91.6
Totals		311	7613.4	100

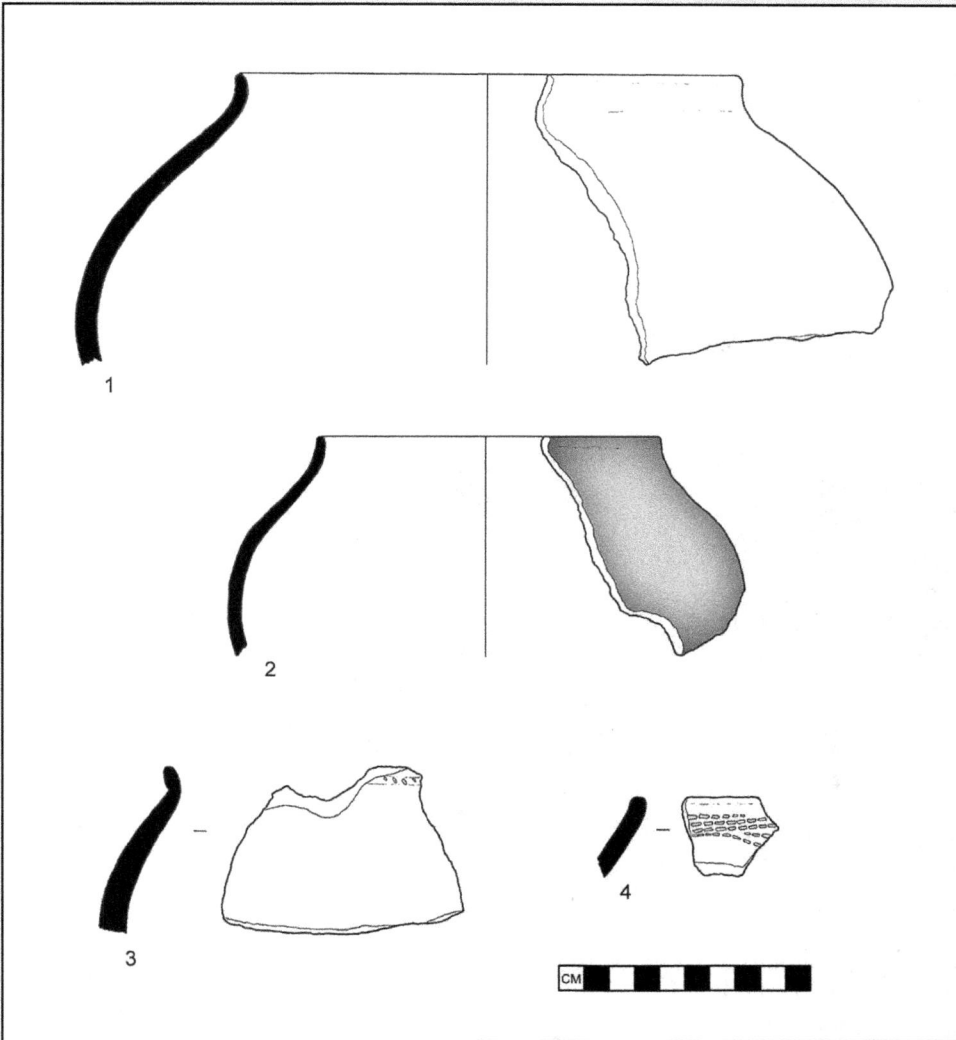

Figure 8.22
Decorated sherds and
representative profiles
from *lapa* M1 of SU26.

Figure 8.22 Ceramic Descriptions

1. Smooth-necked jar, plain. Profile Mode: 1A. Provenance: SU26, M1, Utility Structure 2, interior floor surface. Cat. No. V2.

2. Smooth-necked jar, plain. Natural black colouration. Profile Mode: 1A. Provenance: SU26, M1, Utility Structure 2, interior floor surface. Cat. No. V515.

3. Short-necked jar with horizontal row of punctates on the rim. Profile Mode: 1B. Layout Mode: 2. Decoration Mode: 2. Multi-dimensional Class: 3. Provenance: SU26, M1, Utility Structure 2, interior floor surface. Cat. No. V3.

4. Decorated rim sherd. Horizontal band of comb-stamping on the rim. Profile Mode: 1A. Layout Mode: 2. Decoration Mode: 2. Multi-dimensional Class: 2. Provenance: SU26, M1, Utility Structure 2, wall rubble. Cat. No. V536.

Stone

Two smooth polishing stones (#MAR31 and #MAR33) were retrieved from the Primary Dwelling Structure, and one worn upper grindstone (#MAR32). All were found in the wall rubble (Fig. 8.23). In addition, two upper grindstones were situated on the *lapa* floor surface approximately 1.0 metres away from Utility Structure 1, close to the large lower grindstone. Their positions were noted, but they were not collected (see Fig. 8.16).

Beads

A single corroded iron bead (#MAR78) was recovered from the wall rubble of the Primary Dwelling Structure (Fig. 8.23).

Figure 8.23
Artefacts from the Primary Dwelling Structure in *lapa* M1 of SU26.

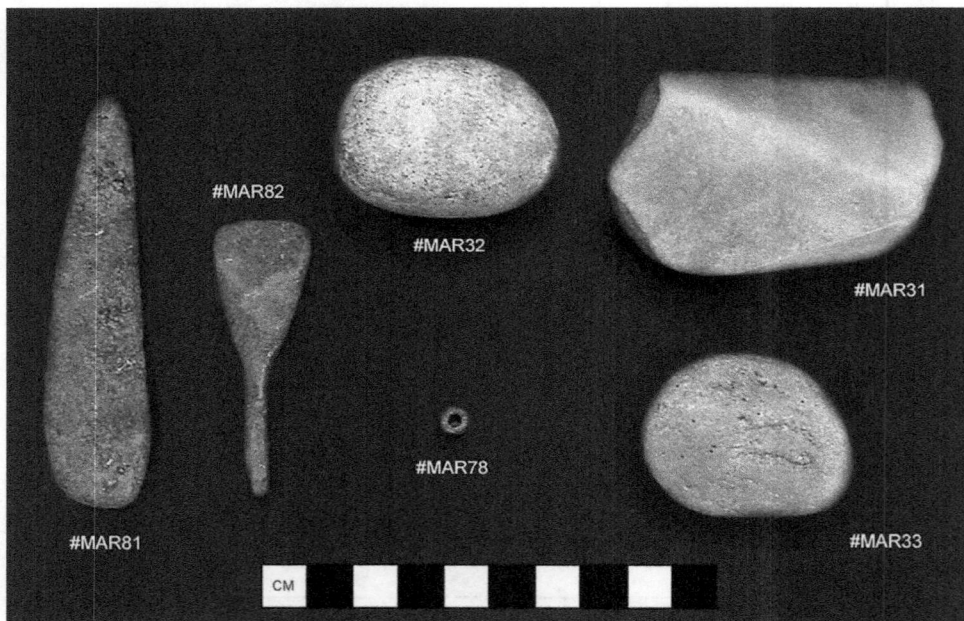

Discussion

The most striking observation from Settlement Unit 26 was the absence of metallurgical debris. The entire homestead, including the three midden excavations, yielded only a single small piece of slag. Apart from this, the only metallurgical debris occurred at the actual copper smelting site behind *lapa* M1. This is a dramatic contrast to the density of metallurgical material at SU25, and the comparison serves to emphasise the intensity of production going on there.

However, there was evidence for other craft production at SU26. The highest density of scraping tools occurred in Midden 1, which contained 100 per excavated cubic metre of deposit. Midden 2 had 57.1 scrapers per cubic metre, and the court midden contained

46.1 scrapers per cubic metre. As at the other homesteads discussed so far, bone was evidently the preferred material. Bone scrapers made up 85.7% of the assemblage, while only 14.3% were ceramic sherds.

The overall density of scrapers from all of the SU26 middens combined was 70.5 per excavated cubic metre. This was less than half of the relative quantity at SU25, which had an average density of 168.7 scrapers per cubic metre. The comparison further emphasises that Settlement Unit 25 was a place of intensive craft production, and that to a degree this applied to hide working as well as to metallurgy (Fig. 8.24).

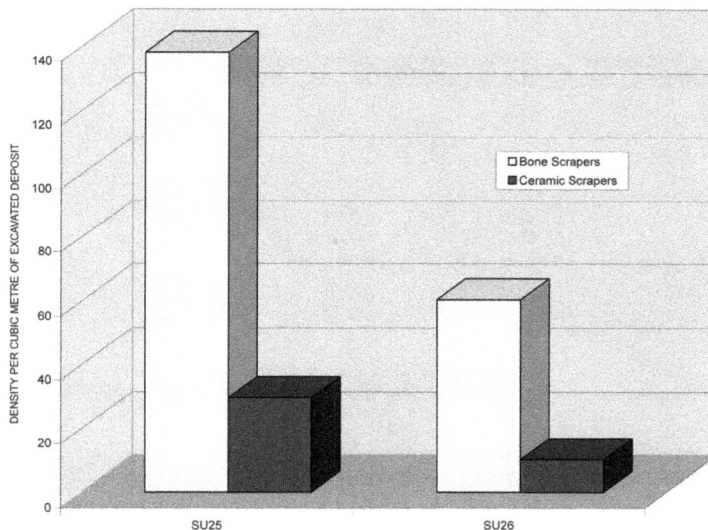

Figure 8.24
Bar chart comparing the density of bone and ceramic scrapers at SU25 and SU26.

The 'tripod' hearths excavated in *lapa* M1 had not been seen elsewhere at Marothodi, although this could be a sampling issue and further excavation might reveal more. A similar use of "fire stones" has been recorded in structures at site OXF1, a 19th century Rolong settlement on the Vogelsrand ridge, near Ventersburg in the Free State (Maggs 1976a: 237), and at site 20/71 at Olifantspoort (Mason 1986: 397). The use of ceramic sherds to make tiled hearth surfaces is most closely paralleled at Olifantspoort. At site 20/71, instead of ceramic sherds, upended pebbles were packed together to create "mosaic" fireplaces inside some of the dwelling structures (Mason 1986: 401). Also at Olifantspoort, at the nearby contemporary site 2/72, the hearth or "firebowl" in Hut P had a surface tiled with sherds that probably performed a similar function (Mason 1986: 487).

It is possible that the 'tripod' hearths reflected the use of charcoal, or perhaps dung as fuel, as opposed to wood. The tiled surfaces might have provided better insulation, making these hearths more efficient. Indeed, wood supplies in the area around Marothodi may have become scarce during the occupation of the capital, especially considering the scale of metal production we have seen here. Sustainability could potentially have been an issue, and more efficient methods of cooking may have been sought. The tiled surfaces of the hearths may have had the additional advantage of being easier to clean after use.

The few decorated sherds from SU26 continue to demonstrate the prominent representation of comb-stamping at Marothodi (Table 8.8). Like the others they are suggestive of the *Uitkomst* ceramic facies (Huffman 2007).

Table 8.8
Decorative techniques on diagnostic sherds from SU26.

Context	Comb-stamping	Rim-nicking	Punctates	Coloured bands	Appliqué
Midden 1	2	1	1	0	0
Midden 2	1	0	0	0	0
Utility Structure 2	0	0	1	0	0
Total	3	1	2	0	0

Table 8.9
Ceramic profile types from SU26.

Context	Smooth-necked jar (1A)	Short-necked jar (1B)	Straight open bowl (2B)	Necked bowl (2A)	Pot Lid (3)	Undetermined
Midden 1	33	1	6	1	2	2
Midden 2	20	0	4	0	0	2
Court Midden	6	0	0	0	0	0
Prim Dwell Structure	1	0	0	0	0	0
Sec Dwell Structure	7	0	0	0	0	0
Utility Structure 1	3	0	0	0	0	0
Utility Structure 2	10	1	1	0	5	0
Lapa surface	9	0	1	0	0	0
Copper Smelt Site	6	0	0	0	0	0
Total	95	2	12	1	7	4

Table 8.10
Multi-dimensional analysis of ceramics from SU26.

Vessel	Context	Class	Vessel	Decoration	Decoration	Description
536	SU26 Utility Structure 2	2	1A	2	2	Smooth-necked jar with a single horizontal band of comb-stamping on the rim
3	SU26 Utility Structure 2	3	1B	2	2	Short-necked jar with a horizontal band of nicking on the rim

Figure 8.25
Domestic scenes like this would have been familiar at Marothodi. Here, Ngwato women thresh and stamp grain in the 1890s, at 'Old Palapye' in Botswana. (W. C. Willoughby)

Chapter Nine
Masters of Iron

T he homesteads explored in Chapters Six, Seven and Eight have all revealed evidence for copper production at Marothodi, an activity that appears to have been comprised of two phases—smelting and refining—both of which were spatially tied to households, and which occurred on a significant scale throughout the town. In Chapter Five we noted that iron production was also going on here, and we drew attention to the different spatial pattern of iron smelting sites or 'precincts'. Generally, in contrast to copper production sites, these appeared to be separated from homesteads (see Fig. 5.7).

As we examine the archaeology of iron production further in this chapter, it begins to clarify specific spatial and organisational differences between iron and copper metallurgy at Marothodi. Once identified, these differences then provide a basis for our discussion of underlying cultural principles in Chapter Ten.

We begin by exploring Settlement Unit 3, a homestead that was chosen for study in light of its proximity to, and evident relationship with, the tree-covered slope immediately to the south (referred to here as 'Smelting Hill' for convenience). Evidence for metal production had been observed on Smelting Hill during preliminary ground survey (see Figs. 5.4 and 5.7). We explore the spatial organisation of SU3, and then discuss the excavations that were undertaken in the midden, and in domestic *lapa* M12. In addition, two iron smelting furnaces were excavated on Smelting Hill, as well as a third furnace near SU22(A), near the southern edge of Marothodi Central.

Spatial organisation of Settlement Unit 3

Settlement Unit 3 is a relatively small homestead on the far northern edge of Marothodi (Fig. 5.4) and was almost completely obscured by tree and bush cover on the aerial photographs. For this reason, the stone walls of SU3 and the features on Smelting Hill were surveyed using EDM (Figs. 9.1 and 9.2). The homestead extends approximately 90 metres from north to south, and 70 metres east to west, making it comparable in size to Settlement Unit 25.

The Cattle Kraals and Court Complex

In the centre of SU3 there are five enclosures large enough to be identified as cattle kraals: E2, E4, E5, E7 and E8 (Fig. 9.1). Of these, E2, E4 and E8 stand out as the largest and most centrally located. All entrances to SU3 through which cattle could have been driven are located on the eastern side of the homestead.

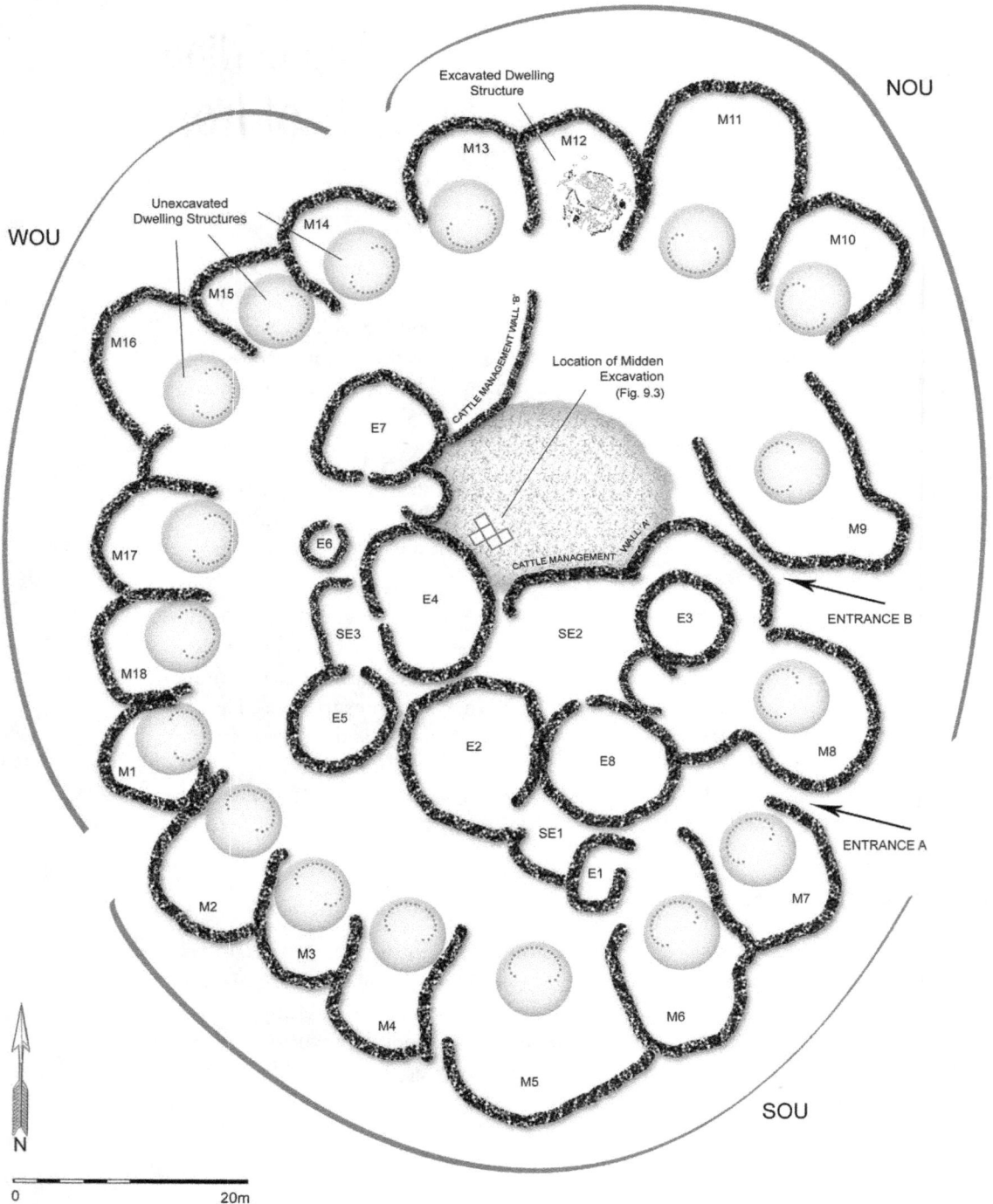

Figure 9.1

Map of Settlement Unit 3, indicating the extent of the three occupation units, the position of the excavated *lapa* M12, and the location of the sample midden excavation.

Figure 9.2
SU3 was mapped using
Electronic Distance
Measuring (EDM).
Here, members of the
Marothodi field team
are surveying with
a Total Station.

E2 is the largest enclosure, and at face value, might be interpreted as a kraal for the head-man's herd. It is most directly accessible through Entrance A on the south-east side (Fig. 9.1) which is clearly a formal entranceway to the homestead. If cattle entered here, they would pass in front of *malapa* M7 and M6, and enter the narrow opening between the walls of E1 and E8. This leads into a small secondary enclosure, SE1, from which access is gained to the E2 enclosure. This would, however, lead the animals very close to domestic households, and it might be more logical to interpret Entrance A as a pedestrian entrance only.

In any case, the spatial relationship between this formal entrance to the homestead, and the largest enclosure suggests that the intermediate spaces, SE1 and E1, may have been components of the court complex. Indeed, E2 may have been large enough to accommo-date the *kgotla* of such a small homestead. No dung was discernable on the surface of E2, although it could have been obscured by the movement of the unstable turf soil below.

The close proximity of the largest *lapa*, M5, certainly supports the recognition of the southern area of the homestead as the locus of political authority at SU3. This is further reinforced by the position of the hill slope immediately to the south, and the fact there is a direct entrance/exit from the back courtyard of M5 to this area. Given the conceptual link between elevation and status (Huffman 1986b: 301; Hall 1996: 317), the most senior members of SU3 are likely to have positioned themselves closest to the hill, at the southern end of the homestead. Furthermore, the red soil here also provided a stable ground surface, in contrast to the problematic black turf soil upon which the households on the northern side were situated. The small enclosure E1 may have been the headman's private *kamore*. It was not possible to identify a distinctive court midden during the initial survey of the court complex, but it might be located with further sample excavations.

A second entrance to the homestead, Entrance B, is situated on the east side of SU3, a short distance to the north of Entrance A (Fig. 9.1). This seems more likely to have been the main entrance for cattle. Here, the addition of 'cattle management wall A' creates a narrow passageway on the south side of *lapa* M9, which leads across the central midden and, via a narrow opening, into the central secondary enclosure, SE2. From SE2, access is gained to kraal E8, and through a narrow alley to the west it is possible to access E4, E5 and E7. The gap between *malapa* M9 and M10 could also have been an entrance for cattle, but this seems unlikely because M9 would be vulnerable to wandering animals, and there are no cattle management walls here to control their movement.

A number of distinct kraal groups might be identified, based on the spatial organisation of access routes. Firstly, E2 (if it was a kraal) has a very private entrance from the M5 to M7 area, and may have been exclusively for the headman's cattle. Secondly, kraals E4, E5 and E7 are likely to have been reached from Entrance B, with cattle walking across the midden, through SE2, and approaching the kraals from the east. 'Cattle management wall B', which extends northward from kraal E7, seems to have been intended to prevent cat-tle that entered the homestead through Entrance B from wandering into households of the WOU, and indicates that they were not herded in that direction to reach those kraals (Fig. 9.1). Finally, kraal E8 is entered from SE2, which could also be most directly accessed from Entrance B. It is possible that the kraal groups represent two or three different own-ers of cattle in the homestead.

The Domestic Sphere

SU3 contains 18 domestic *malapa*, which can be subdivided into three groups (Fig. 9.1). The Southern Occupation Unit (SOU) (*malapa* M7 to M2) is associated with the proposed court complex, the largest *lapa*, and a slightly higher elevation, and is therefore likely to be the senior group in this homestead. *Malapa* M1 to M14 form the Western Occupation Unit (WOU), which has a clear spatial relationship with kraals E4 to E7. The Northern Occupation Unit (NOU) includes *malapa* M13 to M8.

Although M8 seems to be spatially separate, the design of its southern wall clearly indicates that it is distinct from the senior SOU to the south. M8 has a close spatial relationship with kraal E8, which was probably the kraal also used by other occupants of the NOU. The 'cattle management wall A' connected to *lapa* M8 was designed to prevent livestock from trampling into the domestic courtyard as they were herded between Entrance B and kraal E8 (Fig. 9.1). Its position appears to be strategic, and should not distort our perception of the relationship between M8 and the rest of the NOU.

The position of the large midden in the centre of the homestead (Fig. 9.3) seems to suggest that it was used more or less exclusively by the NOU, although no other substantial middens were noted in other locations within or around SU3. It is possible that the unstable turf soil upon which the homestead was built, combined with the movement of modern cattle, may have obscured the visibility of other middens. The proximity of the slope of Smelting Hill on the southern side, and the neighbouring homestead to the west, limited the space available for midden deposition. Consequently one would expect other middens to be somewhere in front of the SOU and WOU *malapa*. Little trace of midden was observed on the external northern or eastern edges of the homestead, although again, they may have been obscured by post-depositional disturbances.

Figure 9.3
The SU3 Midden during excavation, viewed from the west
(see Figs. 9.4 and 9.5).

Excavations at Settlement Unit 3

During the preliminary survey of SU3, a pile of iron smelting slag was observed on the ground in *malapa* M12, suggesting that this household may have been associated with smelting activity. Consequently, M12 was excavated, along with a portion of the domestic midden in the centre of SU3. Here, the aim was to collect a sample of material for comparison with other middens, and to ascertain the quantity and composition of metallurgical debris represented in the deposit. We discuss the midden excavation first.

Midden

An excavation trench of 5.0 square metres was marked out where the deepest part of the midden appeared to be, close to enclosure E4 (Fig. 9.4). The deposit was excavated in arbitrary spits of 0.05 m thick, down to the underlying natural turf soil which was encountered at a maximum depth of 0.46 m. The total volume of excavated deposit was 2.18 cubic metres. Irregular patches of lighter ash were encountered within the main compact grey ashy deposit, with corresponding lenses in the sections. These represented single episodes of deposition. Occasional traces of reddish-brown soil were also visible in the sections. These may have been capping layers of the kind seen in middens at SU25, although here they were patchy and more ephemeral. The two longest trench sections were recorded (Fig. 9.5).

Figure 9.4
Plan of the trench excavated into the SU26 midden, showing the sections illustrated in Fig. 9.5.

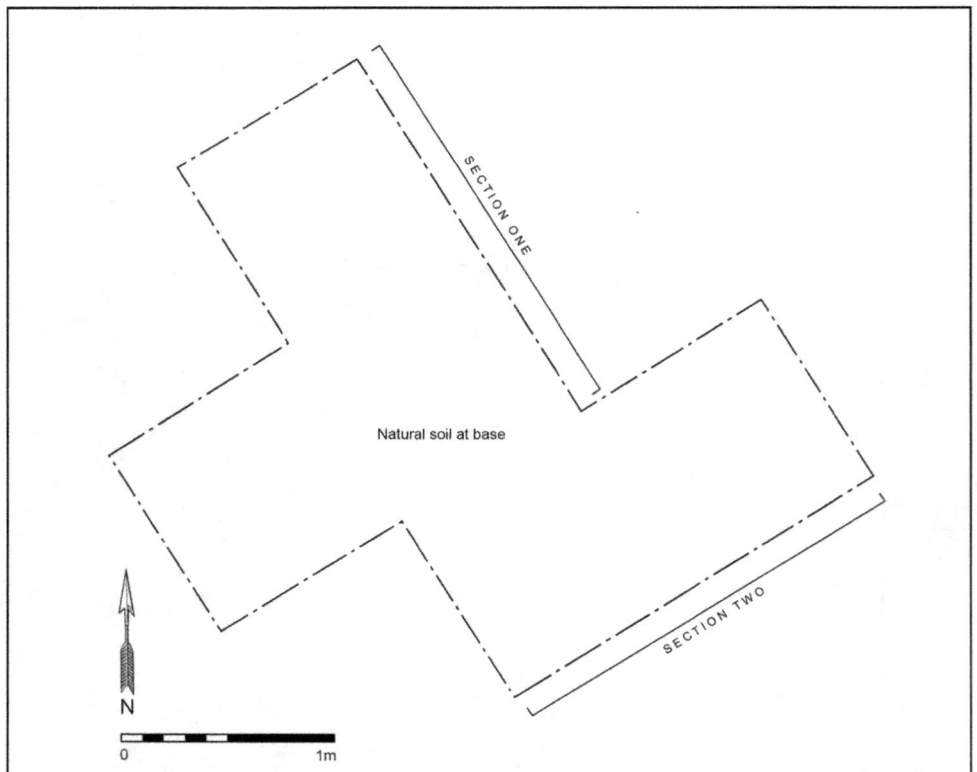

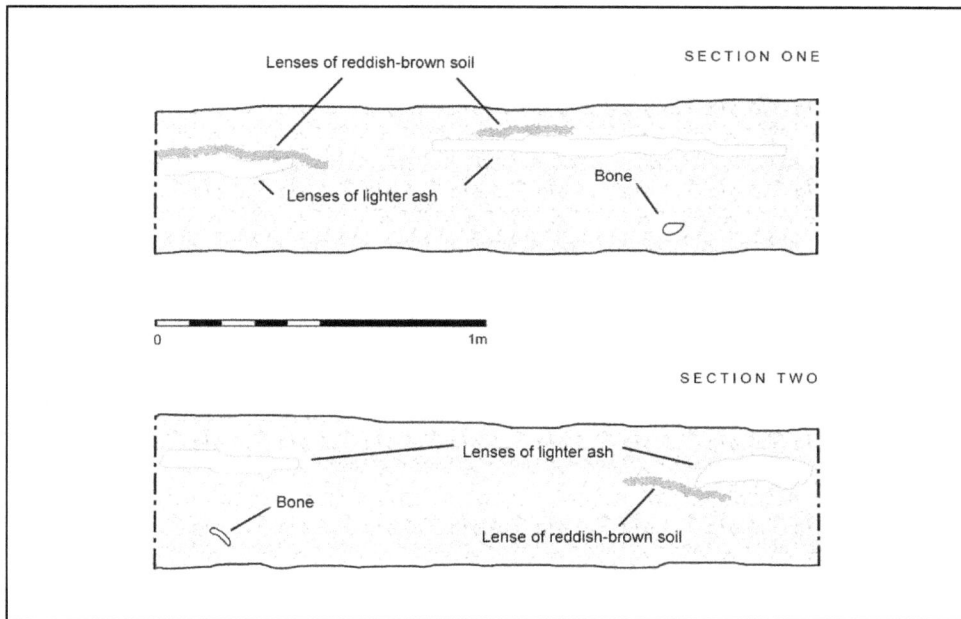

Figure 9.5
Sections 1 and 2 from the midden excavation in SU3 (see Fig. 9.4).

Artefacts from the Midden

Ceramics

A total of 863 (7165.4g) sherds were recovered from the midden, of which 57 were diagnostic (Table 9.1). The overall density was 3286.9g of sherds per cubic metre of excavated deposit. No sherds were suitable for multi-dimensional analysis (Fig. 9.6).

Metallurgy

The only piece of metallurgical debris retrieved from the midden was a single piece of 'smelting/flow' slag, with a mass of 319.2g.

Scraping Tools

The midden yielded 49 abraded sherd scrapers. At the time of writing, the bone scrapers from this midden are still with the general faunal collection and have yet to be quantified.

	Sherds	Mass (g)	Mass (g) per m³	% of total sherds
Diagnostic	57	404.6	185.6	6.6
Adiagnostic	806	6760.8	3101.3	93.4
Total	863	7165.4	3286.9	100

Table 9.1
Quantities of ceramic sherds from the Midden of SU3.

Figure 9.6
Decorated sherds and
representative profiles from
the Midden of SU3.

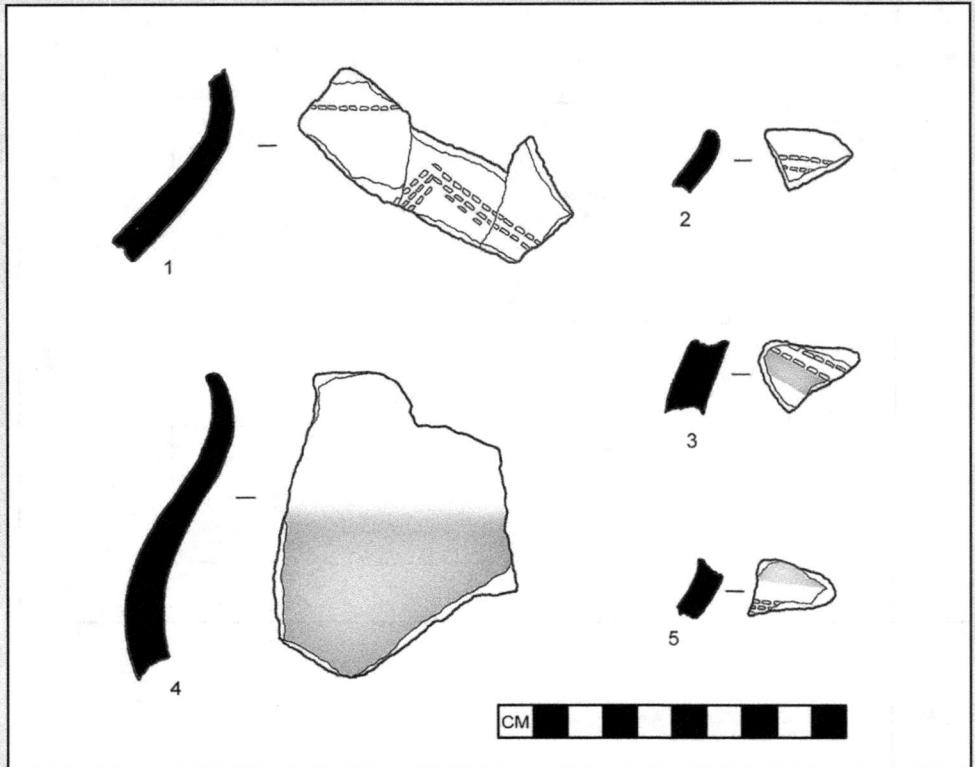

Figure 9.6 Ceramic Descriptions

1. Decorated smooth-necked jar. Horizontal band of comb-stamping above pendant triangles with comb-stamped outlines. Profile Mode: 1A. Insufficient profile for full placement analysis. Provenance: SU3, Midden, Square A, Level 6. Cat. No. V642.

2. Decorated rim sherd, insufficient profile. Horizontal band of comb-stamping. Provenance: SU3, Midden, Square A, Level 6. Cat. No. V640.

3. Decorated sherd, no profile information. Band of comb-stamping (possibly pendant triangle) above black graphite. Provenance: SU3, Midden, Square E, Level 3. Cat. No. V678.

4. Smooth-necked jar, plain with darker lower half (possibly singed). Profile Mode: 1A. Provenance: SU3, Midden, Square F, Level 2. Cat. No. V676.

5. Decorated sherd, no profile information. Band of comb-stamping below black graphite. Provenance: SU3, Midden, Square A, Level 1. Cat. No. V692.

Beads

A total of 8 beads were recovered from the midden, of which 7 were either complete or partial disc-shaped ostrich eggshell beads. The other was a larger disc-shaped bead with a diameter of 16 mm (#MAR91) and is possibly ivory (Fig. 9.7).

Clay Figurines

Four fragments of moulded clay were found, including a cow horn (#MAR126), and what might be a horned head (#MAR122). The largest piece (#MAR127) was amorphous, but clearly moulded. The remaining piece (#MAR123) was burnt black, and had one moulded surface (Fig. 9.8).

Stone

The midden yielded four upper grindstones, including one piece of large-grained pyroxenite with an abraded surface (#MAR308), two rounded stones that had significant wear on all surfaces (#MAR121 and #MAR12), and an oval-shaped stone (#MAR309) that had been slightly smoothed on one surface (Fig. 9.9).

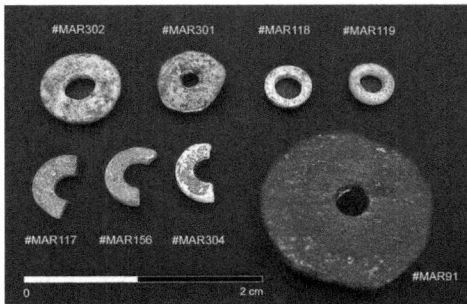

Figure 9.7
Beads from the
Midden of SU3.

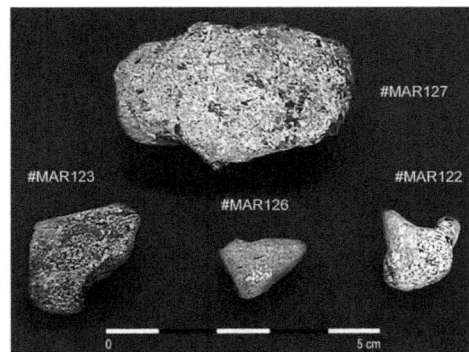

Figure 9.8
Fragments of moulded clay
from the Midden.

Figure 9.9
Stone artefacts from the
Midden.

Domestic *lapa* M12

M12 is a relatively small *lapa*, and the area enclosed by its walling measures only 9.0 x 10.0 m (Fig. 9.1). It is located on the northern fringe of SU3, furthest from the red soil of the hill, and there is evidence that it was affected by the instability of the underlying turf soil in this area. These factors suggest that the occupants were of comparatively low status.

Although M12 was small and relatively poorly preserved, the decision to excavate it was made because of the scatter of iron smelting slag on the ground surface of the courtyard. Excavation revealed the core of this scatter to be a distinct 'cache' situated close to the right hand front veranda wall on the outside of the dwelling structure (Fig. 9.10). The slag may originally have been stored here in an organic container. Its presence indicates that some smelting slags were being kept, possibly so that any small pieces of smelted iron trapped within them could be broken out for forging.

The dwelling structure itself occupied nearly one-third of the courtyard space. It was characterised by the use of both cobbling and larger paving stones beneath the floor surfaces, both in the inner room and on the front veranda. The occupants of this *lapa* clearly experienced problems with the unstable turf soil beneath their dwelling, and this has contributed to the slightly distorted appearance of the structural remains.

Only faint traces of the wall daga survive, and the outline of the structure is recognisable primarily from the upright foundation stones. The base stones of the door slide survive almost *in situ*, although their original alignment seems to have been disturbed (Fig. 9.10).

Artefacts from *lapa* M12

Ceramics

In total, 783 sherds (11202.9g) were recovered from *lapa* M12, most of which were mixed up in the wall rubble (Table 9.2). Twenty-one sherds were found on the front veranda floor, some of which appear to be from a single vessel. Another 13 were scattered around a possible pot stand situated just outside the house on the north-west side. A total of 6 sherds were diagnostic. None were decorated or suitable for multi-dimensional analysis (Fig. 9.11).

Metallurgy

The metallurgical material retrieved from *lapa* M12 was dominated by iron smelting/flow slag (85.6%) most of which was from the cache outside the front veranda (Fig. 9.12). Furnace base slag and tabular slag, both of which are associated with furnace structure, were also represented in the assemblage (7% and 4.9% respectively). The remainder was made up of tuyere fragments (2.5%) (Table 9.3).

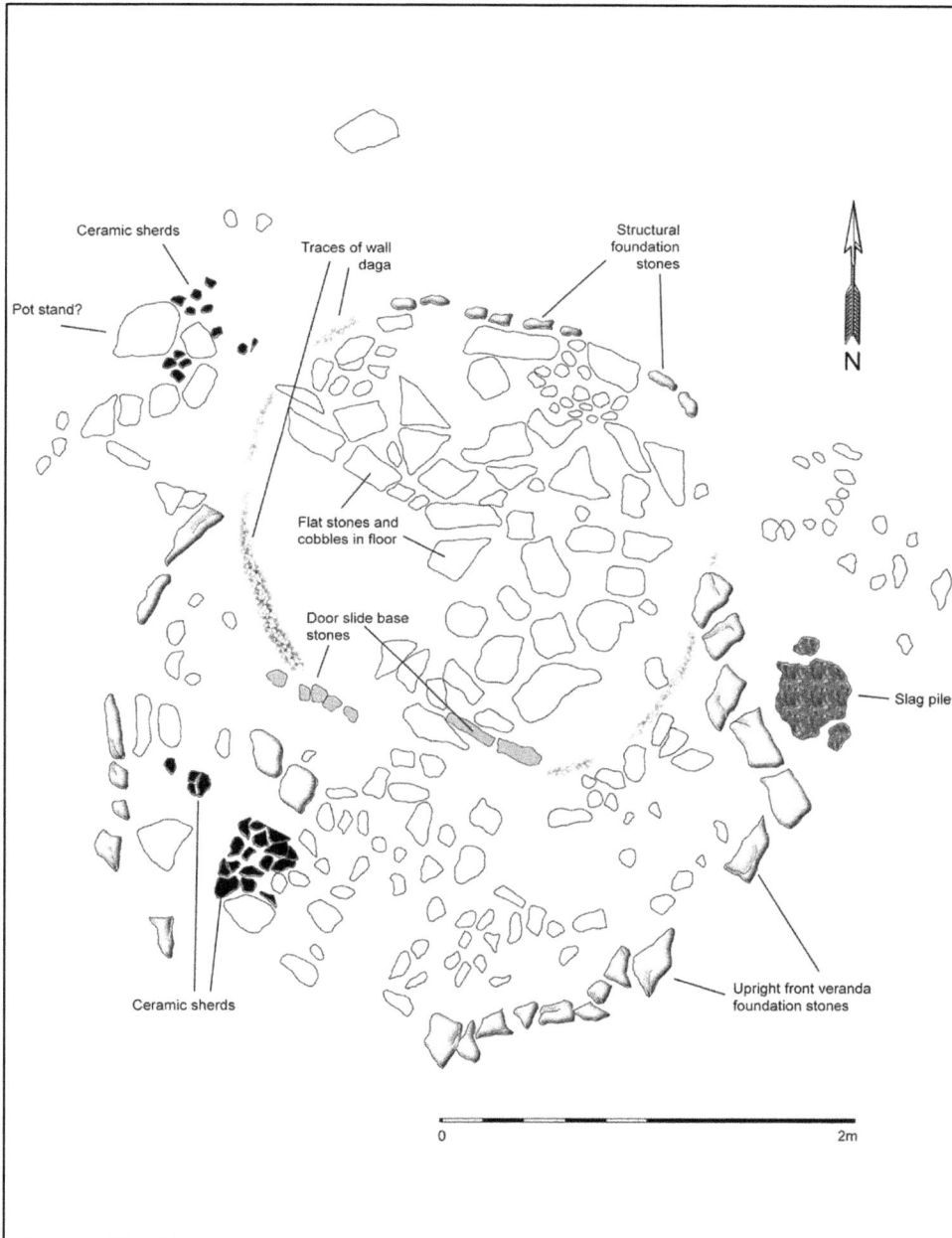

Figure 9.10
Plan of the excavated floor
and foundations of the
Dwelling Structure in *lapa*
M12 of SU3.

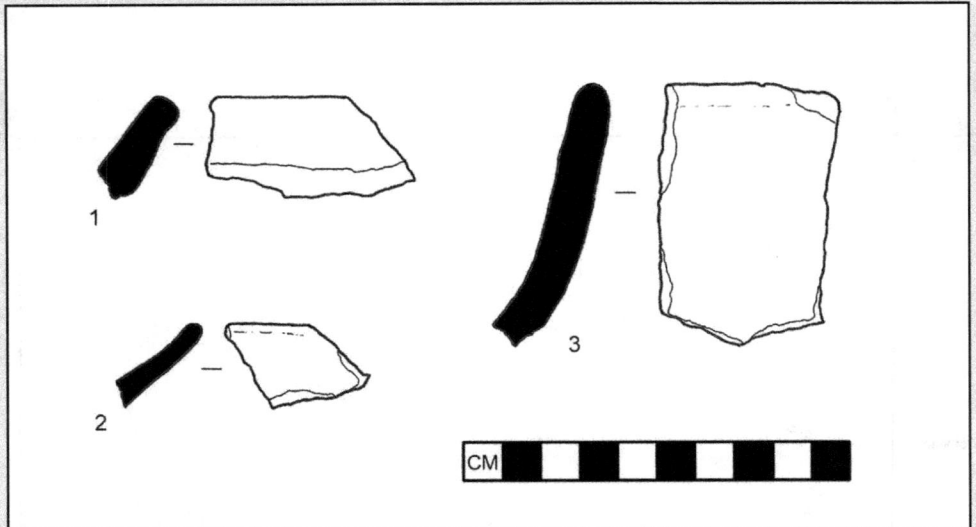

Figure 9.11 Representative ceramic profiles from *lapa* M12 of SU3.

Figure 9.11 Ceramic Descriptions

1. Smooth-necked jar, plain. Profile Mode: 1A. Provenance: SU3, M12, Dwelling Structure, Pot Stand. Cat. No. V636.

2. Smooth-necked jar, plain. Profile Mode: 1A. Provenance: SU3, M12, Dwelling Structure, wall rubble. Cat. No. V637.

3. Straight-necked jar, plain. Profile Mode: 1C. Provenance: SU3, M12, Dwelling Structure, front veranda floor. Cat. No. V631.

		Sherds	Mass (g)	% of total sherds
Wall rubble	Diagnostic	2	32.6	0.3
	Adiagnostic	747	10575.1	95.4
Front veranda floor	Diagnostic	3	14.2	0.4
	Adiagnostic	18	163.7	2.3
Rear pot stand	Diagnostic	1	194.7	0.1
	Adiagnostic	12	222.6	1.5
Subtotals	Diagnostic	6	241.5	0.8
	Adiagnostic	777	10961.4	99.2
Totals		783	11202.9	100

Table 9.2
Quantities of ceramic sherds
from *lapa* M12 of SU3.

Material Type	Mass (g)	% of total mass
Smelting/flow slag	10417.3	85.6
Furnace base slag	851.1	7.0
Tabular slag	591.0	4.9
Tuyere fragments	302.7	2.5
Total	12168.4	100

Table 9.3
Quantities of metallurgical
debris from *lapa* M12.

Context	Comb-stamping	Rim-nicking	Punctates	Coloured bands	Appliqué
Midden 1	6	0	0	0	0
M12	0	0	0	0	0
Total	6	0	0	0	0

Table 9.4
Decorative techniques on
sherds from the Midden
and *lapa* M12 of SU3.

Context	Smooth-necked jar (1A)	Short-necked jar (1B)	Straight open bowl (2B)	Necked bowl (2A)	Pot Lid (3)	Undetermined
Midden 1	40	0	10	0	0	3
M12	3	0	0	0	0	0
Total	43	0	10	0	0	3

Table 9.5
Ceramic profile types
from the Midden and
lapa M12 of SU3.

Figure 9.12
A sample of the iron
smelting slags from
the Dwelling Structure
of *lapa* M12.

Iron smelting precincts

The small excavations at SU3 demonstrated that this homestead, or at least some families within it, were associated with iron production. The smelting precincts on the nearby Smelting Hill are a clearly a possible focus for this activity. In the remainder of this chapter, we discuss the excavation of two iron smelting furnaces on Smelting Hill, and a third furnace located about half a kilometre to the south, close to Settlement Unit 22(A) (see Fig. 5.7). We begin with a description of Smelting Hill.

Smelting Hill

Along the southern edge of SU3 there is a flat 'corridor', approximately 3 metres wide, between the back of the SOU *malapa* and the basal contour of Smelting Hill. It can be entered through an opening in the back courtyard wall of *lapa* M5. This offers the most direct route from the interior of SU3 to Smelting Hill, which rises gently to the south (Fig. 9.13).

Hilltop Enclosure 1 is 16 metres to the south of this entrance. This is a small stone walled enclosure situated on the upper slope of the hill. Its perimeter wall incorporates a standing monolith about a metre in height. In light of the other evidence for iron smelting in the vicinity, Hilltop Enclosure 1 was probably a smelting site. However, as the interior of the enclosure was smothered by a large termite mound it was not explored archaeologically (Fig. 9.14).

To the north-west of Hilltop Enclosure 1 there is a clearing, some 16 metres in diameter, defined by an irregular, roughly oval shaped arrangement of stones, within which large quantities of scattered slag were observed. This space, on a blunt promontory overlooking *malapa* M2 and M3, is referred to here as the 'Smelting Precinct' (Fig. 9.13). Within the clearing, a smaller stone enclosure, 3.5 m in diameter, surrounds 'Iron Smelting Furnace A'. These enclosing stones are arranged irregularly, but despite their informal appearance they look as though they supported a fence or screen. This division of space is a repeated pattern at Marothodi iron smelting sites. The furnaces themselves are always surrounded by individual screen enclosures, and sometimes the wider activity area is also fenced in.

Approximately 70 metres to the south of Hilltop Enclosure 1 and the Smelting Precinct are two small stone walled enclosures, each approximately 4.0 m in diameter (Fig. 9.13). Scattered slag can be seen on the ground around these enclosures. The surface within Hilltop Enclosure 2, the north-westerly of the two, is a flat bedrock slab. Three metres to the south-east, Hilltop Enclosure 3 contained 'Iron Smelting Furnace B'. We will now examine these features in more detail.

Iron Smelting Furnace A

The interior of the Smelting Precinct, within which Iron Smelting Furnace A was situated, was cleared by trowel and brush. Archaeological materials were collected from both the precinct interior and from the immediate vicinity. The circle of large stones that surrounds Iron Smelting Furnace A is situated on the northern side of the precinct, close to the edge of the hill (Figs. 9.15 and 9.16).

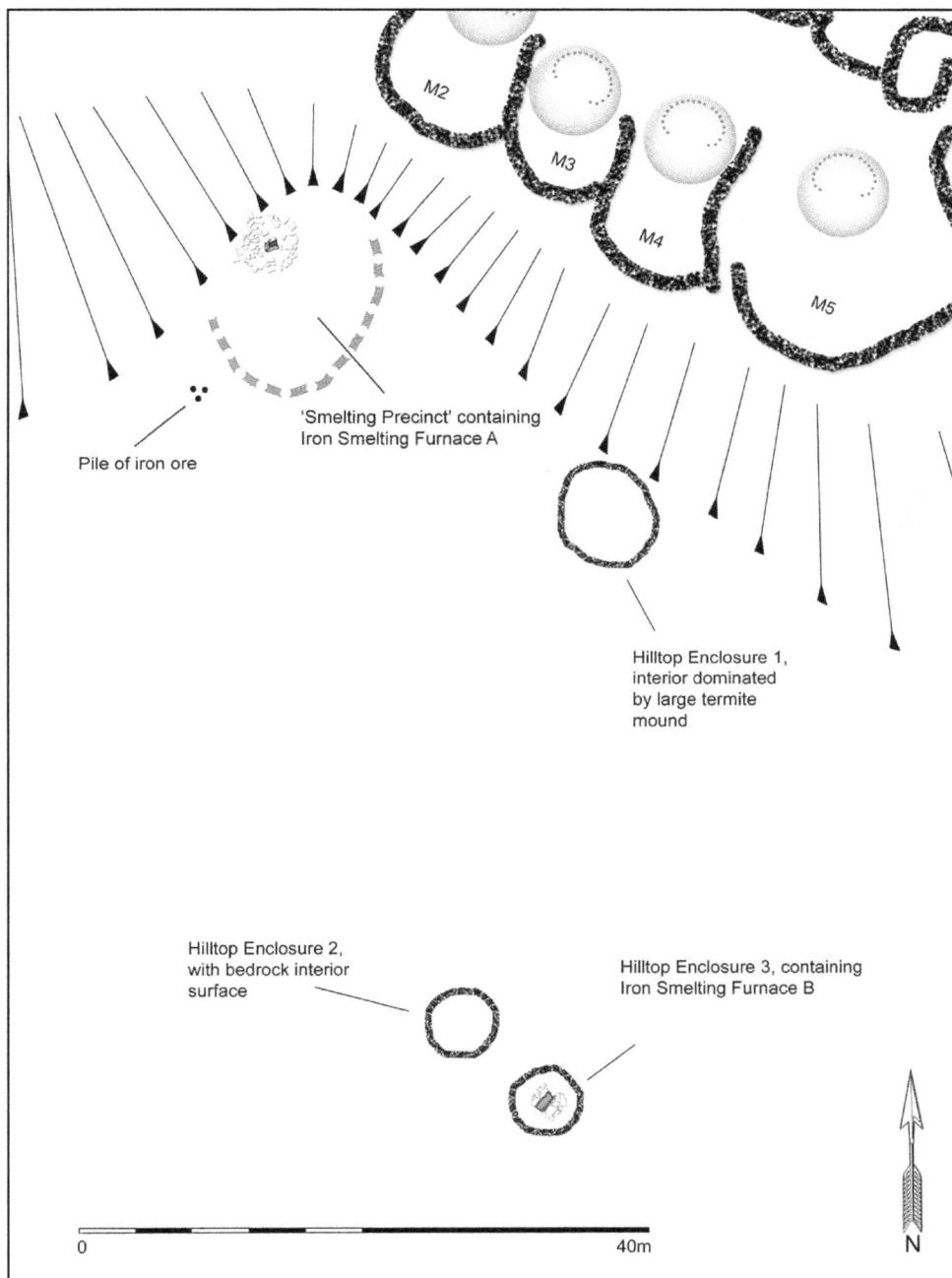

Figure 9.13
Map of the northern slope
of Smelting Hill close to
SU3, showing the location
of Iron Smelting Furnaces
A and B.

M2

M3

M4

M5

Pile of iron ore

'Smelting Precinct' containing
Iron Smelting Furnace A

Hilltop Enclosure 1,
interior dominated
by large termite
mound

Hilltop Enclosure 2,
with bedrock interior
surface

Hilltop Enclosure 3, containing
Iron Smelting Furnace B

0   40m

N

Figure 9.14
Hilltop Enclosure 1
viewed from the south
(see Fig. 9.13). The
monolith is shown in
the right foreground,
while the termite mound
dominates the interior.

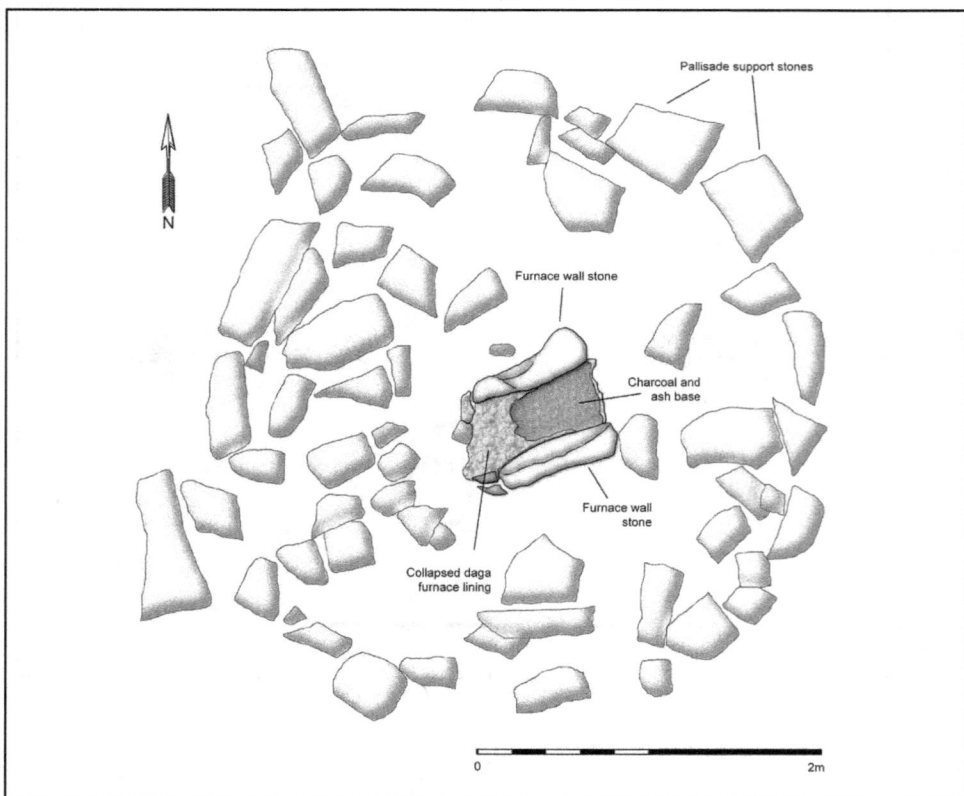

Figure 9.15
Plan of Iron Smelting
Furnace A after excavation,
showing the surrounding
palisade support stones.

Excavation revealed the furnace structure to be a roughly oval shaped cavity sunk into the ground (Fig. 9.15). Two large upright stone slabs were set approximately 0.30 m into the ground, and protruded some 0.12 m above the current ground surface. The slabs provided the outer furnace lining. They were set along the longest axis of the furnace, and spaced 0.30 m apart. The inner walls of the slabs and the furnace cavity were smeared with a daga lining. The base of the furnace was ashy with small pieces of charcoal, but there was no surviving daga floor. This may have been broken out when the iron bloom was removed.

Preservation of Iron Smelting Furnace A was relatively poor. Much of the daga structure was missing, and most of what remained was in a state of collapse. Consequently, there were no obvious traces of tuyere openings, and it was not possible to ascertain the shape of any superstructure (Fig. 9.17).

Figure 9.16
A view of Iron Smelting Furnace A (centre) during excavation, showing the surrounding palisade support stones.

Figure 9.17
Looking into the excavated cavity of Iron Smelting Furnace A. While the two stone slabs still stand, much of the daga lining has collapsed. Grey ash is visible at the base.

Artefacts from Iron Smelting Furnace A

Metallurgy

The metallurgical debris gathered from the 'Smelting Precinct' was dominated by smelting/flow slag (48.5%) and iron ore (39.5%) (Table 9.6). The majority of the ore (10084.4g) was found in a cache just outside the southern perimeter of the precinct. It had been broken up into small pieces, and was presumably being stored there prior to being added to the furnace. The minimal presence of furnace base slag might be a reflection of its removal from the precinct to parts of SU3 where, as we saw in *lapa* M12, it was probably processed to retrieve embedded iron particles.

Table 9.6
Quantities of metallurgical debris from the Smelting Precinct and Iron Smelting Furnace A.

Material Type	Mass (g)	% of total mass
Smelting/flow slag	15050.0	48.5
Iron ore (magnetite)	12264.1	39.5
Tabular slag	1868.4	6.0
Tuyere fragments	1787.9	5.8
Furnace base slag	80.2	0.2
Total	31050.6	100

Iron Smelting Furnace B

Located approximately 70 metres to the south-east of Iron Smelting Furnace A, Iron Smelting Furnace B is also surrounded by a circle of stones (see Fig. 9.13). In this case, however, the walling is more similar to the type used to surround small livestock enclosures in homesteads than those used as palisade supports. There is no evidence for this wall having supported a screen. While the wall clearly defined a boundary around the furnace, there was no attempt to prevent visual access to the furnace inside. Two monoliths stand outside the wall on the south-east perimeter. Although the walling is collapsed, there is a suggestion of an entrance to the enclosure immediaely to the left of one of the monoliths (Fig. 9.18).

The furnace structure was similar in form to Iron Smelting Furnace A, and relatively well preserved (Fig. 9.19). A rectangular cavity was sunk into the gound, with large stone slabs supporting the structure on its north-west and south-east sides. A smaller stone slab at the south-west end may have supported a tuyere. Around the inside walls there were at least two layers of daga on all sides.

The interior cavity measures 0.80 m long by 0.28 m wide, with a maximum depth of 0.48 m from the top of the supporting slabs to the solid daga base. The base was flat, and covered with a layer of ash and charcoal approximately 0.03 m thick (Fig. 9.20). No evidence for additional superstructure was observed, and no metallurgical debris or other artefacts were recovered, indicating that the furnace had been cleaned out completely.

Figure 9.18
A view from the south-
east of Hilltop Enclosure 3
surrounding Iron Smelting
Furnace B. The monoliths
are shown in the left and
right foreground.

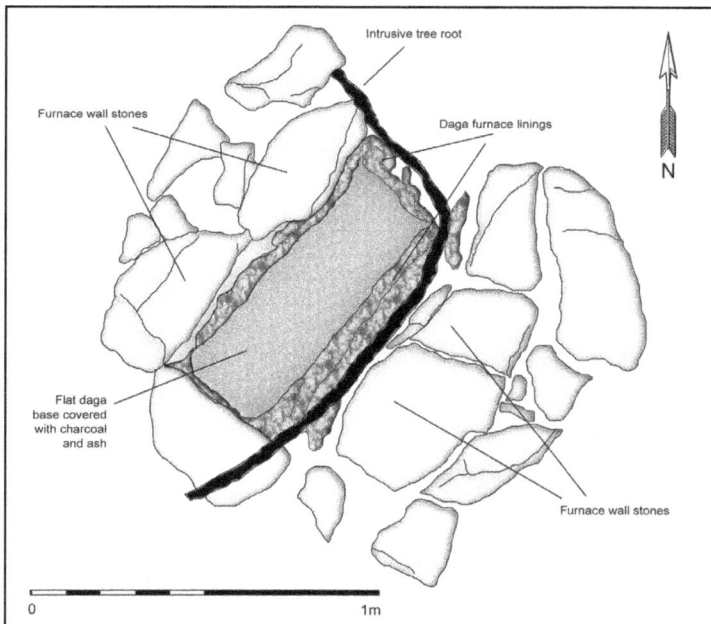

Figure 9.19
Plan of Iron Smelting
Furnace B, showing
the multiple daga
linings and the large
supporting stone slabs.

Figure 9.20
View into Iron Smelting
Furnace B after excavation,
showing the ash covered
daga base.

Settlement Unit 22(A) Iron Smelting Furnace

Half a kilometre away on the southern edge of Marothodi Central, a third iron smelting furnace was excavated, which provided a comparison to Iron Smelting Furnaces A and B on Smelting Hill. This furnace is situated some 7 metres from the western end of Settlement Unit 22, which is one of the larger homesteads at Marothodi (see Figs. 5.4 and 5.7). SU22 is actually made up of of three homesteads—A, B and C—which were integrated to form a coherent whole. This type of 'multi-homestead' structure was probably a result of the expansion of the family or families that lived here (see Sanderson 1981; Huffman 1986b).

The map of SU22 was made from aerial photographs of the site combined with ground survey, but apart from this no archaeological research was conducted within its walls and its features were not recorded in detail.

Nevertheless, metallurgical evidence was observed on the surface of two *malapa* on the western edge of SU22(A). On the front veranda of one of the dwelling structures here, a cache of iron ore was found. It looked like it may have been kept in an organic container, and had been leaning up against the outside wall of the main dwelling structure at the join between the front veranda and the main house wall. In another household nearby to the north, a pile of slag was found at the back of an unexcavated dwelling structure (Fig. 9.21). This evidence clearly implicates these households with certain stages of iron production.

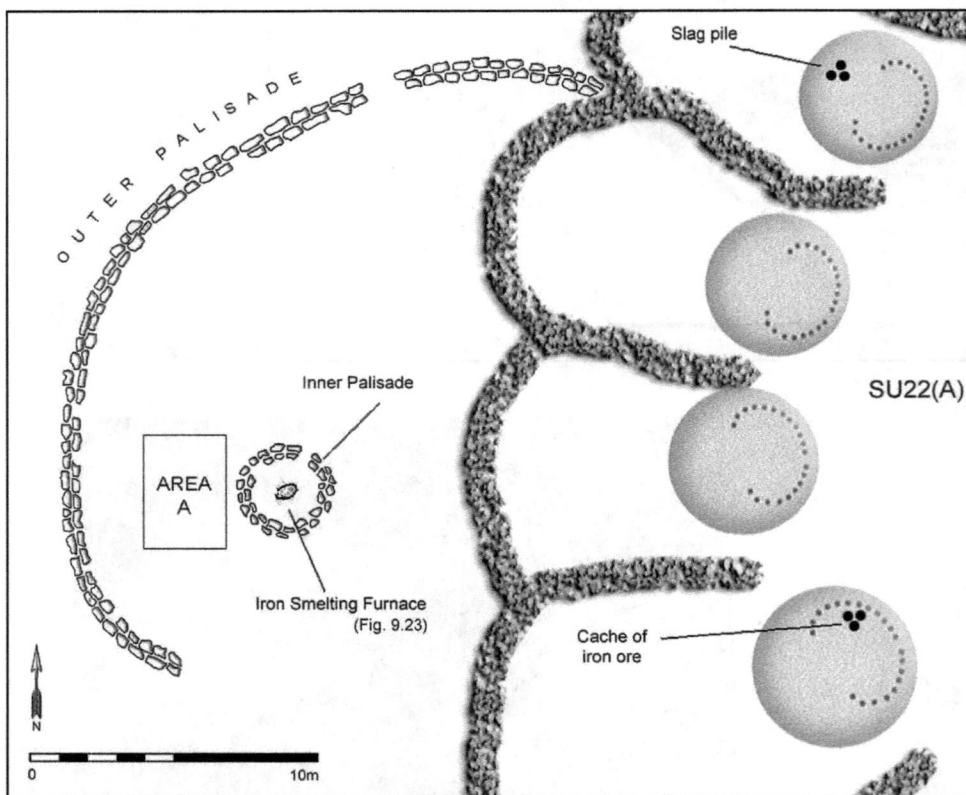

Figure 9.21
Map of the western edge of SU22(A) showing the inner and outer palisades surrounding the iron smelting furnace, and the location of 'Area A'.

From the outside edge of one of the *malapa* walls of SU22(A), a double row of stone blocks arcs in a south-westerly direction for approximately 25 metres, partially enclosing a space some 15 metres wide on the outside of the homestead (Fig. 9.21). As we have seen elsewhere at Marothodi, these blocks supported a wooden pole fence or palisade. Here, they clearly represent an attempt to conceal this 'precinct' from the surrounding homesteads. A gap in the screen provided a point of access into the precinct from the north side, but to the south, where there were no other homesteads, the precinct was open.

Within the screened area, a second stone palisade support forms a full circle approximately 4 metres in diameter, with a narrow opening on the north-east side. The iron smelting furnace was situated in the centre of this fenced circle (Figs. 9.21 and 9.22). Large quantities of slag were scattered both within and around the circle, especially on the western side. Here, a 3.0 x 4.0 m grid was laid out, labelled 'Area A', within which the surface was carefully trowelled and all archaeological material recovered (Fig. 9.21).

Excavation of the furnace revealed its cavity to be roughly rectangular in shape, 0.66 m long and 0.44 m wide. The structure was supported by upright stone slabs on three of its four sides, and the base was 'cobbled' with small stones. The interior was lined around the edges with at least two layers of daga, varying in thickness up to 0.10 m. In the centre of the base there is a hole in the cobbling, 0.20 m in diameter, which may have been created during the removal of the iron bloom at the end of the smelting process. The base was covered with a thin layer of ash, but no artefactual material was recovered from inside the furnace cavity (Figs. 9.23 and 9.24).

Although the furnace structure was disturbed and parts of the daga lining had collapsed, it was still possible to identify an opening at the western end, presumably through which a tuyere was placed. It is possible that a similar opening existed at the opposite end, but the daga here was too disturbed to be conclusive. Certainly, the occurrence of a tuyere at either end of the furnace would be in line with other archaeological examples of Sotho-Tswana furnaces observed in the western/central trans-Vaal region, such as that those at Buispoort and Melville Koppies (Mason 1971; Friede & Steel 1985) and at Magozastad (Miller *et al*. 1995: 40).

Figure 9.22
The support stones of the circular 'inner palisade' surrounding the SU22(A) iron smelting furnace, prior to excavation.

Figure 9.23
Plan of the iron smelting
furnace at SU22(A).

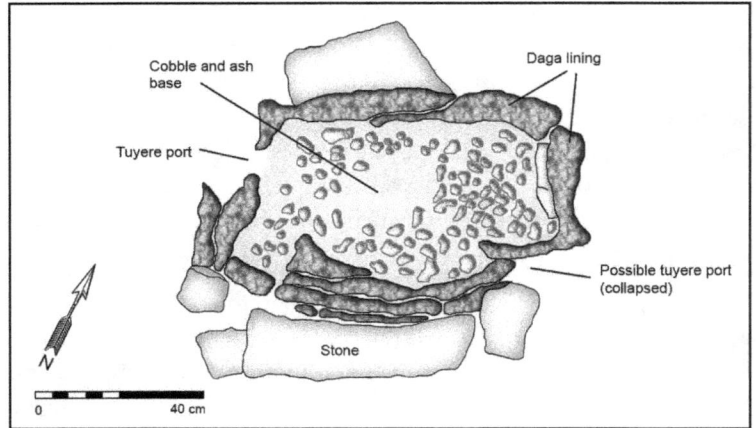

Figure 9.24
A view into the excavated
Iron Smelting Furnace at
SU22(A), showing the daga
linings and cobbled base.

Artefacts from Settlement Unit 22(A) Iron Smelting Furnace

Ceramics

A total of 115 ceramic sherds (846g) were recovered from the vicinity of the SU22(A) furnace, the vast majority of which were retrieved from 'Area A' just outside the furnace enclosure. Four sherds were recovered from inside the enclosure. Nine sherds were diagnostic,
but none were suitable for multi-dimensional analysis (Table 9.7). They were all plain rims
of smooth-necked jars, and are not illustrated here.

Table 9.7
Quantities of ceramic
sherds from the Iron
Smelting Furnace and
'Area A' at SU22(A).

		Sherds	Mass (g)	% of total sherds
Area A	Diagnostic	8	70.2	7.0
	Adiagnostic	103	695.8	89.5
Enclosure interior	Diagnostic	1	56.6	0.9
	Adiagnostic	3	23.4	2.6
Subtotals	Diagnostic	9	126.8	7.8
	Adiagnostic	106	719.2	92.2
Totals		115	846.0	100

Metallurgy

The metallurgical debris collected from the furnace enclosure and from the adjacent 'Area A' amounted to 8429.1g in total, and was composed primarily of smelting/flow slag (60.5%) and iron ore (30.6%). This is not surprising given that this is clearly a primary smelting site. Two small pieces of iron bloom were also found, one in 'Area A' and the other within the furnace enclosure. They were covered in slag, and probably missed by the smelters as they broke open the furnace. The rest of the debris is consistent with that observed from the other iron smelting furnaces, and includes 'tabular' slag, tuyere fragments, small quantities of 'frothy/glassy' slag and hollow slag droplets (Table 9.8).

Material Type	Mass (g)	% of total mass
Smelting/flow slag	5097.4	60.5
Iron ore (magnetite)	2580.3	30.6
Tabular slag	585.2	6.9
Tuyere fragments	76.9	0.9
Iron bloom	65.0	0.8
Frothy glassy slag	16.7	0.2
Hollow slag droplets	7.6	0.1
Total	8429.1	100

Table 9.8 Quantities of metallurgical debris from the Iron Smelting Furnace and 'Area A' at SU22(A).

Beads

A single black glass bead (#MAR116) was retrieved from 'Area A', adjacent to the iron smelting furnace (Fig. 9.25).

#MAR116

|——————| 1 cm

Figure 9.25 Black glass bead from 'Area A' next to the Iron Smelting Furnace at SU22(A).

Discussion

The iron smelting furnaces excavated at Marothodi shared similar structural characteristics. All were semi-rectangular or oval shaped cavities sunk into the ground, supported on the two longest sides by large stone slabs against which the daga lining was smeared. A stone slab at one of the short ends might also be a consistent feature, and may be related to the position of a tuyere. The design of the furnaces at Marothodi might be most closely compared with the shape of the furnace excavated at Melville Koppies, although here more of the superstructure was intact (see Mason 1971; Friede & Steel 1985). The lack of above-ground superstructure among the Marothodi furnaces is a recurring characteristic. This might be an issue of preservation, or an indication that they did not have much superstructure originally.

The most noticeable difference between the furnaces is seen in the nature of their surrounding enclosures, which clearly represented a desire to conceal the smelting activity. The varying degree of effort put into the outer screening seems to correlate with the proximity of the furnace to, or accessibility from, nearby homesteads. On Smelting Hill, for example, Iron Smelting Furnace B is enclosed by a rubble wall that seems unlikely to have supported a fence. On its own, it would not have prevented visual access to the furnace, and there is no evidence for an outer screen that concealed the wider activity area. But as the furnace is situated just over the crest of the hill, and is not overlooked by any homesteads, its location may have naturally fulfilled the need for seclusion without the addition of an outer fence (see Fig. 9.13).

Iron Smelting Furnace A on the northern edge of Smelting Hill was at least partially enclosed by fencing of some sort, although here the loose arrangement of the supporting stones suggests that any screens may have been relatively informal or ad-hoc. While this furnace is physically closer to SU3, it is elevated above it. The presence of the hill slope may have provided a natural restriction to the movement of people around the furnace area, and would have limited any view of the smelting activity from the homestead. While fences may have added to the effect, much of the necessary seclusion was created by the topographical context of the furnace.

By contrast, the furnace at SU22(A) is situated in close proximity to the 'Primary' *Kgosing* on its northern side, and SU21 is also nearby to the west (see Fig. 5.4). With no topography to create the necessary seclusion, more effort was put into creating it artificially. It is here that we see how formally arranged stones supported both an inner circular fence around the furnace structure, and also an outer fence that screened off the wider smelting precinct—a 'double membrane' of fencing (Fig. 9.21). This pattern was also observed around furnaces at the eastern end of SU22, although these have not yet been mapped. With the use of additional fencing, the need for seclusion was maintained despite the close proximity of homesteads.

But why were the smelters trying to conceal their furnaces, and from whom? The need to separate the process of iron smelting from the general community was underpinned by Tswana cultural principles. As a 'male' activity involving transformation through heat, iron smelting was deemed conceptually volatile and dangerous, and it needed to be carefully controlled (Herbert 1993; Collett 1993). In the following chapter we discuss these cultural principles in more depth, and consider how they were expressed through aspects of the organisation of production at Marothodi.

Chapter Ten
Organisation of Production

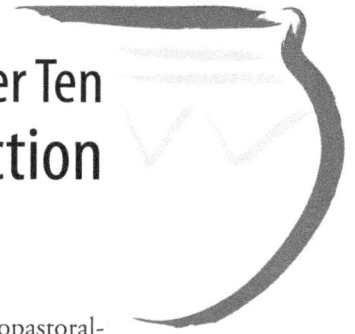

The primary focus of production for 19th century Tswana towns was agropastoralism. Life revolved around the seasonal agricultural cycle, and the management of cattle. As we have seen, these processes were reflected in the fundamental organisation of each homestead, which were repeated patterns designed around agropastoral concerns.

The density of Tswana towns in the Pilanesberg/Magaliesberg region attests to the agropastoral potential of the area, and we have discussed the ecological advantages of this Premium Biophysical Landscape. But the historical records from early travellers and Tswana oral traditions do record inter-chiefdom hostility focused on cattle raiding and the theft of crops. They serve as a reminder that, despite the agropastoral potential of the region, food production and food security in the late 18th and early 19th centuries could not be taken for granted. If such day-to-day needs were not satisfied, the development of complimentary forms of intense craft production, such as metallurgy, may have been hindered.

At Marothodi, however, we have seen that the position of the Tlokwa capital on the landscape was a strategic choice influenced primarily by economic considerations, and not by a concern for physical defence. As discussed in Chapter Four, this suggests that the Tlokwa were politically confident during their occupation here. This observation, combined with other factors such as the very large cattle kraals at the royal homesteads, indicates that they must have been successfully meeting their basic agropastoral needs. With this "material base" in place, other forms of production could develop and flourish (Comaroff 1985: 62).

These would include industries such as hide working, represented at Marothodi by the bone and pot sherd scraping tools recovered from middens, and of course, ceramic production. Indeed, pottery was produced in very large amounts, but although the results are visible archaeologically in the high quantities of ceramic sherds, the production process itself has not yet been identified archaeologically at Marothodi. Ethnography indicates that pots were made by women in back courtyards, and then fired in pit kilns outside the homestead (Van der Merwe & Scully 1971).

As we have seen, the most visible evidence for production outside of agriculture at Marothodi relates to metallurgy. The simultaneous production of both copper and iron, in such high quantities at a single town, provides a valuable opportunity to examine both the technology and the organisation of the production of each metal.

Metal production in sub-Saharan Africa was underpinned by a set of cultural principles which centred on a key theme: smelting as a transformative process involving heat was conceptually dangerous. It could only be performed by men, and taboos and ritual observances surrounded the activity to protect the community from its dangers. These included a need for seclusion, and the avoidance of women, who were inherently carriers of dangerous 'heat' themselves (Cline 1937; Hammond-Tooke 1981; Comaroff 1985; Herbert 1993; Schmidt 1997).

When exploring the organisation of metallurgy at Marothodi, however, we must bear in mind that this was a recently aggregated capital with a population of several thousand. By contrast, Tswana homesteads of earlier phases were small and relatively dispersed, and cultural principles such as seclusion, around which metal production was organised, could perhaps have been implemented more easily. The process of aggregation was a significant change in the Tswana world, and brought with it a new set of practical constraints. Suddenly there were many homesteads situated in close proximity to each other, and all forms of production occurred on a much larger scale, requiring greater labour and creating new demands for efficient coordination.

Nevertheless, the spatiality of metal production at Marothodi, and importantly, the differences in the spatial organisation of copper and iron, indicates that the production of both metals took place under the guidance of a cultural structure.

In this chapter we address three issues. Firstly, we examine the technology of iron and copper production as it is represented in the archaeology of Marothodi. We then explore the extent to which the cultural principles mentioned above influenced the spatial organisation of iron and copper production, and how these were adapted to the context of living in a high density town environment. Finally, we focus on the politics of production, with some discussion of the movement of metals within the town and how this may have reflected economic hierarchies.

The technology of metal production

As we have seen, two stages of iron production are represented at Marothodi; smelting, and forging or smithing. While one likely iron forge has been identified, it has not received detailed archaeological attention. The majority of analysis and discussion therefore focuses primarily on smelting at Marothodi, with a brief summary of iron forging processes to follow.

Evidence for copper production at Marothodi represents a process that also consists of two phases: a primary smelting phase in which ore is reduced to a copper matte; and a secondary 'refining' process that re-melts the copper matte to remove impurities and unwanted elements. The result of the refining process is metallic copper or copper alloy that is suitable for casting as ingots or working into objects or ornaments. The smelting and refining phases can be archaeologically distinguished, and both phases can occur at a single homestead.

Our discussion of metallurgical technology begins here with iron.

Iron smelting

In some parts of sub-Saharan Africa, where the only available ores are poor-grade and relatively difficult to reduce to workable metal, a two-step process of smelting and refining iron is necessary (Miller 1997). Most of the evidence from the iron furnaces at Marothodi, however, seems to indicate that there was only a single smelting event, suggesting that the ore used to produce the iron was sufficiently high-grade to render a refining stage unnecessary. This is supported by the results of optical microscopy and chemical analyses, which indicate that the majority of the ore retrieved from the iron furnace at SU22(A), as an example, was a pure, massive iron oxide with low titanium content. If adequately fluxed, this ore would have produced a workable iron bloom after only one smelt (Hall *et al*. 2006). As we saw in Chapter Nine, however, slag was evidently kept and perhaps processed in at least one household adjacent to the SU22(A) iron smelting precinct, and also in the excavated *lapa* M12 at SU3. As previously suggested, this slag was probably broken up to extract small pieces of smelted iron that had failed to separate from it.

It is interesting to note that, of the finished iron objects from Marothodi subjected to XRF analysis, most possess a high magnesium oxide (MgO) content that contrasts significantly with the low MgO of the iron slags. Consequently, it would appear that the Tlokwa community at Marothodi had acquired at least some of their iron tools from smelters elsewhere, who were using a different type of ore (Hall *et al*. 2006). The source, or sources, of iron ore used by the Marothodi smelters has not yet been identified.

In terms of morphology, the iron smelting furnaces at Marothodi were generally rectangular in shape, insulated by thick daga walls to maintain the high temperatures necessary to smelt iron (see Merkell 1990). Despite having slightly different dimensions, the three excavated iron furnaces were relatively consistent in design and form. All were supported on the two longest sides by large stone slabs, with another stone built into at least one of the shorter end walls. This may have supported one of the tuyeres, although detailed interpretation is hampered by the uneven preservation of the three structures. From the traces of other iron furnaces that are visible above ground, such as the groups to the north-west

Figure 10.1
John Campbell's sketch of a Hurutshe iron smelting furnace, from his visit to Kaditshwene in 1820.

of SU33 and to the east of SU22(C), iron furnaces at Marothodi seem to have been fairly consistent in their basic design and construction. The excavation of more examples would be expected to confirm this.

The iron ore was initially prepared by being broken up into small pieces suitable for adding to the furnace. Like the processing of slag, this could be undertaken within domestic household space as suggested by the small cache of broken-up ore on the front veranda of a dwelling structure in SU22(A) (see Fig. 9.21). In light of the 'maleness' of metal production, this may have been one of the few stages of the process that women were permitted to perform (Haaland *et al.* 2002).

Successive deposits of charcoal and ore were tipped into the furnace, and the temperature was controlled throughout the smelt by bellows attached to tuyeres, which entered the furnace through apertures in the daga structure. Due to post-depositional warping and missing superstructure, the tuyere apertures are not easily identifiable in the Marothodi iron smelting furnaces, but it seems likely that they originally had two tuyeres. One tuyere entered the furnace at each of the short ends, as demonstrated by more complete examples excavated at other Tswana sites (Mason 1971; Freide & Steel 1985; Miller *et al.* 1995).

Chemical reduction of iron ore can theoretically occur at around 800°C, but it is also necessary for the slag produced to melt and separate from the forming bloom, and this requires temperatures of between 1100 to 1300°C. The quality of the metal produced depends largely on the composition of gasses inside the furnace, which is in turn dependent upon the temperature, and the ratio of ore to fuel (Herbert 1993; Miller 1997). The perfection of this technique would have taken a great deal of experience, and trial and error with a particular ore type. The product formed by a successful smelt was a spongy mass of metallic iron, often containing pieces of slag waste and other impurities, but nevertheless suitable for working by a smith.

Two small pieces of iron bloom were recovered from the vicinity of the iron smelting furnace at SU22(A), which had presumably been either lost or discarded after different smelts. Analysis of the blooms revealed that each piece had significantly different titanium and carbon levels, indicating they originated from ore nodules with varied mineral composition, and that conditions inside the furnace were slightly different for each one (Hall *et al.* 2006).

Figure 10.2
An engraving of a Tlhaping iron forger at work, by William Burchell from his visit to Dithakong in 1812.

Small, manually operated bloomery furnaces such as these would have varied considerably in the ratio of ore to fuel, and in the rate of air flow, from smelt to smelt. Such volatility highlights the importance of skill and experience in successfully producing workable iron.

Iron forging

As described in Chapter Seven, the feature observed on the south-east edge of Settlement Unit 25 (see Fig. 7.1) has been identified as an iron forge in light of a range of archaeological evidence visible on the surface in the immediate vicinity that might be characteristic of a forging site (see Huffman 1993, 2007). This included scatters of small, broken pieces of slag, large stones with flat, hammered and dimpled surfaces, and a small iron object that might be identified as a hammer head. The feature incorporates some naturally outcropping rocks and, as we have seen, the wall of the nearby *lapa* M25 was built to respect it spatially. It seems likely that closer examination and excavation, would confirm the identity of this feature as a forge.

Forge 'ovens' are typically shallow circular bowls in the ground in which charcoal was burned (Fig. 10.2). The temperature was maintained at around 900°C by means of bellows, which were operated by an assistant using either hands or feet. The iron bloom was placed in the oven for an initial heating process to melt off any adhering slag, and to soften the metal. When it was soft and relatively pure, the temperature was lowered to between 730 and 850°C, and the metal was shaped using stone or iron hammers on a flat stone anvil. Tempering by plunging the metal into water and then reheating it was not typically practiced by sub-Saharan smiths, who preferred to let the metal air-cool between phases of reheating (Campbell 1822; Miller & Van der Merwe 1994; Miller 1997; Hall *et al.* 2006).

Primary copper smelting

Evidence for primary copper smelting has been observed at many locations within Marothodi, being frequently visible on the ground surface. The smelting sites always occur outside the back walls of domestic *malapa*, and are characterised by scatters of slag, fragments of green-streaked gossan, and a reddish soil, coloured by fragmented furnace daga. In Chapter Eight we examined one such site at the rear of *lapa* M1 in SU26 (Fig. 8.21), and in Chapter Seven we described the excavation of a smelting site and furnace at the rear of *lapa* M12 at SU25 (Fig. 7.33).

Excavation at the SU25 copper smelting site revealed an example of the small sunken bowl-shaped furnaces in which the primary smelting took place. The fragments of ore found in association with the furnaces and in the SU25 middens were composed of iron-rich opaline gossan with inclusions of green-coloured malachite—the material that forms the weathered gossan capping of the nickel sulphide pipes on the north-east side of the town (Wagner 1924; Hall *et al.* 2006).

In common with most ancient sub-Saharan copper smelters, the malachite inclusion was the desired copper-carbonate ore element (Herbert 1984; Vogel 2000). The malachite concentration was enhanced by crushing the gossan and removing superfluous elements of the gangue before smelting. The crushing process could have been undertaken close to the ore source (Herbert 1984), or within domestic *malapa* as suggested by the presence of the flat beaten stone in M1 of SU26 (Fig. 8.13). This is also indicated at other Marothodi homesteads, such as SU4 (see Fig. 5.4) where caches of copper ore have been observed behind dwelling structures in some *malapa*. It is also likely that further beneficiation of the ore occurred at the smelting site, as suggested by the flat stone adjacent to the SU25 furnaces (Fig. 7.33), although this stone may also have been used to break off the slag sticking to the copper matte after smelting. In any case, the evidence from Marothodi shows that neither iron nor copper ore preparation was confined to the smelting locales, but that domestic areas were also considered appropriate for this stage in the process.

The ore pieces recovered at SU25 were probably fragments discarded as unsuitable for smelting. Indeed, analysis of the ore indicated that it was quite low-grade, and that the smelters at Marothodi probably needed to beneficiate the material substantially to make it productive (Hall *et al.* 2006). It would seem that the nickel sulphide pipes had already yielded their most productive ore, and that the mines were nearing the end of their use life. But despite the extra effort required to collect and beneficiate this material, the process was clearly still considered to be economically worthwhile, and the labour required did not constrain production.

A certain percentage of the gangue, being rich in iron oxide, would have been retained to facilitate self-fluxing and the achievement of more efficient separation of copper from slag (Crump 1925; Vogel 2000). Gauging the precise ratio of flux material to include would have been essential to the success of the smelt, and as with iron smelting, must have been a skill acquired through trial and error with this particular ore. A long history of smelting by the Tlokwa and others that pre-dates Marothodi, may have provided that experience.

The smelting reaction for malachite can occur in a reducing atmosphere with temperatures as low as 700 to 800°C, but in order to create a slag fluid enough to separate efficiently from the copper, it would have been necessary to maintain a temperature at least as high as 1083°C (Bisson 1997; Vogel 2000).

It was also desirable to prevent the furnace from becoming so hot that too much iron contained in the ore was reduced along with the copper. This would have reduced the malleability of the copper produced. A certain amount of accidental iron reduction was almost unavoidable, as it would start to occur at 1100°C which is not much hotter than the temperature required to smelt copper (Merkell 1990). It is therefore not surprising that the copper smelting slags from Marothodi contain some metallic iron particles (Hall *et al.* 2006). They confirm that the Marothodi copper furnaces operated at temperatures above 1100°C, in common with all other known copper furnaces on the continent (Bisson 1997).

Maintaining tight control over furnace temperature was only made possible with the use of bellows and tuyeres to manage air flow. Although bellows rarely survive archaeologically, being made largely from organic materials (Fig. 10.3) the tuyere tips survive well when they become vitrified during smelting. As we have seen, there are many tuyere fragments associated with the smelting sites examined at Marothodi. In light of the small size of the excavated furnace at SU25, it seems likely that a single tuyere was used rather than the double tuyeres noted during some copper smelting re-enactments (Miller 1994). As noted in Chapter Seven, the tuyere of the SU25 furnace probably entered the structure at the northern end.

At the southern end, where the daga is intact up to the ground surface, there is no in-dication of a tap hole for the release of molten copper or slag. It is therefore likely that the copper sank to the base of the furnace, and was retrieved after the smelt by breaking the furnace open, as is the case with many other copper smelting furnace types (see Stayt 1931: 64; Chaplin 1961: 56; Herbert 1984: 58; Bisson 1997: 129). Observations of cop-per smelting re-enactments suggest that it would have taken less than an hour for the smelting process to be completed from the lighting of the furnace to the extraction of the metal (Miller 1994). After removing the copper, and when it had sufficiently cooled, it was probably necessary to break off the main bits of slag that were sticking to it (see Bisson 1997; Vogel 2000) on the flat stone nearby. The furnace linings could then be repaired and the furnaces used again, as indicated by the multiple daga linings of the SU25 furnace.

Given the surviving physical characteristics of the SU25 furnace, it is possible that the original structure was similar in design to the furnace recorded at Phalaborwa (Schwellnus 1937; van der Merwe & Scully 1971). This "bowl-shaped oven" was oval in shape, with a single arched tuyere hole at one end and a circular shaft on top. The walls extended some 0.20 m above the ground surface, and appear to have been approximately 0.10 m thick (Schwellnus 1937: 909). The absence of a daga base is an attribute also shared by the Marothodi furnace, which has a layer of ash at the bottom instead of a solid 'floor'. It is not clear whether the ash was simply a by-product of the smelting process, or whether, as suggested ethnographically, it was deliberately placed inside the furnace during its con-struction to prevent the smelted copper from mixing with the soil underneath and to aid its removal (Chaplin 1961; Herbert 1984). In any case, it is conceivable that, with the su-perstructure broken away, the remains of the Phalaborwa furnace would closely resemble the surviving furnace remains at SU25.

Copper refining

The end result of the primary smelting phase is a matrix composed of slag, metallic cop-per prills, and other impurities such as iron. The removal of the superfluous elements was achieved by first mechanically removing slag and dirt to expose the trapped copper, and then refining it through a process of re-melting. At Marothodi, copper refining furnaces

Figure 10.3
A pair of goat skin bellows connected to a fragment of clay tuyere.

are relatively easy to distinguish from primary smelting furnaces. As described in Chapter Six, an example of a Copper Refining Annex was excavated behind M1 of the 'Secondary' *Kgosing*, and another was identified behind *lapa* M2 of the 'Primary' *Kgosing*.

In the example at the 'Secondary' *Kgosing*, five small oval-shaped furnaces are arranged in a circular formation within an 'annex', enclosed by a double row of stones that are interpreted as supports for a wooden fence or palisade. Flat 'anvil' stones with beaten surfaces occur within the annex, suggesting that the smelted copper was subjected to further mechanical processing here before being refined in the crucibles.

The furnaces themselves are described in detail in Chapter Six. They consisted of oval arrangements of stones within which a 2-3 cm thick layer of daga was smeared to form a shallow dish, with an opening at one end to accommodate the tuyere (Fig. 6.23). According to ethnographic accounts of copper refining practices, it is likely that a large ceramic sherd was placed on the daga dish, to act as a crucible. A tuyere was placed just above it, and the crucible was filled with charcoal. When the charcoal was lit, bellows pumped air into the crucible to create the necessary temperature, and pieces of previously smelted copper were added. The copper melted, and gradually coalesced in the crucible. During this process the copper was homogenised and consolidated, iron and slag inclusions were removed, and a workable quantity of copper was produced that was suitable for casting, or for drawing into wire (Fig. 10.4). Afterwards, the ash was brushed away, the crucible was removed, and the molten copper could be poured from it (Stayt 1931; Chaplin 1961; Bisson 1997).

The 'casting' process—the pouring of molten copper from the crucibles into ingot moulds—was a continuation of this stage of copper production. The presence of crucible

Figure 10.4
A Venda man making copper wire bracelets in the early 1900s. (H. Stayt)

sherds here suggests that this may also have taken place within the refining annex. If this was the case, the specific evidence for this process (i.e. the presence of ingot moulds) has not yet been identified archaeologically at Marothodi.

The spatiality of metal production

Our discussion of the technology of copper and iron production has demonstrated that, with the exception of some minor differences in furnace design, the number of tuyeres used, and the presence or absence of a refining process, there was little significant difference in the smelting technology of the two metals. It seems likely that a skilled copper smelter would also be capable of successfully smelting iron, and *visa versa*.

At Marothodi, the possibility of a compartmentalisation of skills is difficult to discern, but some hints may arise from the location of iron and copper production sites and their association with specific homesteads, and at a finer scale, with specific households. We now turn to a discussion of the spatiality of metal production at Marothodi, in which we explore both the cultural principles that may underpin this, and the political relationships around which this production was organised.

The cultural structure of iron production

In Chapter Five we observed that iron production areas were predominantly detached from homesteads, and tended to 'float' in the spaces between them or on the outskirts of the town. In Chapter Nine, the practice of secluding all iron furnaces by means of at least one, and sometimes two, surrounding screens was described, which reflected a desire to control both visual and physical access to the iron smelting process. The presence of the 'inner' circular screen surrounding each iron smelting furnace occurs so consistently that it is a key physical characteristic of the feature that helps to identify them. The use of an outer or second screen seems to be related to the proximity of homesteads. The closer the smelting furnace to a homestead, the more elaborate and extensive the outer screens were.

The need for this isolation and separation from homesteads is guided by a set of cultural principles that are largely shared, with some variation in expression, by most Bantu-speaking African communities. Ethnography directly related to Tswana iron production is scarce compared to other areas in Bantu-speaking Africa. Much of our discussion concerning the cultural structure of this craft is drawn from the ethnography of other areas, or sometimes from other cultural domains not explicitly linked to metalworking.

Nevertheless, this is sufficient to realistically account for the persistent separation of iron smelting 'precincts' from homesteads. At the core of the discussion are the concepts of iron smelting as a process of transformation through heat, and the conceptual parallels between smelting and childbirth (Cline 1937; Herbert 1993; Schmidt 1997).

According to Tswana worldview, heat can be a source of danger, volatility and pollution. If it is not controlled, isolated or countered it has the potential to disrupt the order of society and lead to imbalance, drought, illness and death. For this reason, heat-producing activities tend to be seasonally controlled to avoid the summer months, as they might deter rainfall.

Women are seen as being inherently predisposed to the 'carrying' of heat, and consequently their physical activities are subject to tight conceptual controls (Hammond-Tooke 1981; Comaroff 1985). They are particularly 'dangerous' when menstruating, and during pregnancy. When in these states, a woman is subject to varying degrees of physical and conceptual isolation, and her activities are restricted in an attempt to control the unstable 'heat' of her condition, and to prevent it from diffusing to other members of society—particularly men who are conceptually 'cool' and stable. Activities in the world of men, such as rainmaking, male initiation, cattle management and communication with the ancestors, were all potentially vulnerable to the disruptive heat of the female (Comaroff 1985).

The cosmological context is further elaborated by Bantu-speakers' perception of iron smelting itself as a process of transformation through heat, and its conceptual parallels with the process of childbirth (Cline 1937; Collett 1993; Herbert 1993; Schmidt 1997) which was "a subsocial process, occurring in domestic seclusion" (Comaroff 1985: 97). Smelting furnaces were seen as women, a parallel that is made more explicit among some Bantu-speakers like the Karanga (Shona) who designed their furnaces with aspects of female anatomy (Collett 1993). Some smelters, such as the Chisinga (Bemba), were conceptually 'married' to the furnace for the duration of the smelting process, and for this reason "the man does not sleep in his wife's hut or have sexual intercourse with her until the smelting is finished" (Brelsford 1949: 28).

The clay tuyeres represent the male element of the process of conception (Blacking 1969), and as ritually charged objects their disposal may need to be carefully controlled after the smelt to prevent their procurement by malevolent forces who might use them for witchcraft (Schmidt 1997).

The iron bloom is gradually 'gestated' within the womb of the furnace during the reduction process, throughout which it could be disastrous for any conceptually 'inappropriate' persons to engage with the furnace or the smelters. Men who are 'hot' from recent sexual activity, and all women of childbearing age, by virtue of their innate propensity to carry heat, must stay away from the furnace and the smelters during this time. As the evidence from Marothodi has suggested, women can be involved in certain preparations for the smelt, such as gathering, transporting and beneficiating ore and fuel. But the screens suggest that they were required to steer clear of the actual smelting process. Women who are pregnant or menstruating must not come into contact with any aspect of the production process at all, including the preparation of materials (Schmidt 1997).

If a smelt failed to produce iron successfully, it would be assumed that one or more of these taboos had been contravened, and that the resulting permeation of disruptive heat had caused a 'miscarriage' of the bloom. It is to maximise the chances of preventing such disruption that iron smelting among Bantu-speaking people is usually conducted in a context of seclusion, secrecy and separation from everyday domestic life. Although the spatial scale over which these principles are evident at Marothodi is relatively small, the spatiality of iron smelting precincts indicates that they were applied.

By contrast, these principles do not apply to the comparatively open practice of iron forging. In many Bantu-speaking societies the smith did not necessarily need to possess the same spiritual knowledge or 'power' as the smelter of metals, and could be any man who possessed the required skills. The process of forging itself was rarely guided by the same taboos as the smelting process. It was not conceptually tied to childbirth, as a delicate and potentially dangerous transformation through heat, but was more associated with the raising of the child – the 'post-birth' socialisation in which the whole community played a role.

Consequently, forges are often observed in central, public spaces in homesteads (Stayt 1931; Herbert 1993; Huffman 1993, 2007). For example, the iron forges identified at site ZK001, a mid-19th century Tswana settlement near present-day Brits, are associated with the central kraals as well as "the veld directly outside the borders of the settlement" (Pistorius & Steyn 1995: 72). These spatial contexts emphasise the public nature of forging, and at face value it therefore seems appropriate that no obvious attempt had been made to conceal the forge on the south-east edge of Settlement Unit 25 at Marothodi, although this detail requires further research.

The cultural structure of copper production

Although two distinct phases of copper production can be identified archaeologically at Marothodi, both primary smelting and refining sites share the same spatial context: they are always intimately associated with homesteads, and more specifically, are situated immediately behind the back courtyards of domestic *malapa*. This recurring attachment of both copper smelting and refining areas to the back courtyards of individual households raises questions as to what cultural values or principles underpin this consistent association.

As discussed in Chapter Four, domestic *malapa* are a conceptually female domain (Huffman 1986b; Hall 1998, 2000). Back courtyards were, in particular, acutely private spaces where food was stored and prepared, and young children were raised. "It was, in other words, the site of the transformation of presocial elements into more decidedly social form" (Comaroff 1985: 58).

At face value, therefore, the association of copper smelting with 'female' space may seem at odds with what we know of Tswana cultural values. As we have discussed, metallurgy is a 'male' activity involving dangerous processes of transformation conceptually parallel to procreation, and as such should be conducted in seclusion (Herbert 1993; Huffman 2001). The 'feminine' could be a potent source of 'pollution' and a danger to such transformative processes (Comaroff 1985; Hammond-Tooke 1993).

However, most African ethnography from which we draw our understanding of the cultural structure of metallurgy relates only to iron production. The association we have identified between back courtyards and copper smelting suggests that there must be somewhat different cultural values tied to copper, and these might be understood in terms of the symbolic gender of this metal. In contrast to the white hardness of 'male' iron, the red softness of copper is symbolically associated with the feminine, rendering it conceptually 'female'. Its use as a material of personal adornment, often symbolising concepts of fertility, further imbues copper with feminine significance (Herbert 1984).

We have recognised the Tswana household, and especially the back courtyard, as a space that encloses processes associated with female labour and transformation, such as food preparation and making pottery. If copper production is seen as a feminine transformation, metaphorically associated with childbirth, then we begin to glimpse a cultural code that legitimately places copper production close to this back courtyard space.

Our developing association between copper production and female space at Marothodi can be elaborated if we step outside the town to include an historical observation from the contemporary Hurutshe capital of Kaditshwene, recorded by the missionary John Campbell in 1820:

> The Marootzee (Hurutshe) are confidently reported by other nations to smelt copper; they profess the same themselves, and they abound in copper articles more than the other nations. They asserted also that copper furnaces were behind the houses of some of their captains (Headmen), but we never could obtain a sight of them. They did not flatly refuse, but put it off from time to time. Perhaps they acted thus on the principle of the Birmingham and Sheffield manufacturers, being jealous lest others should obtain a knowledge of the art. (Campbell 1822: 275-276)

This source attests to the location of copper production at the rear of households, and also potentially elaborates the privacy of these areas as exclusively female space. It was probably these factors that were behind the reluctance of Campbell's hosts to show him the copper furnace, rather than an attempt to protect industrial secrets as Campbell suspected (Campbell 1822). He was, by contrast, given free access to an iron smelting furnace (see Fig. 10.1).

Furthermore, the association between copper production and back courtyard space appears to have considerable time depth. A copper furnace was observed in a back courtyard at a 16th century Madikwe (ancestral Tswana) homestead in the Madikwe Game Reserve, in present-day North West Province (Hall 2000). This association was therefore a persistent cultural principle.

Thus, it can be demonstrated that the principles guiding the spatial organisation of metal production are different for each metal, and we can suggest that this is a reflection of the gendered nature of iron as male and copper as female. In order to explore this distinction further and build confidence in these ideas, it is instructive to briefly review the spatiality of another domain of transformation in the Tswana world. This is the process of male and female initiation, for which there is considerably more ethnographic information.

Initiation schools were seasonal events, typically scheduled during the winter months to avoid conflicting with the demands of the agricultural cycle (Schapera 1978; Comaroff 1985). We might therefore expect that for the same reasons, metal production was also performed according to a seasonal calendar.

Male initiation is composed of two main ceremonies: first the 'white' *bogwêra*; followed by the 'black' *bogwêra*. The former is where the most significant transformative processes occurred, where the "initiates' childhood identity was to be reduced to its natural substrate and shaped anew", and from which they emerged as socially functional men (Comaroff 1985: 95).

As with all processes of transformation, 'white' *bogwêra* is conducted in an atmosphere of great secrecy, far from the settlement, in the seclusion of the bush (Schapera 1953;

Mönnig 1967; Hammond-Tooke 1981)—a "liminal capsule outside of social space and time" where "social beings" were forged (Comaroff 1985: 95, 98). Women and uninitiated men are forbidden to approach or even look upon the initiation lodge, and the men associated with the ceremonies had to refrain from sexual contact for the duration of the proceedings, lest they harm the initiates with the "heat generated by adult sexuality" (Comaroff 1985: 91). Such observations underline the conceptual and structural parallel with iron smelting which, like 'white' *bogwêra*, is a male process, closely linked to the theme of childbirth and subject to many of the same taboos.

The second rite of male initiation, 'black' *bogwêra* commenced several months after the conclusion of the 'white' *bogwêra*, and by contrast was conducted largely in the central cattle kraal near the *kgotla*, in a public context (Schapera 1953). With the primary transformation from boys to men having already been accomplished in seclusion, this rite centred on the "subsequent impression on them of collective norms" (Comaroff 1985: 87). To extend the analogy of childbirth, this phase might be considered structurally parallel to the public, communal process of 'raising' a child and as such it is possible to recognise conceptual ties to the process of iron forging—the crafting of a socially meaningful 'object' (Herbert 1993).

In contrast to the main transformational processes of male initiation, the corresponding rites of female initiation, *bojale*, were considerably less elaborate and were spatially tied to the homestead. There was only one phase of the initiation, and this was conducted primarily "at the margins of, rather than outside, the community" (Comaroff 1985: 116) usually "in the village itself, in certain selected homesteads" (Schapera 1955: 116). There was less need for seclusion and elaborate ritual, because the development of the female was seen as more of a natural process guided by her physical development, and consequently no elemental or potentially 'dangerous' transformation was occurring. Instead, women were "incompletely socialized, capable of producing value but not of transforming it into enduring social form" (Comaroff 1985: 114).

The spatial context of *bojale* rites, and the subdued levels of ceremony and taboo surrounding them, resonate with what we have observed of the spatial organisation of copper production at Marothodi. As we have seen, both primary copper smelting and refining activities are closely tied to the household, being conducted on the margins of homesteads, and tightly linked to female back courtyard space. Primary copper smelting seems to have been conducted without screens which, as previously discussed, suggests less of a concern for the seclusion and secrecy within which, by contrast, iron smelting was shrouded.

This potential parallel might strengthen the suggestion that the primary smelting of copper, like *bojale*, was not considered to be a fundamental transformation from the natural to the socially meaningful. It consistently played out in the domestic domain, rather than traversing from the deeply liminal to the social and political core.

Thus, we can begin to recognise metal production at Marothodi as being structurally parallel to Tswana rites of male and female initiation. The spatial organisation of iron smelting, iron forging and copper production are guided by some of the same cultural principles that underpin 'white' and 'black' *bogwêra* for males, and *bojale* for females.

The hierarchy of production

Our discussion has hitherto focussed upon the cultural values directing the organisation of metal production at Marothodi. Another aspect of this organisation may have been underpinned by political hierarchy within the Tlokwa community, and we will now consider some of these dynamics.

We begin with the observation made earlier that at both the 'Primary' *Kgosing* and the 'Secondary' *Kgosing*, the supreme high status homesteads, the only evidence for metal production is related to copper refining, and there is only one refining annex at each *kgosing*. There is no sign of primary copper smelting at either of the two royal homesteads, and there are no other palisade supports to indicate the presence of additional refining annexes.

The absence of primary smelting indicates that the *kgosing* copper refiners received their unrefined copper matte from other homesteads where primary smelting did occur. This may have been a form of tribute collected by the chief from all homesteads involved in primary smelting, or from specific homesteads that were 'designated suppliers' to the *kgosing*. In Chapter Seven, for example, it was suggested that SU25—a large scale producer of primary copper—might have had some type of formal association with the 'Secondary' *Kgosing* that was reflected in the spatial relationship between the two.

Furthermore, the output of only a single copper refining annex at each *kgosing* would have been relatively small scale. It is highly unlikely that they produced sufficient finished copper for the consumption of all the residents of the *kgosing* to which they were attached. It would therefore seem reasonable to suggest that the 'royal refiners' at the *kgosing* were producing copper only for the core of the royal family—perhaps just for the chief and his wives, or potentially just for the chief himself. This was copper production for the 'Court', and was not for general consumption.

It is also possible that the metallurgists who conducted the copper refining at the two *kgosing* were not themselves residents of the royal homesteads, but were specialists who performed this task specifically for the chief. Such a craftsman/client relationship might help to explain the lack of physical access from the refining annexes into the *malapa* to which they were connected, as discussed in Chapter Six. The metallurgists entered and left the refining annexes from outside the royal homesteads. This contrasts with the arrangement at commoner homesteads, such as SU25 and SU26, where there do appear to be entrances from back courtyards that lead directly into, or close to, rear annexes.

The absence of any other production sites at either of the two *kgosing* suggests that other residents were not permitted either to smelt or refine their own copper at the royal homestead, but had to obtain their copper goods from outside, either from copper producers at Marothodi or from other towns. The exclusivity of production at the *kgosing* serves to heighten the significance of the 'royal copper' as an elite, prestige product.

It is significant that despite the overall scale of copper production at Marothodi, some of the copper objects found in the 'Primary' *Kgosing* were actually tin bronzes (see Hall *et al.* 2006). This material probably originated from Rooiberg, some 100 km north of Marothodi, and these items were likely to have been imported from other copper producers. Their presence in the *kgosing* is perhaps a reflection of its elite status.

At commoner homesteads, primary smelting sites have been observed behind *malapa* of different sizes, including some small ones which are likely to have been occupied by people of relatively low status. This is particularly clear in M12 at SU25, which is not only small, but also located opposite the high status households identified on the southern side of the homestead. The implication is that primary smelting was not restricted exclusively to high status members of the community, but that any man who possessed the necessary skills could potentially participate in this phase of copper production.

By contrast, the copper refining sites at commoner homesteads seem to be associated primarily with large, and by extension senior, *malapa*. This pattern is recognised at SU25, and possibly at SU26. It has also been observed more explicitly along the northern perimeter of SU22 (see Fig. 5.4) where a series of annexes, as yet unmapped, occur in association with large *malapa*. The relative seniority of these households is emphasised by their position on slightly elevated ground and their proximity to the court of the 'Primary' *Kgosing*.

This observation suggests that the secondary phase in the production process, where the raw matrix produced by the primary smelt was purified and made into valuable, workable copper, took place within tighter cultural and political frameworks than primary smelting. The coordination of non-elite metal production, and possibly distribution, at the level of the headman of each commoner homestead would be in keeping with ethnographically described systems of power in Tswana society, wherein individual homesteads enjoyed relative autonomy over their own political and economic affairs (Schapera 1953, 1955; Mönnig 1967; Hammond-Tooke 1993).

It is noteworthy that there is no evidence for any iron production at either of the two *kgosing*. In contrast to the keeping of 'royal copper refiners', it would appear that the elites obtained iron from the same producers as other members of the community, either as tribute or through purchase. This may also have come from iron producers at Marothodi, or from elsewhere. As discussed earlier, some of the iron objects found at Marothodi seem to have been imported from outside the town (Hall *et al.* 2006).

By the very nature of its spatial organisation it can be difficult to link iron smelting with specific homesteads, but some suggestions can be made. For example, the proximity of SU3 to the iron furnaces on Smelting Hill, and the presence of a cache of slag in *lapa* M12 of this homestead, indicates an association with iron smelting in this part of the town. Even more directly, the slag and ore caches in some *malapa* on the western perimeter of SU22(A) clearly link this homestead to the smelting furnace a few metres outside its walls, and the palisade support stones physically connect it to the smelting area here.

Summary

In Chapter Three we discussed some of the changing regional economic realities, such as increasing competition for resources and burgeoning demands for trade goods, which may have encouraged the Tlokwa to develop practices of high-quantity metal output. The evidence for metal production at Marothodi, particularly copper, certainly indicates an output that exceeded the needs of this community alone. Production on such a scale might be described as economic specialisation, and this is alluded to in historical records.

Tswana oral traditions and the journals of early travellers record that the Hurutshe, for example, were known as accomplished copper manufacturers (Campbell 1822; Breutz 1953b). This was an early hint that, where the necessary resources were available to Tswana communities, some of them seized the opportunity to become specialist producers.

At Marothodi, as we have seen, there is evidence for specific homesteads specialising in the production of one metal or another. Certainly, SU25 seems to have specialised in copper production to the extent that its economic focus on cattle was subsumed. Other homesteads such as SU22 and SU3 were heavily involved with iron production. Based on the observation of annexes attached to homesteads like SU22, it is possible that some specialised in both iron and copper, but further excavation would be needed to elaborate this suggestion.

As we have discussed in this chapter, however, the development of economic specialisation and the high-quantity output of surplus goods did not cause the abandonment of the cultural principles that had historically directed the organisation of metal production. Instead, these were reworked to facilitate growth in the scale of production, and were adapted to the logistical challenges of life in a high density town environment.

Furthermore, the archaeology indicates that despite the considerable scale of metal production at Marothodi, this community still obtained copper and iron objects from elsewhere. This, in combination with the evidence for their own surplus generation, suggests that the Tlokwa were participants in a regional copper trade, which was described as thriving by early European travellers (Lichtenstein 1815; Campbell 1822; Burchell 1824).

In the concluding chapter we return to a consideration of these regional dynamics, and review some of the key outcomes of this research.

Chapter Eleven
Origins, Prosperity and Prospects

One of the primary aims of this book has been to establish the importance of exploring Tswana towns of the 18th and early 19th centuries against the backdrop of their specific historical, political and environmental contexts. Employing an interdisciplinary approach that incorporates historical, ethnographic and archaeological data is critical for the development of our understanding of the social and economic strategies being played out by Tswana communities as they experienced a period of significant turbulence and transformation.

While regional historical studies, lineage-specific oral traditions and site-specific archaeological research offer different scales of historical data, and each have their limitations, the combination of these sources can lead to insights and conclusions that reach beyond those obtainable from any discipline in isolation (Deetz 1998; Lane & Reid 1998; Behrens & Swanepoel 2008). The early 19th century Tlokwa capital at Marothodi, for which there is reasonable historical resolution, has been studied here to demonstrate the value of this approach towards Tswana towns of the 18th and early 19th centuries. In this concluding chapter, we highlight some of the main issues from this work.

The archaeology of identity

As discussed in Chapter Three, the Tlokwa oral traditions are relatively silent before the mid-18th century, when the lineage is described emerging through the Magaliesberg into the Rustenburg area from the south-east. This oral evidence for a south-eastern origin has been supported archaeologically at earlier sites in the Tlokwa sequence. Now, as demonstrated in Chapters Six to Nine, excavation at Marothodi has confirmed that the dominant ceramic style associated with the Tlokwa in the early 19th century is representative of the *Uitkomst* facies, which is part of the Fokeng cluster. In the ceramic sequence, as we have discussed, *Uitkomst* is derived from *Nstuanatsatsi*, demonstrating a link between the Marothodi Tlokwa and the first group of Bantu-speakers to cross the Vaal River from the KwaZulu-Natal region in the south-east. These early Fokeng originated among Northern Nguni people (Huffman 2007).

Thus, although Marothodi is essentially a 'Tswana-ised' town by the early 1800s, the ceramic profile of the capital still contrasts sharply with that of neighbouring contemporary towns, such as the Kwena capital of Molokwane and the Hurutshe capital Kaditshwene (see Figure 5). There, ceramics are characterised by the rim nicking, linear incisions and coloured bands representative of the *Buispoort* facies, which is more typically representative of western Sotho-Tswana (Mason 1986; Pistorius 1992; Boeyens 2000; Huffman 2007).

The Nguni origins of the Tlokwa are reflected in other archaeological features at Marothodi, such as the deposition of middens in the centre of homesteads, and the periodic sealing of some of those middens with soil capping layers. As discussed in Chapter Seven, these are practices that would seem to be derived from an Nguni concept of ash as a potentially dangerous substance that needs to be protected (Huffman & Steel 1996; Schoeman 1998).

Thus, Marothodi must be understood against an historical backdrop somewhat different to those of the neighbouring aggregated towns inhabited by western Sotho-Tswana in the region. Instead, we glimpse a process of 'Tswana-isation' somewhere along their journey north-westward, possibly beginning soon after their arrival in the Pilanesberg, which eventually resulted in the cultural expression we see at Marothodi in the early 19th century. While *Uitkomst* remains the dominant ceramic style at Marothodi, a trajectory of increasing interaction with other regional communities is represented in elements of imported *Buispoort* pottery appearing in the assemblages, and in the adoption of a western Tswana worldview so vividly demonstrated in the culturally-driven organisation of settlement space and commodity production.

The *Uitkomst* affiliation also carries implications for understanding the development of Tlokwa walling style. In Chapter Five the observation was made that the overall layout of Marothodi was less condensed than contemporary Tswana towns in the region, with more open space between individual homesteads than we see at Molokwane or Kaditshwene. While this may be, as suggested, partly associated with diachronic processes of aggregatation, we should now also consider that the Marothodi walling style derived from the 'Type N' and 'Klipriviersberg' forms, which are associated with earlier Fokeng/*Uitkomst* sites (Huffman 2007). These settlements, even when clustered, tended to be arranged in a looser, less condensed pattern than the Molokwane type walling arrangements of western Sotho-Tswana groups (Maggs 1976a; Huffman 2007).

By the early 19th century town phase, this stylistic premise would have been morphologically influenced by interaction with Tswana groups and by Marothodi's expanding population.

Production and trade

Life in a densely populated town presented new challenges for the organisation of metal production, particularly in relation to iron. With such a high number of smelters engaged in the craft, it had become impractical for all of them to seek environmental seclusion on hilltops or in forests outside the settlement, as had been perhaps been possible in earlier times. Iron smelting now had to be conducted closer to the settlement, but as we saw in Chapter Nine, extra efforts were made to create the necessary seclusion artificially through the use of strategically placed screens. The consistent employment of this strategy at Marothodi demonstrates the resilience of the cultural principles that guided it.

Although oral traditions tend to emphasise inter-chiefdom hostility, regional interchange must also have been important. The archaeology of metallurgy, the most visible form of craft production at Marothodi, encourages a consideration of this regional framework. We have seen that the scale of copper and possibly iron production here exceeded the needs of the Tlokwa community, and this raises questions about regional trade and economic relationships with other chiefdoms. The increasing scale of production is particularly evident in relation to copper, as almost every homestead at Marothodi was apparently involved in either primary smelting, refining, or in some cases, both. In the case of Settlement Unit 25 an entire homestead seems to have been dedicated to specialist copper production.

Tracing the distribution of copper from Marothodi will be facilitated by the unique nickel signature of the local ore, which makes it easy to identify when analysed (Hall *et al.* 2006). With the exception of historical references to the Hurutshe as prolific metallurgists (Campbell 1822) few contemporary Tswana communities in the area appeared to have produced their own metals. Archaeological research and ground survey at the neighbouring Kwena capital of Molokwane, for example (Fig. 11.1) has hitherto revealed no indication of primary metal production despite its significant size and regional status (Pistorius 1992, 1996a).

Considering the scale of Molokwane, this observation is highly significant. With over 150 homesteads and a population of about 12,000, Molokwane was considerably larger than Marothodi, and all aspects of consumption—including of metals—must have been substantial here. Identifying the origin of the metal artefacts at Molokwane, and at other contemporary towns, could shed light on the regional economic and political relationships between the major Tswana polities of the early 19th century.

Figure 11.1
The author examines stone walling at Molokwane. Although larger than Marothodi, no evidence for metal production has yet been observed at this contemporary Tswana town.

The probability that the Tlokwa participated in regional trade networks raises questions about what they received in return for their produce. As we have seen, there are very few glass trade beads from Marothodi, which suggests that beads were not a dominant medium

of exchange here. Among most Tswana peoples, glass beads were prized as a currency because they could be stored, their value could be manipulated (Saitowitz 1996; Wood 2008), and they could be traded for cattle—the ultimate form of 'wealth' in the Tswana world.

It could be argued that these values applied equally to copper which, as a currency in its own right (Bisson 1975; Herbert 1984) may have provided the Tlokwa with an economic substitute for glass beads. The possibility of a direct exchange of copper for cattle may be suggested by the large cattle kraals at Marothodi. The size of these kraals, if an accurate reflection of herd size, would certainly indicate that cattle were procured in relatively high quantities.

As specialist copper producers, the relationship of the Tlokwa at Marothodi with the nearby nickel-copper sulphide pipes was obviously critical. Maintaining access to, and control over, this ore resource must have been a key component in their political economy in such turbulent times, and required them to situate the town in close physical proximity to it. As discussed in Chapter Four, their ability to do so successfully is a reflection of the political confidence they must have enjoyed in the region in the early 19th century, and this may have influenced copper specialists from outside the lineage to join the Tlokwa here, so that they could participate in this industry.

An interdisciplinary approach

The high density of archaeological evidence for metal production at Marothodi could not have been understood in isolation. It was situated within the regional politics of the early 19th century Pilanesberg/Magaliesberg region, and must be viewed against this historical backdrop.

The *organisation* of Tlokwa production was sculpted by their unprecedented need to compromise between guiding cultural principles on the one hand, and the new challenges of high-quantity output and aggregated town life on the other. The *scale* of this production was both influenced and facilitated by increases in regional demand, and importantly, by maintaining control over the nearby ore source. Consequently, both the organisation and scale of production revealed in the archaeology of Marothodi, as well as the location of the settlement itself, must reflect a period of ascendant political confidence for the Tlokwa at this specific time in their history—a conclusion that is implicit, but by no means obvious, in the oral accounts of the Tlokwa alliance with the Kgatla and their subsequent military victory over the Fokeng in this period.

Thus, the Marothodi study has demonstrated how a full consideration of historical context has powerfully informed and enhanced our interpretation of the archaeology. The combination has, in this case, led to our recognition of shifts in the dynamics of regional political power among Tswana polities of the Pilanesberg/Magaliesberg region in the early 19th century. Neither the histories, nor the archaeological data could have yielded such an interpretation by themselves.

Directions for future research

On a site as extensive and archaeologically rich as Marothodi the current work has, inevitably, barely scratched the surface. Much more basic archaeological exploration needs to be conducted around the central and outlying portions of the town, with an emphasis on copper and iron production sites and the retrieval of larger ceramic samples. The suggestions put forward here in relation to themes of scale and organisation of production and the archaeological expression of identity must be tested and elaborated upon by targeting more homesteads and households in different parts of the settlement.

The issue of independent dating methods is also critical here. As noted in the Preface, the impracticality of radiocarbon techniques for this period means that an alternative method for establishing precise archaeological chronology is required, and optically stimulated luminescence (OSL) appears to offer the most promising solution (Rosenstein 2008).

The Tlokwa sequence in the region traverses a period of significant transformation in the Tswana world, and Marothodi represents a strategic response to these challenges during a 'snapshot' of time and place. In order to understand the developments in political scale and economic emphases represented at Marothodi, the town must be securely placed within the context of the broader Tlokwa sequence. To this end it will be vital to archaeologically examine sites that were occupied by the Tlokwa both before and after Marothodi, and to compare scales of production at these settlements.

As described in Chapter Three, the oral records identify the main settlements in the regional sequence as Bôte, Mankwe, Itlholanoga, Maruping, and Kolontwane before Marothodi, and subsequently Letlhakeng, and Tshwene-Tshwene in the Madikwe Game Reserve (Breutz 1953a; Ellenberger 1939). While the oral records offer high geographical resolution, the accessibility or preservation of archaeological residues at these sites cannot be confidently predicted at present. This would need to be assessed via a preliminary archaeological survey in collaboration with currently resident communities.

African pioneers

This book contributes to a process of situating Tswana production within specific historical contexts. It offers a scale of analysis that glimpses a complex world of economic organisation and regional dynamics in early 19th century Tswana society. The work at Marothodi will not be complete until comparative studies of equivalent scale have been conducted, but this offers a rich research future.

From a broader perspective, our study of Marothodi leaves us with an enduring impression of a resilient, resourceful and adaptable African community. In the midst of an increasingly turbulent landscape and unprecedented shifts in their political economy, the Tlokwa managed to thrive and prosper. Their growing political confidence was founded upon an expanding specialist economy, and the prosperity of the chiefdom must have seemed assured. We are left to speculate on the scale and complexity of their continued development had they not found themselves uprooted by war, and swept cataclysmically into the colonial era from the later 19th century.

Figure 11.2
Direct descendents of the
community at Marothodi.
Tlokwa girls stamp grain
at Tlokweng in Botswana,
during the reign of
Gaborone in the early
1900s. (Duggan-Cronin)

Figure 11.3 (below)
The author introduces
local school children to the
archaeological legacy of
their Tswana ancestors.

Bibliography

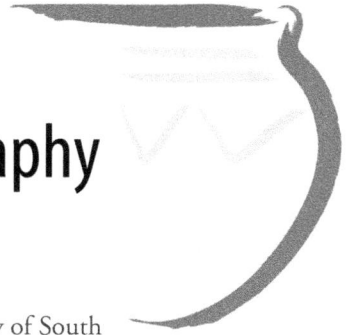

Acocks, J. P. H. 1988. *Veld Types of South Africa*. Memoirs of the Botanical Survey of South Africa, No. 57.

Anderson, M. S. 2005. *The Archaeology of Marothodi, North West Province, South Africa*. Paper delivered at the 12th Congress of the PanAfrican Archaeological Association for Prehistory and Related Studies. Gaborone, Botswana.

Anderson, M. S. 2009. *The Historical Archaeology of Marothodi: Towards an understanding of space, identity and the organisation of production at an early 19th century Tlokwa capital in the Pilanesberg region of South Africa*. PhD Thesis, University of Cape Town.

Barker, P. 1997. *Techniques of Archaeological Excavation*. Routledge, London.

Barrow, J. 1806. *A Voyage to Cochinchina*. Cadell & Davies, London.

Behrens, J. 2007. A New Initiative in Southern African Archaeology. *South African Archaeological Bulletin* 62.

Behrens, J. and Swanepoel, N. 2008. Historical archaeologies of southern Africa: precedents and prospects. In Swanepoel *et al.* (eds), *Five Hundred Years Rediscovered: Southern African Precedents and Prospects*. Wits University Press, Johannesburg.

Bisson, M. S. 1975. Copper currency in central Africa: the archaeological evidence. *World Archaeology* 6 (3): 276-292.

Bisson, M. S. 1997. Copper Metallurgy. In Vogel. J (ed.), *Encyclopedia of Precolonial Africa*. Altamira Press, Walnut Creek.

Blacking, J. 1969. Songs, dances, mimes and symbolism of Venda girls' initiation schools: part 3, Domba. *African Studies* 28: 149-99.

Blokhuis, W. A. 2002. Vertisols. In Lal, R. (ed.), *Encyclopaedia of Soil Science*. Marcel Dekker Inc., New York.

Boeyens, J. C. A. 2000. In Search of Kaditshwene. *South African Archaeological Bulletin* 55: 3-17.

Boeyens, J. C. A. 2003. The Late Iron Age sequence in the Marico and early Tswana history. *South African Archaeological Bulletin* 58: 63-78.

Boeyens, J. C. A. 2004. *Oral tradition and historical identity at Marothodi*. Southern African Association of Archaeologists Biennial Conference, Kimberley.

Boeyens, J. C. A. 2006. *Kaditshwene: a portrait of an early nineteenth-century Tswana capital in the South African interior*. Paper delivered at the 18th Biennial Conference of the Society of Africanist Archaeologists. Calgary, Canada.

Boeyens, J. C. A. and Cole, D. T. 1999. Kaditshwene: What's in a Name? In, Finlayson, R. (ed.), *African Mosaic: Festschrift For JA Louw*. Unisa Press, Pretoria.

Bonner, P., Esterhuysen, A. and Jenkins, T. (eds) 2007. *A Search for Origins*. Witwatersrand University Press, Johannesburg.

Borcherds, P. B. 1861. *An Autobiographical Memoir.* A. S. Robertson, Cape Town.

Bothma, C. V. 1962. *Ntshabeleng Social Structure: A Study of a Northern Transvaal Sotho Tribe.* Department of Bantu Administration and Development, Ethnological Publications 48. The Government Printer, Pretoria.

Bradlow, E. and Bradlow, F. (eds) 1979. *William Somerville's Narrative of his Journeys to the Eastern Cape Frontier and to Lattakoe 1799-1802.* Van Riebeeck Society, Cape Town.

Brelsford, W. V. 1949. Rituals and medicines of Chisinga ironworkers. *Man* 49: 27-29.

Breutz, P-L. 1953a. *The Tribes of the Rustenburg and Pilanesberg Districts.* Ethnological Publications 28. Government Printer, Pretoria.

Breutz, P-L. 1953b. *The Tribes of Marico District.* Ethnological Publications32. Government Printer, Pretoria.

Broadbent, S. 1865. *A Narrative of the Introduction of Christianity among the Barolong Tribe of Bechuanas, South Africa.* Wesleyan Mission House, London.

Brown, J. T. 1921. Circumcision rites of the Becwana Tribes. *Journal of the Royal Anthropological Institute* 51: 419-427.

Burchell, W. J. 1824. *Travels in the Interior of Southern Africa.* (Vol. 2, reprinted in 1953). Batchworth, London.

Butler, G. 1974. *The 1820 Settlers: An illustrated commentary.* Human & Rousseau, Cape Town.

Campbell, J. 1822. *Travels in South Africa… being a Narrative of a Second Journey (1820).* Vols. 1 & 2. Westley, London.

Casalis, E. 1861. *The Basutos.* Reprinted 1965. Struik, Cape Town.

Casalis, E. 1889. *My Life in Basutoland: A story of missionary enterprise in South Africa.* Reprinted 1971. Struik, Cape Town.

Chaplin, J. H. 1961. Notes on traditional smelting in Northern Rhodesia. *South African Archaeological Bulletin* 16: 53-60.

Childs, S. T. 1994. *Society, Culture and Technology in Africa.* MASCA Research papers in Science and Archaeology, supplement to Volume 11. University of Pennsylvania Museum of Archaeology and Anthropology, Philadelphia.

Clarke, D. L. 1977. *Spatial Archaeology.* Academy Press, London.

Cline, W. 1937. *Mining and Metallurgy in Negro Africa.* General Studies in Anthropology No. 5.

Cobbing, J. 1988. The *mfecane* as alibi: thoughts on Dithakong and Mbolompo. *Journal of African History* 29(3): 487-519.

Coetzee, F. P. 2005. The settlement sequence of the Bakgatla Ba Ga Kgafela in the Pilanesberg during the late eighteenth and early nineteenth centuries. *Proceedings of the 12th Congress of the PanAfrican Archaeological Association for Prehistory and Related Studies.* July, Gaborone, Botswana.

Collett, D. P. 1993. Metaphors and representations associated with precolonial iron-smelting in eastern and southern Africa. In Shaw *et al.* (eds), *The Archaeology of Africa: Food, Metals and Towns.* Routledge, London and New York.

Comaroff, J. 1985. *Body of Power, Spirit of Resistance.* University of Chicago Press.

Comaroff, J. and Comaroff, J. 1991. *Of Revelation and Revolution: Volume 1, Christianity and Colonialism in South Africa.* University of Chicago Press.

Comaroff, J. L., Comaroff, J. and James, D. (eds) 2007. *Picturing a Colonial Past: The African photographs of Isaac Schapera*. University of Chicago Press.

Connah, G. 2001. *African Civilizations: An Archaeological Perspective*. Cambridge University Press.

Crump, N. E. 1925. *Copper*. William Rider & Son Ltd., London.

Curtis, B. A., Tyson, P. D. and Dyer, T. G. J. 1978. Dendrochronological age determination of Podocarpus falcatus. *South African Journal of Science* 74: 92-95.

Daniell, W. 1820. *Sketches Representing the Native Tribes, Animals and Scenery of Southern Africa, from drawings made by the late Mr. Samuel Daniell, engraved by William Daniell*. William Daniel, London.

Daubenton, F. 1938. A Preliminary Report on Stone Structures near Steynsrust, Orange Free State. *South African Journal of Science*. Vol. XXXV: 364-370.

Deane, D. J. 1958. *Robert Moffat: The Missionary Hero of Kuruman*. S. W. Partridge & Co., London.

Deetz, J. 1988. American Historical Archeology: Methods and Results. *Science*, 239: 362-367.

Delius, P. and Schoeman, M. H. 2008. Revisiting Bokoni: populating the stone ruins of the Mpumalanga Escarpment. In Swanepoel *et al*. (eds), *Five Hundred Years Rediscovered*. Wits University Press, Johannesburg.

Denbow, J. R. 1979. *Cenchrus ciliaris*: an ecological indicator of Iron Age middens using aerial photography in eastern Botswana. *South African Journal of Science* 75: 405-408.

Department of Agriculture 1957. *Handbook for Farmers in South Africa. Volume 1: Agriculture and Related Services*. The Government Printer, Pretoria.

Department of Environmental Affairs and Tourism (DEAT) 2000. *Environmental Potential Atlas, July 2000*.

Division of Economics and Markets 1948. *Agro-Economic Survey of the Union*. Department of Agriculture. Economic Series No. 34.

Duggan-Cronin, A. M. 1929. *The Bantu Tribes of South Africa, Vol. II, Section I: The Suto-Chuana Tribes, Sub-Group I, The Bechuana*. McGregor Museum. Cambridge University Press.

Du Toit, A. L. 1954. *The Geology of South Africa*. Oliver and Boyd, Edinburgh and London.

Ellenberger, D. F. 1912. *History of the Basuto: Ancient and Modern*. (Translated by J. C. MacGregor). Caxton.

Ellenberger, V. 1939. History of the Batlokwa of Gaberones (Bechuanaland Protectorate). *Bantu Studies* XIII: 165-198.

Ellis, S. and Mellor, A. 1995. *Soils and the Environment*. Routledge, London and New York.

Evers, T. M. 1975. Recent Iron Age research in the eastern Transvaal, South Africa. *South African Archaeological Bulletin* 30: 71-83.

Evers, T. M. 1983. 'Oori' or 'Moloko'? The origins of the Sotho-Tswana on the evidence of the Iron Age of the Transvaal, reply to R. J. Mason. *South African Journal of Science*, 79: 261-264.

Evers, T. M. 1984. Sotho-Tswana and Moloko settlement patterns and the Bantu Cattle Pattern. In Hall, M. J., Avery, G., Avery, M., Wilson, M. and Humphreys, A. (eds), *Frontiers: Southern African Archaeology Today*. British Archaeological Reports International Series, No. 119. Oxford.

FAO, ISRIC and ISSS 1998. *World Reference Base for Soils*. World Soil Resources Reports No. 84. International Society of Soil Science.

Finlayson, R. (ed.) 1999. *African Mosaic: Festschrift For JA Louw.* Unisa Press, Pretoria.

Fouché, L. (ed.) 1937. *Mapungubwe: Ancient Bantu Civilization on the Limpopo.* Cambridge University Press.

Fredriksen, P. D. 2007. Approaching Intimacy: Interpretations of Changes in Moloko Household Space. *South African Archaeological Bulletin* 62 (186): 126-139.

Frescura, F. 1981. *Rural Shelter in Southern Africa: A survey of the architecture, house forms and constructional methods of the black rural peoples of southern Africa.* Ravan Press, Johannesburg.

Friede, H. M. 1977. Iron Age metalworking in the Magaliesberg area. *Journal of the South African Institute of Mining and Metallurgy* 77: 224-232.

Friede, H. M. 1979. Iron-smelting furnaces and metallurgical traditions of the South African Iron Age. *Journal of the South African Institute of Mining and Metallurgy* 79: 372-381.

Friede, H. M. 1983. *Typology of metal-smelting furnaces from Iron Age South Africa.* Archaeological Research Unit Occasional Papers 12. University of the Witwatersrand, Johannesburg.

Friede, H. M. and Steel, R. H. 1976. Tin mining and smelting in the Transvaal during the Iron Age. *Journal of the South African Institute of Mining and Metallurgy* 76: 461-470.

Friede, H. M. and Steel, R. H. 1985. Iron smelting furnaces in the western/central Transvaal – their structure, typology and affinities. *South African Archaeological Bulletin* 40: 45-49.

Friede, H. M. and Steel, R. H. 1986. Traditional wooden drum bellows of south-western Africa. *South African Archaeological Bulletin* 41: 12-16.

Hall, M. 1976. Dendroclimatology, Rainfall and Human Adaptation in the Later Iron Age of Natal and Zululand. *Annals of the Natal Museum,* Vol. 22(3): 693-703.

Hall, M. J., Avery, G., Avery, M., Wilson, M. and Humphreys, A. (eds) 1984. *Frontiers: Southern African Archaeology Today.* British Archaeological Reports International Series 207. Oxford.

Hall, S. 1995a. Archaeological Indicators for Stress in the Western Transvaal Region between the Seventeenth and Nineteenth Centuries. In Hamilton, C. (ed.), *The Mfecane Aftermath.* Witwatersrand University Press. Johannesburg.

Hall, S. 1995b. Review of Pistorius, J. C. C., 1992, *Molokwane: an Iron Age Bakwena Village,* Perskor, Johannesburg. *South African Archaeological Bulletin* 50: 88-89.

Hall, S. 1998. A consideration of gender relations in the Late Iron Age "Sotho" sequence of the Western Highveld, South Africa. In Kent, S. (ed.), *Gender in African Prehistory.* Altamira Press, Walnut Creek.

Hall, S. 2000. Forager lithics and Early Moloko homesteads at Madikwe. *Natal Museum Journal of Humanities* 12: 33-55.

Hall, S. 2007. Tswana History in the Bankenveld. In Bonner, P., Esterhuysen, A. and Jenkins, T. (eds), *A Search for Origins.* Witwatersrand University Press, Johannesburg.

Hall, S., Miller, D., Anderson, M. and Boeyens, J. 2006. An exploratory study of copper and iron production at Marothodi, an early 19th century Tswana town, Rustenburg District, South Africa. *Journal of African Archaeology* 4(1): 3-35.

Hall, S., Anderson, M., Boeyens, J. and Coetzee, F. 2008. Towards an outline of the oral geography, historical identity and political economy of the late precolonial Tswana in the Rustenburg region. In Swanepoel *et al.* (eds), *Five Hundred Years Rediscovered.* Wits University Press, Johannesburg.

Haalland, G., Haaland, R. and Rijal, S. 2002. The Social Life of Iron: A Cross-Cultural Study of Technological, Symbolic, and Social Aspects of Iron Making. *Anthropos* 97: 35-54.

Hamilton, C. (ed.) 1995. *The Mfecane Aftermath: reconstructive debates in southern African history.* Witwatersrand University Press, Johannesburg.

Hammond-Tooke, W. D. (ed.) 1974. *The Bantu-speaking Peoples of Southern Africa.* Routledge & Kegan Paul, London and Boston.

Hammond-Tooke, W. D. 1981. *Boundaries and Belief: The Structure of a Sotho Worldview.* Witwatersrand University Press, Johannesburg.

Hammond-Tooke, W. D. 1993. *The Roots of Black South Africa.* Jonathan Ball Publishers, Johannesburg.

Hanekom, A. J. 1960. *The South African Wool Industry.* South African Wool Board, Pretoria.

Harmse, H. J. von M. 1978. *Schematic Soil Map of Southern Africa South of Latitude 16° 30'S.* The Hague.

Hartley, G. 1995. The Battle of Dithakong and 'Mfecane' Theory. In Hamilton, C. (ed.), *The Mfecane Aftermath.* Witwatersrand University Press, Johannesburg.

Haughton, E. J. and Wells, L. H. 1942. Underground Structures in Caves of the Southern Transvaal. *South African Journal of Science.* Vol. XXXVIII: 319-333.

Henige, D. P. 1974. *The Chronology of Oral Tradition.* Oxford University Press.

Herbert, E. W. 1984. *Red Gold of Africa: Copper in Precolonial History and Culture.* University of Wisconsin Press, Madison.

Herbert, E. W. 1993. *Iron, Gender and Power: Rituals of Transformation in African Societies.* Bloomington, Indiana.

Hester, T. R., Shafer, H. J. and Feder, K. L. 1997. *Field Methods in Archaeology.* Mayfield Publishing Company, California.

Hockly, H. E. 1948. *The Story of the British Settlers of 1820 in South Africa.* Juta & CO. Ltd., Cape Town and Johannesburg.

Hoernlé, R. F. A. and Hoernlé, W. 1930. The Stone-Hut Settlement on Tafelkop, near Bethal. *Bantu Studies* IV: 33-46.

Huffman, T. N. 1980. Ceramics, classification and Iron Age entities. *African Studies* 39(2): 123-174.

Huffman, T. N. 1982. Archaeology and ethnohistory of the African Iron Age. *Annual Review of Anthropology* 11: 133-150.

Huffman, T. N. 1986a. Archaeological evidence and conventional explanations of southern Bantu settlement patterns. *Africa* 56: 280-298.

Huffman, T. N. 1986b. Iron Age settlement patterns and the origins of class distinction in Southern Africa. *Advances in World Archaeology* 5: 291-338.

Huffman, T. N. 1986c. Cognitive studies of the Iron Age in Southern Africa. *World Archaeology*, 18: 84-94.

Huffman, T. N. 1993. Broederstroom and the Central Cattle Pattern. *South African Journal of Science* 89: 220-226.

Huffman, T. N. 1996a. Archaeological Evidence for Climatic Change During the Last 2000 Years in Southern Africa. *Quaternary International*, Vol. 33: 55-60.

Huffman, T. N. 1996b. *Snakes and Crocodiles: Power and Symbolism in Ancient Zimbabwe.* Witwatersrand University Press.

Huffman, T. N. 2001. The Central Cattle Pattern and interpreting the past. *Southern African Humanities* 13: 19-35.

Huffman, T. N. 2002. Regionality in the Iron Age: the case of the Sotho-Tswana. *Southern African Humanities* 14: 1-22.

Huffman, T. N. 2006. Maize grindstones, Madikwe pottery and ochre mining in precolonial South Africa. *Southern African Humanities* 18: 51-70.

Huffman, T. N. 2007. *Handbook to the Iron Age: The Archaeology of Pre-Colonial Farming Societies in Southern Africa.* University of KwaZulu-Natal Press.

Huffman, T. N. and Murimbika, M. 2003. Shona ethnography and Iron Age burials. *Journal of African Archaeology* 1 (2): 237-246.

Huffman, T. N. and Steel, R. H. 1996. Salvage excavations at Planknek, Potgietersrus, Northern Province. *Southern African Field Archaeology* 5: 45-56.

Humphreys, A. J. B. 1976. Note on the southern limits of Iron Age settlement in the Northern Cape. *South African Archaeological Bulletin* 31: 54-57.

Jones, T. R. 1935. Prehistoric Stone Structures in the Magaliesberg Valley, Transvaal. *South African Journal of Science.* Vol. XXXII: 528-536.

Kay, S. 1833. *Travels and Researches in Caffraria.* Mason, London.

Kent, S. (ed.) 1998. *Gender in African Prehistory.* Altamira Press, Walnut Creek.

Kuper, A. 1980. Symbolic dimensions of the southern Bantu Homestead. *Africa* 50 (1): 8-23.

Kuper, A. 1982. *Wives for Cattle: Bridewealth and Marriage in Southern Africa.* Routledge and Kegan Paul, London.

Laidler, P. W. 1935. The Archaeology of Certain Prehistoric Settlements in the Heilbron Area. *Transactions of the Royal Society of South Africa.* Vol. XXIII(1): 23-68.

Lane, P. 1994/5. The Use and Abuse of Ethnography in the Study of the Southern African Iron Age. *Azania,* 29/30.

Lane, P. 1998. Engendered Spaces and Bodily Practices in the Iron Age of Southern Africa. In Kent, S. (ed.), *Gender in African Prehistory.* Altamira Press, Walnut Creek.

Lane, P. and Reid, A. 1998. Historical Archaeology in Botswana. In Lane, P. *et al.* (eds), *Ditswa Mmung: The Archaeology of Botswana.* The Botswana Society, Pula Press.

Lane, P., Reid, A. and Segobye, A. 1998. *Ditswa Mmung: The Archaeology of Botswana.* The Botswana Society, Pula Press.

Lane, P. 2004. Re-Constructing Tswana townscapes: toward a critical historical archaeology. In Reid, A. and Lane, P. (eds), *African Historical Archaeologies.* Kluwer Academic/Plenum Publishers, New York.

Larsson, A. and Larsson, V. 1984. *Traditional Tswana Housing: A study in four villages in eastern Botswana.* Swedish Council for Building Research, Stockholm.

Lal, R. (ed.) 2002. *Encyclopaedia of Soil Science.* Marcel Dekker Inc., New York.

Legassick, M. 1969. The Sotho-Tswana peoples before 1800. In Thompson, L. M. (ed.), *African Societies in Southern Africa: Historical Studies.* London.

Lichtenstein, H. 1928. *Travels in Southern Africa in the years 1803, 1804, 1805 and 1806.* The Van Riebeeck Society, Cape Town. A reprint of the translation from the original German by Anne Plumptre, Vols. 1 and 2.

Lister, M. H. 1949. *Journals of Andrew Geddes Bain.* The Van Riebeeck Society, Cape Town.

Long, U. (ed.) 1956. *The Journals of Elizabeth Lees Price written in Bechuanaland, Southern*

Africa, 1854-1883. Edward Arnold Publishers, London

Loubser, J. N. 1991. The Ethnoarchaeology of Venda-Speakers in Southern Africa. *Navorsinge van die Nasionale Museum, Bloemfontein* 7(8): 146-464.

Loubser, J. N. 1994. Ndebele archaeology of the Pietersburg area. *Navorsinge van die Nasionale Museum, Bloemfontein* 10(2): 61-147.

Low, A. B. and Rebelo, A. G. (eds) 1996. *Vegetation of South Africa, Lesotho and Swaziland*. Department of Environmental Affairs and Tourism, Pretoria.

Lye, W. F. (ed.) 1975. *Andrew Smith's Journal of his Expedition into the Interior of South Africa / 1834-36*. Published for the South African Museum by A. A. Balkema, Cape Town.

Lye, W. F. and Murray, C. 1980. *Transformations on the Highveld: The Tswana and Southern Sotho*. David Philip, Cape Town and London.

Mackenzie, J. 1871. *Ten Years North of the Orange River*. Edmonston and Douglas, Edinburgh.

MacVicar, C. N., De Villiers, J. M., Loxton, R. F., Verster, E., Lambrechts, J. J. N., Merryweather, F. R., Le Roux, J., Van Rooyen, T. H., and Harmse, H. J. van M. 1977. *Soil Classification – A Binomial System for South Africa*. Department of Agricultural Technical Services. Soil and Irrigation Research Institute, Pretoria.

Maggs, T. M. 1972. Bilobial Dwellings: A Persistent Feature of Southern Tswana Settlements. *Goodwin Series* 1: 54-65. South African Archaeological Society.

Maggs, T. M. 1976a. *Iron Age Communities of the Southern Highveld*. Natal Museum, Pietermaritzburg.

Maggs, T. M. 1976b. Iron Age patterns and Sotho history on the southern Highveld: South Africa. *World Archaeology*, 7: 318-332.

Maggs, T. M. 1993a. Sliding doors at Mokgatle's, a nineteenth century Tswana town in the central Transvaal. *South African Archaeological Bulletin* 48: 32-36.

Maggs, T. M. 1993b. Three decades of Iron Age research in South Africa: some personal reflections. *South African Archaeological Bulletin*, 48: 70-76.

Malan, B. D. and Brink, A. S. 1951. Pre-European Ruins on Brodie Hill, No. 1061, Pietersburg. *South African Journal of Science*. Vol. 48: 133-137.

Manson, A. 1995. Conflict on the western Highveld/southern Kalahari. In Hamilton, C. (ed.), *The Mfecane Aftermath*. Witwatersrand University Press. Johannesburg.

Mason, R. J. 1952. South African pottery from the Southern Transvaal. *South African Archaeological Bulletin*, 7: 70-79.

Mason, R. J. 1965. The Origin of South African Society. *South African Journal of Science*, 61: 255-267.

Mason, R. J. 1969. Iron Age Stone Artefacts from Olifantspoort, Rustenburg District and Kaditshwene, Zeerust District. *South Africa Journal of Science*. Vol. 65: 41-44.

Mason, R. J. 1971. *Prehistoric Man at Melville Koppies, Johannesburg*. University of the Witwatersrand, Department of Archaeology. Occasional Paper No. 6.

Mason, R. J. 1983. 'Oori' or 'Moloko'? The origins of the Sotho-Tswana on the evidence of the Iron Age of the Transvaal. *South African Journal of Science*, 79: 261.

Mason, R. J. 1986. *Origins of the Black People of Johannesburg and the Southern Western Central Transvaal, AD 350-1880*. Witwatersrand University Press, Johannesburg.

Mason, R. J. 1989. *South African Archaeology 1922 – 1988*. Witwatersrand University Press, Johannesburg.

Merkel, J. F. 1990. Experimental reconstruction of Bronze Age copper smelting based on archaeological evidence from Timna. In Rothenberg, B. (ed.), *The Ancient Metallurgy of Copper*. Institute for Archaeolo-Metallurgical Studies, London.

Miller, D. 1994. Kaonde copper smelting: technical versatility and the ethnographic record. In Childs, S. T., *Society, Culture and Technology in Africa*. MASCA Research Papers in Science and Archaeology, supplement to Volume 11. University of Pennsylvania Museum of Archaeology and Anthropology, Philadelphia.

Miller, D. 1997. Ironworking Technology. In Vogel. J. (ed.), *Encyclopedia of Precolonial Africa*. Altamira Press, Walnut Creek.

Miller, D., Boeyens, J. and M. Küsel. 1995. Metallurgical analyses of slags, ores, and metal artefacts from archaeological sites in the North-West Province and Northern Transvaal. *South African Archaeological Bulletin* 50: 39-46.

Miller, D. and Killick, D. 2004. Slag identification at southern African archaeological sites. *Journal of African Archaeology* 2 (1): 23-47.

Miller, D. and Van der Merwe, N. J. 1994. Early metal working in sub-Saharan Africa: a review of recent research. *Journal of Africa History* 35: 1-36.

Moffat, R. 1842. *Missionary Labours and Scenes in Southern Africa*. John Snow, London.

Mönnig, H. O. 1967. *The Pedi*. J. L. van Schaik Limited, Pretoria.

Mucina, L., Rutherford, M. C. and Pourie, L. W. 2005. *Vegetation Map of South Africa, Lesotho and Swaziland*. South African National Biodiversity Institute.

Nash, M. D. 1987. *The Settler Handbook: A new list of the 1820 settlers*. Chameleon Press, Diep River.

Nkhasi, M. E. 2008. *Investigating the Nature of Aggregation and Variability in Late Iron Age Settlements in the Vredefort Dome: A Geographic Information Systems Application*. MSc Thesis, University of Cape Town.

Orser, C. E. 1996. *A Historical Archaeology of the Modern World*. Plenum Press, New York and London.

Parsons, N. 1995. Prelude to Difaqane in the Interior of Southern Africa c.1600-c.1822. In Hamilton, C. (ed.), *The Mfecane Aftermath*. Witwatersrand University Press, Johannesburg.

Pauw, B. A. 1960. *Religion in a Tswana Chiefdom*. Oxford University Press.

Phillipson, D. W. 2005. *African Archaeology*. Cambridge University Press.

Pistorius, J. C. C. 1992. *Molokwane: an Iron Age Bakwena village*. Perskor, Johannesburg.

Pistorius, J. C. C. 1994. Molokwane, a seventeenth century Tswana village. *South African Journal of Ethnology* 17: 38-54.

Pistorius, J. C. C. and Steyn, M. 1995. Iron working and burial practices amongst the Kgatla-Kwena of the Mabyanamatshwana complex. *Southern African Field Archaeology* 4: 68-77.

Pistorius, J. C. C. 1996a. Spatial expressions in the *kgosing* of Molokwane. *South African Journal of Ethnology* 19(4): 143-164.

Pistorius, J. C. C. 1996b. The Matabele village which eluded history (Part 1). *South African Journal of Ethnology* 20 (1): 26-38.

Pistorius, J. C. C. 1997. The Matabele village which eluded history (Part 2). *South African Journal of Ethnology* 20 (2): 43-55.

Pitje, G. M. 1950a. Traditional systems of male education among Pedi and cognate tribes,

Part 1. *African Studies* 9(2): 53-76.

Pitje, G. M. 1950b. Traditional systems of male education among Pedi and cognate tribes, Part 2. *African Studies* 9(3): 105-124.

Pitje, G. M. 1950c. Traditional systems of male education among Pedi and cognate tribes, Part 3. *African Studies* 9(4): 194-201.

Pullen, R. A. 1942. Remains from stone-hut settlements in the Frankfort District, O.F.S. *South African Journal of Science,* 38: 334-344.

Randall, S. 2005/6. Digging in South Africa. *Current Archaeology Handbook 2005/2006*: 32-33.

Raum, O. 1973. *The Social Functions of Avoidances and Taboo among the Zulu.* Walter de Gruyter, Berlin.

Reid, A. and Lane, P. 2004. African Historical Archaeologies: An Introductory Consideration of Scope and Potential. In Reid, A. M. and Lane, P. J. (eds), *African Historical Archaeologies.* Kluwer Academic/Plenum Publishers, New York.

Reid, A. M. and Lane, P. J. (eds) 2004. *African Historical Archaeologies.* Kluwer Academic/ Plenum Publishers, New York.

Rivett-Carnac, D. E. 1963. *Thus Came the English in 1820.* Howard Timmins, Cape Town.

Robertshaw, P. 1990. *A History of African Archaeology.* Heinemann.

Rosenstein, D. 2008. *Sorting Out Ceramics: Correlating change in the technology of ceramic production with the chronology of 18th and early nineteenth century western BaTswana towns.* MSc thesis, University of Cape Town.

Roskams, S. 2002. *Excavation.* Cambridge University Press.

Rothenberg, B. 1990. *The Ancient Metallurgy of Copper: Archaeology-Experiment-Theory.* Institute for Archaeolo-Metallurgical Studies, London.

Saitowitz, S. J. 1996. *Glass Beads as Indicators of Contact and Trade in Southern Africa ca. AD 900 – AD 1250.* PhD Thesis, University of Cape Town.

Sanderson, J. 1981. *Memoranda of a Trading Trip into the Orange River (Sovereignty) Free State and the Country of the Transvaal Boers.* State Library, Pretoria.

Saunders, C. C. 1966. Early knowledge of the Sotho: seventeenth and eighteenth century accounts of the Tswana. *Quarterly Bulletin of the South African Library* 20 (3): 60-70.

Schaetzl, R. J. and Anderson, S. 2005. *Soils: Genesis and Geomorphology.* Cambridge University Press.

Schapera, I. (ed.) 1940. *Ditirafalo tsa Batswana.* Lovedale Press, Alice.

Schapera, I. 1942. A Short History of the BaNgwaketse. *African Studies* 1 (1): 1-26.

Schapera, I. (ed.) 1946. Some features in the social organization of the Tlôkwa (Bechuanaland Protectorate). *Southwestern Journal of Anthropology* 2: 16-47.

Schapera, I. (ed.) 1951. *Apprenticeship at Kuruman: being the journals and letters of Robert and Mary Moffat 1820-1828.* Chatto & Windus, London.

Schapera, I. 1953. *The Tswana.* International African Institute, London.

Schapera, I. 1955. *A Handbook of Tswana Law and Custom.* Frank Cass, London.

Schapera, I. 1971. *Rainmaking Rites of Tswana Tribes.* African Studies Centre, Cambridge.

Schapera, I. 1978. *Bogwera: Kgatla Initiation.* Phuthadikobo Museum, Botswana.

Schapera, I. 1979. Kgatla notions of ritual impurity. *African Studies* 38(1): 3-15.

Schapera, I. 1980. *A History of the Bakgatla-bagaKgafêla.* Puthadikobo Museum, Mochudi.

Schmidt, P. 1997. *Iron Technology in East Africa: Symbolism, Science, and Archaeology.* Indiana

University Press, Bloomington.

Schoeman, M. H. 1998. Excavating Ndzunda Ndebele identity at KwaMuza. *Southern African Field Archaeology* 7 (1): 42-52.

Schofield, J. F. 1948. *Primitive Pottery.* South African Archaeological Society, Cape Town.

Schulze, R. E. 1997. *South African Atlas of Agrohydrology and –Climatology.* Water Research Commission, Pretoria. Report TT82/96.

Schwellnus, C. M. 1935. *The Nickel-Copper Occurrence in the Bushveld Igneous Complex West of the Pilandsbergen.* Geological Series Bulletin No. 5. The Government Printer, Pretoria.

Schwellnus, C. M. 1937. Short notes on the Palaboroa smelting ovens. *South African Journal of Science* 33: 904-912.

Seddon, J. D. 1966. Kurrechane: a Late Iron Age site in the western Transvaal. *African Studies* 25(4): 227-233.

Seddon, J. D. 1968. An aerial survey of settlement and living patterns in the Transvaal Iron Age: preliminary report. *African Studies,* 27: 189-194.

Shaw, T., Sinclair, P. J. J., Andah, B. and Okpoko, A. (eds) 1993. *The Archaeology of Africa: Food, Metals and Towns.* Routledge, London and New York.

Soil Classification Working Group 1991. *Soil Classification - A Taxonomic System for South Africa.* Department of Agricultural Development, Pretoria.

Soil Survey Staff 1998. *Keys to Soil Taxonomy: 8ᵗʰ Edition.* United States Department of Agriculture. Natural Resources Conservation Service, Washington, DC.

Stayt, H. 1931. *The BaVenda.* Oxford University Press.

Stow, G. W. 1905. *The Native races of South Africa.* Sonenschein, London.

Swanepoel, N., Esterhuysen, A. and Bonner, P. 2008. *Five Hundred years Rediscovered: Southern African Precedents and Prospects.* Wits University Press, Johannesburg.

Tainton, N. M. 1999. *Veld Management in South Africa.* University of Natal Press, Pietermaritzburg.

Taylor, M. O. V. 1979. *Late Iron Age Settlements on the Northern Edge of the Vredefort Dome.* MA Thesis, University of the Witwatersrand.

Taylor, M. O. V. 1984. Southern Transvaal Stone Walled Sites. In Hall, M. *et al.* (eds), *Frontiers: Southern African Archaeology Today.* BAR International Series 207: 248-251.

Theal, G. M. 1919. *Ethnography and Condition of South Africa Before A.D. 1505.* George Allen & Unwin, London.

Thompson, G. 1967. *Travels and Adventures in Southern Africa.* The Van Riebeeck Society, Cape Town. (Edited by V. S. Forbes)

Thompson, L. M. (ed.) 1969. *African Societies in Southern Africa: Historical Studies.* London.

Tlou, T. 1974. *The Nature of Batswana States: The Batawana Case.* University of Botswana, Lesotho and Swaziland.

TNAD 1905. *Short History of the Native Tribes of the Transvaal.* Transvaal Native Affairs Department. The Government Printing and Stationary Office, Pretoria.

Tyson, P. D. and Lindesay, J. A. 1992. The climate of the last 2000 years in southern Africa. *The Holocene* 2: 271-278.

Van der Merwe, N. J. and Scully, T. K. 1971. The Phalaborwa story: archaeological and ethnographic investigation of a South African Iron Age group. *World Archaeology* 3(2): 178-196.

Van Riet Lowe, C. 1927. A preliminary report on the stone huts of Vechtkop. *Journal of the*

Royal Anthropological Institute, 57: 217:233.

Vansina, J. 1961. *Oral Tradition: A Study in Historical Methodology.* (Translated by H. M. Wright). Routledge & Kegan Paul, London.

Vansina, J. 1971. Once Upon a Time: Oral Traditions as History in Africa. *Daedalus,* Vol. 100, No. 2: 442-468.

Viljoen, M. J. and Reimold, W. U. 1999. *An Introduction to South Africa's Geological and Mining Heritage.* Mintek, Randburg.

Vogel, J. C. and Fuls, A. 1999. Spatial distribution of radiocarbon dates for the Iron Age in southern Africa. *South African Archaeological Bulletin* 54: 97-101.

Vogel. J. (ed) 1997. *Encyclopedia of Precolonial Africa.* Altamira Press, Walnut Creek.

Vogel, J. (ed) 2000. *Ancient African Metallurgy: The Socio-Cultural Context.* Altamira Press, Walnut Creek.

Wagner, P. A. 1924. *Magmatic Nickel Deposits of the Bushveld Complex in the Rustenburg District, Transvaal.* Geological Survey Memoir No. 21. The Government Printer, Pretoria.

Walker, N. 1997. In the footsteps of the ancestors: the Matsieng creation site in Botswana. *South African Archaeological Bulletin* 52: 95-104.

Wallace, J. P. R. (ed.) 1945. The Matabele Journals of Robert Moffat, 1829-1860, 2 vols. Chatto & Windus, London.

Walton, J. 1953. An early Fokeng-Hlakoana settlement at Metlaeeng, Basutoland. *South African Archaeological Bulletin,* 8: 3-11.

Walton, J. 1956a. Early Bafokeng Settlement in South Africa. *African Studies,* 15: 37-43.

Walton, J. 1956b. *African Village.* Schaik, Pretoria.

Walton, J. 1958. Sotho Cattle-kraals. *South African Archaeological Bulletin* 13: 133-148.

Wells, L. H. 1933. A Report on the Stone Structures on the Platberg near Klerksdorp. *South Africa Journal of Science.* Vol. XXX: 582-584.

Willems, J. 1964. A Brief Outline of the Geology of the Bushveld Igneous Complex. In Haughton, S. H. (ed.), *The Geology of Some Ore Deposits in Southern Africa,* Vol. 2. The Geological Society of South Africa, Johannesburg.

Willoughby, W. C. 1900. *Native Life on the Transvaal Border.* Simpkin, Marshall, Hamilton, Kent & Co., Ltd., London.

Willoughby, W. C. 1909. Notes on the initiation ceremonies of the Becwana. *Journal of the Royal Anthropological Institute* 39: 228-245.

Wilson, K. J. 1976. *Godfather to the Griquas: An outline of the early history of the Griqua people and the life of their missionary, Peter Wright.* Original Typescript. MSB 805,1. South African National Library, Cape Town.

Wilson, M. and Thompson, L. (eds) 1969; 1971. The Oxford History of South Africa, Vols. 1 and 2. Oxford University Press.

Wood, M. 2000. Making connections: relationships between international trade and glass beads from the Shashe-Limpopo area. *South African Archaeological Society Goodwin Series* 8: 78-90.

Wood, M. 2008. Post-European contact glass beads from the southern African interior: a tentative look at trade, consumption and identities. In Swanepoel *et al.* (eds), *Five Hundred Years Rediscovered.* Wits University Press, Johannesburg.

Sources of Illustrations

All photographs, maps and illustrations © 2009 Mark Steven Anderson, except those used by permission from the following sources/contributors:

Figure 6.17 and front cover (upper): © Christian Biggi.
Figures 3, 6.9, 6.22, 9.3, 9.16 and 11.2: © Sarah Court.
Figure 10.4 (Hugh Stayt): © International African Institute.
Figures 6, 5.1, 7.2 and back cover (top): © Revil Mason/School of Geography, Archaeology and Environmental Studies, University of the Witwatersrand.
Figures 3.2 and 11.3: (Alfred Duggan-Cronin) © McGregor Museum Kimberley, Duggan-Cronin collection.
Figures 1.9 and 1.10, and back cover (third from top): (Charles Bell) Museum Africa, Johannesburg.
Figures 4, 1.1 (inset) and 4.5 satellite map imagery, and page xxii Planet Earth/African Continent: National Aeronautics and Space Administration (NASA).
Figure 8.20 (Isaac Schapera) © Royal Anthropological Institute, London.
Figures 7.7(a), 7.29, 7.32, 8.4(c), 9.2(b) and back cover (fifth from top): (Neil Rusch) © Department of Archaeology, University of Cape Town.
Front cover (lower) (photographer unknown), Figures 1.5, 10.1 (John Campbell) and 1.9 (artist unknown): South African National Library Special Collections, Cape Town.

The following images are from published works now in the public domain, and are listed in the Bibiliography:

Figure 1.4(a) (Barrow 1806); Figure 1.2 (Borcherds 1861); Figures 1.3, 1.4(b), 1.5 and 10.2 (Burchell 1824); Figures 1.6 and 1.7 (Campbell 1822); Figure 1.4(c) (Kay 1833); Figures 6.3, 8.22 and back cover (second from top) (Willoughby 1900).

Other permissions/credits:

Epigraph on page vi adapted from V. Ellenberger (1939) with permission from Wits University Press, Johannesburg. Plans of Molokwane on pages 75 and 165 adapted from the originals with permission from J. Pistorius. Plan of Kaditshwene on page 87 adapted from the original with permission from J. Boeyens. Plan of Boschoek on page 126 adapted from the original with permission from T. Huffman. Badfontein walling on page 127 adapted from the original with permission from J. Loubser.

Painted vessel motif © Atikkam Media Ltd.

Index

www.ingramcontent.com/pod-product-compliance
Lightning Source LLC
Chambersburg PA
CBHW080415270326
41929CB00018B/3042